MY HERO ACADEMIA

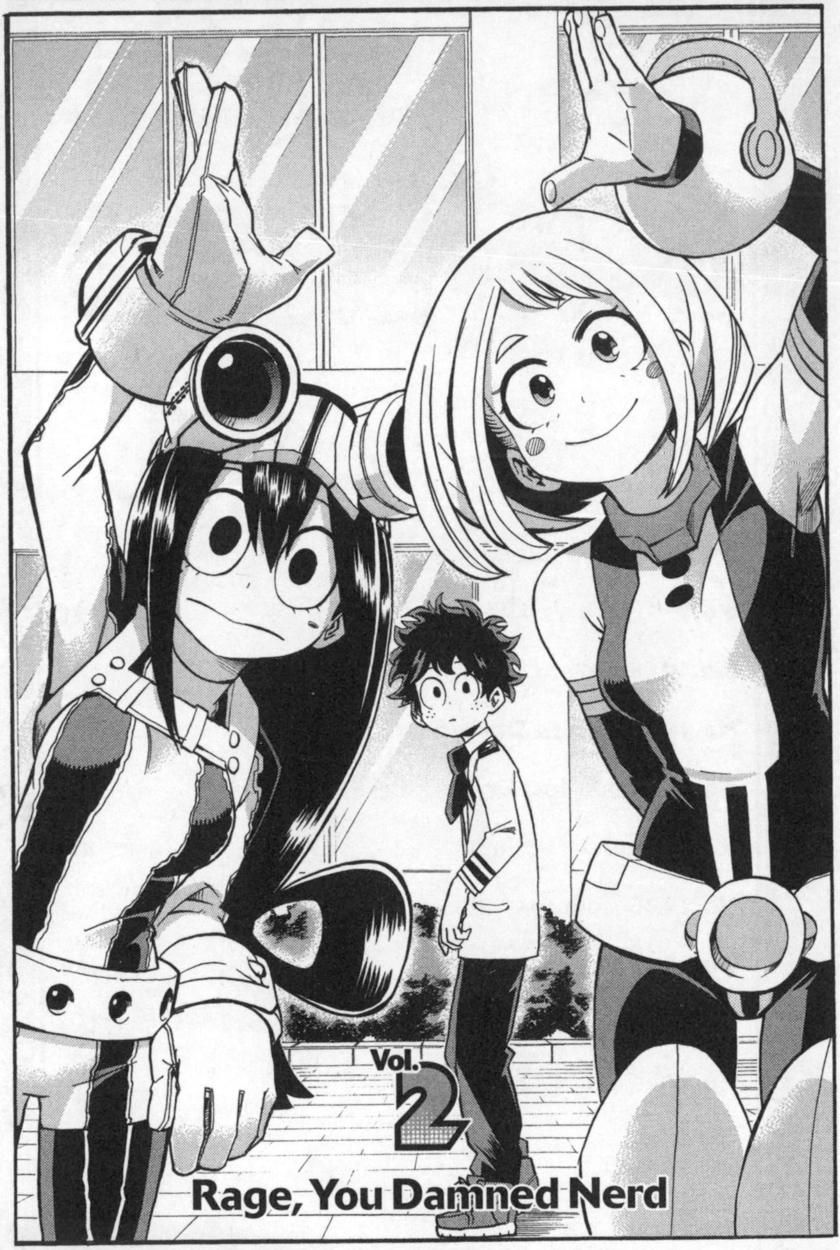
Vol. 2
Rage, You Damned Nerd

KOHEI HORIKOSHI

Vol. 2

MY HERO ACADEMIA

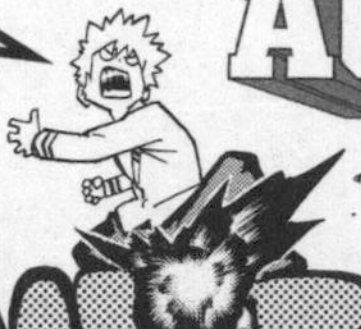

CONTENTS

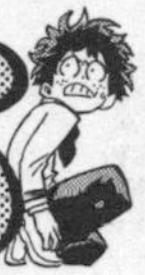

Rage, You Damned Nerd

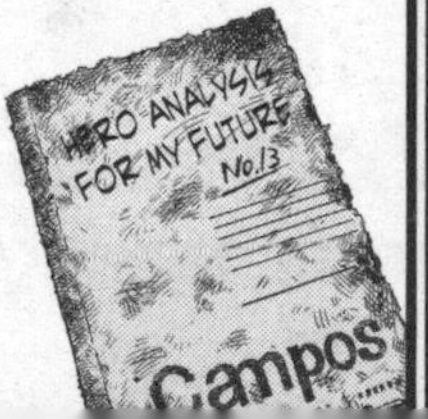

HERO ANALYSIS FOR MY FUTURE
No.13
Campos

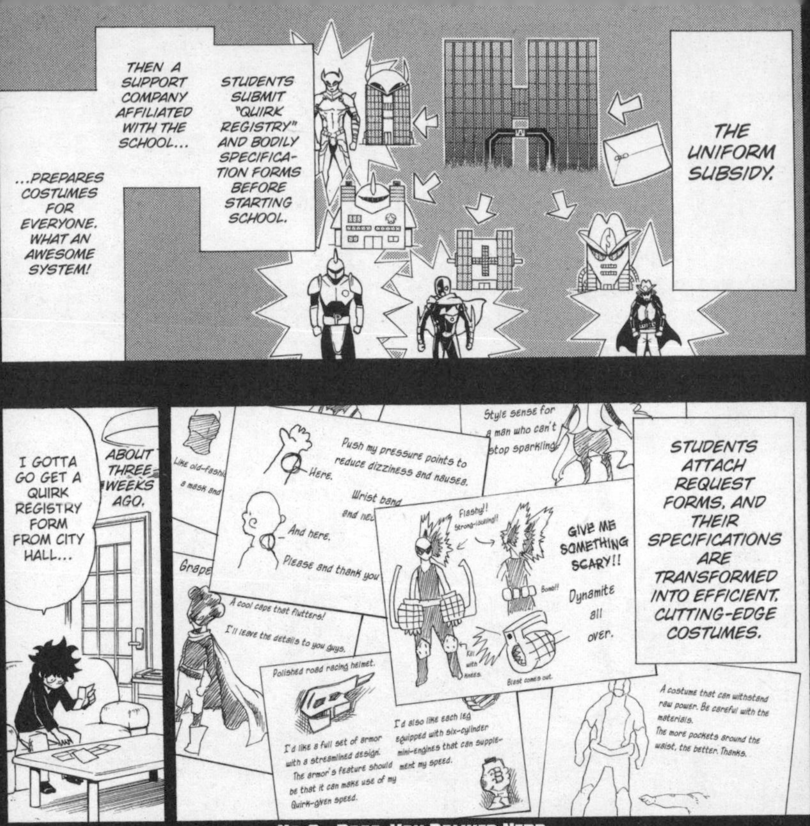
THE UNIFORM SUBSIDY.
STUDENTS SUBMIT "QUIRK REGISTRY" AND BODILY SPECIFICATION FORMS BEFORE STARTING SCHOOL.
THEN A SUPPORT COMPANY AFFILIATED WITH THE SCHOOL...
...PREPARES COSTUMES FOR EVERYONE. WHAT AN AWESOME SYSTEM!
STUDENTS ATTACH REQUEST FORMS, AND THEIR SPECIFICATIONS ARE TRANSFORMED INTO EFFICIENT, CUTTING-EDGE COSTUMES.
Style sense for a man who can't stop sparkling
A costume that can withstand raw power. Be careful with the materials.
The more pockets around the waist, the better. Thanks.
GIVE ME SOMETHING SCARY!!
Dynamite all over.
Flashy!!
Strong-looking!!
Bomb!!
Blast comes out.
Push my pressure points to reduce dizziness and nausea.
Here.
And here.
Please and thank you
A cool cape that flutters!
I'll leave the details to you guys.
Polished road racing helmet.
I'd like a full set of armor with a streamlined design. The armor's feature should be that it can make use of my Quirk-given speed.
I'd also like each leg equipped with six-cylinder mini-engines that can supplement my speed.
ABOUT THREE WEEKS AGO.
I GOTTA GO GET A QUIRK REGISTRY FORM FROM CITY HALL...

NO.8 - RAGE, YOU DAMNED NERD

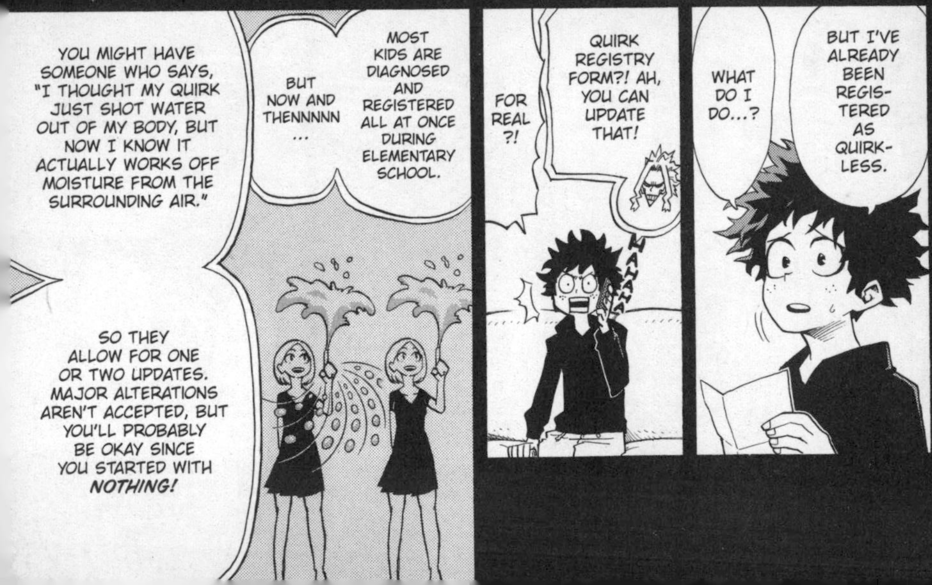
BUT I'VE ALREADY BEEN REGISTERED AS QUIRKLESS.
WHAT DO I DO...?
QUIRK REGISTRY FORM?! AH, YOU CAN UPDATE THAT!
FOR REAL?!
HAHAHA
MOST KIDS ARE DIAGNOSED AND REGISTERED ALL AT ONCE DURING ELEMENTARY SCHOOL.
BUT NOW AND THENNNNN...
YOU MIGHT HAVE SOMEONE WHO SAYS, "I THOUGHT MY QUIRK JUST SHOT WATER OUT OF MY BODY, BUT NOW I KNOW IT ACTUALLY WORKS OFF MOISTURE FROM THE SURROUNDING AIR."
SO THEY ALLOW FOR ONE OR TWO UPDATES. MAJOR ALTERATIONS AREN'T ACCEPTED, BUT YOU'LL PROBABLY BE OKAY SINCE YOU STARTED WITH NOTHING!

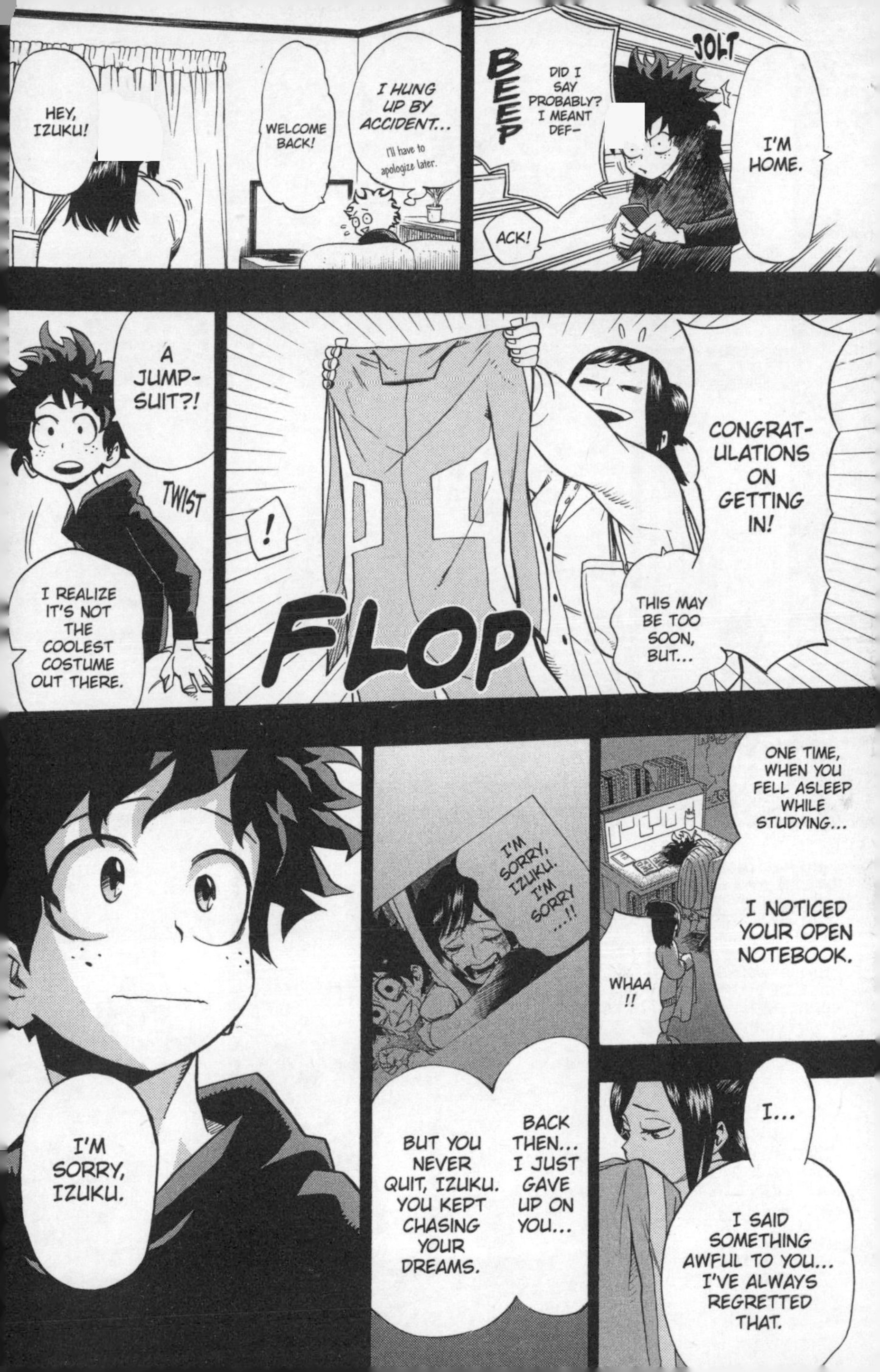
JOLT
I'M HOME.
BEEP
DID I SAY PROBABLY? I MEANT DEF–
ACK!
I HUNG UP BY ACCIDENT...
I'll have to apologize later.
WELCOME BACK!
HEY, IZUKU!
CONGRAT-ULATIONS ON GETTING IN!
THIS MAY BE TOO SOON, BUT...
!
FLOP
A JUMP-SUIT?!
TWIST
I REALIZE IT'S NOT THE COOLEST COSTUME OUT THERE.
ONE TIME, WHEN YOU FELL ASLEEP WHILE STUDYING...
I NOTICED YOUR OPEN NOTEBOOK.
WHAA!!
I...
I SAID SOMETHING AWFUL TO YOU... I'VE ALWAYS REGRETTED THAT.
I'M SORRY, IZUKU. I'M SORRY...!!
BACK THEN... I JUST GAVE UP ON YOU...
BUT YOU NEVER QUIT, IZUKU. YOU KEPT CHASING YOUR DREAMS.
I'M SORRY, IZUKU.

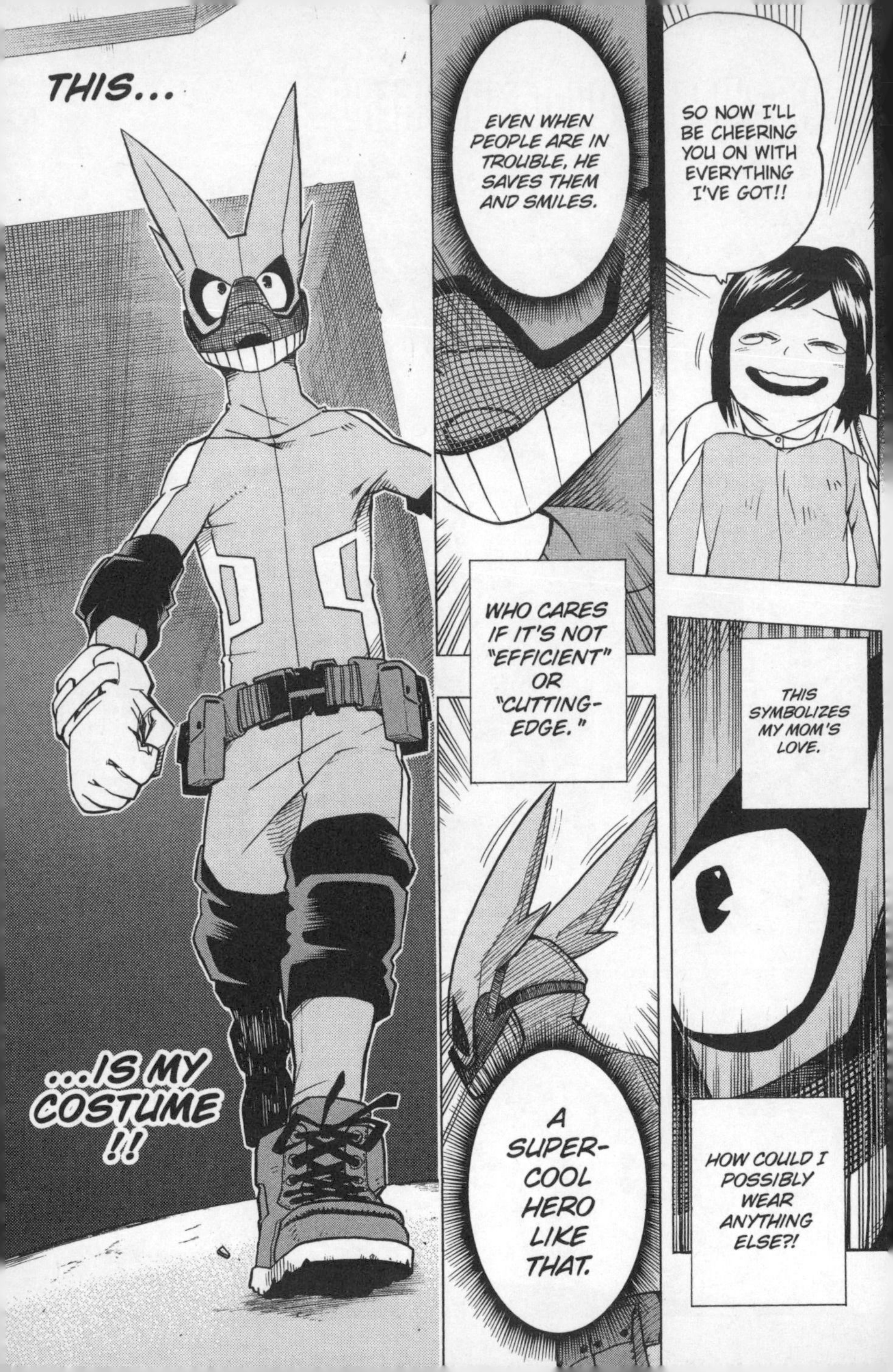
SO NOW I'LL BE CHEERING YOU ON WITH EVERYTHING I'VE GOT!!
THIS SYMBOLIZES MY MOM'S LOVE.
HOW COULD I POSSIBLY WEAR ANYTHING ELSE?!
EVEN WHEN PEOPLE ARE IN TROUBLE, HE SAVES THEM AND SMILES.
WHO CARES IF IT'S NOT "EFFICIENT" OR "CUTTING-EDGE."
A SUPER-COOL HERO LIKE THAT.
THIS...
...IS MY COSTUME!!

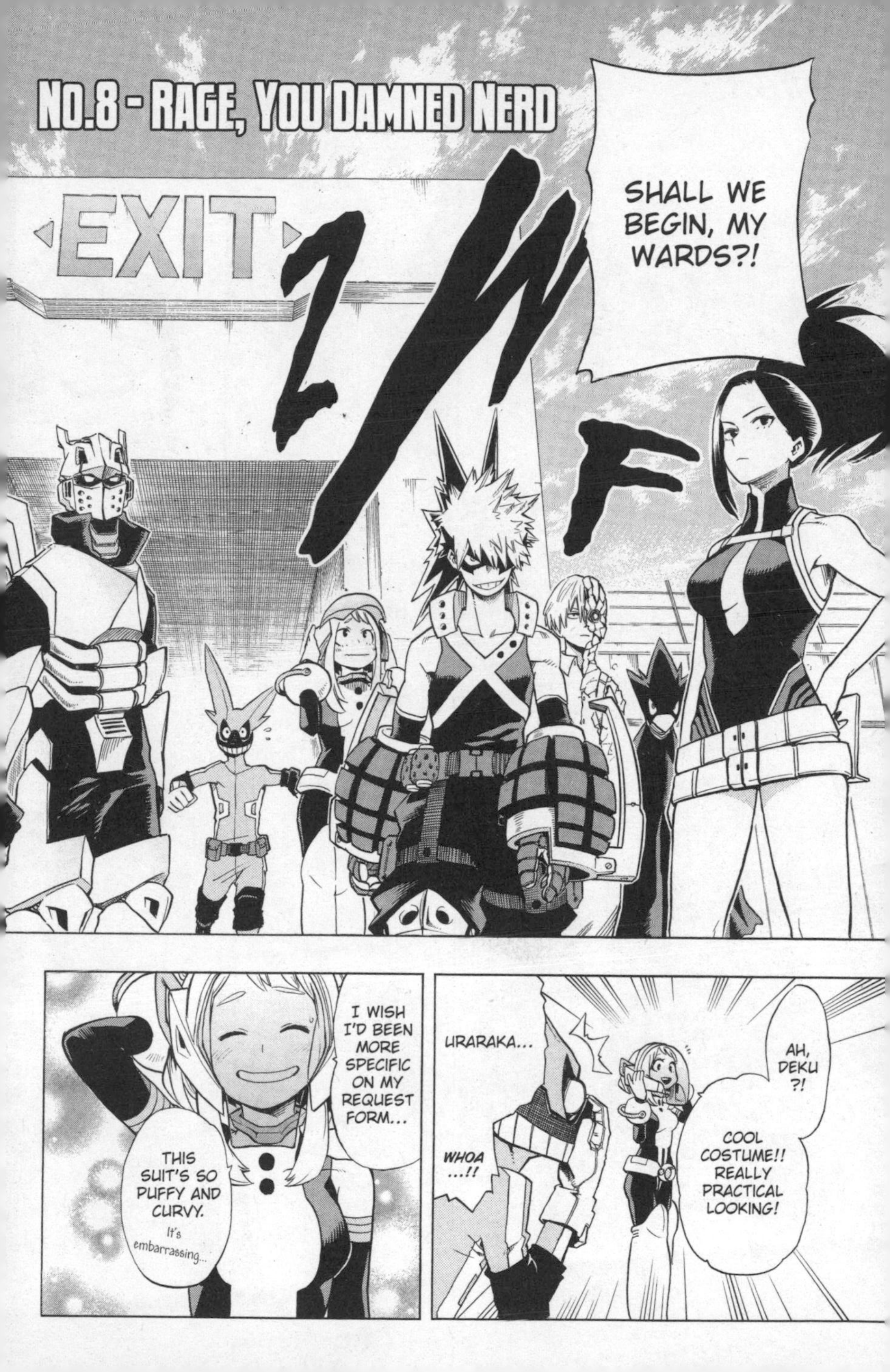
No.8 - Rage, You Damned Nerd
SHALL WE BEGIN, MY WARDS?!
AH, DEKU ?!
COOL COSTUME!! REALLY PRACTICAL LOOKING!
URARAKA...
WHOA ...!!
I WISH I'D BEEN MORE SPECIFIC ON MY REQUEST FORM...
THIS SUIT'S SO PUFFY AND CURVY.
It's embarrassing...

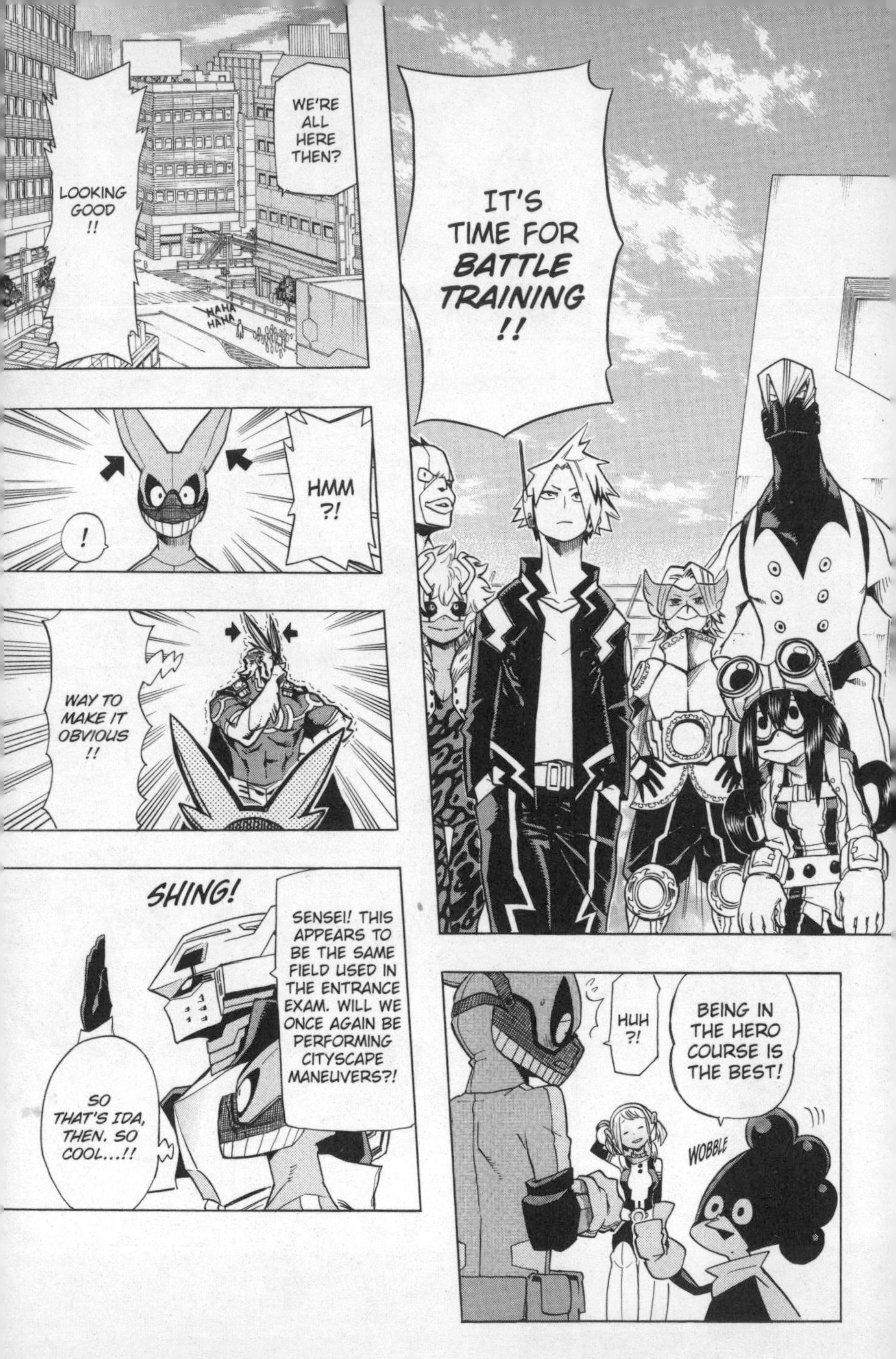
IT'S TIME FOR BATTLE TRAINING!!
WE'RE ALL HERE THEN?
LOOKING GOOD!!
HAHA HAHA
HMM?!
!
WAY TO MAKE IT OBVIOUS!!
BEING IN THE HERO COURSE IS THE BEST!
HUH?!
WOBBLE
SENSEI! THIS APPEARS TO BE THE SAME FIELD USED IN THE ENTRANCE EXAM. WILL WE ONCE AGAIN BE PERFORMING CITYSCAPE MANEUVERS?!
SHING!
SO THAT'S IDA, THEN. SO COOL...!!

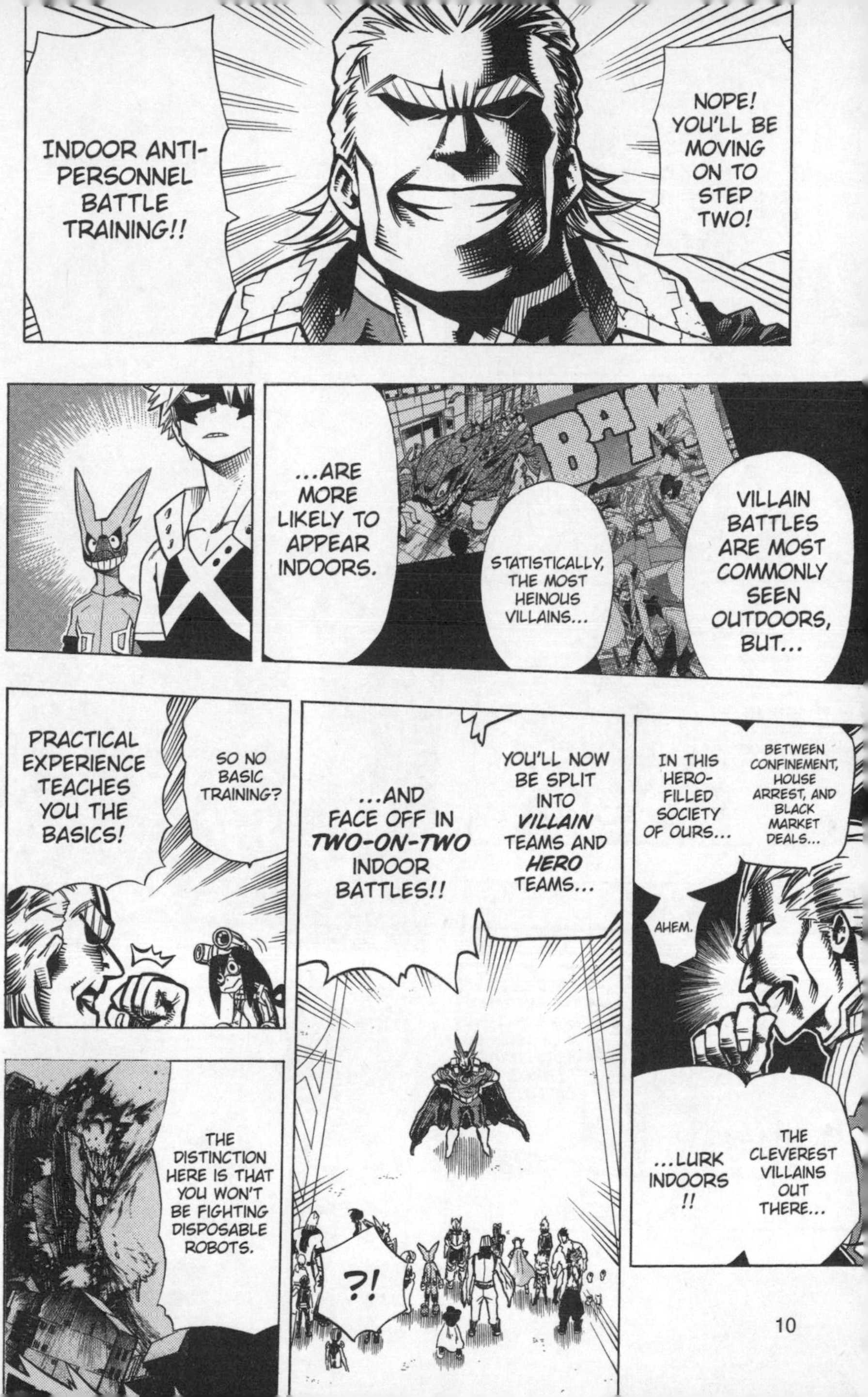
NOPE! YOU'LL BE MOVING ON TO STEP TWO!
INDOOR ANTI-PERSONNEL BATTLE TRAINING!!
VILLAIN BATTLES ARE MOST COMMONLY SEEN OUTDOORS, BUT...
STATISTICALLY, THE MOST HEINOUS VILLAINS...
...ARE MORE LIKELY TO APPEAR INDOORS.
BETWEEN CONFINEMENT, HOUSE ARREST, AND BLACK MARKET DEALS...
IN THIS HERO-FILLED SOCIETY OF OURS...
AHEM.
THE CLEVEREST VILLAINS OUT THERE...
...LURK INDOORS!!
YOU'LL NOW BE SPLIT INTO VILLAIN TEAMS AND HERO TEAMS...
...AND FACE OFF IN TWO-ON-TWO INDOOR BATTLES!!
?!
SO NO BASIC TRAINING?
PRACTICAL EXPERIENCE TEACHES YOU THE BASICS!
THE DISTINCTION HERE IS THAT YOU WON'T BE FIGHTING DISPOSABLE ROBOTS.

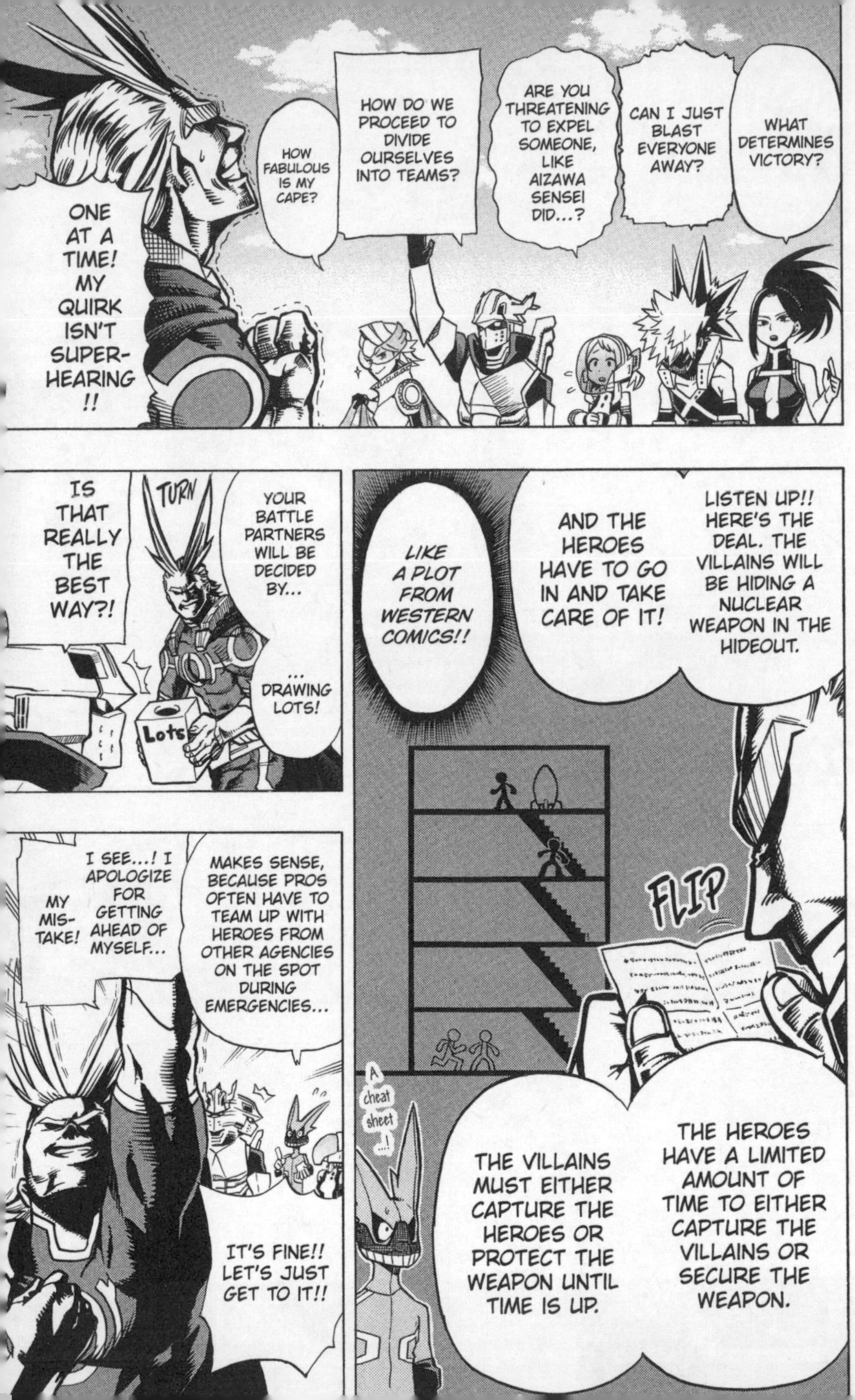
WHAT DETERMINES VICTORY?
CAN I JUST BLAST EVERYONE AWAY?
ARE YOU THREATENING TO EXPEL SOMEONE, LIKE AIZAWA SENSEI DID...?
HOW DO WE PROCEED TO DIVIDE OURSELVES INTO TEAMS?
HOW FABULOUS IS MY CAPE?
ONE AT A TIME! MY QUIRK ISN'T SUPER-HEARING!!
LISTEN UP!! HERE'S THE DEAL. THE VILLAINS WILL BE HIDING A NUCLEAR WEAPON IN THE HIDEOUT.
AND THE HEROES HAVE TO GO IN AND TAKE CARE OF IT!
LIKE A PLOT FROM WESTERN COMICS!!
FLIP
THE HEROES HAVE A LIMITED AMOUNT OF TIME TO EITHER CAPTURE THE VILLAINS OR SECURE THE WEAPON.
THE VILLAINS MUST EITHER CAPTURE THE HEROES OR PROTECT THE WEAPON UNTIL TIME IS UP.
A cheat sheet...!
YOUR BATTLE PARTNERS WILL BE DECIDED BY...
TURN
IS THAT REALLY THE BEST WAY?!
... DRAWING LOTS!
Lots
MAKES SENSE, BECAUSE PROS OFTEN HAVE TO TEAM UP WITH HEROES FROM OTHER AGENCIES ON THE SPOT DURING EMERGENCIES...
I SEE...! I APOLOGIZE FOR GETTING AHEAD OF MYSELF...
MY MISTAKE!
IT'S FINE!! LET'S JUST GET TO IT!!

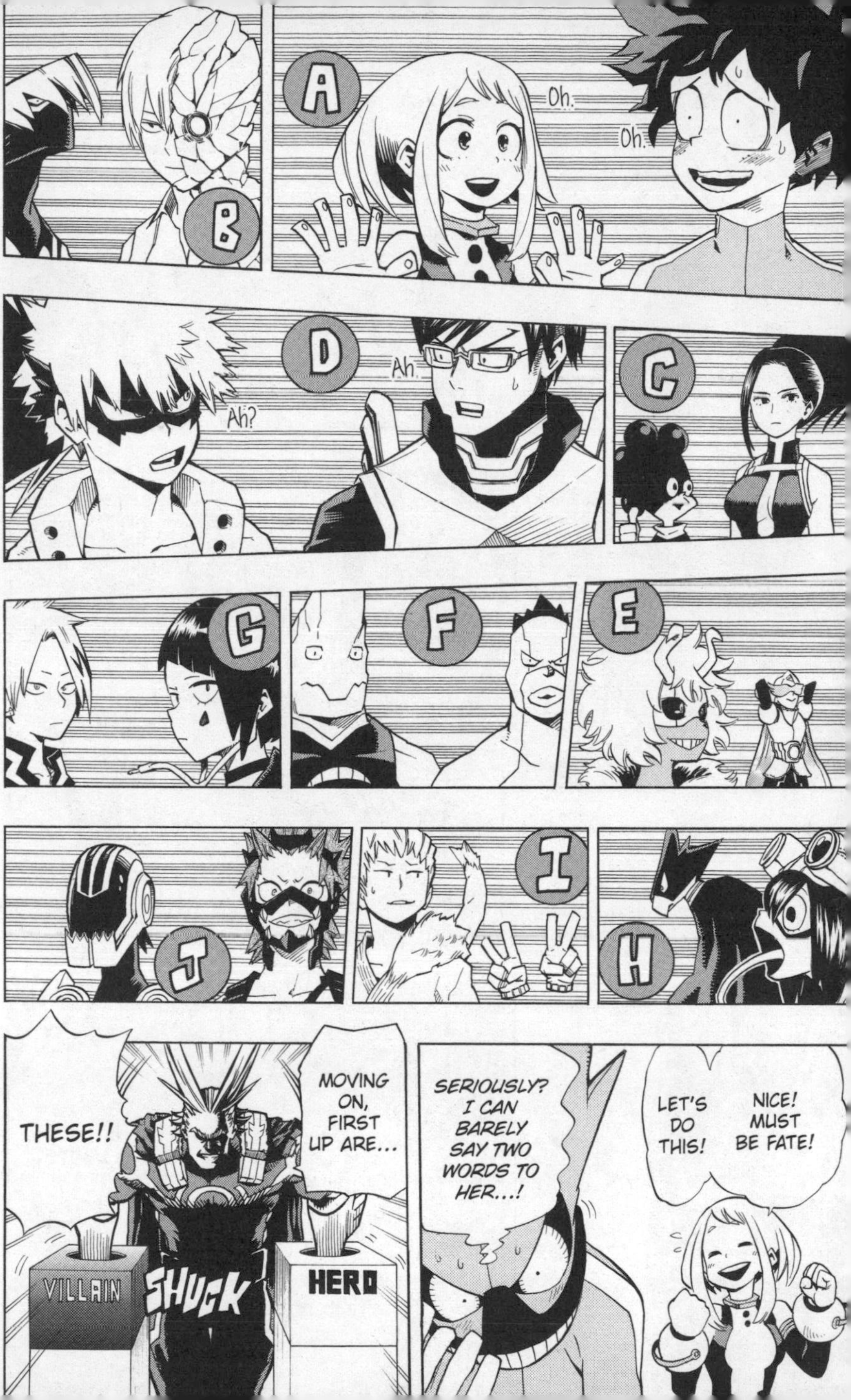

Oh.
Oh.
A
B
C
D
Ah.
Ah?
E
F
G
H
I
J
NICE! MUST BE FATE!
LET'S DO THIS!
SERIOUSLY? I CAN BARELY SAY TWO WORDS TO HER...!
MOVING ON, FIRST UP ARE...
THESE!!
HERO
SHUCK
VILLAIN

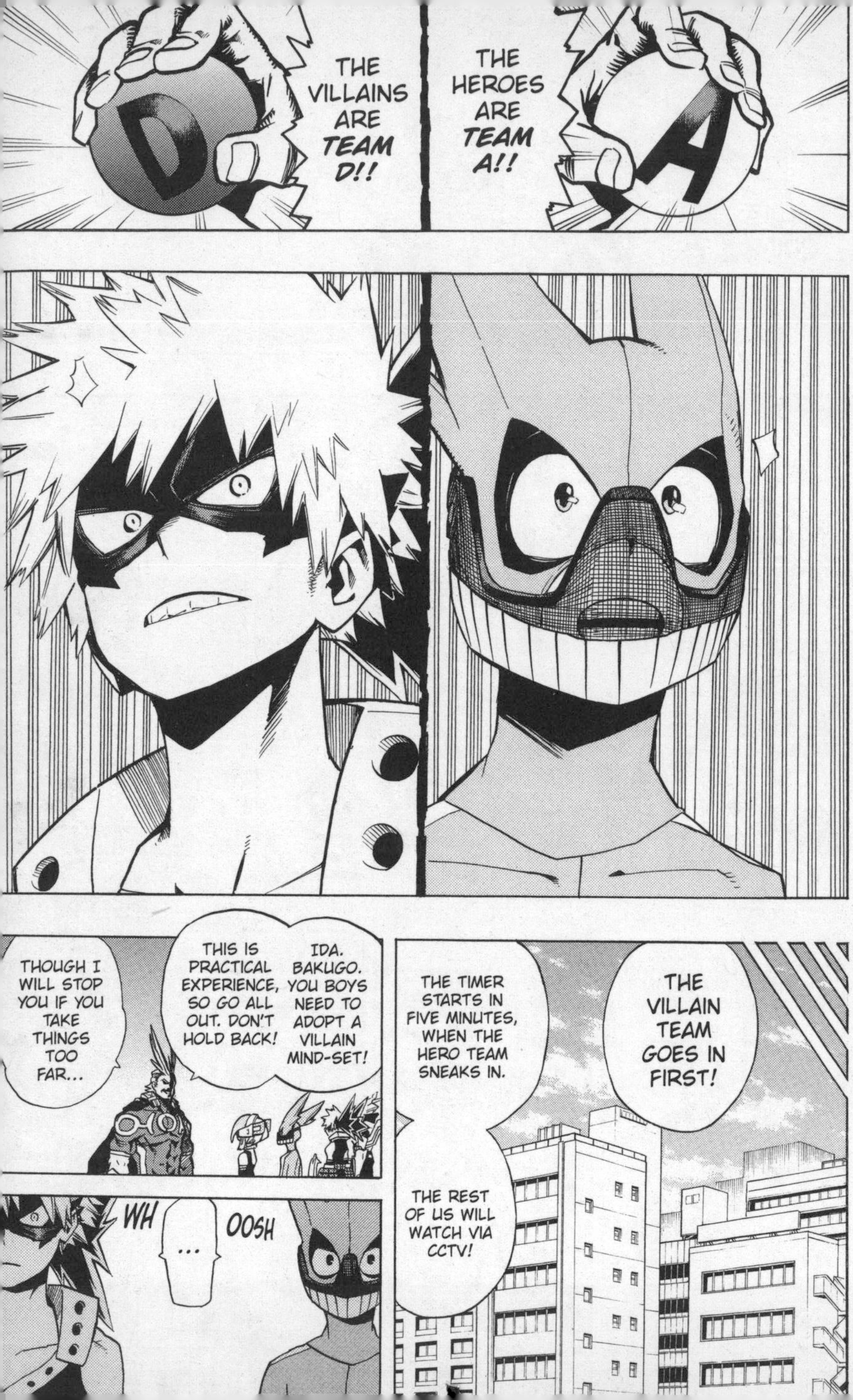
THE HEROES ARE TEAM A!!
THE VILLAINS ARE TEAM D!!
THE VILLAIN TEAM GOES IN FIRST!
THE TIMER STARTS IN FIVE MINUTES, WHEN THE HERO TEAM SNEAKS IN.
THE REST OF US WILL WATCH VIA CCTV!
IDA. BAKUGO. YOU BOYS NEED TO ADOPT A VILLAIN MIND-SET!
THIS IS PRACTICAL EXPERIENCE, SO GO ALL OUT. DON'T HOLD BACK!
THOUGH I WILL STOP YOU IF YOU TAKE THINGS TOO FAR...
WH OOSH
...

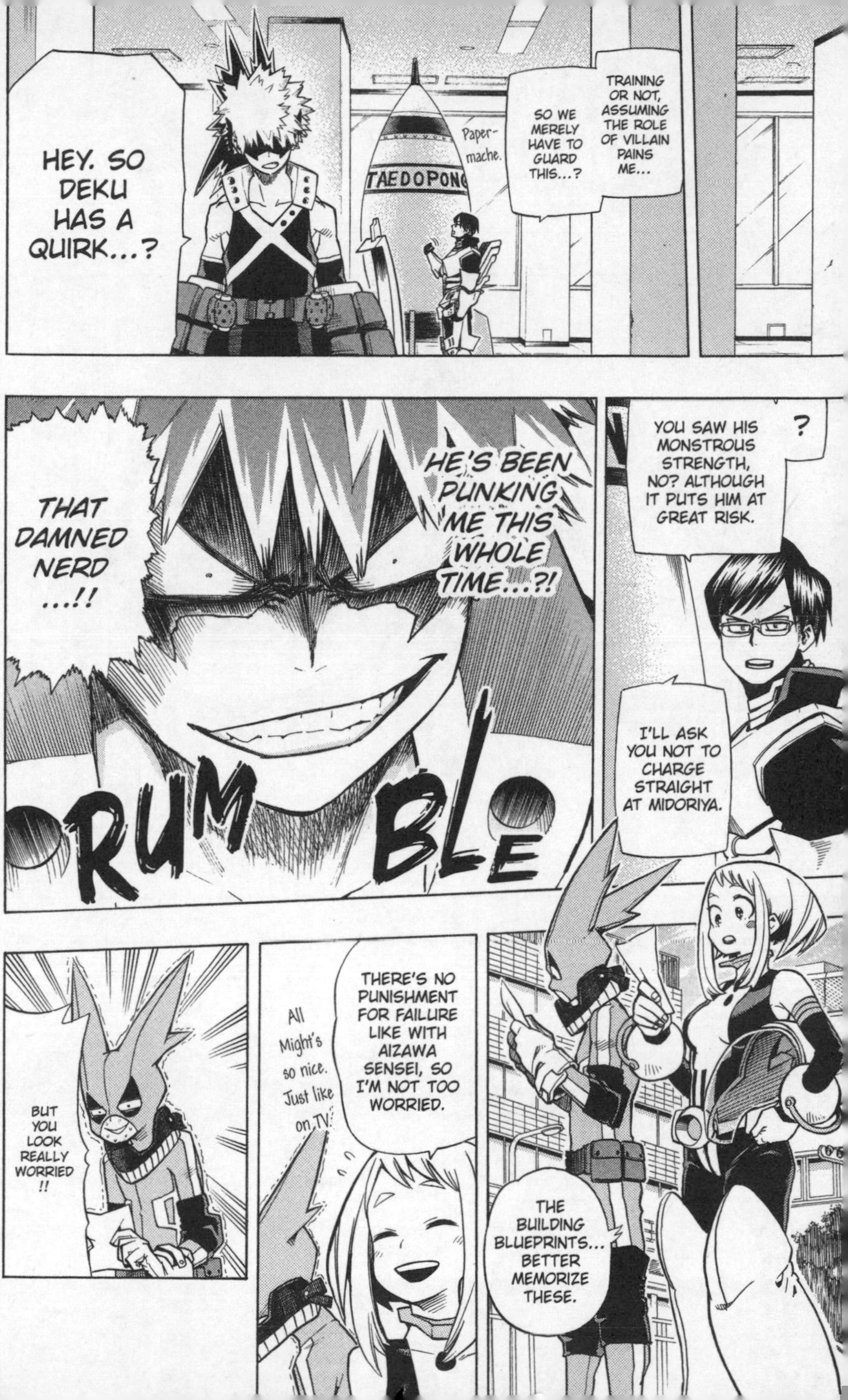
TRAINING OR NOT, ASSUMING THE ROLE OF VILLAIN PAINS ME...
SO WE MERELY HAVE TO GUARD THIS...?
Paper-mache.
TAEDOPONG
HEY. SO DEKU HAS A QUIRK...?
?
YOU SAW HIS MONSTROUS STRENGTH, NO? ALTHOUGH IT PUTS HIM AT GREAT RISK.
I'LL ASK YOU NOT TO CHARGE STRAIGHT AT MIDORIYA.
HE'S BEEN PUNKING ME THIS WHOLE TIME...?!
THAT DAMNED NERD ...!!
RUMBLE
THE BUILDING BLUEPRINTS... BETTER MEMORIZE THESE.
THERE'S NO PUNISHMENT FOR FAILURE LIKE WITH AIZAWA SENSEI, SO I'M NOT TOO WORRIED.
All Might's so nice. Just like on TV.
BUT YOU LOOK REALLY WORRIED !!

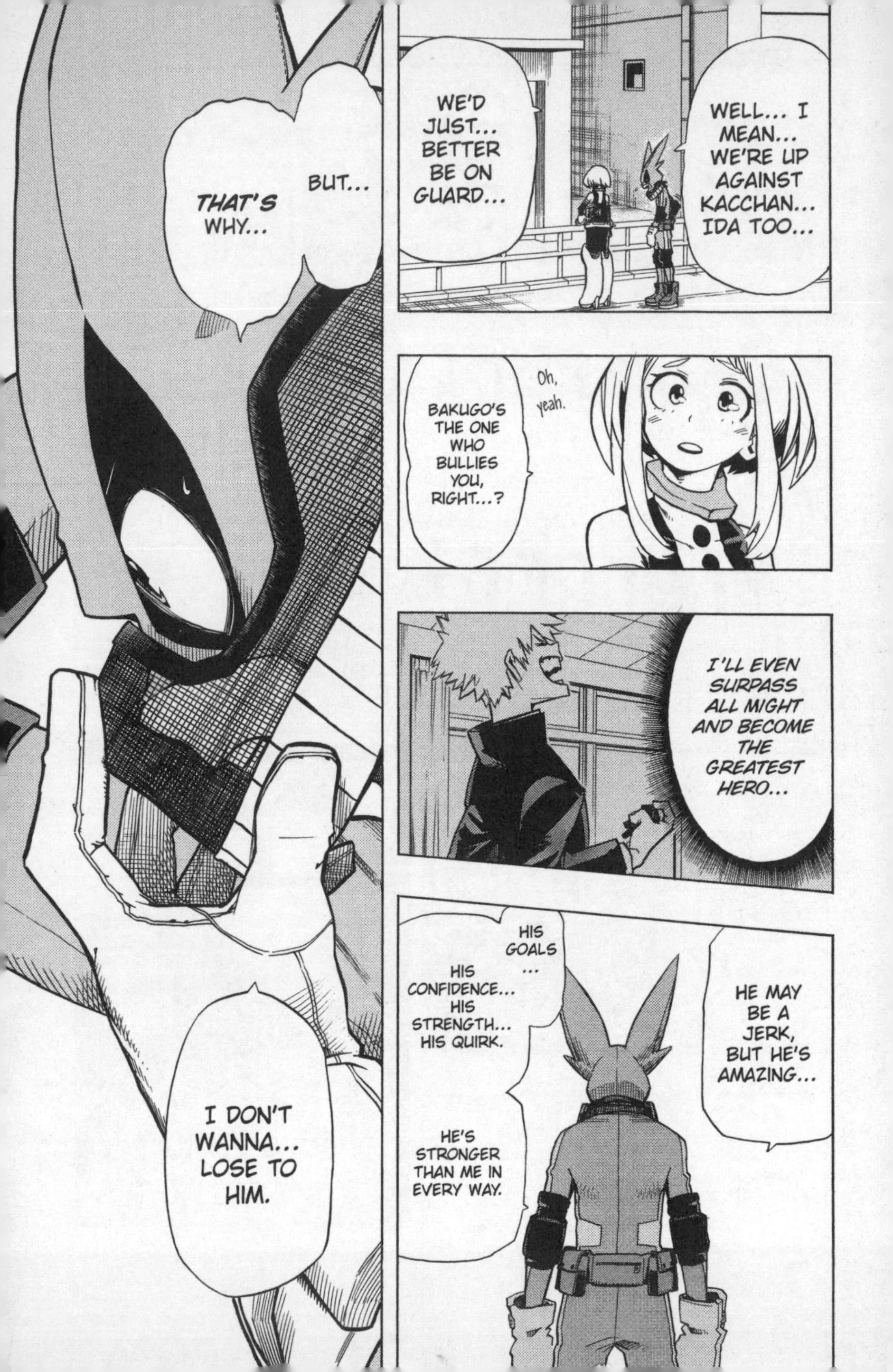
WELL... I MEAN... WE'RE UP AGAINST KACCHAN... IDA TOO...
WE'D JUST... BETTER BE ON GUARD...
Oh, yeah.
BAKUGO'S THE ONE WHO BULLIES YOU, RIGHT...?
I'LL EVEN SURPASS ALL MIGHT AND BECOME THE GREATEST HERO...
HE MAY BE A JERK, BUT HE'S AMAZING...
HIS GOALS...
HIS CONFIDENCE... HIS STRENGTH... HIS QUIRK.
HE'S STRONGER THAN ME IN EVERY WAY.
BUT...
THAT'S WHY...
I DON'T WANNA... LOSE TO HIM.

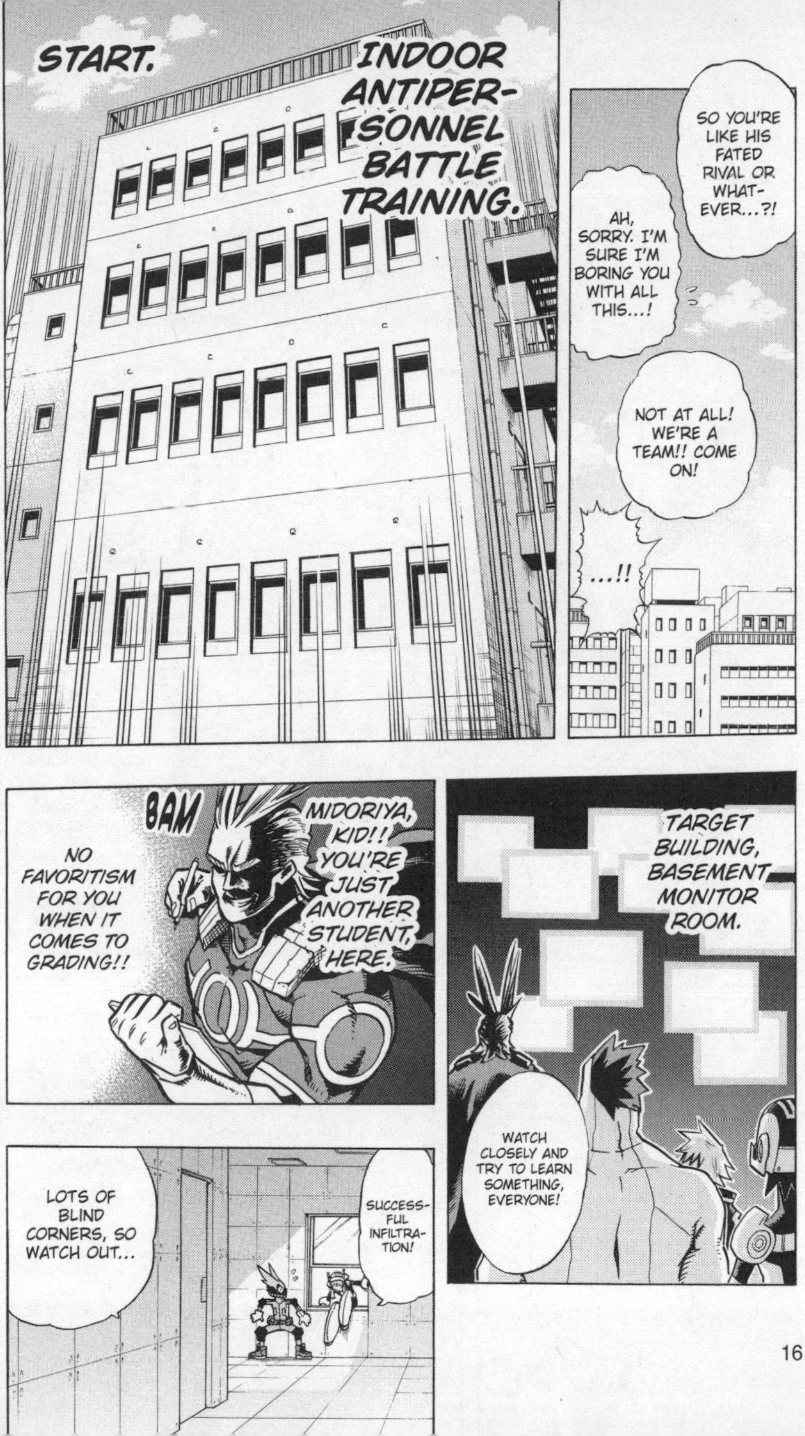
SO YOU'RE LIKE HIS FATED RIVAL OR WHAT-EVER...?!
AH, SORRY. I'M SURE I'M BORING YOU WITH ALL THIS...!
NOT AT ALL! WE'RE A TEAM!! COME ON!
...!!
INDOOR ANTIPER-SONNEL BATTLE TRAINING.
START.
TARGET BUILDING, BASEMENT MONITOR ROOM.
WATCH CLOSELY AND TRY TO LEARN SOMETHING, EVERYONE!
BAM
MIDORIYA, KID!! YOU'RE JUST ANOTHER STUDENT, HERE.
NO FAVORITISM FOR YOU WHEN IT COMES TO GRADING!!
SUCCESS-FUL INFILTRA-TION!
LOTS OF BLIND CORNERS, SO WATCH OUT...

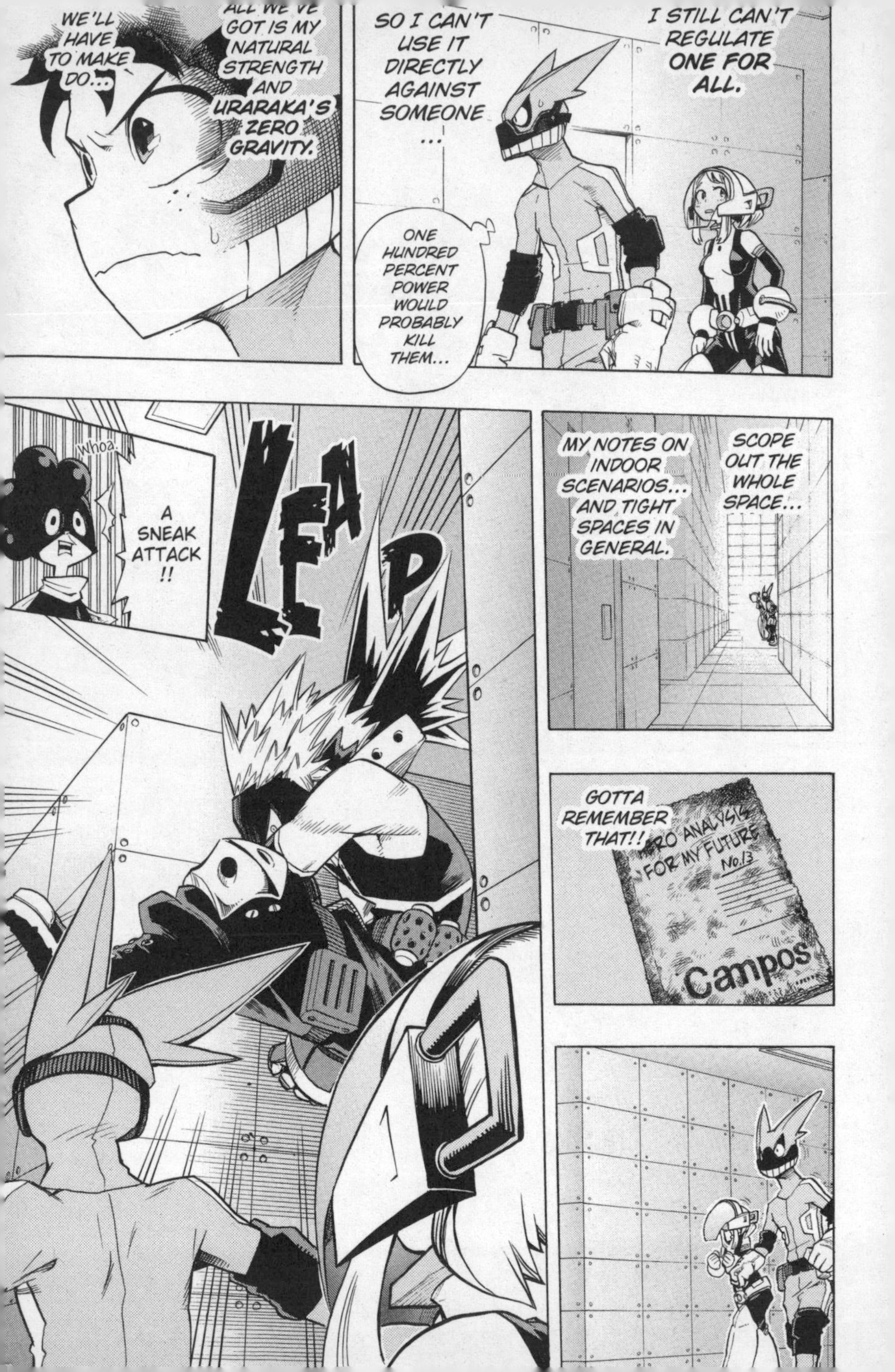
I STILL CAN'T REGULATE ONE FOR ALL.
SO I CAN'T USE IT DIRECTLY AGAINST SOMEONE ...
ONE HUNDRED PERCENT POWER WOULD PROBABLY KILL THEM...
ALL WE'VE GOT IS MY NATURAL STRENGTH AND URARAKA'S ZERO GRAVITY.
WE'LL HAVE TO MAKE DO...
SCOPE OUT THE WHOLE SPACE...
MY NOTES ON INDOOR SCENARIOS... AND TIGHT SPACES IN GENERAL.
GOTTA REMEMBER THAT!!
RO ANALYSIS FOR MY FUTURE No.13
Campos
LEAP
Whoa.
A SNEAK ATTACK !!

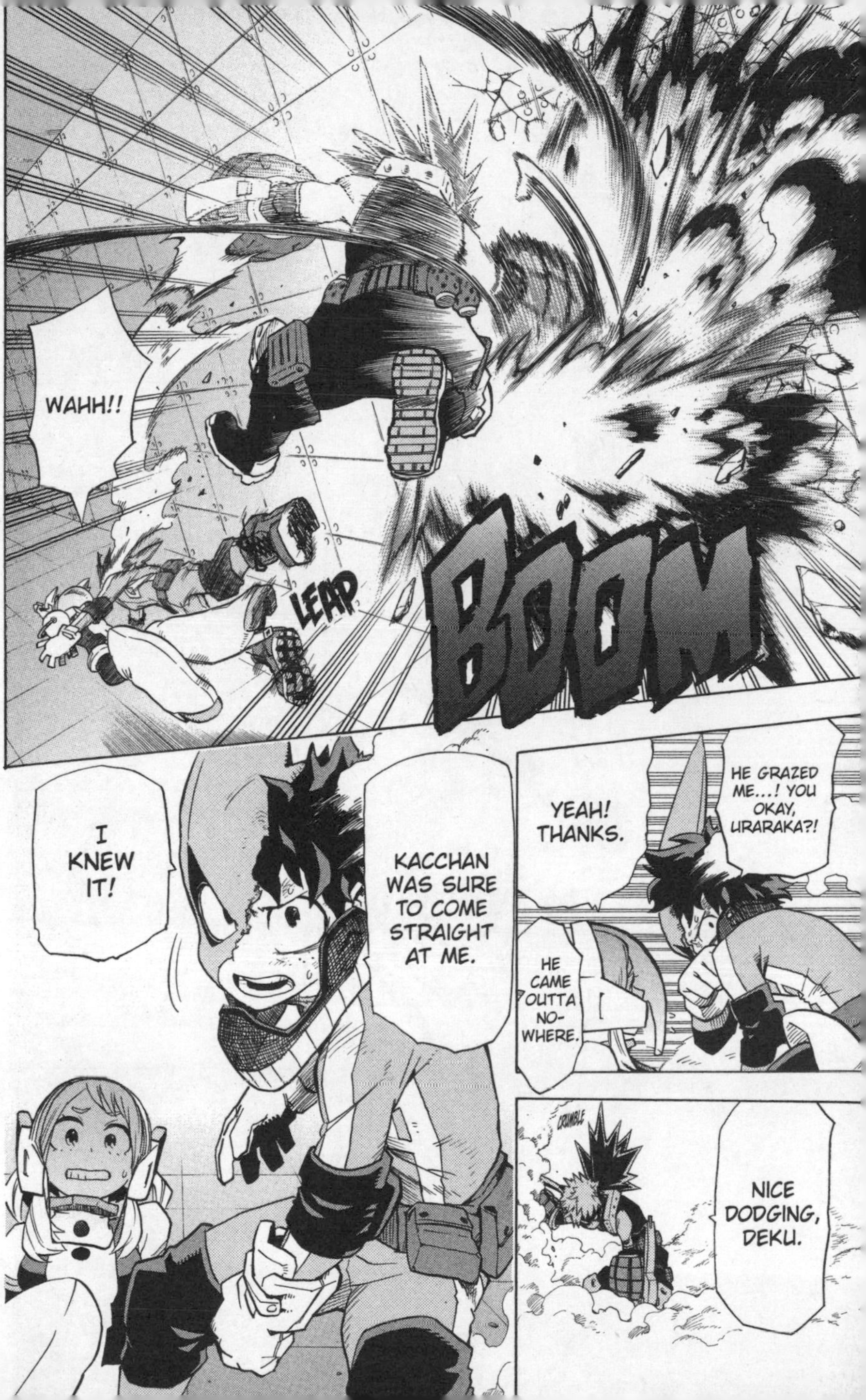
WAHH!!
BOOM
LEAP
HE GRAZED ME...! YOU OKAY, URARAKA?!
YEAH! THANKS.
HE CAME OUTTA NO-WHERE.
CRUMBLE
NICE DODGING, DEKU.
KACCHAN WAS SURE TO COME STRAIGHT AT ME.
I KNEW IT!

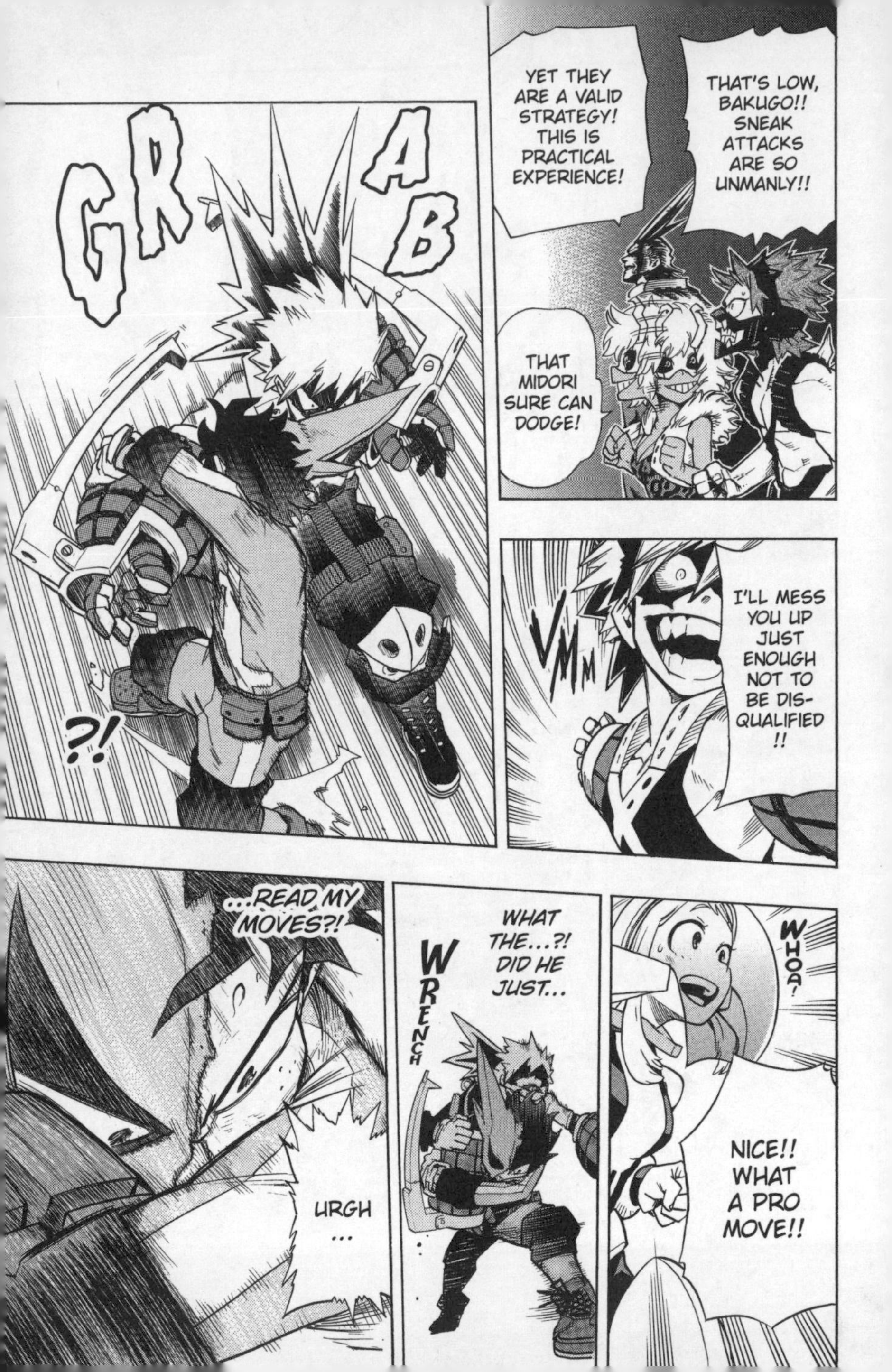
THAT'S LOW, BAKUGO!! SNEAK ATTACKS ARE SO UNMANLY!!
YET THEY ARE A VALID STRATEGY! THIS IS PRACTICAL EXPERIENCE!
THAT MIDORI SURE CAN DODGE!
I'LL MESS YOU UP JUST ENOUGH NOT TO BE DIS-QUALIFIED!!
VMM
GRAB
?!
WHOA!
NICE!! WHAT A PRO MOVE!!
WHAT THE...?! DID HE JUST...
WRENCH
...READ MY MOVES?!
URGH...

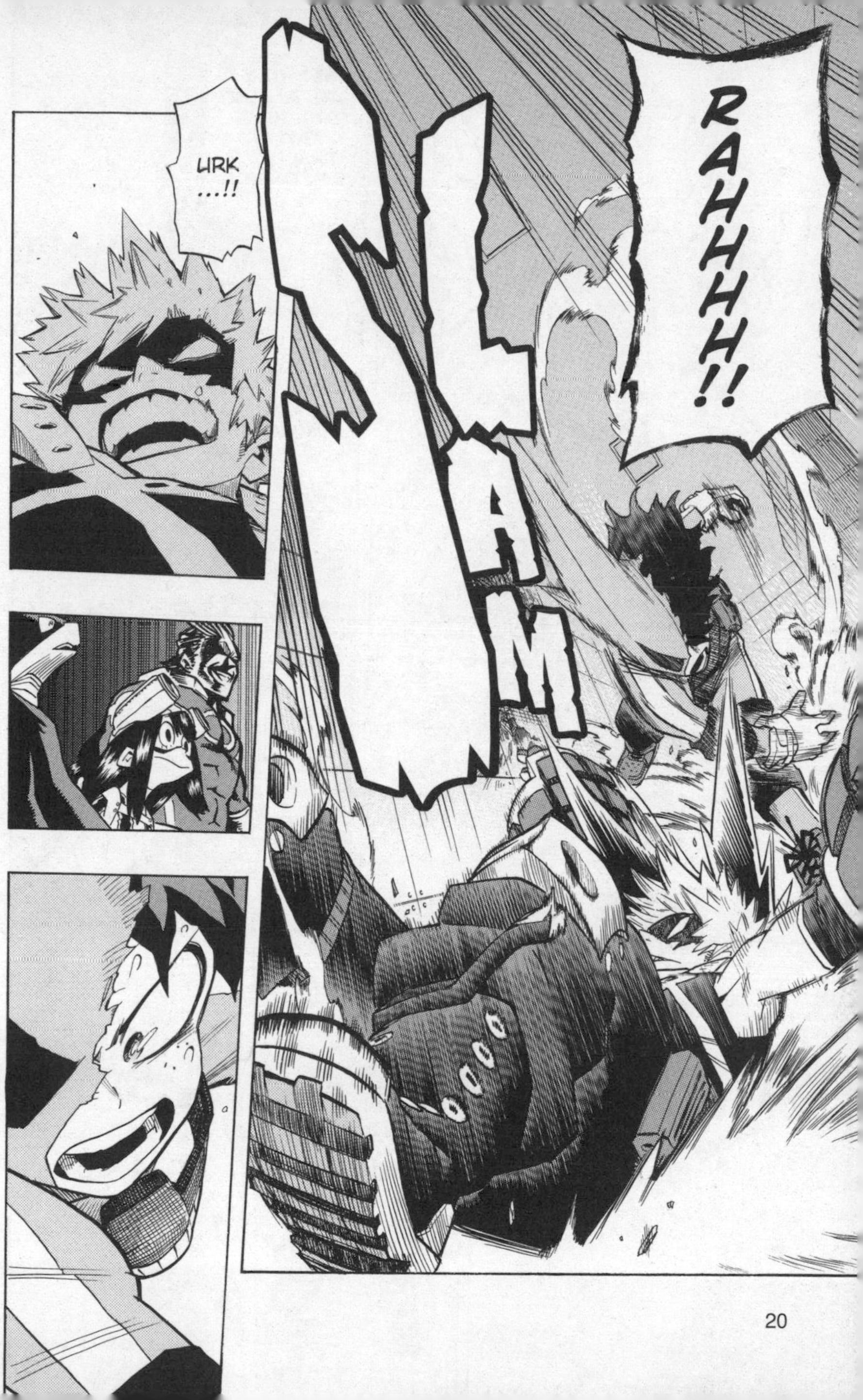
RAHHHHH!!
SLAM
URK ...!!

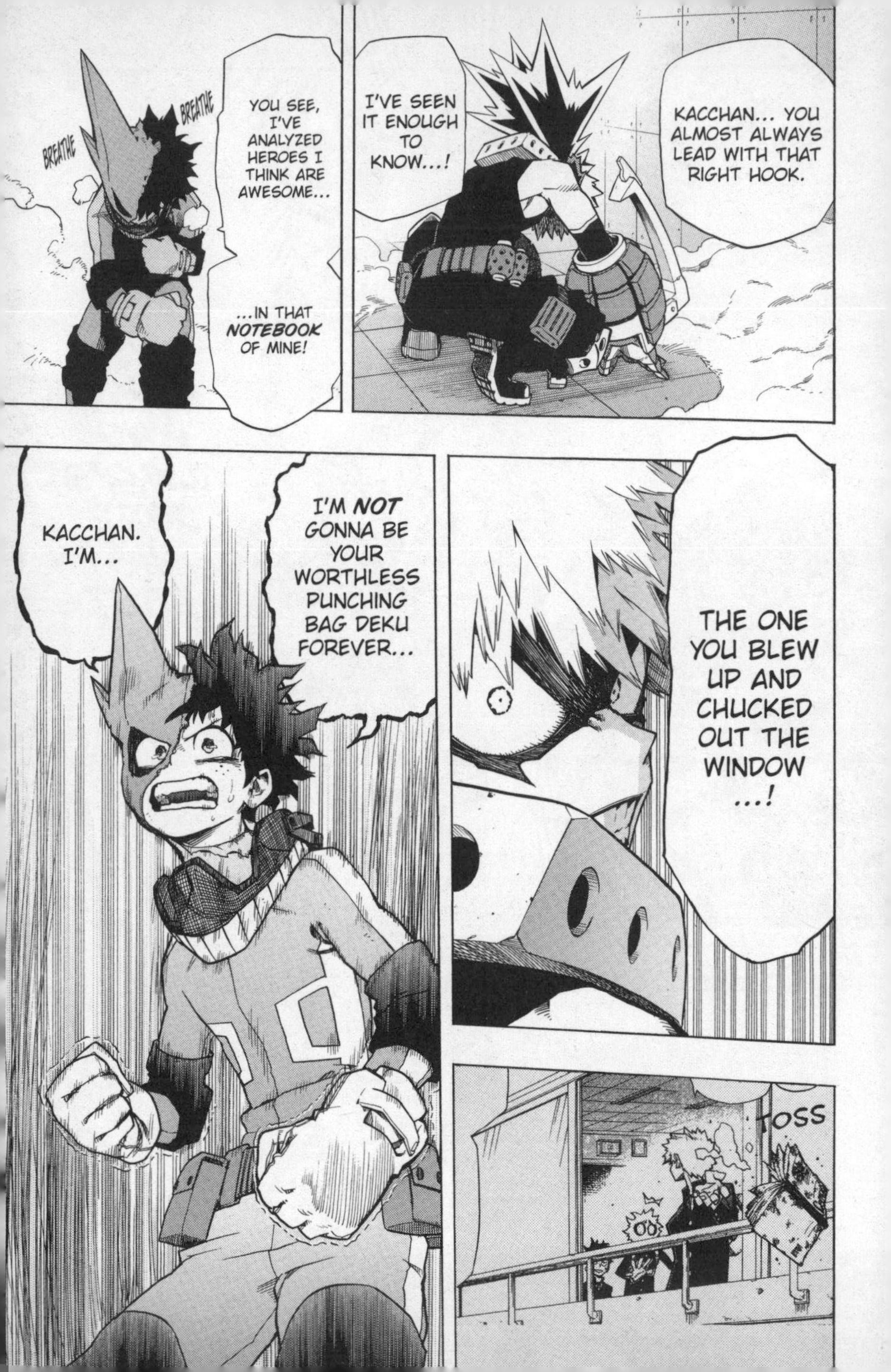
KACCHAN... YOU ALMOST ALWAYS LEAD WITH THAT RIGHT HOOK.
I'VE SEEN IT ENOUGH TO KNOW...!
BREATHE
BREATHE
YOU SEE, I'VE ANALYZED HEROES I THINK ARE AWESOME...
...IN THAT **NOTEBOOK** OF MINE!
THE ONE YOU BLEW UP AND CHUCKED OUT THE WINDOW ...!
TOSS
KACCHAN. I'M...
I'M **NOT** GONNA BE YOUR WORTHLESS PUNCHING BAG DEKU FOREVER...

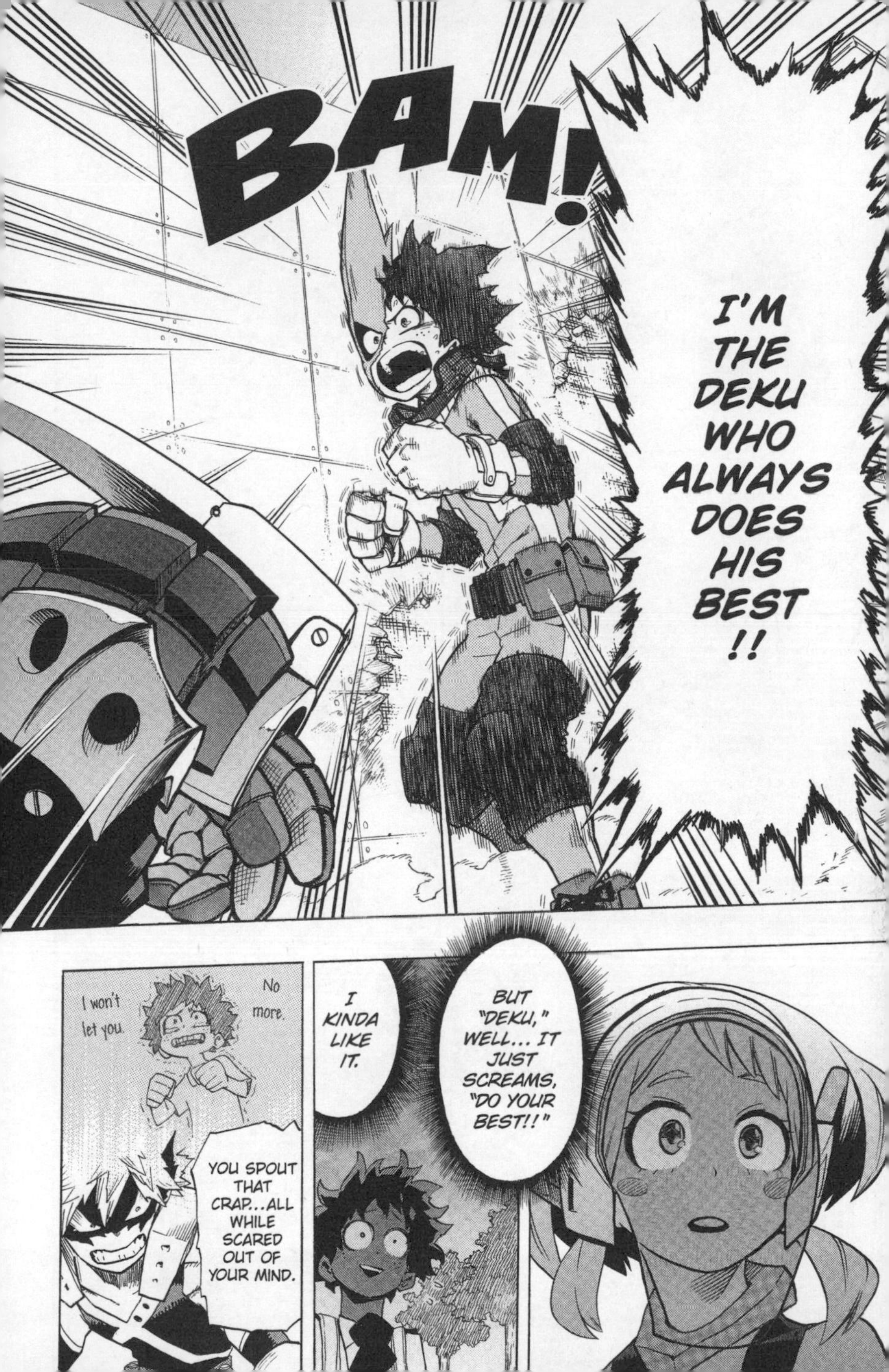
I'M THE DEKU WHO ALWAYS DOES HIS BEST!!
BAM!
BUT "DEKU," WELL... IT JUST SCREAMS, "DO YOUR BEST!!"
I KINDA LIKE IT.
No more.
I won't let you.
YOU SPOUT THAT CRAP...ALL WHILE SCARED OUT OF YOUR MIND.

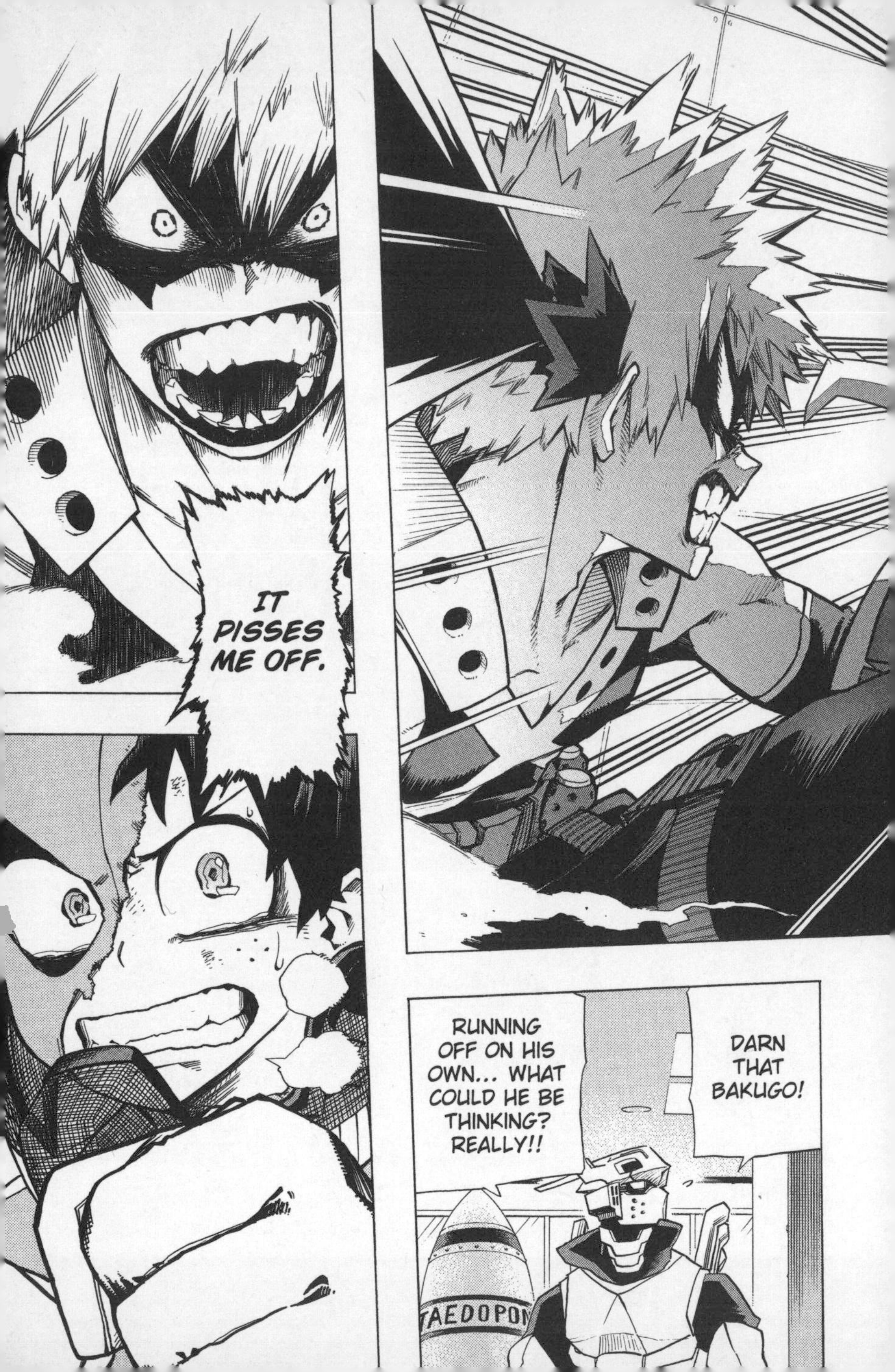
IT PISSES ME OFF.
DARN THAT BAKUGO!
RUNNING OFF ON HIS OWN... WHAT COULD HE BE THINKING? REALLY!!

PRESENT MIC (30)

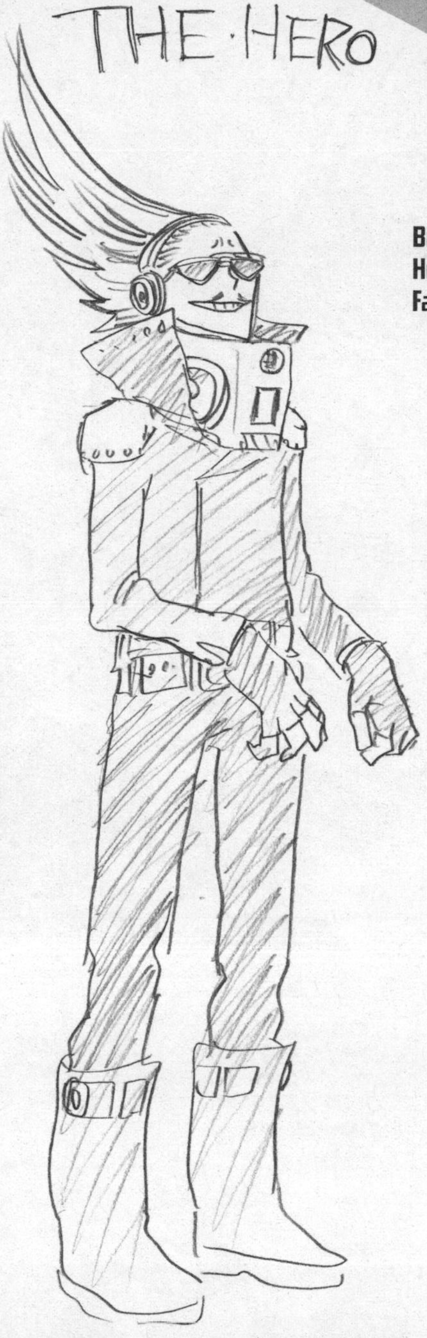
THE HERO

Birthday: 7/7
Height: 185 cm
Favorite Things: Radio, TV

BEHIND THE SCENES

This guy debuted in chapter 3. At first he was just this chubby old man who made announcements, but that was really boring, so I transformed him into the amped-up character he is today.

He graduated in the same class as Eraser Head.

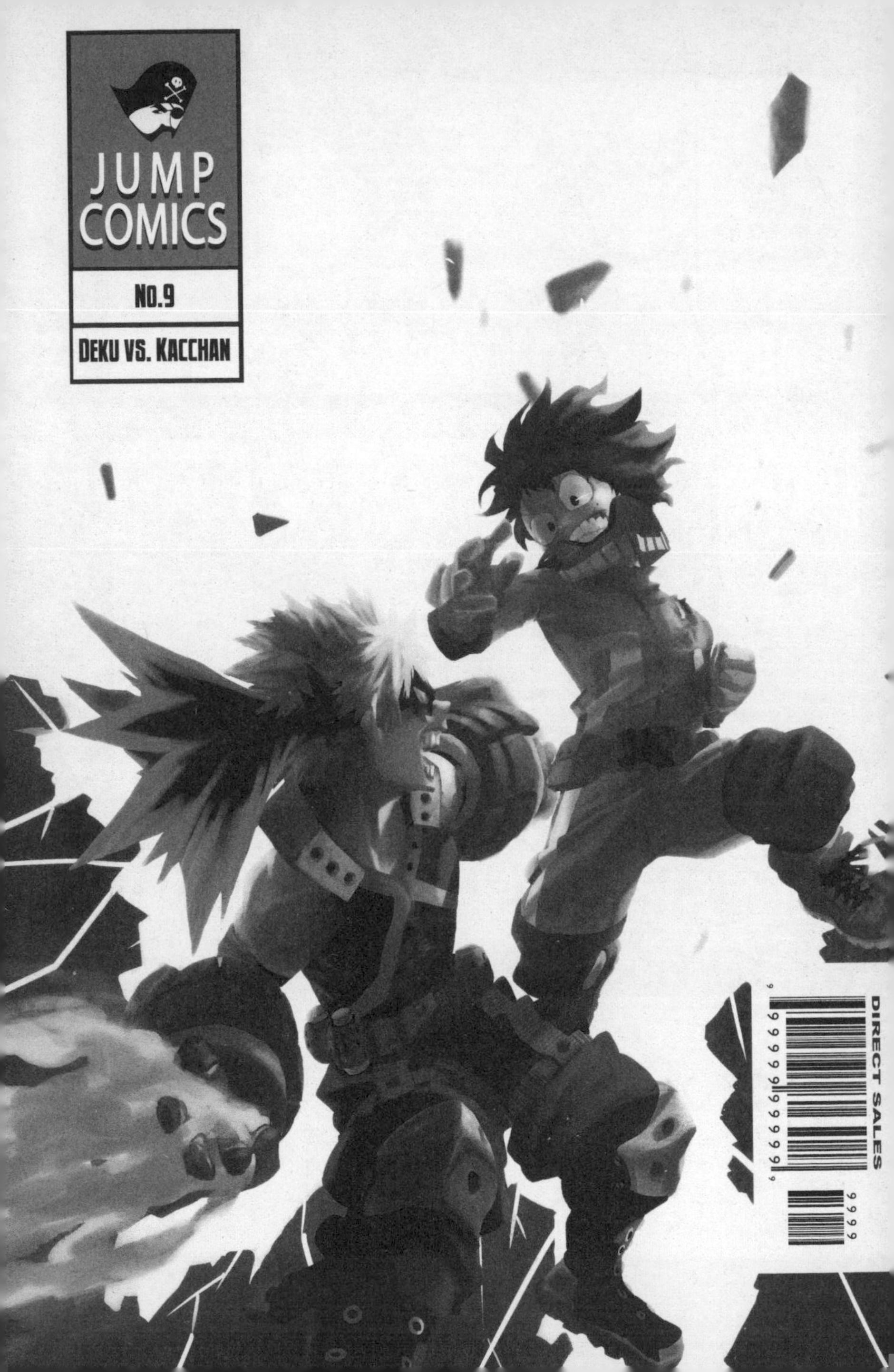
JUMP
COMICS
No.9
DEKU VS. KACCHAN
DIRECT SALES

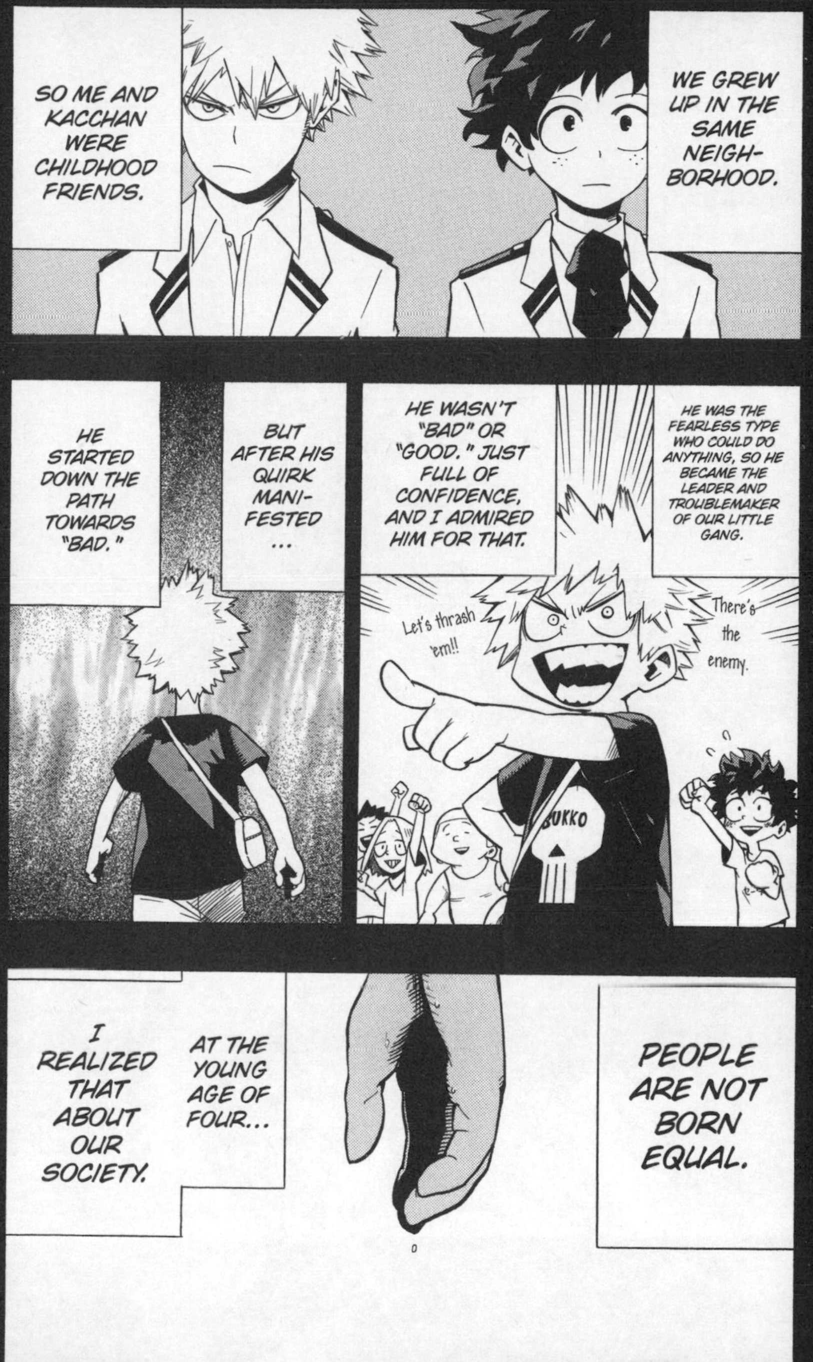
WE GREW UP IN THE SAME NEIGH-BORHOOD.
SO ME AND KACCHAN WERE CHILDHOOD FRIENDS.
HE WAS THE FEARLESS TYPE WHO COULD DO ANYTHING, SO HE BECAME THE LEADER AND TROUBLEMAKER OF OUR LITTLE GANG.
HE WASN'T "BAD" OR "GOOD." JUST FULL OF CONFIDENCE, AND I ADMIRED HIM FOR THAT.
There's the enemy.
Let's thrash 'em!!
BUKKO
BUT AFTER HIS QUIRK MANI-FESTED...
HE STARTED DOWN THE PATH TOWARDS "BAD."
PEOPLE ARE NOT BORN EQUAL.
AT THE YOUNG AGE OF FOUR...
I REALIZED THAT ABOUT OUR SOCIETY.

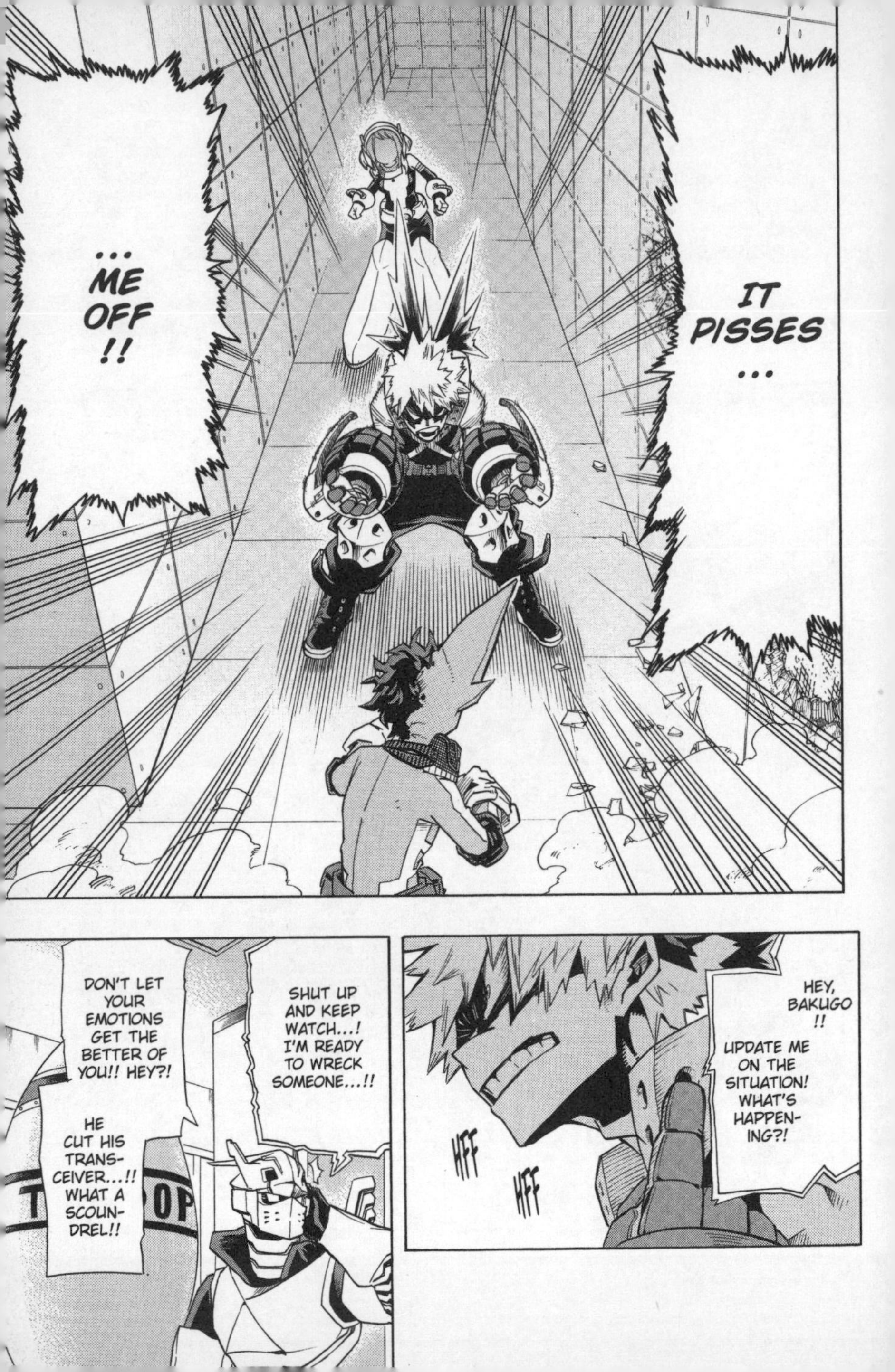
IT PISSES ...
... ME OFF !!
HEY, BAKUGO !!
UPDATE ME ON THE SITUATION! WHAT'S HAPPEN-ING?!
HFF
HFF
SHUT UP AND KEEP WATCH...! I'M READY TO WRECK SOMEONE...!!
DON'T LET YOUR EMOTIONS GET THE BETTER OF YOU!! HEY?!
HE CUT HIS TRANS-CEIVER...!! WHAT A SCOUN-DREL!!

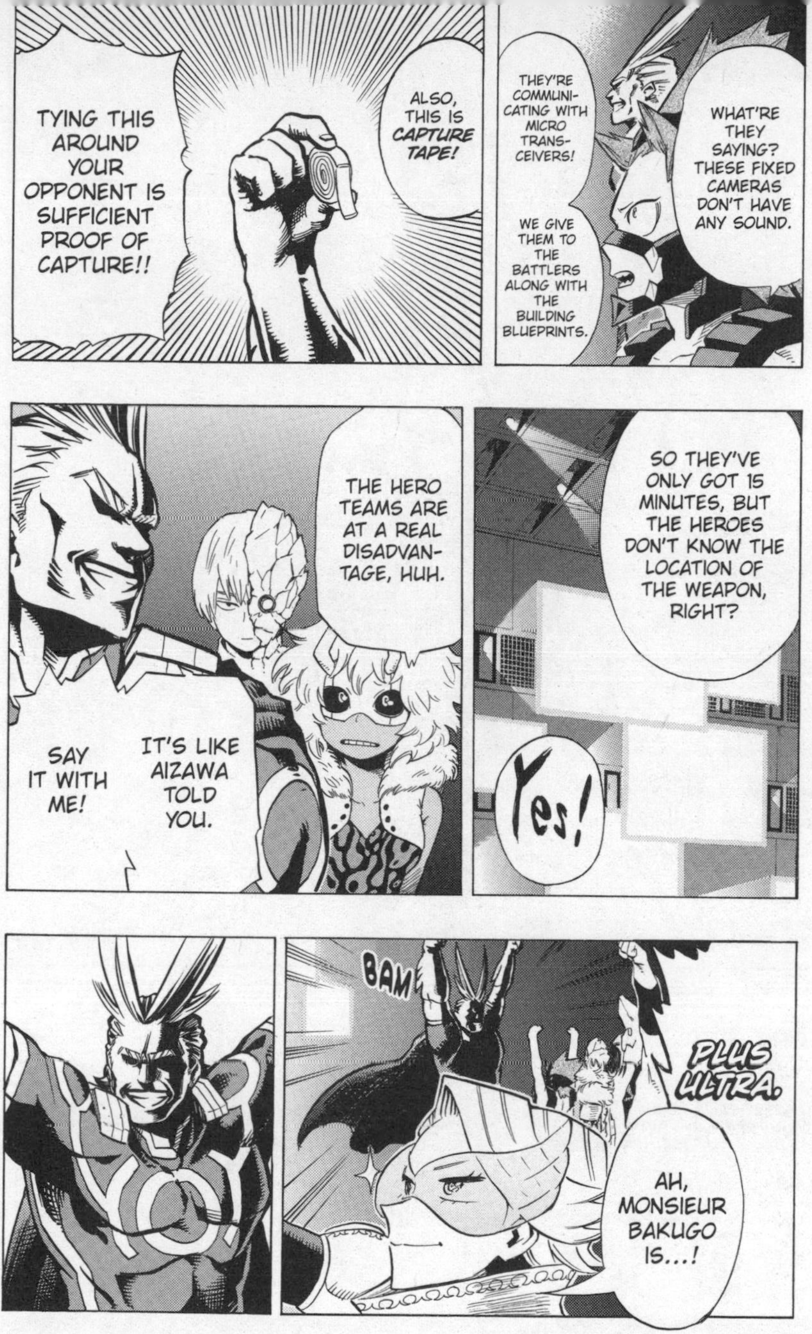
WHAT'RE THEY SAYING? THESE FIXED CAMERAS DON'T HAVE ANY SOUND.
THEY'RE COMMUNI-CATING WITH MICRO TRANS-CEIVERS!
WE GIVE THEM TO THE BATTLERS ALONG WITH THE BUILDING BLUEPRINTS.
ALSO, THIS IS *CAPTURE TAPE!*
TYING THIS AROUND YOUR OPPONENT IS SUFFICIENT PROOF OF CAPTURE!!
SO THEY'VE ONLY GOT 15 MINUTES, BUT THE HEROES DON'T KNOW THE LOCATION OF THE WEAPON, RIGHT?
Yes!
THE HERO TEAMS ARE AT A REAL DISADVAN-TAGE, HUH.
IT'S LIKE AIZAWA TOLD YOU.
SAY IT WITH ME!
BAM
PLUS ULTRA.
AH, MONSIEUR BAKUGO IS...!

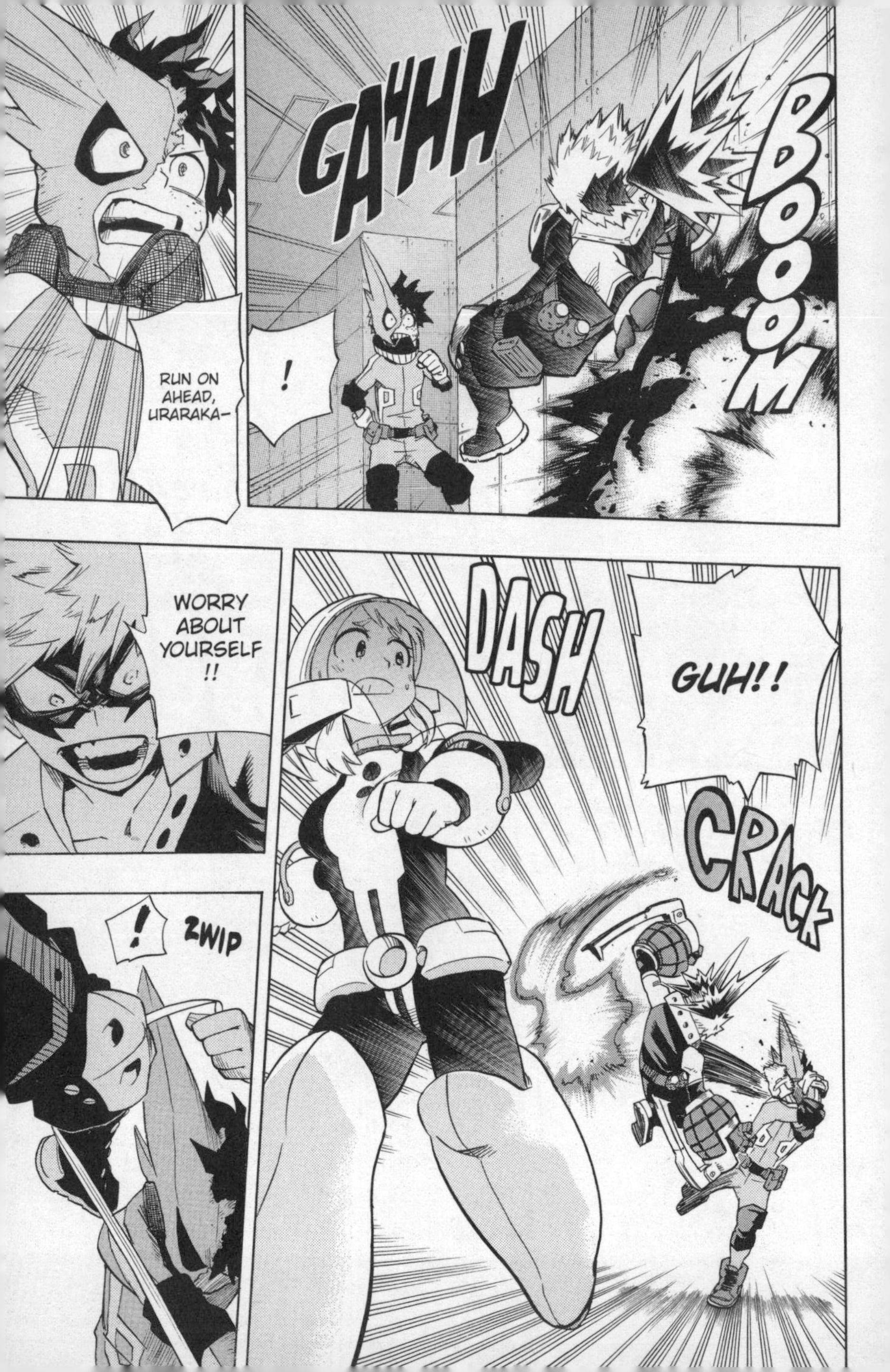
BOOOOM
GAHHH
!
RUN ON AHEAD, URARAKA-
GUH!!
DASH
CRACK
WORRY ABOUT YOURSELF!!
ZWIP
!

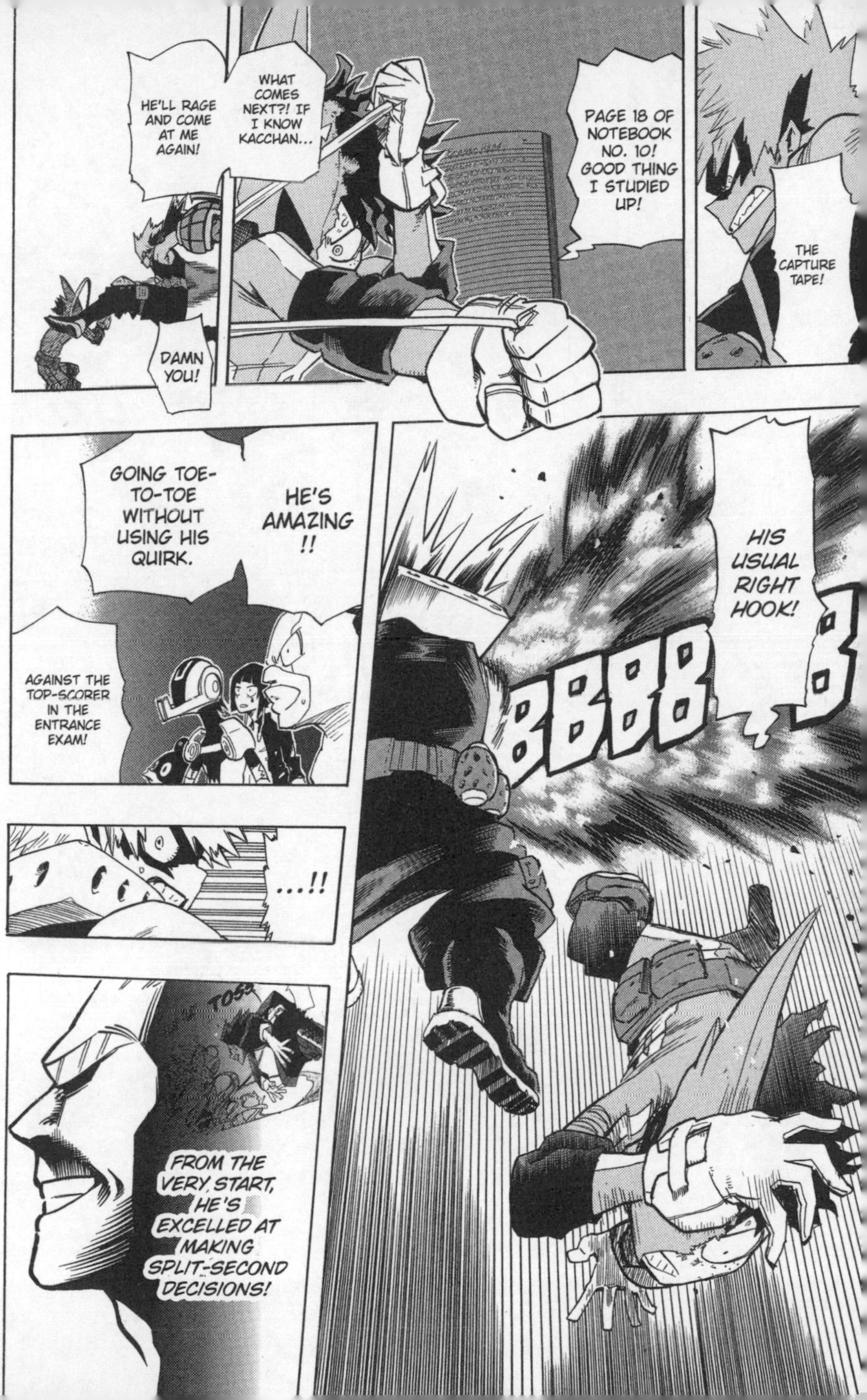
THE CAPTURE TAPE!
PAGE 18 OF NOTEBOOK NO. 10! GOOD THING I STUDIED UP!
WHAT COMES NEXT?! IF I KNOW KACCHAN...
HE'LL RAGE AND COME AT ME AGAIN!
DAMN YOU!
HIS USUAL RIGHT HOOK!
BBBB
HE'S AMAZING!!
GOING TOE-TO-TOE WITHOUT USING HIS QUIRK.
AGAINST THE TOP-SCORER IN THE ENTRANCE EXAM!
...!!
TOSS
FROM THE VERY START, HE'S EXCELLED AT MAKING SPLIT-SECOND DECISIONS!

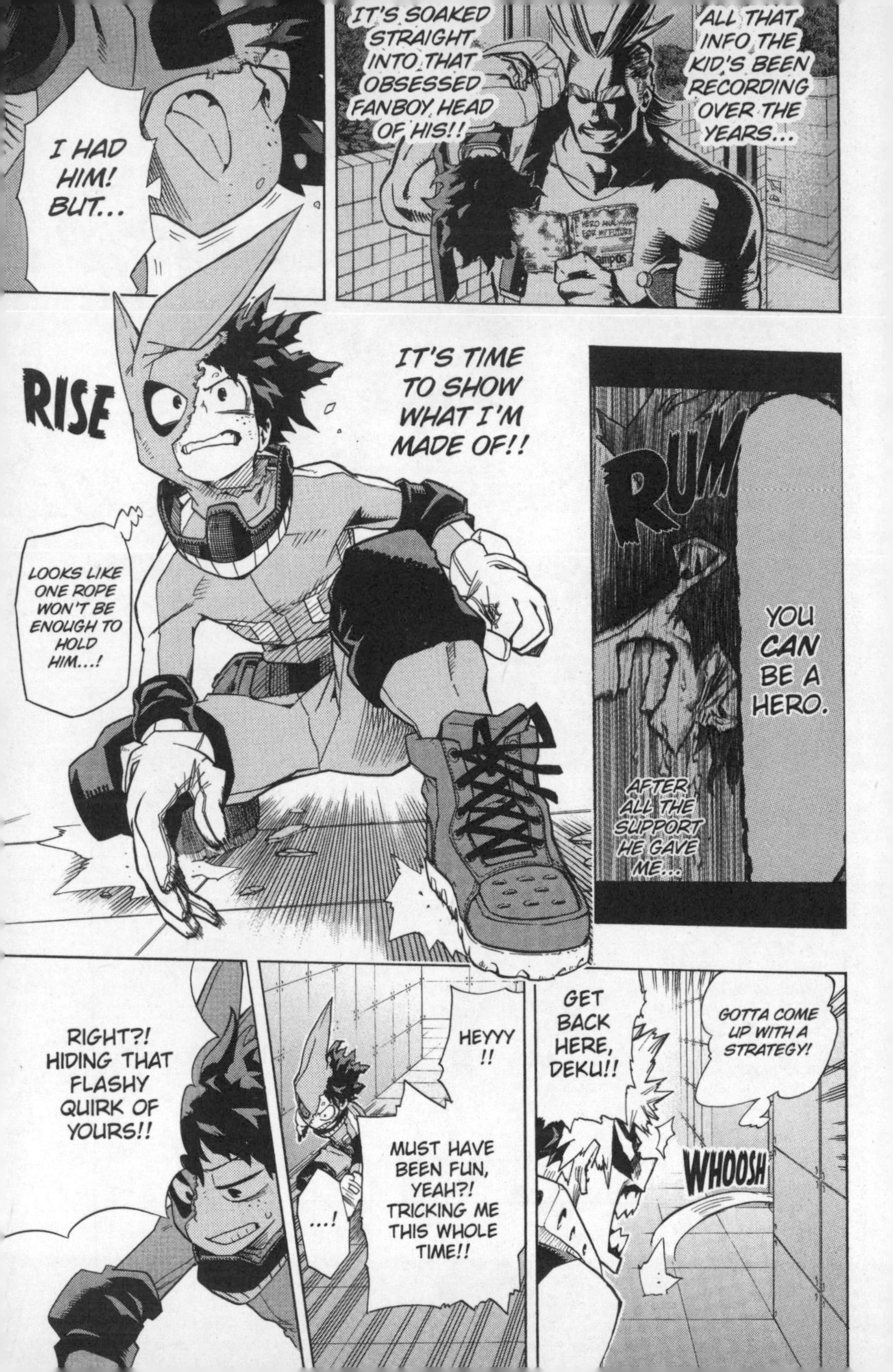
ALL THAT INFO THE KID'S BEEN RECORDING OVER THE YEARS...
IT'S SOAKED STRAIGHT INTO THAT OBSESSED FANBOY HEAD OF HIS!!
I HAD HIM! BUT...
YOU CAN BE A HERO.
RUM
AFTER ALL THE SUPPORT HE GAVE ME...
IT'S TIME TO SHOW WHAT I'M MADE OF!!
RISE
LOOKS LIKE ONE ROPE WON'T BE ENOUGH TO HOLD HIM...!
GOTTA COME UP WITH A STRATEGY!
GET BACK HERE, DEKU!!
WHOOSH
HEYYY!!
MUST HAVE BEEN FUN, YEAH?! TRICKING ME THIS WHOLE TIME!!
...!
RIGHT?! HIDING THAT FLASHY QUIRK OF YOURS!!

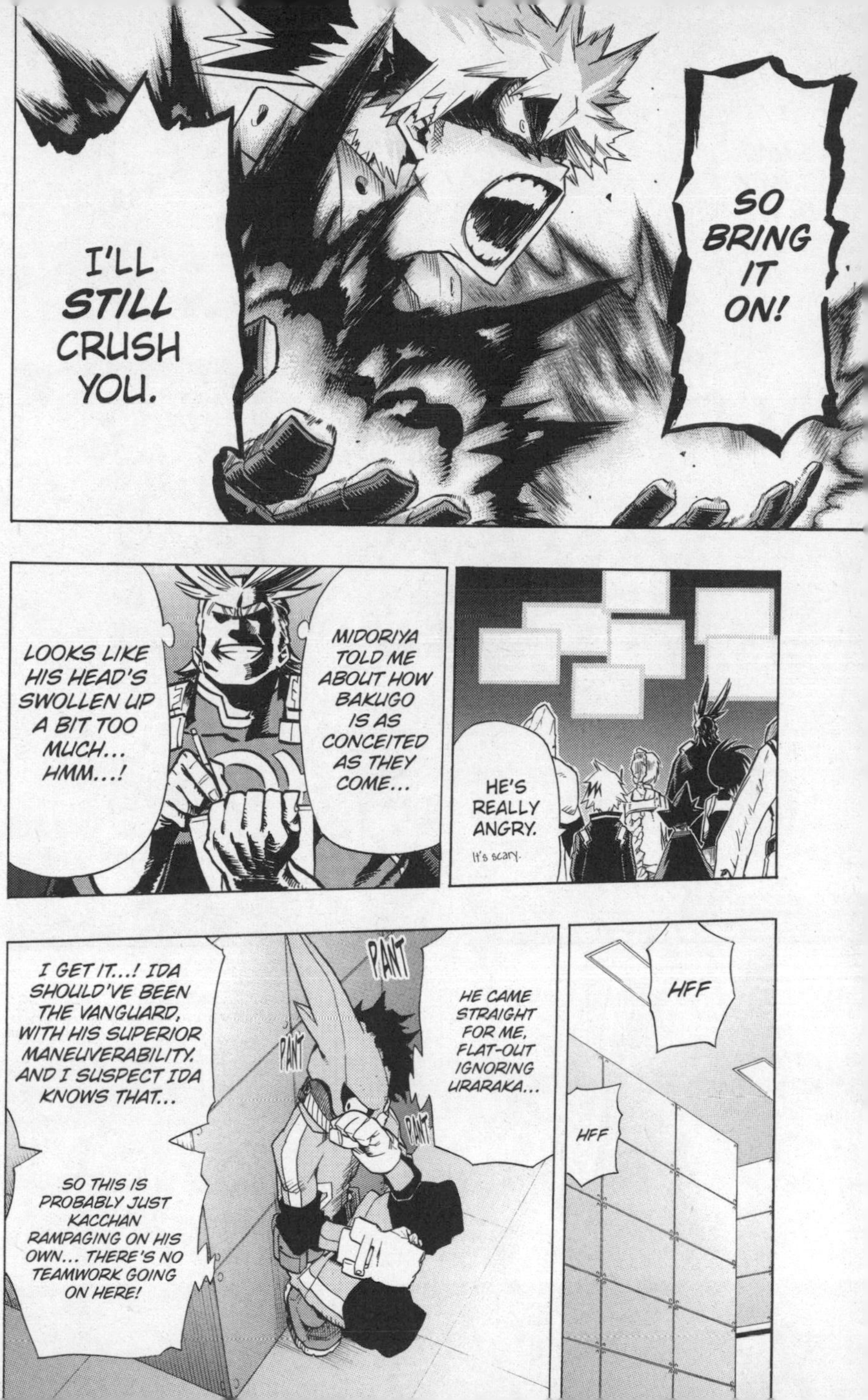
SO BRING IT ON!
I'LL STILL CRUSH YOU.
HE'S REALLY ANGRY.
It's scary.
MIDORIYA TOLD ME ABOUT HOW BAKUGO IS AS CONCEITED AS THEY COME...
LOOKS LIKE HIS HEAD'S SWOLLEN UP A BIT TOO MUCH... HMM...!
HFF
HFF
PANT
HE CAME STRAIGHT FOR ME, FLAT-OUT IGNORING URARAKA...
I GET IT...! IDA SHOULD'VE BEEN THE VANGUARD, WITH HIS SUPERIOR MANEUVERABILITY. AND I SUSPECT IDA KNOWS THAT...
PANT
PANT
SO THIS IS PROBABLY JUST KACCHAN RAMPAGING ON HIS OWN... THERE'S NO TEAMWORK GOING ON HERE!

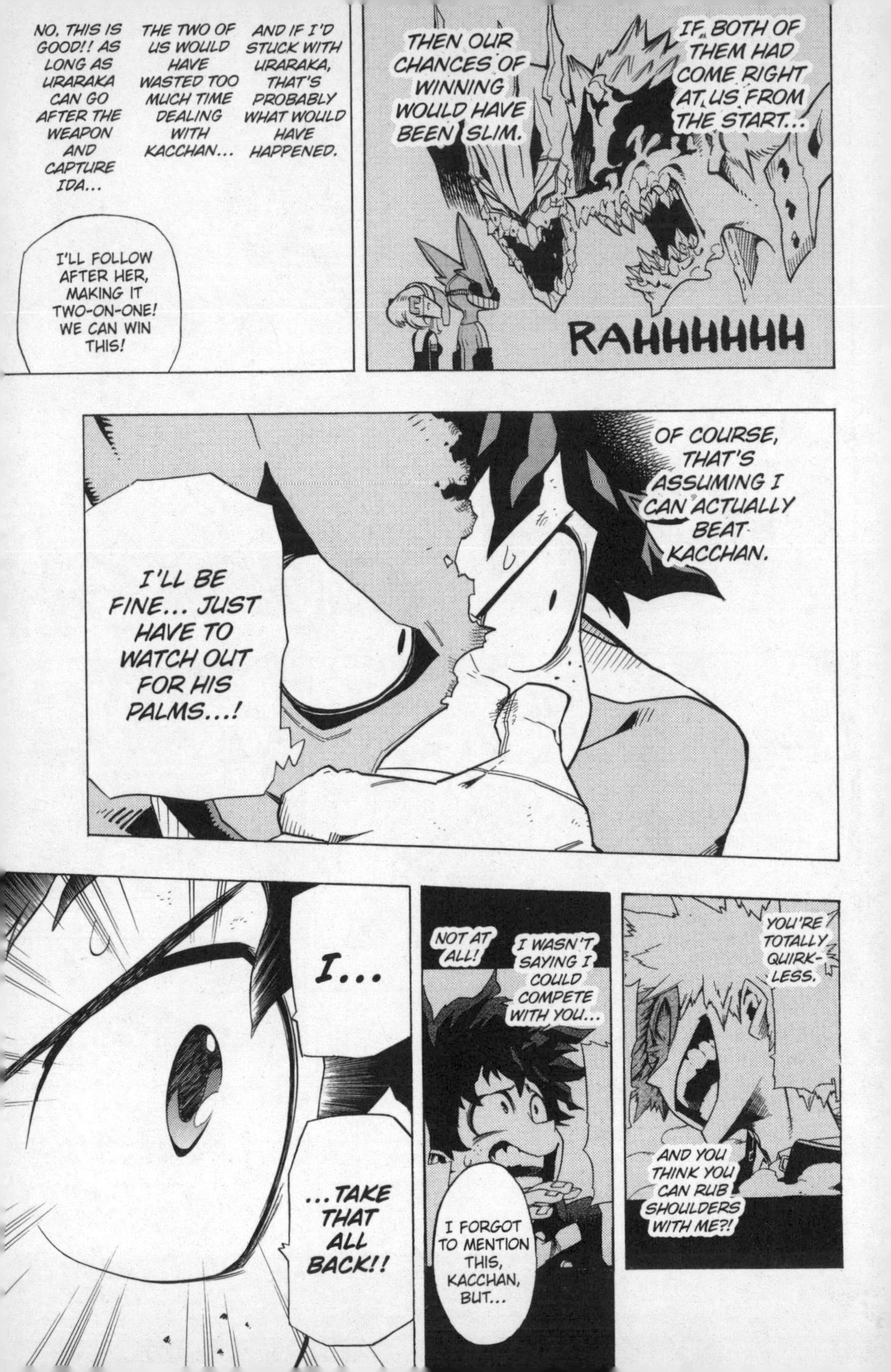
IF BOTH OF THEM HAD COME RIGHT AT US FROM THE START...
THEN OUR CHANCES OF WINNING WOULD HAVE BEEN SLIM.
RAHHHHHH
NO, THIS IS GOOD!! AS LONG AS URARAKA CAN GO AFTER THE WEAPON AND CAPTURE IDA...
THE TWO OF US WOULD HAVE WASTED TOO MUCH TIME DEALING WITH KACCHAN...
AND IF I'D STUCK WITH URARAKA, THAT'S PROBABLY WHAT WOULD HAVE HAPPENED.
I'LL FOLLOW AFTER HER, MAKING IT TWO-ON-ONE! WE CAN WIN THIS!
I'LL BE FINE... JUST HAVE TO WATCH OUT FOR HIS PALMS...!
OF COURSE, THAT'S ASSUMING I CAN ACTUALLY BEAT KACCHAN.
YOU'RE TOTALLY QUIRKLESS.
AND YOU THINK YOU CAN RUB SHOULDERS WITH ME?!
NOT AT ALL!
I WASN'T SAYING I COULD COMPETE WITH YOU...
I FORGOT TO MENTION THIS, KACCHAN, BUT...
I...
...TAKE THAT ALL BACK!!

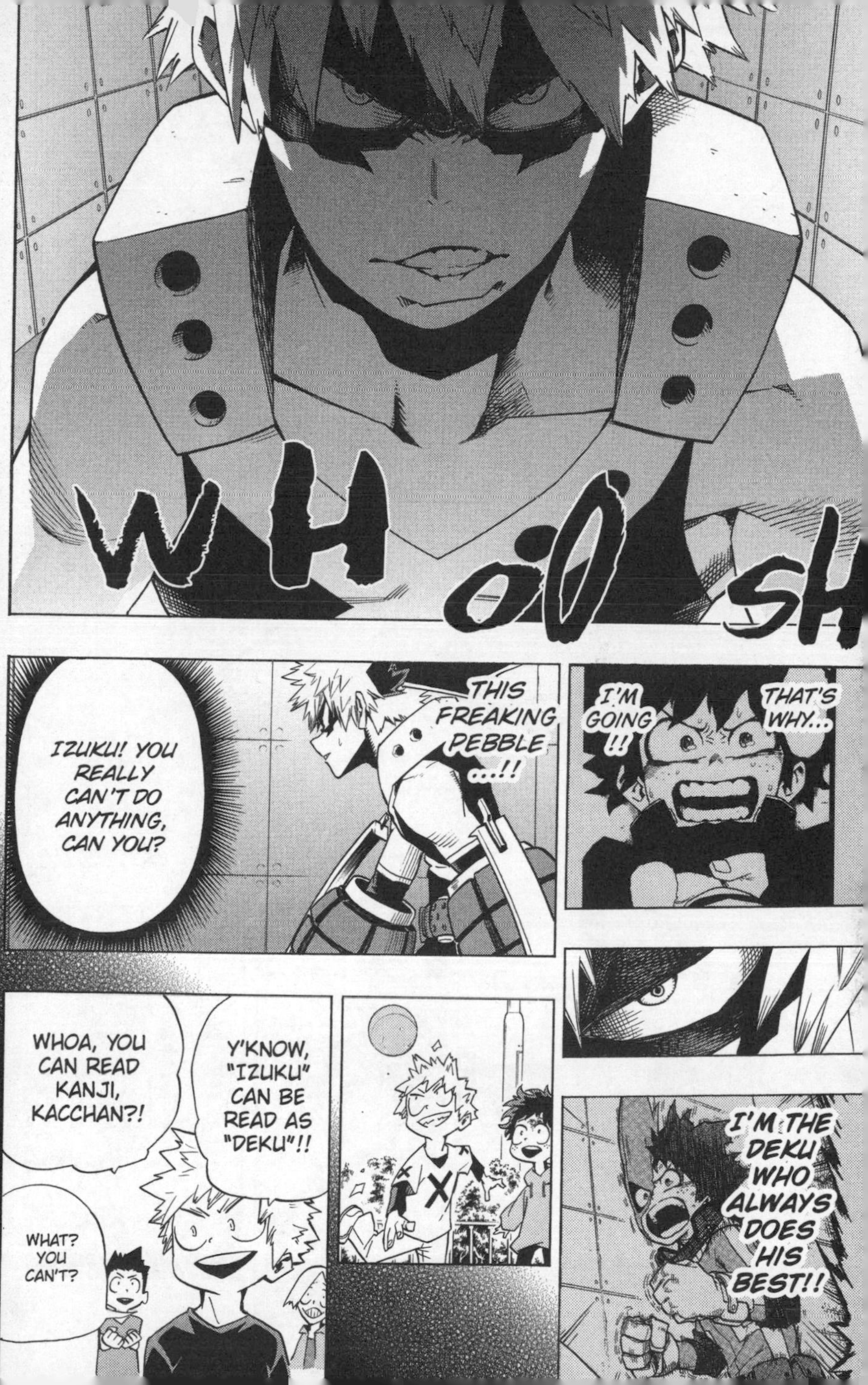
WHOOSH
THAT'S WHY...
I'M GOING!!
THIS FREAKING PEBBLE ...!!
IZUKU! YOU REALLY CAN'T DO ANYTHING, CAN YOU?
I'M THE DEKU WHO ALWAYS DOES HIS BEST!!
Y'KNOW, "IZUKU" CAN BE READ AS "DEKU"!!
WHOA, YOU CAN READ KANJI, KACCHAN?!
WHAT? YOU CAN'T?

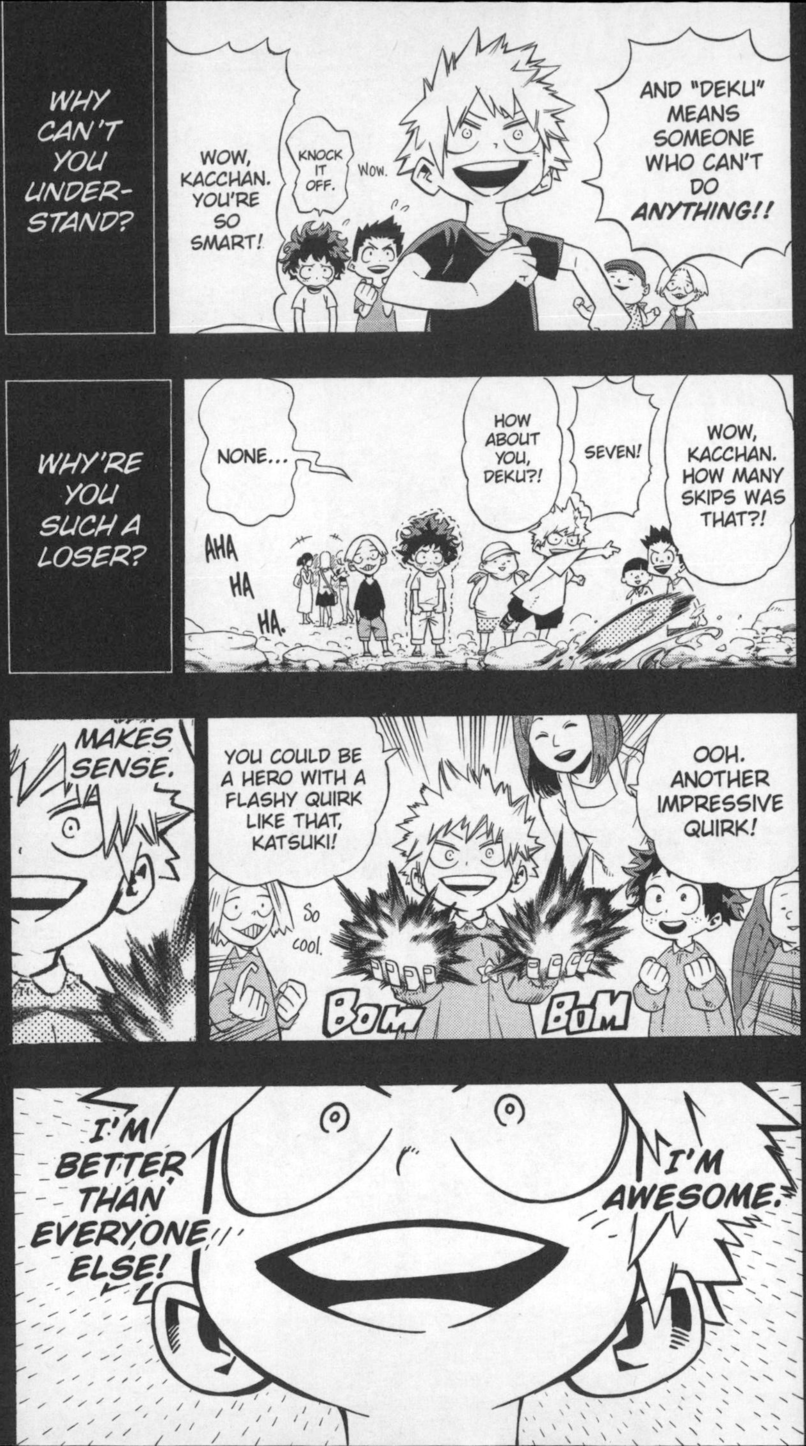
AND "DEKU" MEANS SOMEONE WHO CAN'T DO ANYTHING!!
WOW.
KNOCK IT OFF.
WOW, KACCHAN. YOU'RE SO SMART!
WHY CAN'T YOU UNDERSTAND?
WOW, KACCHAN. HOW MANY SKIPS WAS THAT?!
SEVEN!
HOW ABOUT YOU, DEKU?!
NONE...
AHA HA HA.
WHY'RE YOU SUCH A LOSER?
OOH. ANOTHER IMPRESSIVE QUIRK!
YOU COULD BE A HERO WITH A FLASHY QUIRK LIKE THAT, KATSUKI!
SO COOL.
BOM
BOM
MAKES SENSE.
I'M AWESOME.
I'M BETTER THAN EVERYONE ELSE!

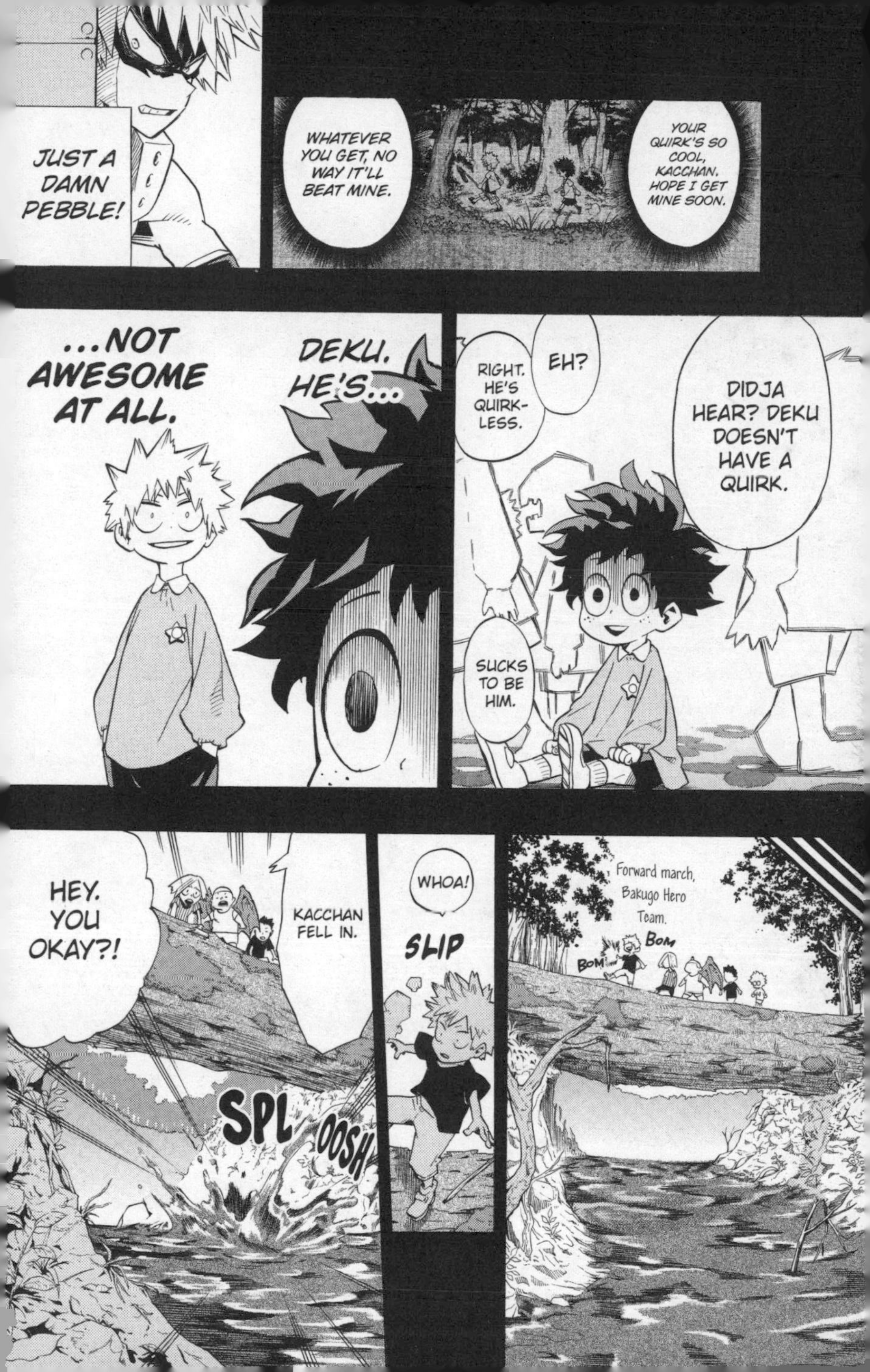
YOUR QUIRK'S SO COOL, KACCHAN. HOPE I GET MINE SOON.
WHATEVER YOU GET, NO WAY IT'LL BEAT MINE.
JUST A DAMN PEBBLE!
DIDJA HEAR? DEKU DOESN'T HAVE A QUIRK.
EH?
RIGHT. HE'S QUIRK-LESS.
SUCKS TO BE HIM.
DEKU. HE'S...
...NOT AWESOME AT ALL.
Forward march, Bakugo Hero Team.
BOM
BOM
WHOA!
SLIP
KACCHAN FELL IN.
HEY. YOU OKAY?!
SPLOOSH

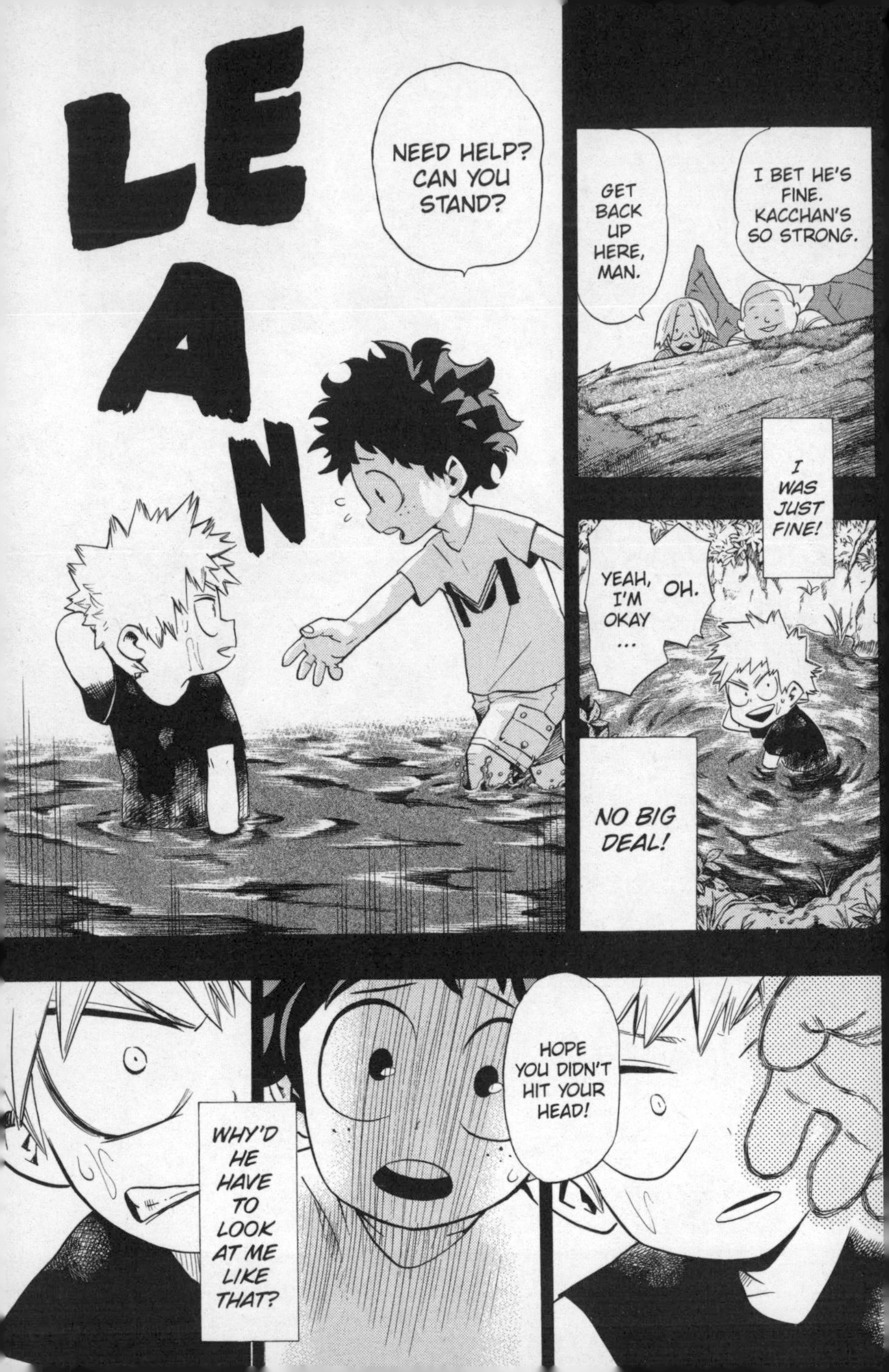
I BET HE'S FINE. KACCHAN'S SO STRONG.
GET BACK UP HERE, MAN.
I WAS JUST FINE!
OH.
YEAH, I'M OKAY ...
NO BIG DEAL!
NEED HELP? CAN YOU STAND?
LEAN
HOPE YOU DIDN'T HIT YOUR HEAD!
WHY'D HE HAVE TO LOOK AT ME LIKE THAT?

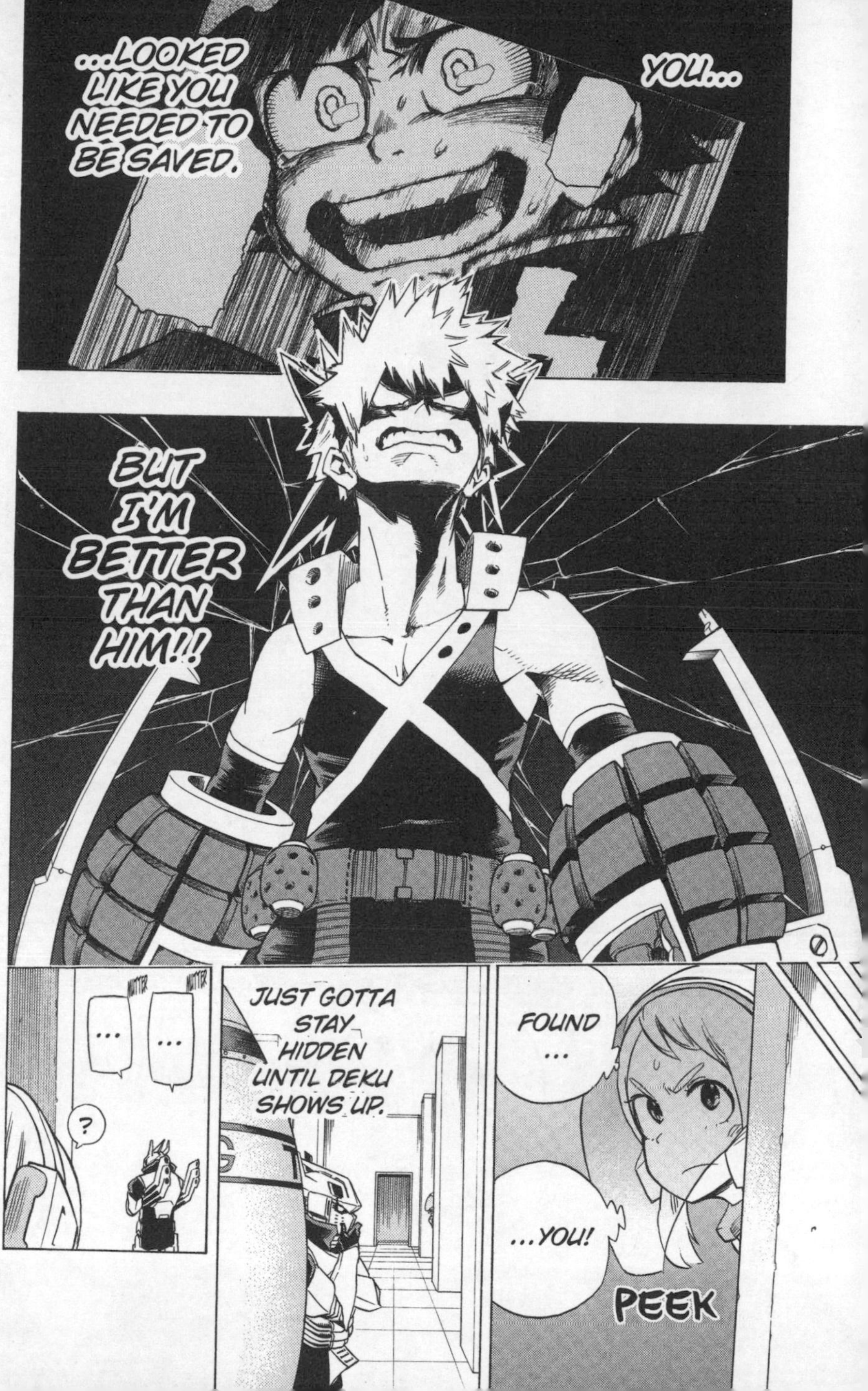
YOU...
...LOOKED LIKE YOU NEEDED TO BE SAVED.
BUT I'M BETTER THAN HIM!!
FOUND ...
...YOU!
PEEK
JUST GOTTA STAY HIDDEN UNTIL DEKU SHOWS UP.
MUTTER
MUTTER
...
...
?

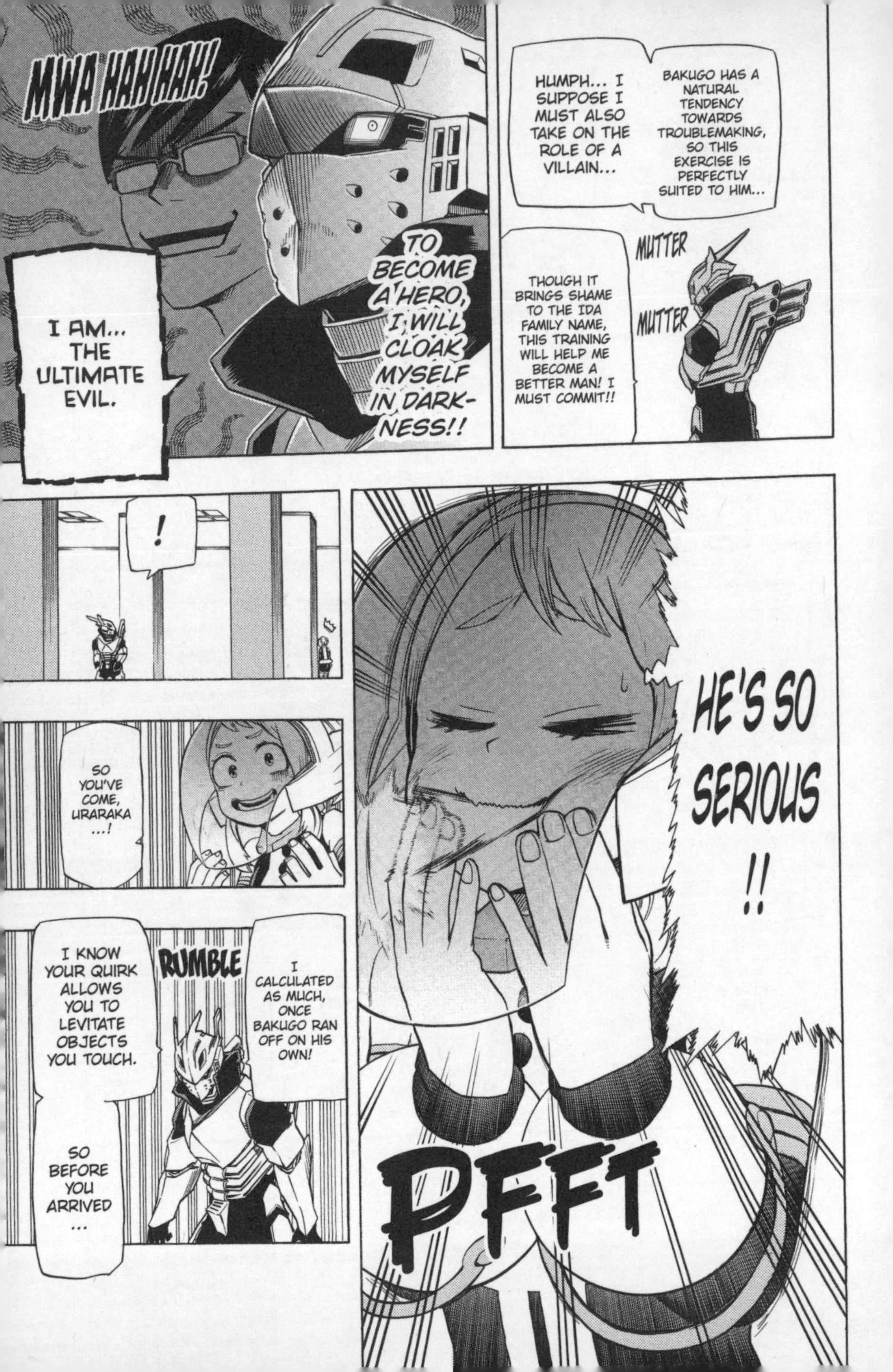
BAKUGO HAS A NATURAL TENDENCY TOWARDS TROUBLEMAKING, SO THIS EXERCISE IS PERFECTLY SUITED TO HIM...
HUMPH... I SUPPOSE I MUST ALSO TAKE ON THE ROLE OF A VILLAIN...
MUTTER
MUTTER
THOUGH IT BRINGS SHAME TO THE IDA FAMILY NAME, THIS TRAINING WILL HELP ME BECOME A BETTER MAN! I MUST COMMIT!!
MWA HAH HAH!
TO BECOME A HERO, I WILL CLOAK MYSELF IN DARK-NESS!!
I AM... THE ULTIMATE EVIL.
HE'S SO SERIOUS !!
PFFT
!
SO YOU'VE COME, URARAKA ...!
I CALCULATED AS MUCH, ONCE BAKUGO RAN OFF ON HIS OWN!
RUMBLE
I KNOW YOUR QUIRK ALLOWS YOU TO LEVITATE OBJECTS YOU TOUCH.
SO BEFORE YOU ARRIVED ...

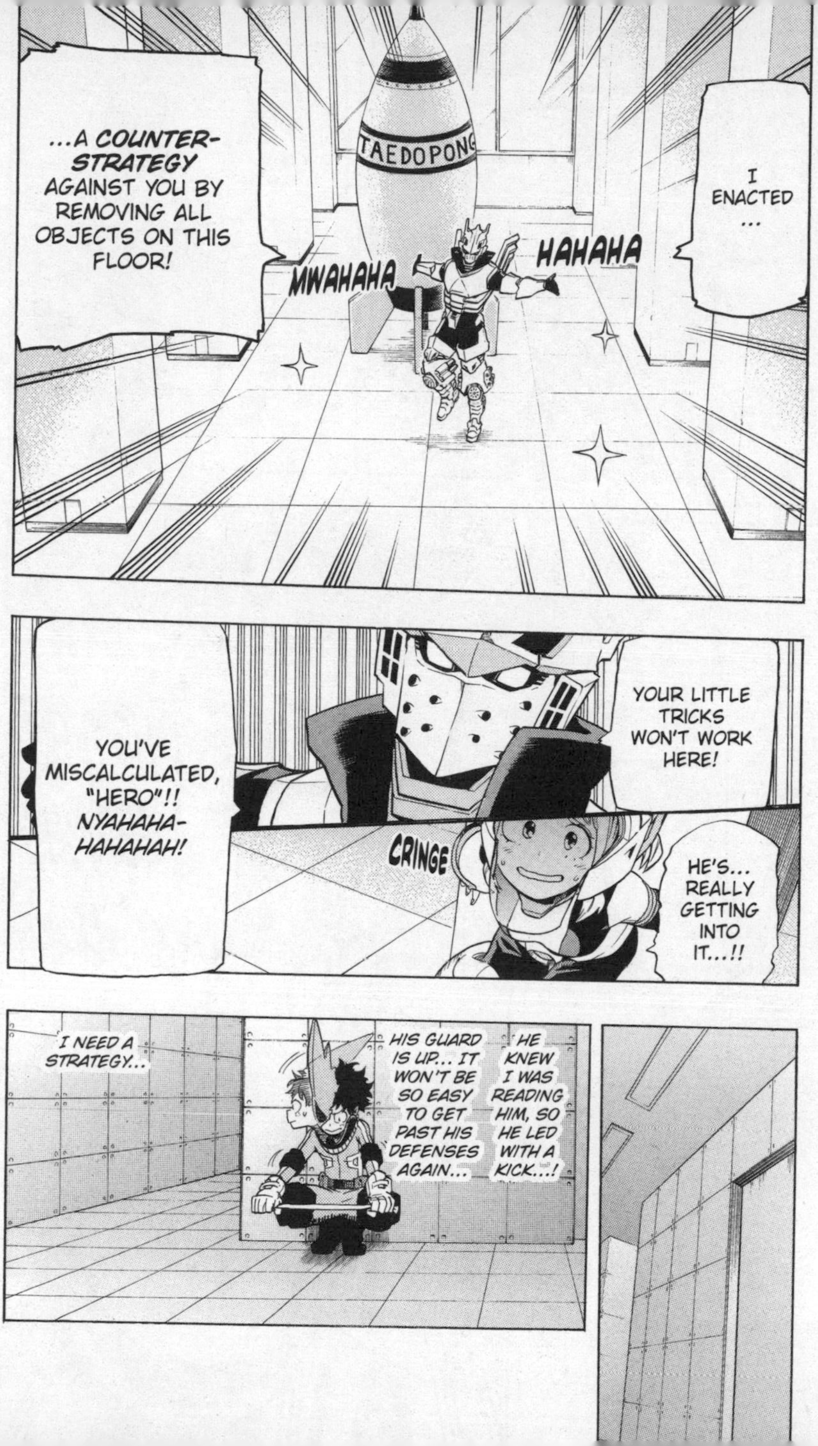
I ENACTED ...
...A COUNTER-STRATEGY AGAINST YOU BY REMOVING ALL OBJECTS ON THIS FLOOR!
HAHAHA
MWAHAHA
YOUR LITTLE TRICKS WON'T WORK HERE!
YOU'VE MISCALCULATED, "HERO"!! NYAHAHA-HAHAHAH!
CRINGE
HE'S... REALLY GETTING INTO IT...!!
HE KNEW I WAS READING HIM, SO HE LED WITH A KICK...!
HIS GUARD IS UP... IT WON'T BE SO EASY TO GET PAST HIS DEFENSES AGAIN...
I NEED A STRATEGY...

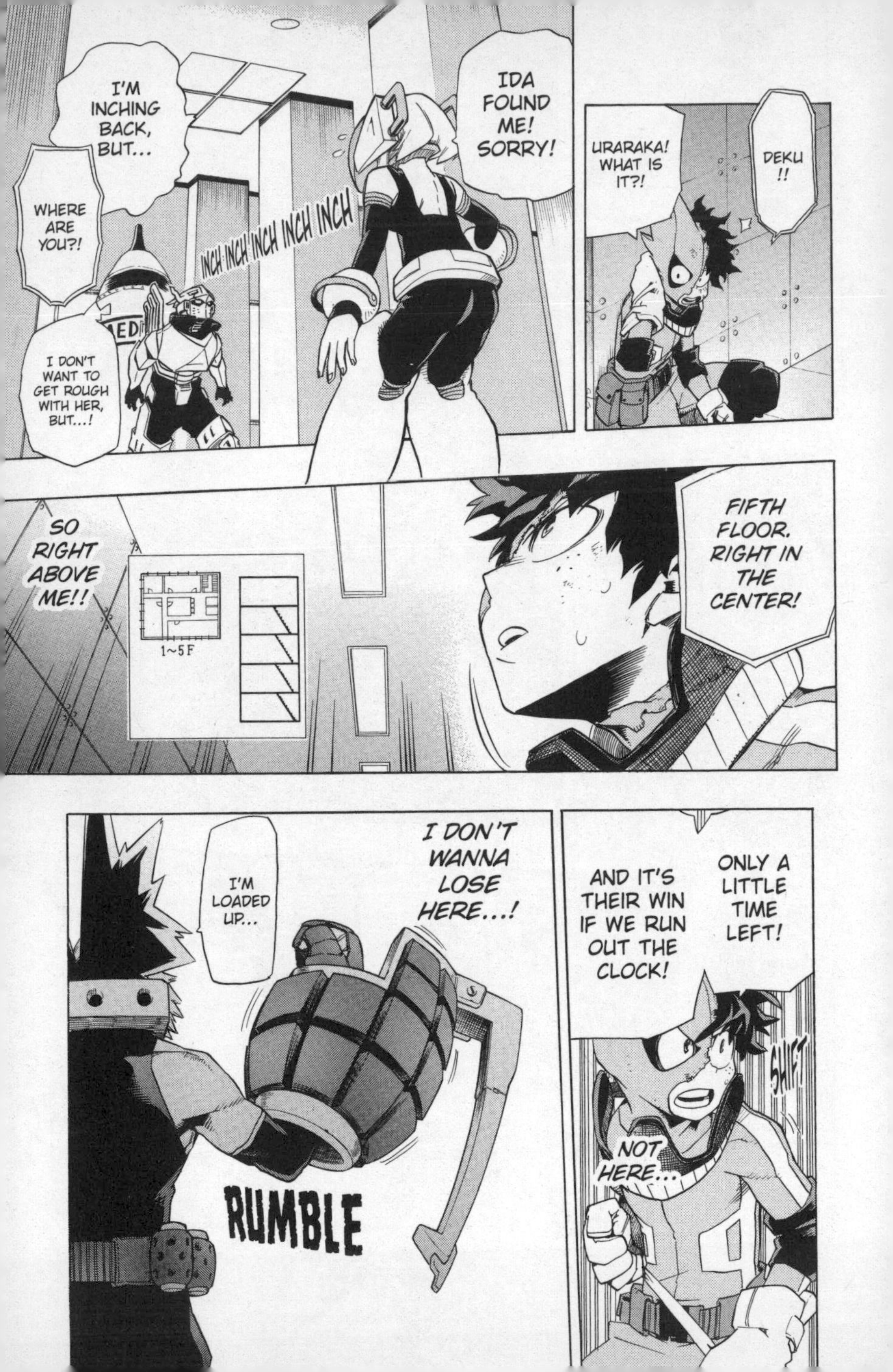
DEKU!!
URARAKA! WHAT IS IT?!
IDA FOUND ME! SORRY!
INCH INCH INCH INCH INCH
I'M INCHING BACK, BUT...
WHERE ARE YOU?!
I DON'T WANT TO GET ROUGH WITH HER, BUT...!
FIFTH FLOOR. RIGHT IN THE CENTER!
SO RIGHT ABOVE ME!!
1~5F
ONLY A LITTLE TIME LEFT!
AND IT'S THEIR WIN IF WE RUN OUT THE CLOCK!
SHIFT
NOT HERE...
I DON'T WANNA LOSE HERE...!
I'M LOADED UP...
RUMBLE

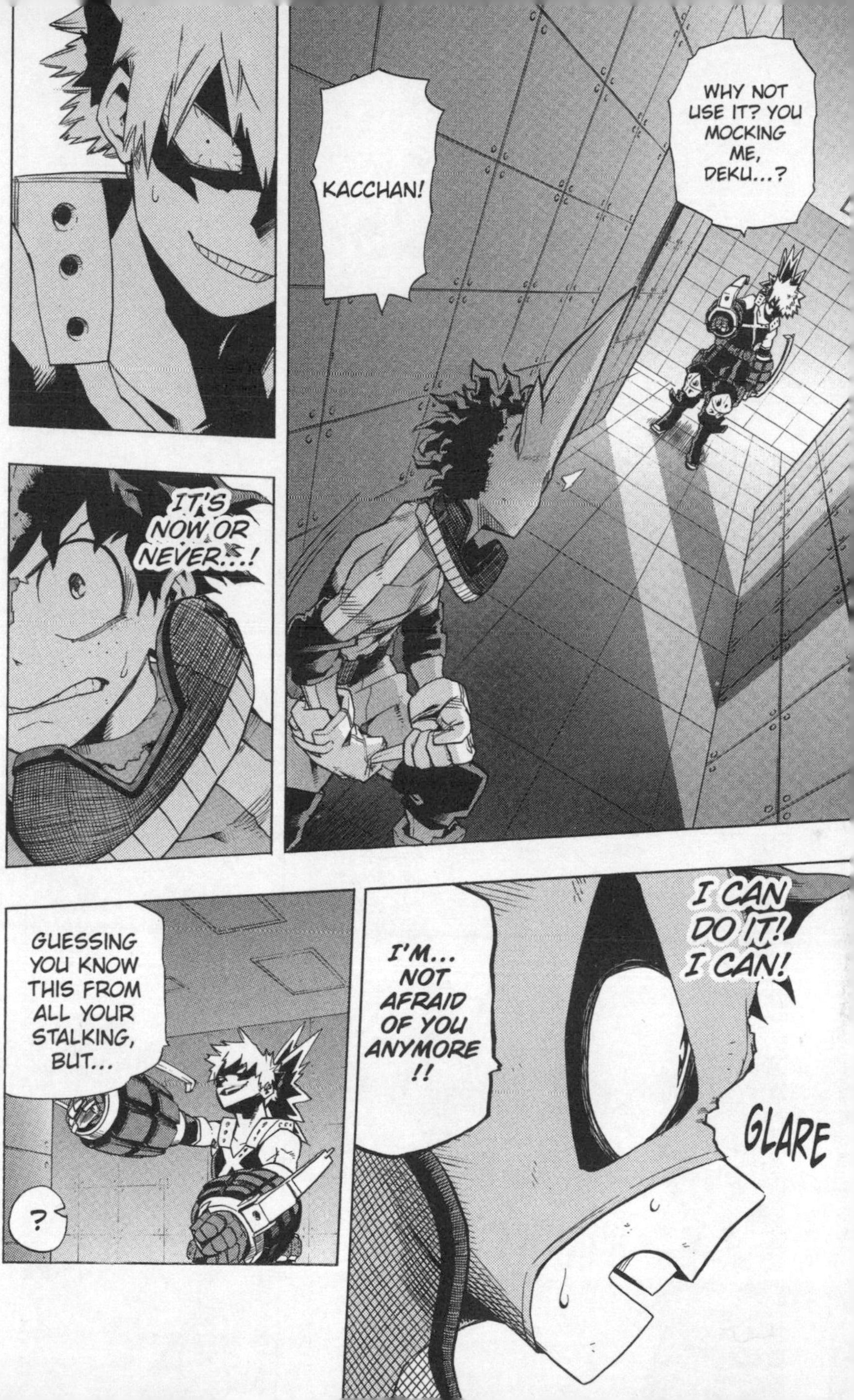
WHY NOT USE IT? YOU MOCKING ME, DEKU...?
KACCHAN!
IT'S NOW OR NEVER...!
I CAN DO IT! I CAN!
I'M... NOT AFRAID OF YOU ANYMORE!!
GLARE
GUESSING YOU KNOW THIS FROM ALL YOUR STALKING, BUT...
?

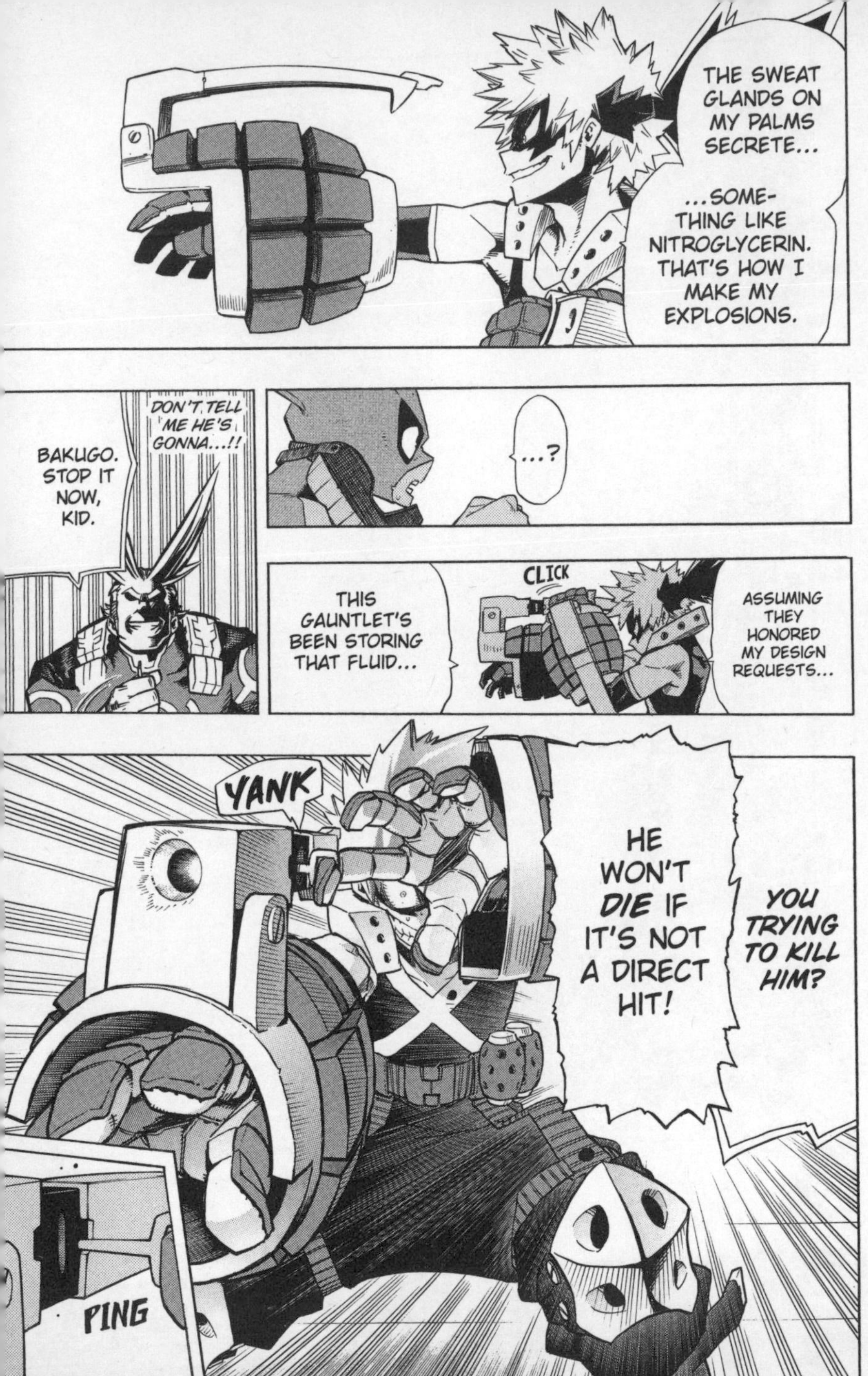
THE SWEAT GLANDS ON MY PALMS SECRETE...
...SOMETHING LIKE NITROGLYCERIN. THAT'S HOW I MAKE MY EXPLOSIONS.
...?
ASSUMING THEY HONORED MY DESIGN REQUESTS...
CLICK
THIS GAUNTLET'S BEEN STORING THAT FLUID...
DON'T TELL ME HE'S GONNA...!!
BAKUGO. STOP IT NOW, KID.
YOU TRYING TO KILL HIM?
HE WON'T DIE IF IT'S NOT A DIRECT HIT!
YANK
PING

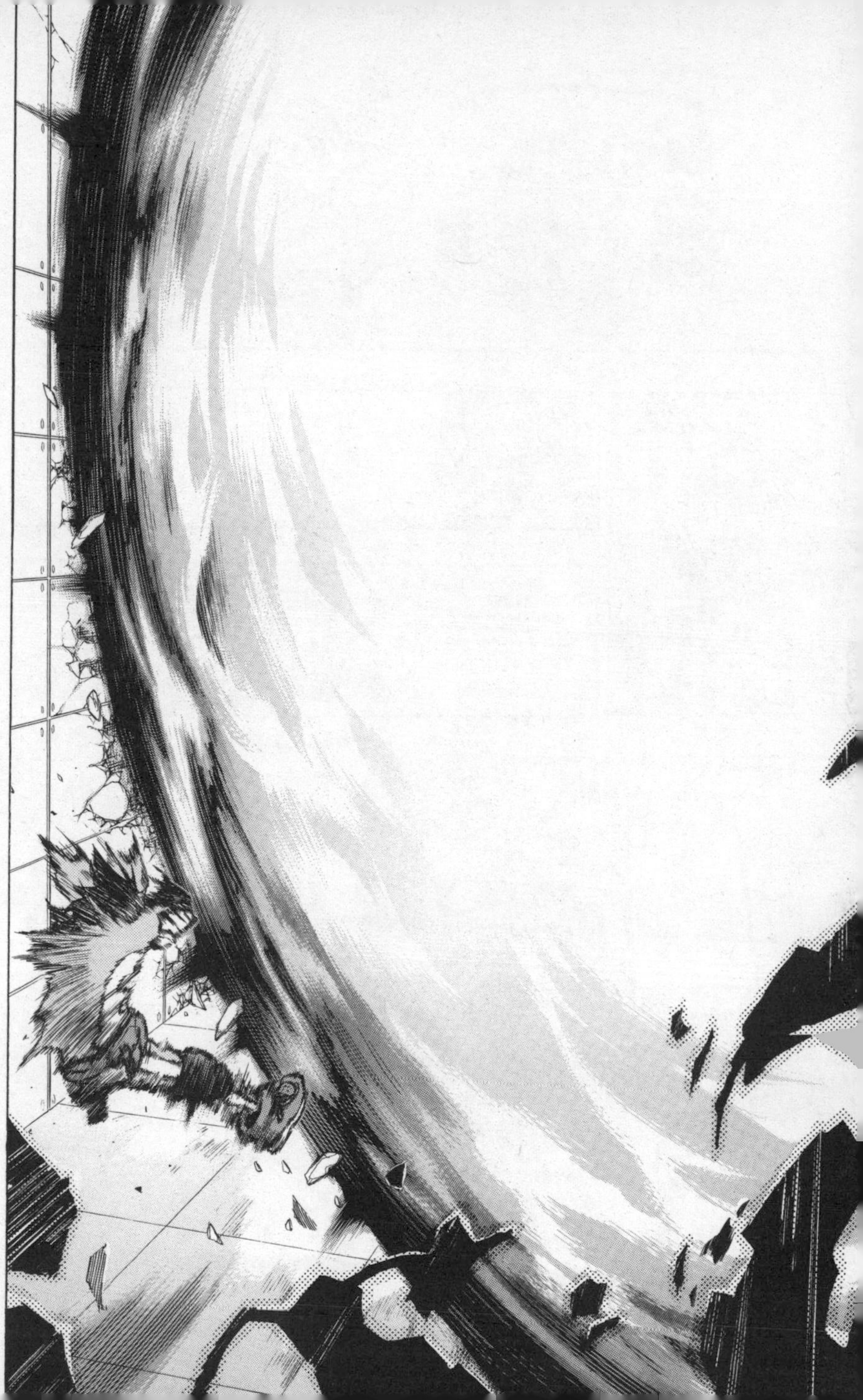

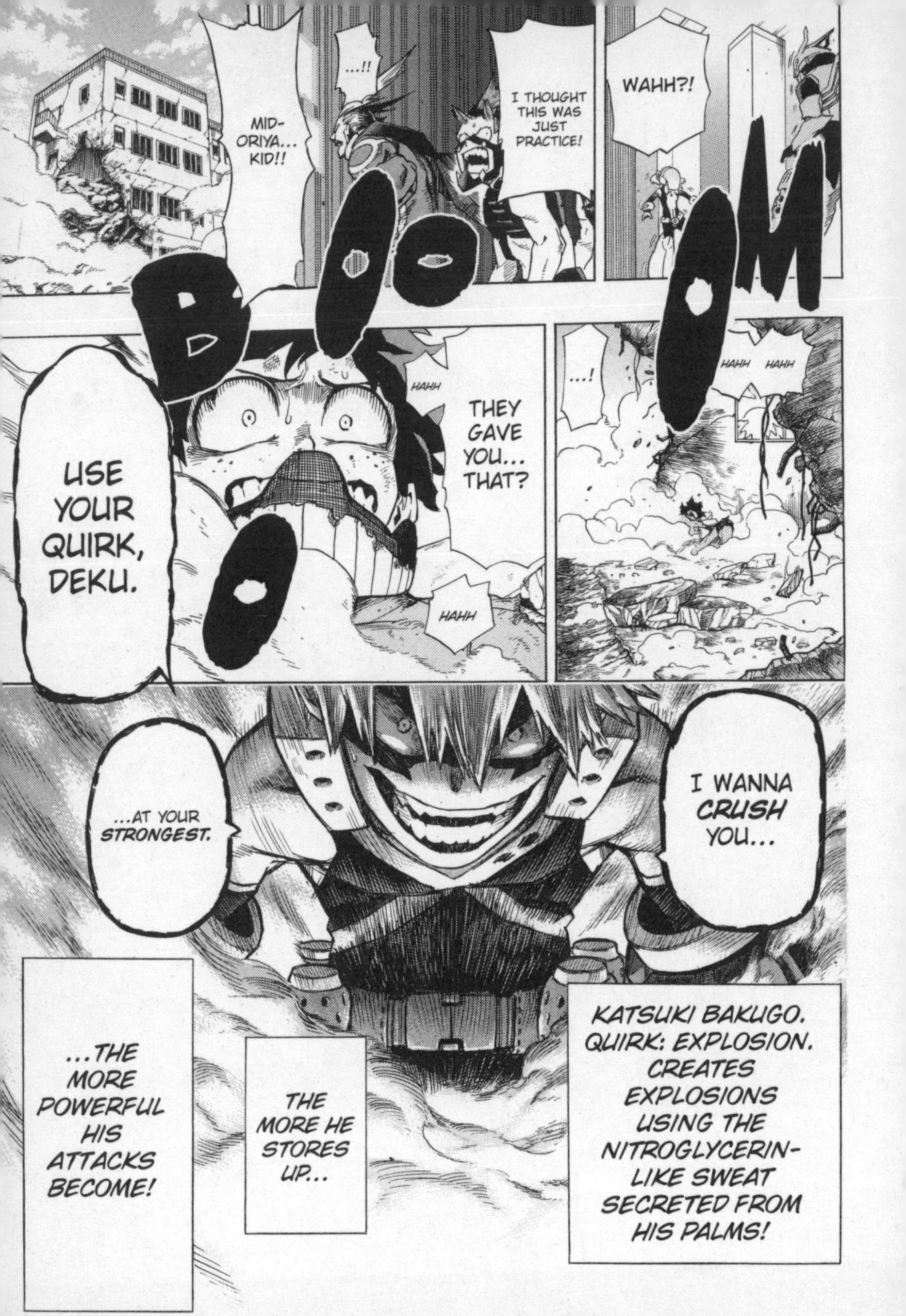
WAHH?!
I THOUGHT THIS WAS JUST PRACTICE!
...!!
MID-ORIYA... KID!!
BOOOOM
...!
HAHH HAHH
THEY GAVE YOU... THAT?
HAHH
USE YOUR QUIRK, DEKU.
HAHH
I WANNA CRUSH YOU...
...AT YOUR STRONGEST.
KATSUKI BAKUGO. QUIRK: EXPLOSION. CREATES EXPLOSIONS USING THE NITROGLYCERIN-LIKE SWEAT SECRETED FROM HIS PALMS!
THE MORE HE STORES UP...
...THE MORE POWERFUL HIS ATTACKS BECOME!

YUGA AOYAMA (15)

STREET CLOTHES

Birthday: 5/30
Height: 168 cm
Favorite Thing: Himself

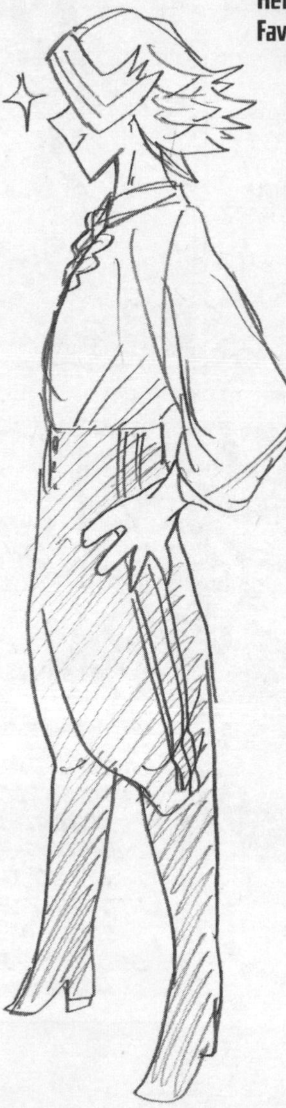

BEHIND THE SCENES

I don't really understand this guy, myself. But he's always fun to draw, so that's nice!!

NO.10 - BREAKING BAKUGO

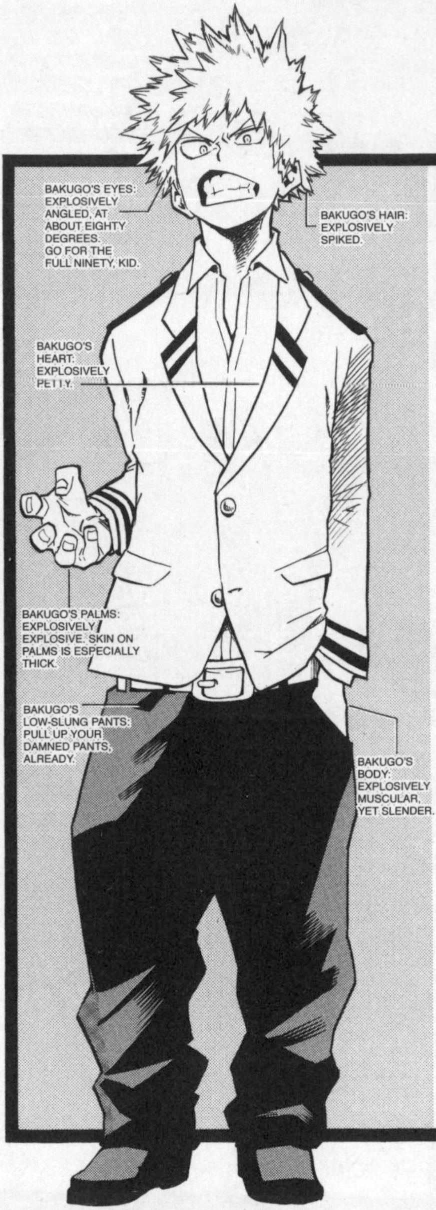
BAKUGO'S EYES: EXPLOSIVELY ANGLED, AT ABOUT EIGHTY DEGREES. GO FOR THE FULL NINETY, KID.
BAKUGO'S HAIR: EXPLOSIVELY SPIKED.
BAKUGO'S HEART: EXPLOSIVELY PETTY.
BAKUGO'S PALMS: EXPLOSIVELY EXPLOSIVE. SKIN ON PALMS IS ESPECIALLY THICK.
BAKUGO'S LOW-SLUNG PANTS: PULL UP YOUR DAMNED PANTS, ALREADY.
BAKUGO'S BODY: EXPLOSIVELY MUSCULAR, YET SLENDER.

U.A.FILE.02

CLASS No.17

KATSUKI BAKUGO

Quirk

EXPLOSION

He's got specialized sweat glands on his palms! They secrete nitroglycerin-like sweat that he can detonate at will. Although he can control the flow of sweat to an extent, his glands still retain their original function, meaning that Bakugo is explosively strong in the summer and a slow starter in the winter! The more he sweats, the stronger his Quirk is! It's a powerful, flashy ability with no big downsides! This delinquent's future looks bright!

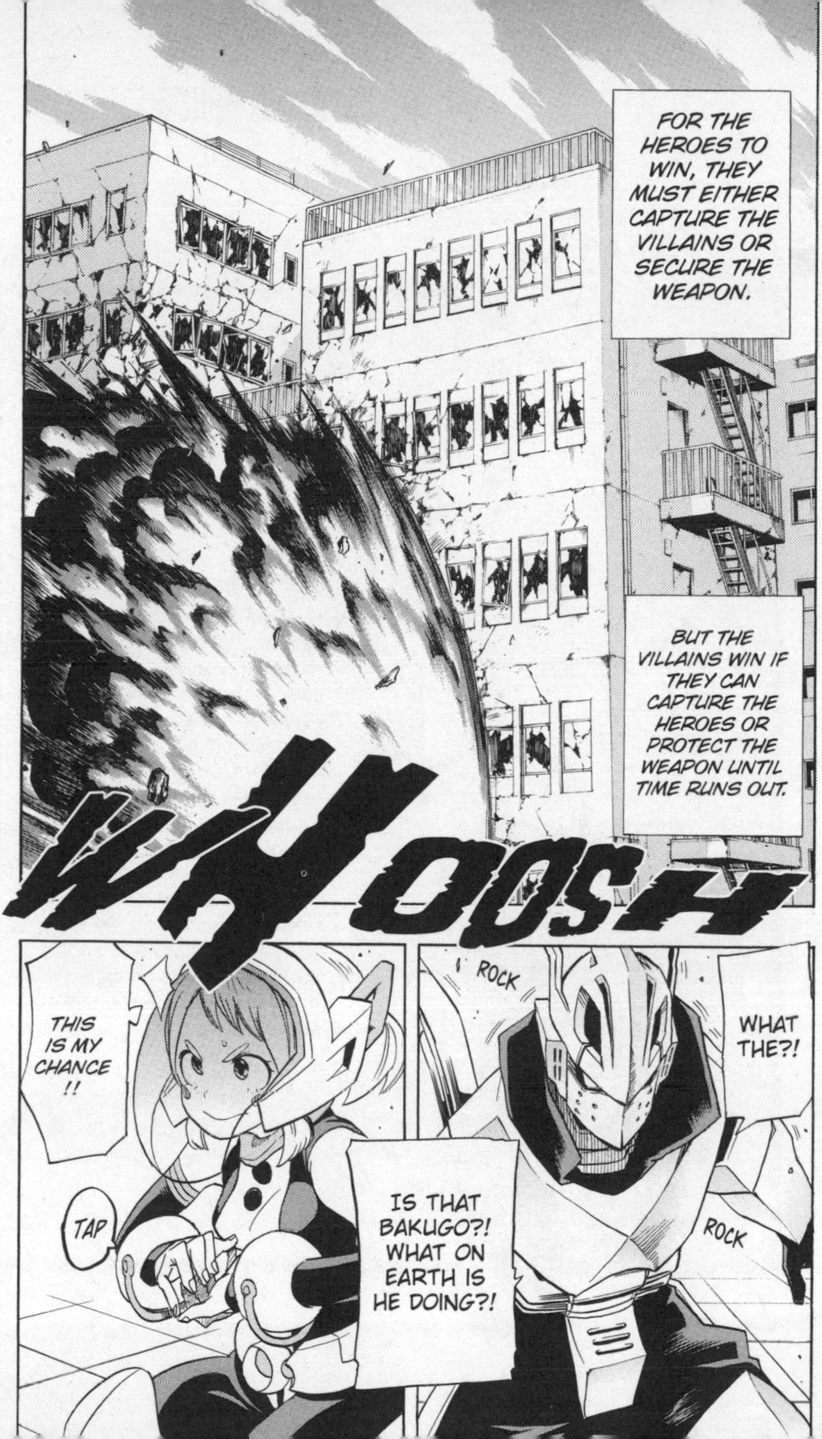
FOR THE HEROES TO WIN, THEY MUST EITHER CAPTURE THE VILLAINS OR SECURE THE WEAPON.
BUT THE VILLAINS WIN IF THEY CAN CAPTURE THE HEROES OR PROTECT THE WEAPON UNTIL TIME RUNS OUT.
WHOOSH
ROCK
WHAT THE?!
IS THAT BAKUGO?! WHAT ON EARTH IS HE DOING?!
ROCK
THIS IS MY CHANCE!!
TAP

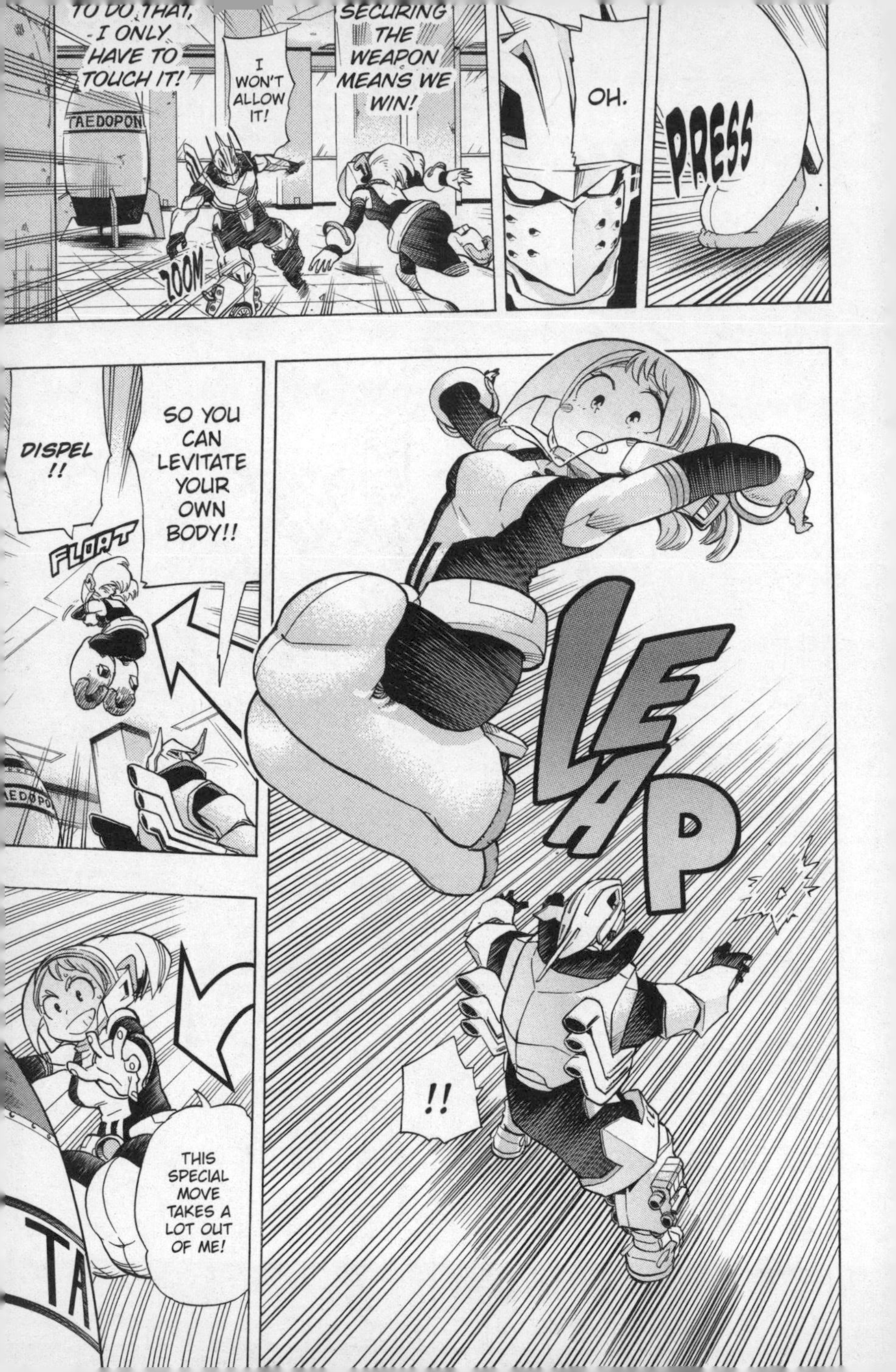
PRESS
OH.
SECURING THE WEAPON MEANS WE WIN!
TO DO THAT, I ONLY HAVE TO TOUCH IT!
I WON'T ALLOW IT!
TAEDOPON
ZOOM
LEAP
!!
SO YOU CAN LEVITATE YOUR OWN BODY!!
DISPEL!!
FLOAT
TAEDOPON
THIS SPECIAL MOVE TAKES A LOT OUT OF ME!
TA

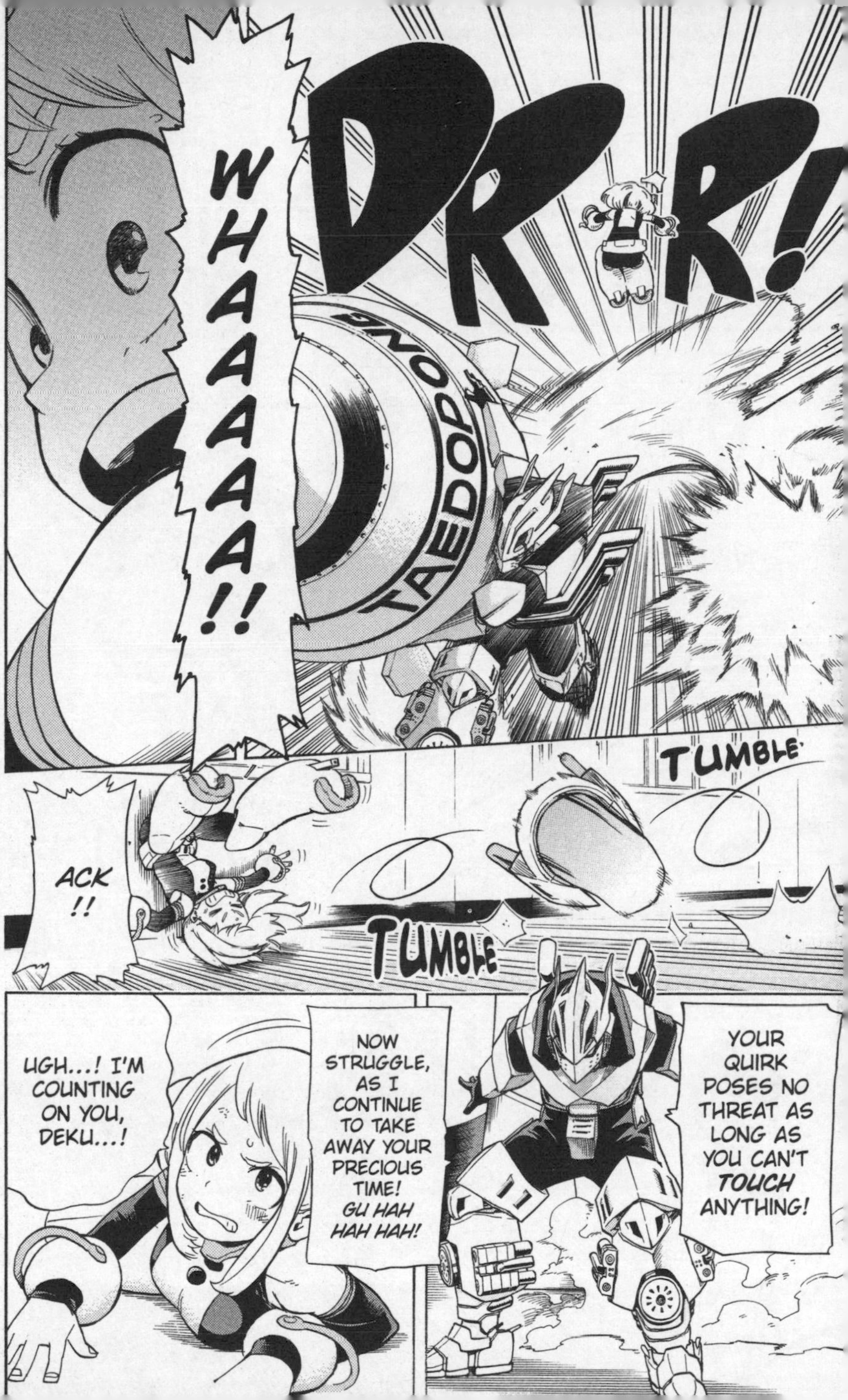
DRRR!
TAEDOPONG
WHAAAAA!!
TUMBLE
TUMBLE
ACK!!
YOUR QUIRK POSES NO THREAT AS LONG AS YOU CAN'T *TOUCH* ANYTHING!
NOW STRUGGLE, AS I CONTINUE TO TAKE AWAY YOUR PRECIOUS TIME! *GU HAH HAH HAH!*
UGH...! I'M COUNTING ON YOU, DEKU...!

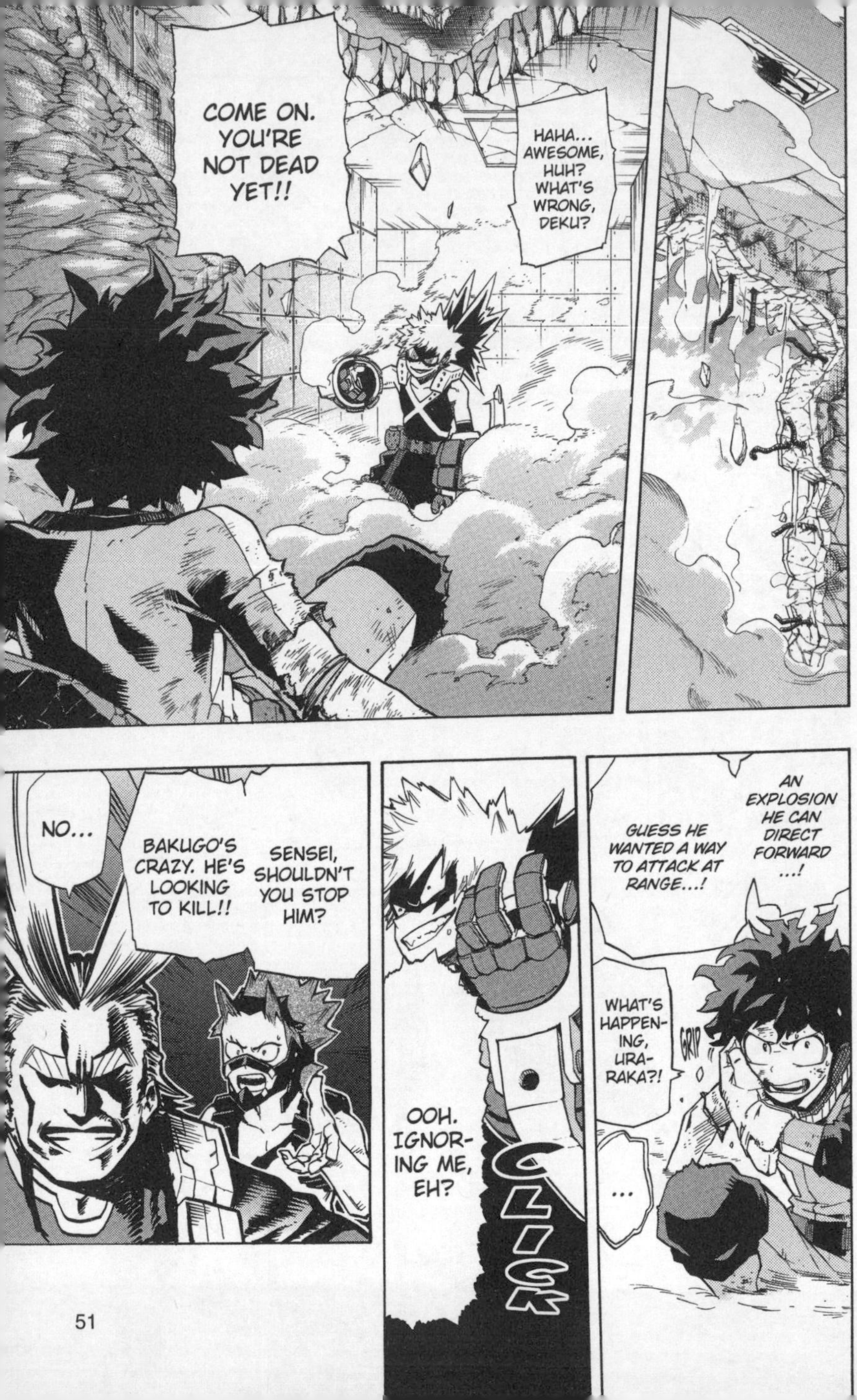

HAHA... AWESOME, HUH? WHAT'S WRONG, DEKU?
COME ON. YOU'RE NOT DEAD YET!!
AN EXPLOSION HE CAN DIRECT FORWARD ...!
GUESS HE WANTED A WAY TO ATTACK AT RANGE...!
GRIP
WHAT'S HAPPEN-ING, URA-RAKA?!
...
OOH. IGNOR-ING ME, EH?
CLICK
SENSEI, SHOULDN'T YOU STOP HIM?
BAKUGO'S CRAZY. HE'S LOOKING TO KILL!!
NO...

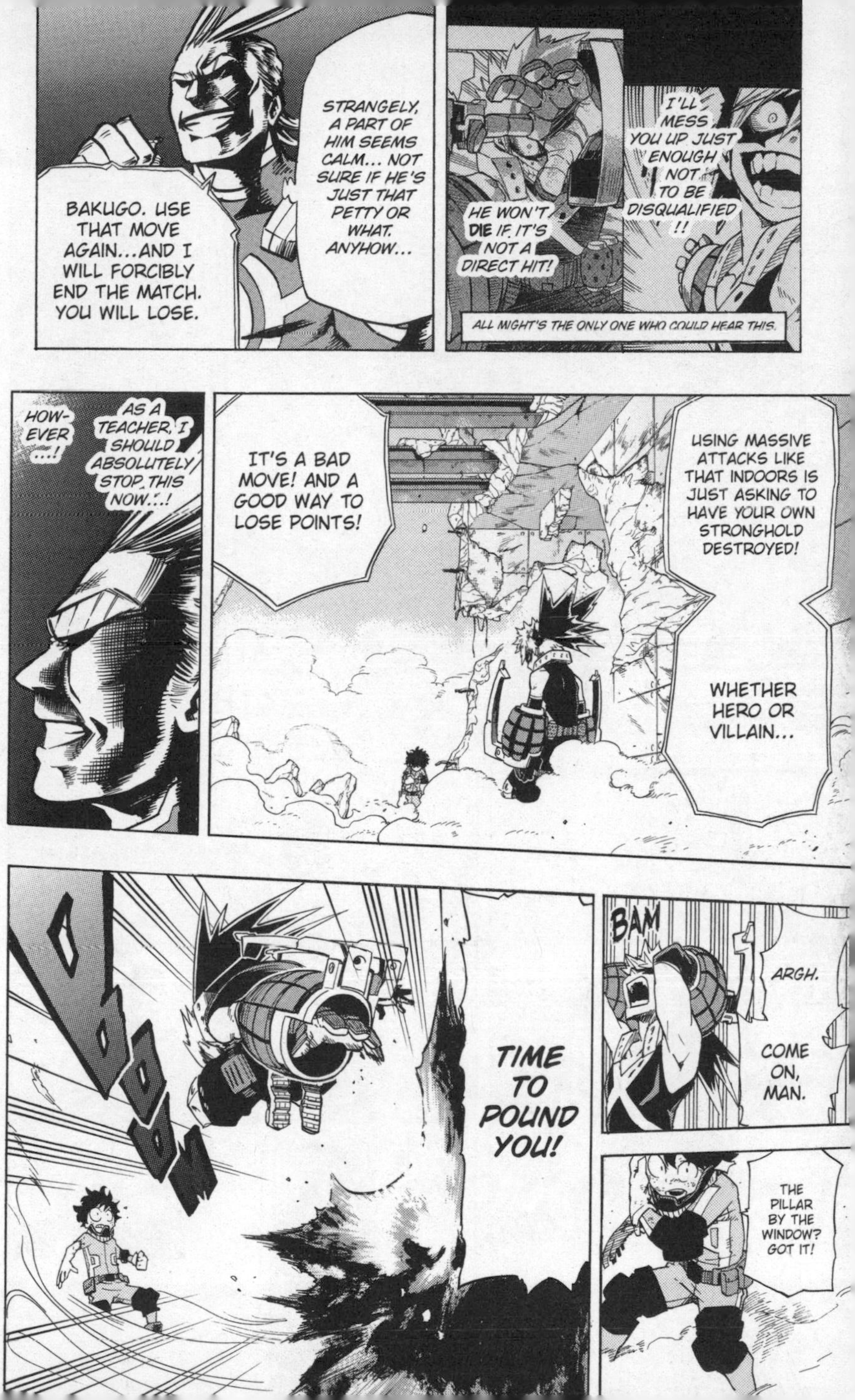
I'LL MESS YOU UP JUST ENOUGH NOT TO BE DISQUALIFIED!!
HE WON'T DIE IF IT'S NOT A DIRECT HIT!
ALL MIGHT'S THE ONLY ONE WHO COULD HEAR THIS.
STRANGELY, A PART OF HIM SEEMS CALM... NOT SURE IF HE'S JUST THAT PETTY OR WHAT. ANYHOW...
BAKUGO. USE THAT MOVE AGAIN...AND I WILL FORCIBLY END THE MATCH. YOU WILL LOSE.
USING MASSIVE ATTACKS LIKE THAT INDOORS IS JUST ASKING TO HAVE YOUR OWN STRONGHOLD DESTROYED!
IT'S A BAD MOVE! AND A GOOD WAY TO LOSE POINTS!
WHETHER HERO OR VILLAIN...
AS A TEACHER, I SHOULD ABSOLUTELY STOP THIS NOW...!
HOW-EVER...!
BAM
ARGH.
COME ON, MAN.
THE PILLAR BY THE WINDOW? GOT IT!
TIME TO POUND YOU!

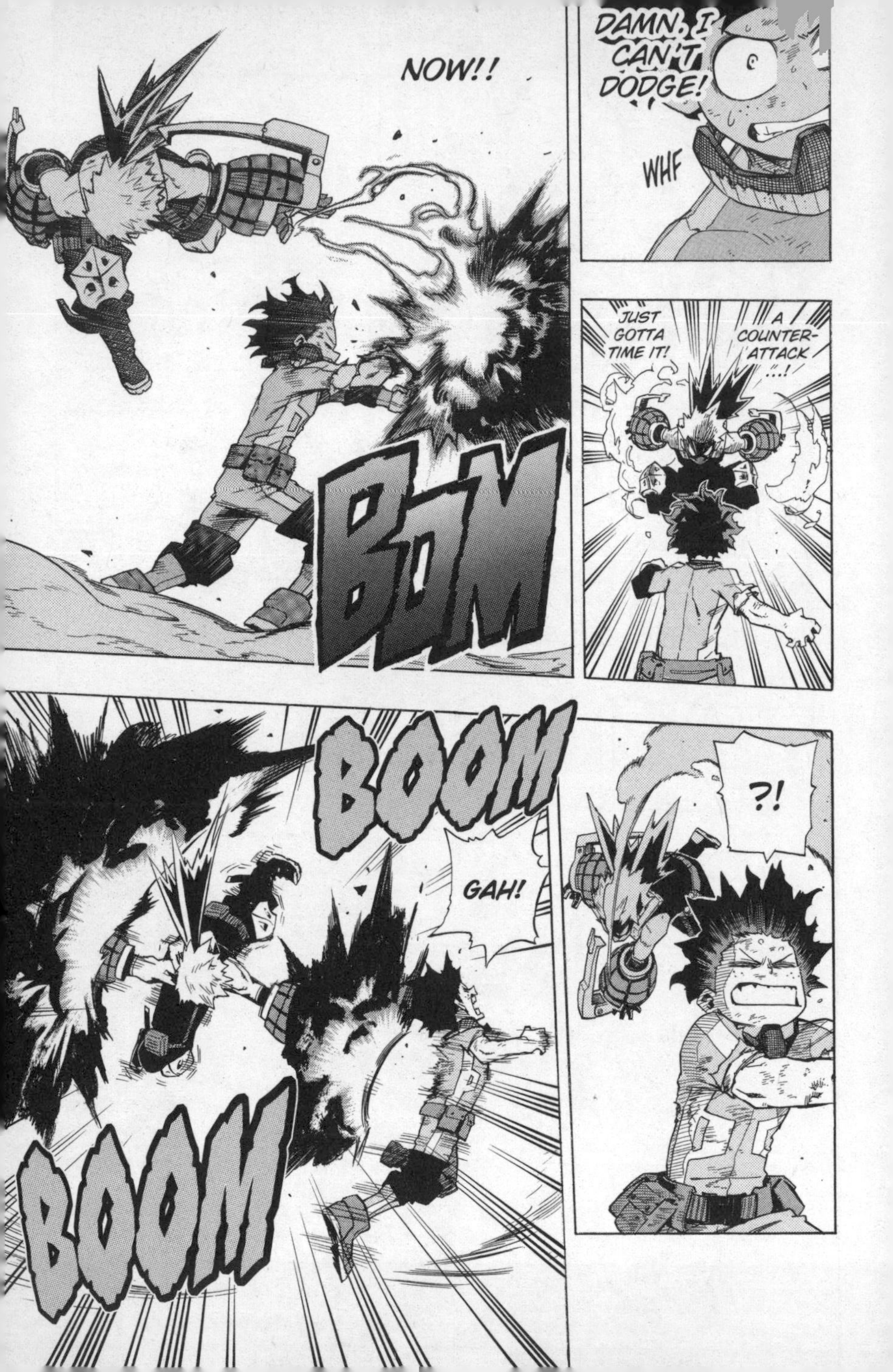
DAMN, I CAN'T DODGE!
WHF
A COUNTER-ATTACK...!
JUST GOTTA TIME IT!
NOW!!
BOOM
?!
BOOM
GAH!
BOOM

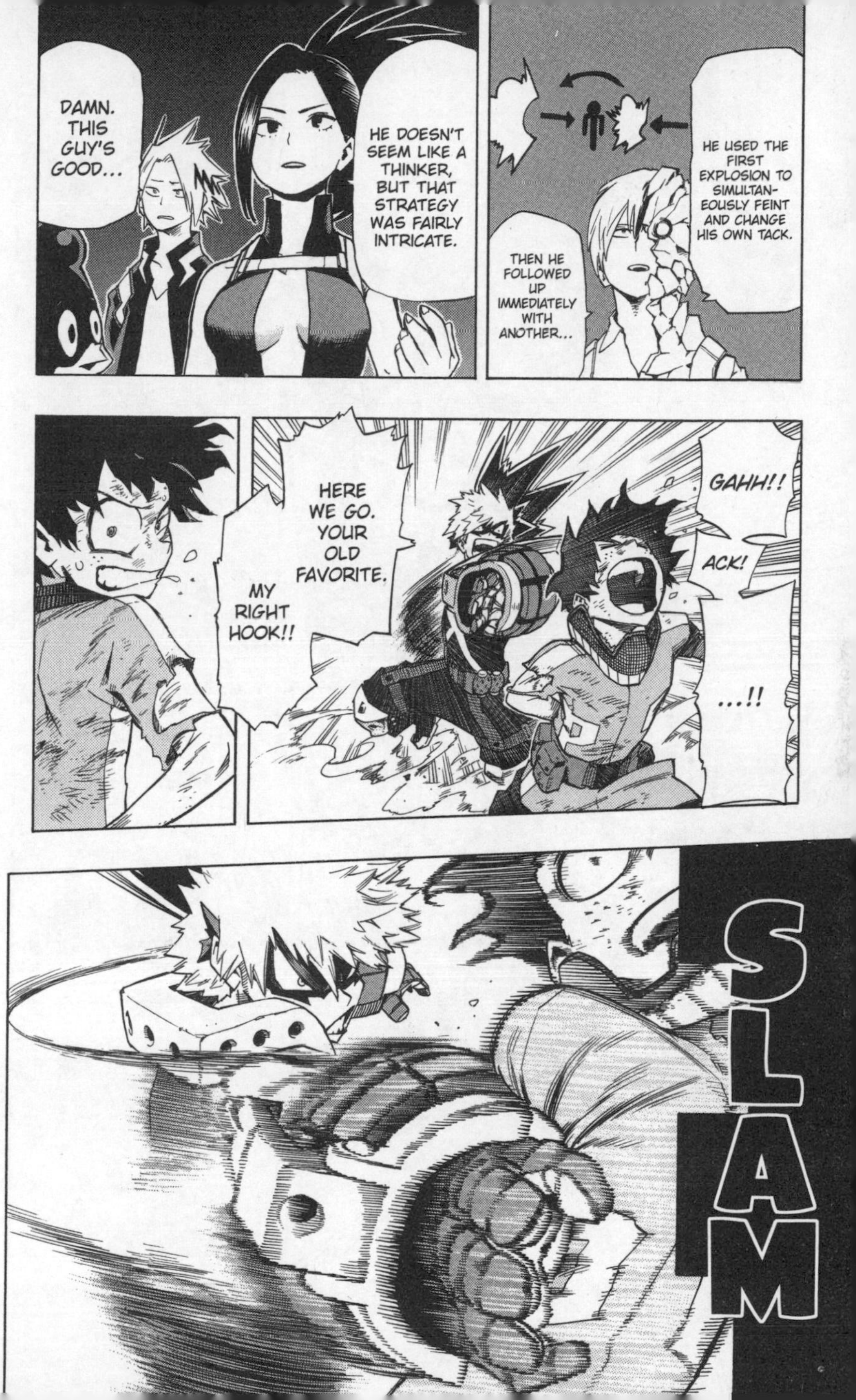
HE USED THE FIRST EXPLOSION TO SIMULTANEOUSLY FEINT AND CHANGE HIS OWN TACK.
THEN HE FOLLOWED UP IMMEDIATELY WITH ANOTHER...
HE DOESN'T SEEM LIKE A THINKER, BUT THAT STRATEGY WAS FAIRLY INTRICATE.
DAMN. THIS GUY'S GOOD...
GAHH!!
ACK!
HERE WE GO. YOUR OLD FAVORITE.
...!!
MY RIGHT HOOK!!
SLAM

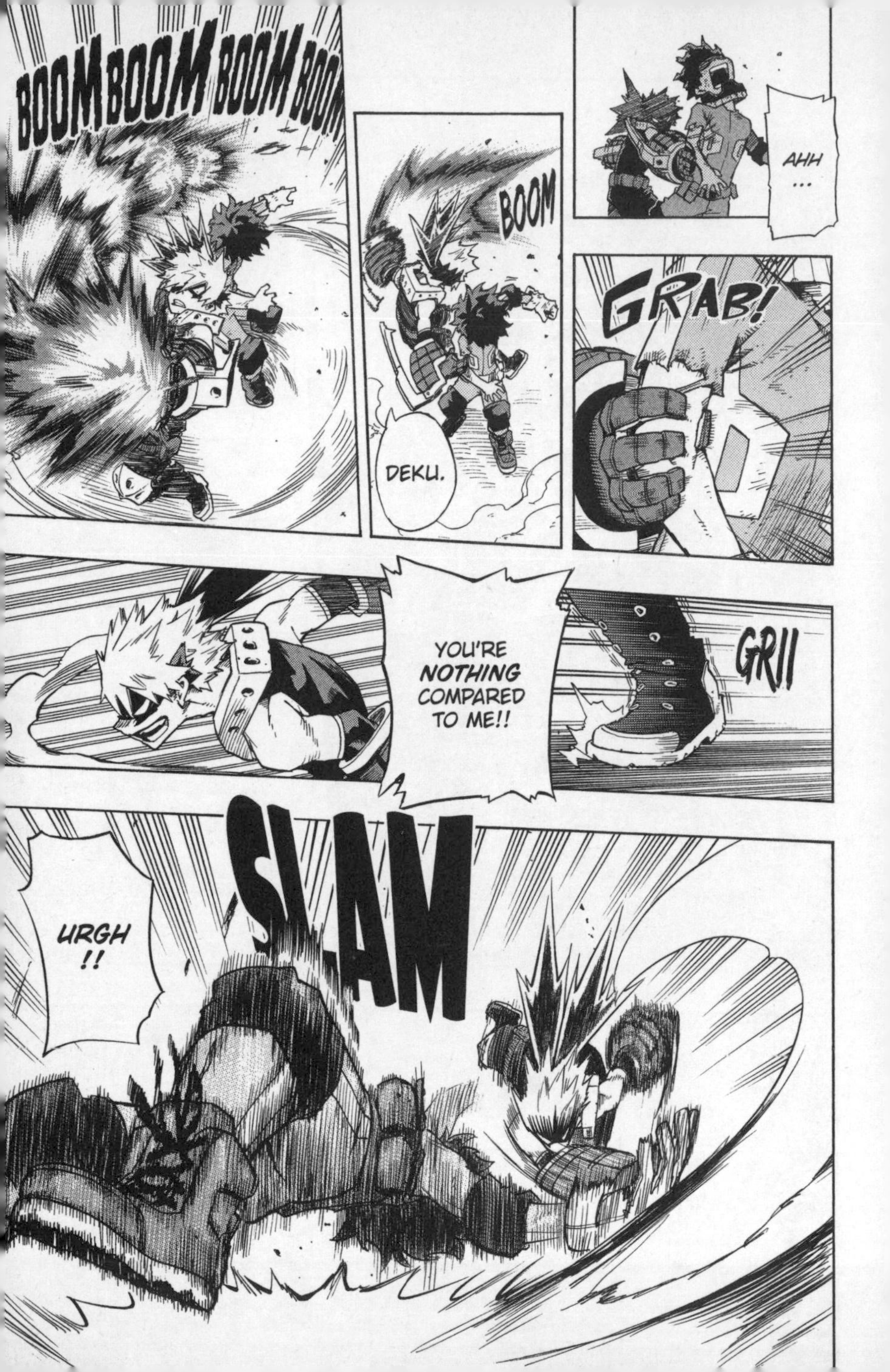
AHH ...
GRAB!
BOOM
DEKU.
BOOM BOOM BOOM BOOM
GRII
YOU'RE *NOTHING* COMPARED TO ME!!
SLAM
URGH !!

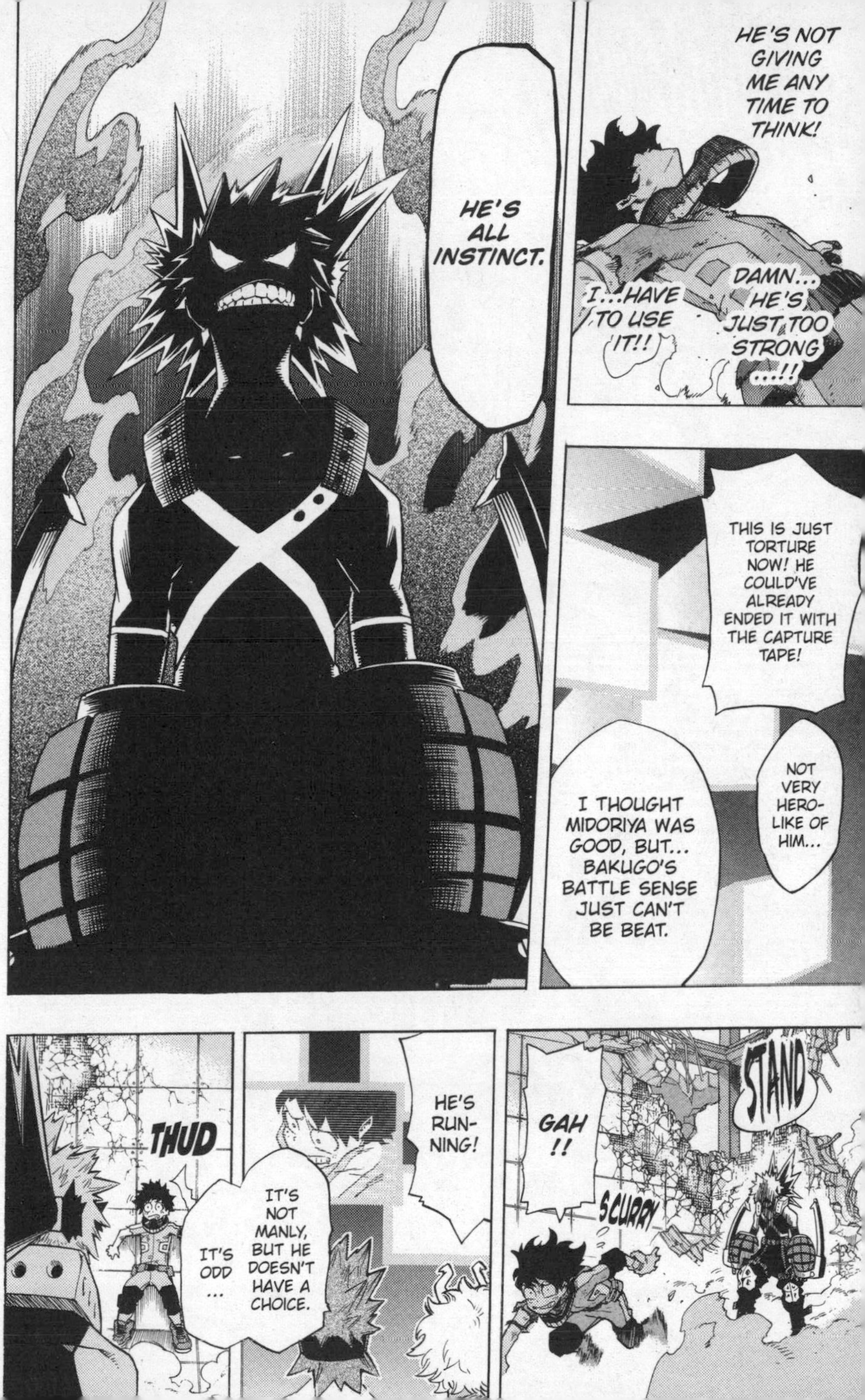
HE'S NOT GIVING ME ANY TIME TO THINK!
DAMN... HE'S JUST TOO STRONG ...!!
I...HAVE TO USE IT!!
THIS IS JUST TORTURE NOW! HE COULD'VE ALREADY ENDED IT WITH THE CAPTURE TAPE!
NOT VERY HERO-LIKE OF HIM...
I THOUGHT MIDORIYA WAS GOOD, BUT... BAKUGO'S BATTLE SENSE JUST CAN'T BE BEAT.
HE'S ALL INSTINCT.
STAND
GAH !!
SCURRY
HE'S RUN-NING!
IT'S NOT MANLY, BUT HE DOESN'T HAVE A CHOICE.
IT'S ODD ...
THUD

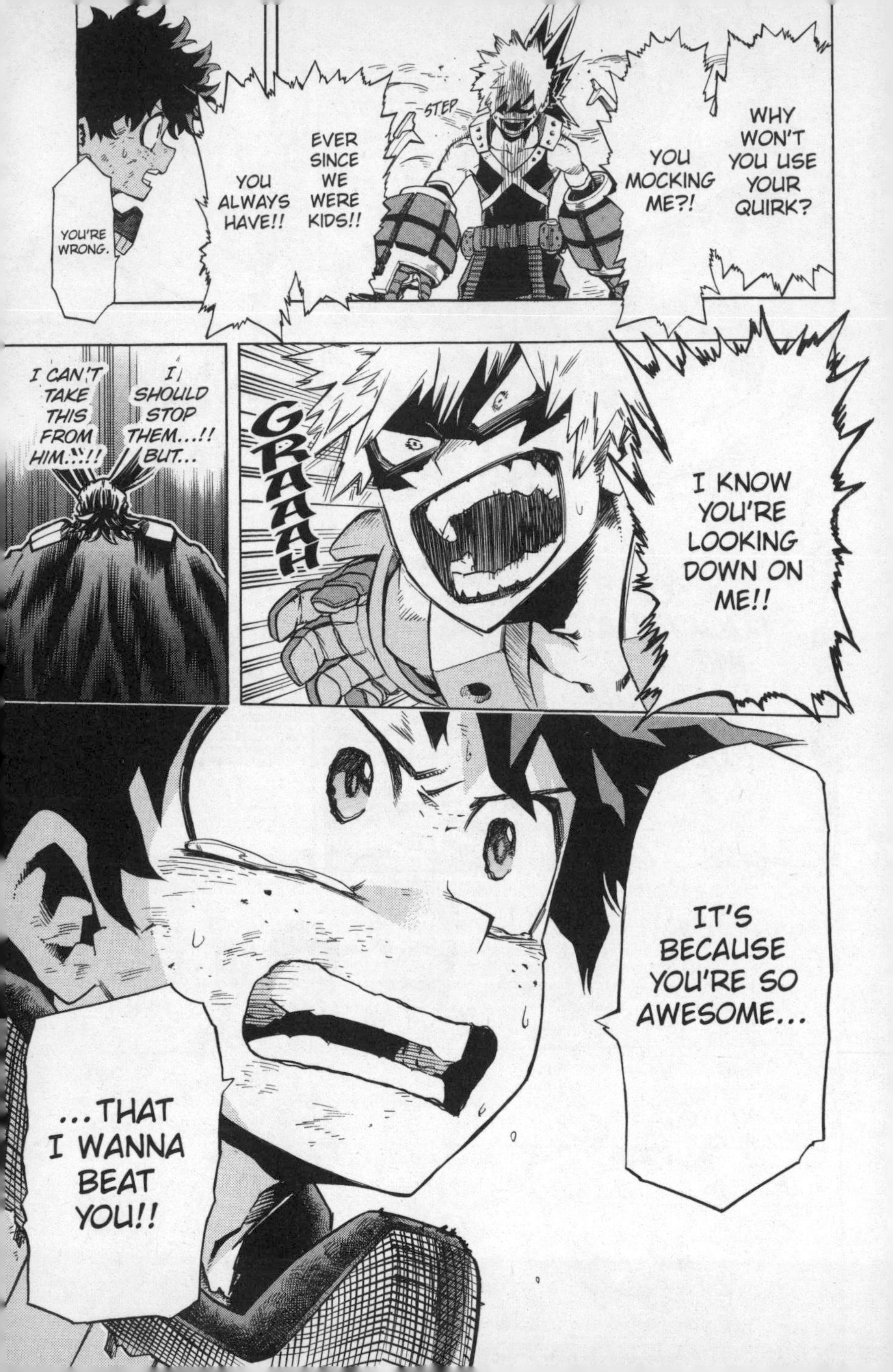
WHY WON'T YOU USE YOUR QUIRK?
YOU MOCKING ME?!
STEP
EVER SINCE WE WERE KIDS!!
YOU ALWAYS HAVE!!
YOU'RE WRONG.
I KNOW YOU'RE LOOKING DOWN ON ME!!
GRAAAAH
I SHOULD STOP THEM...!! BUT...
I CAN'T TAKE THIS FROM HIM...!!
IT'S BECAUSE YOU'RE SO AWESOME...
...THAT I WANNA BEAT YOU!!

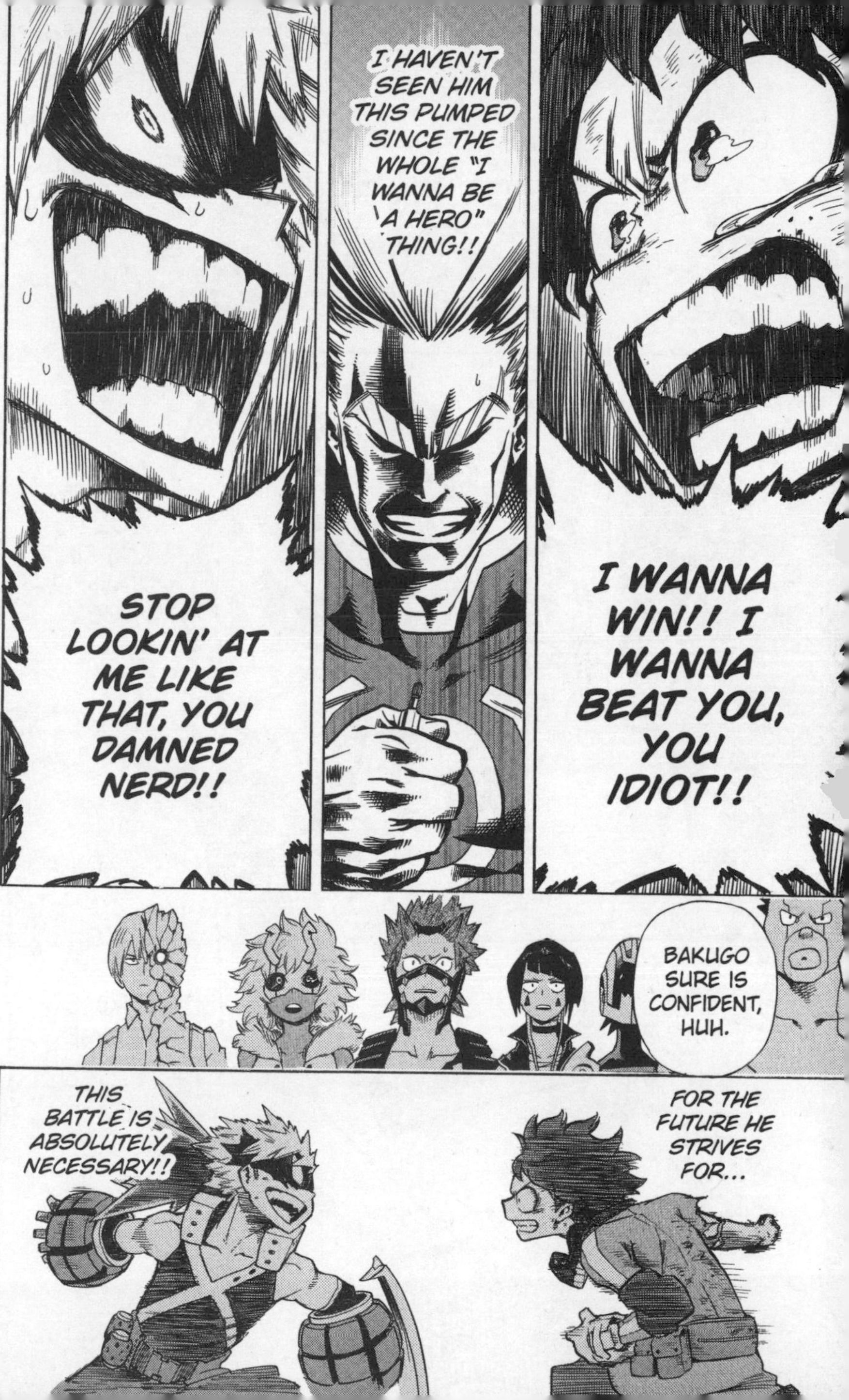
I WANNA WIN!! I WANNA BEAT YOU, YOU IDIOT!!
I HAVEN'T SEEN HIM THIS PUMPED SINCE THE WHOLE "I WANNA BE A HERO" THING!!
STOP LOOKIN' AT ME LIKE THAT, YOU DAMNED NERD!!
BAKUGO SURE IS CONFIDENT, HUH.
FOR THE FUTURE HE STRIVES FOR...
THIS BATTLE IS ABSOLUTELY NECESSARY!!

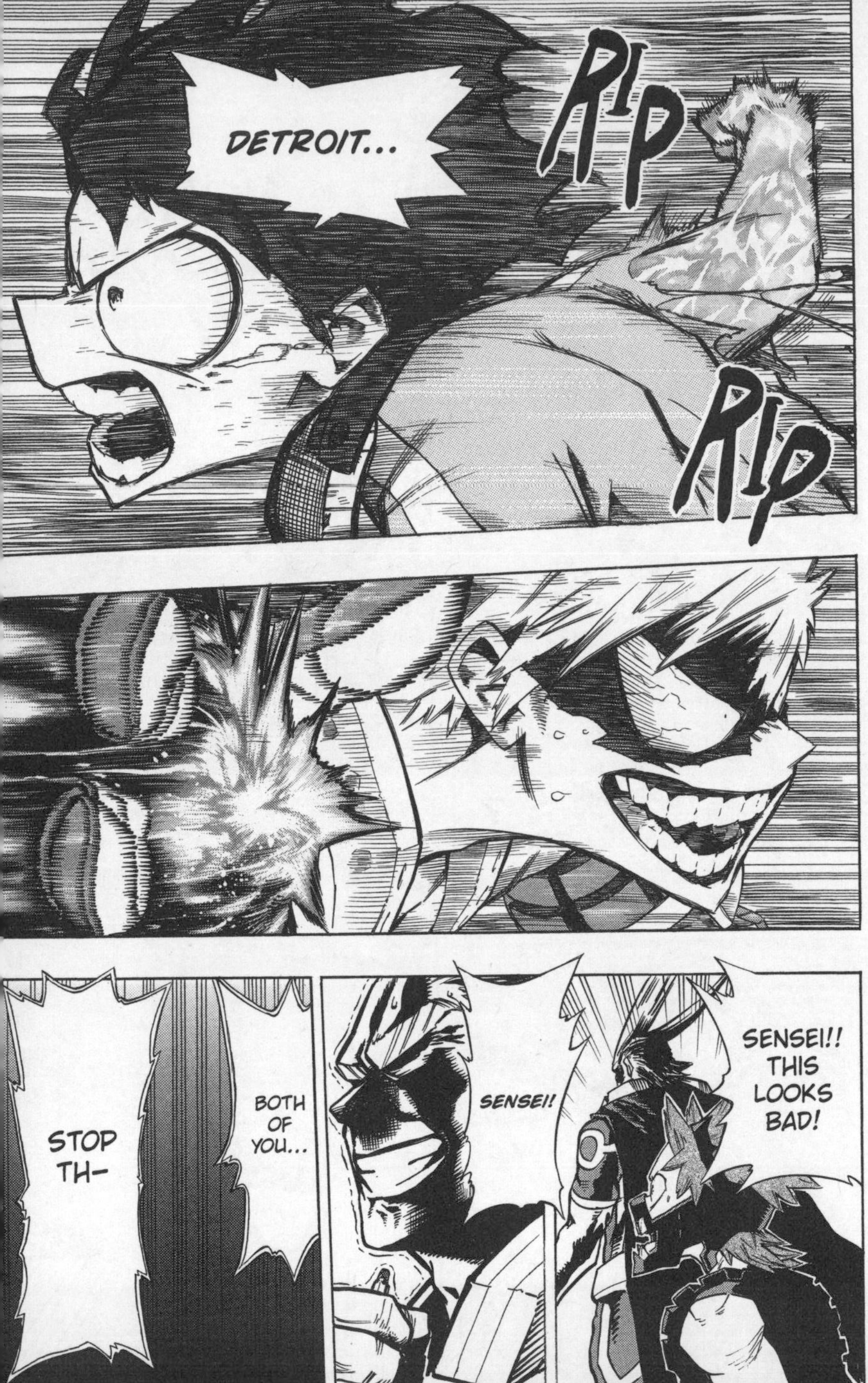
RIP
DETROIT...
RIP
SENSEI!! THIS LOOKS BAD!
SENSEI!
BOTH OF YOU...
STOP TH-

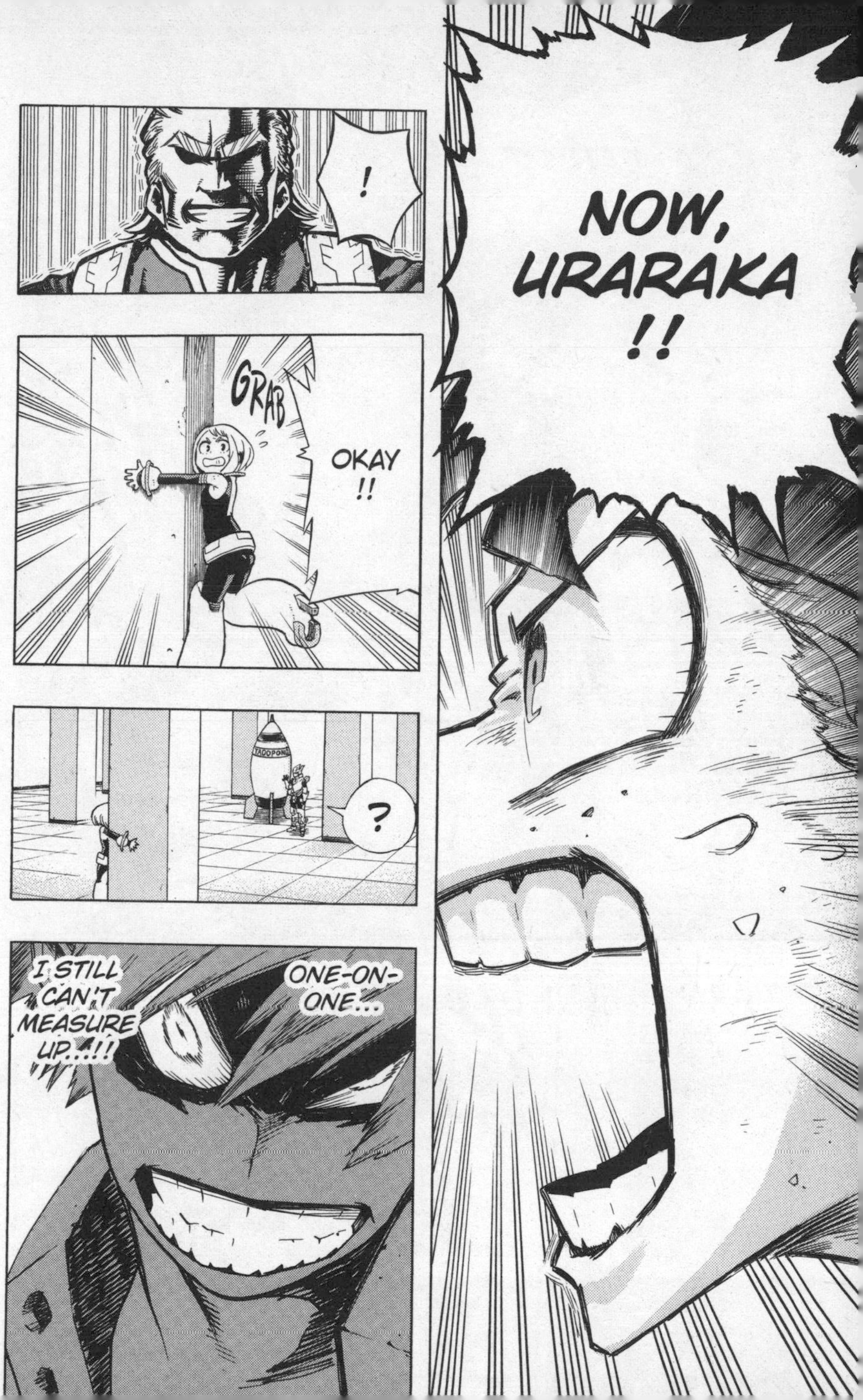
NOW, URARAKA !!
!
GRAB
OKAY !!
?
ONE-ON-ONE...
I STILL CAN'T MEASURE UP...!!

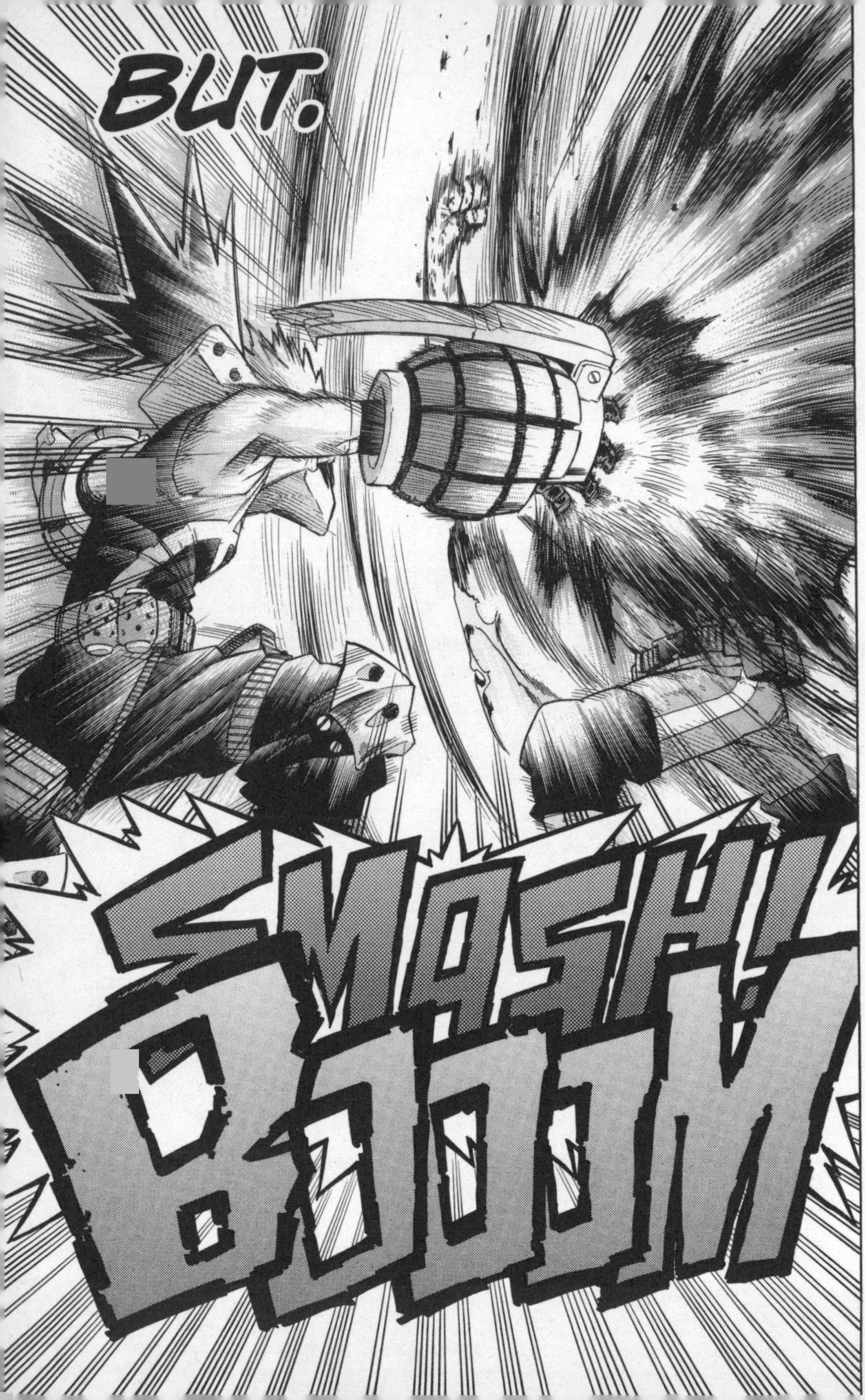
BUT.
SMASH!
BOOM

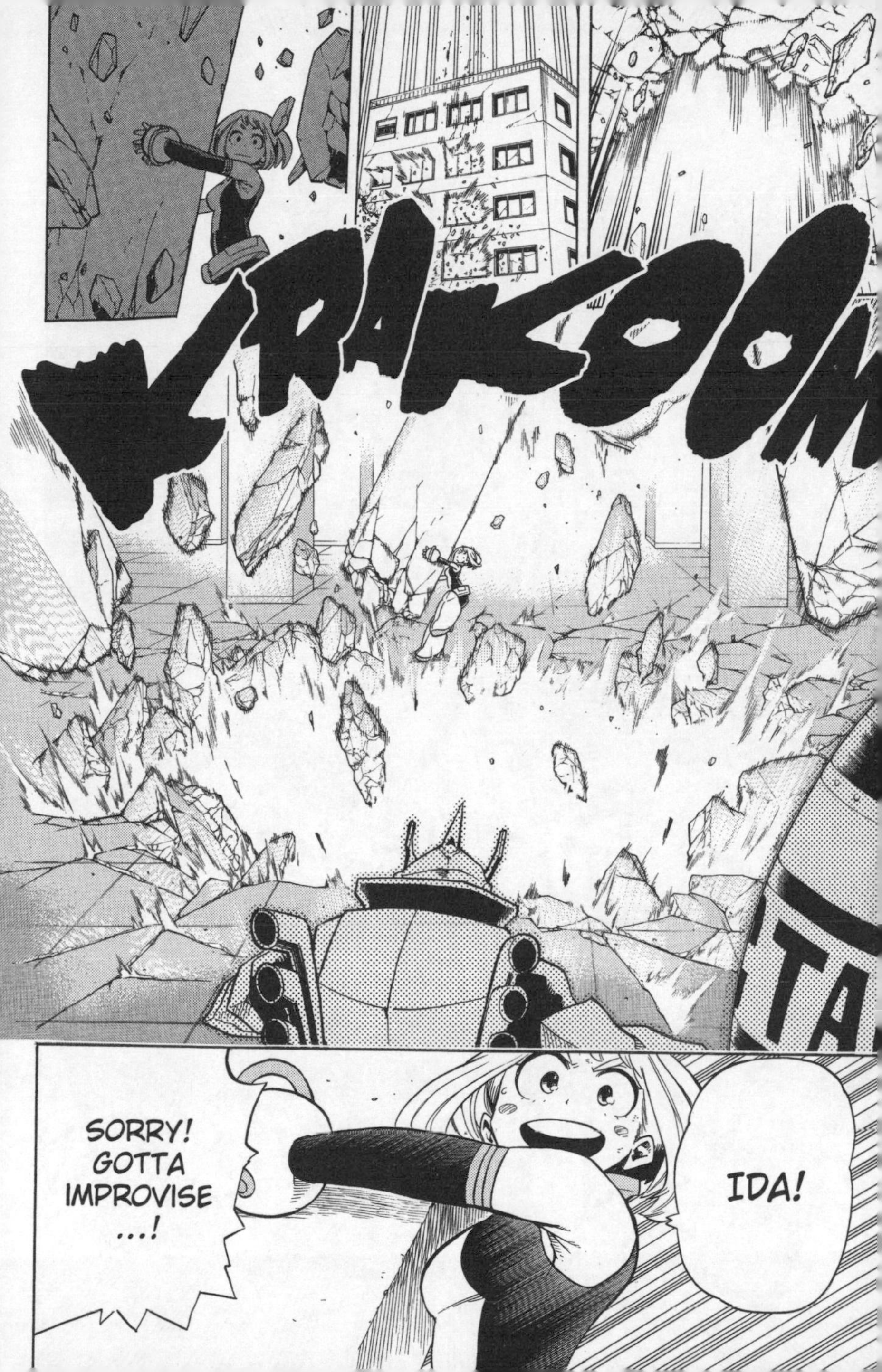
KRAKOOM
IDA!
SORRY! GOTTA IMPROVISE ...!

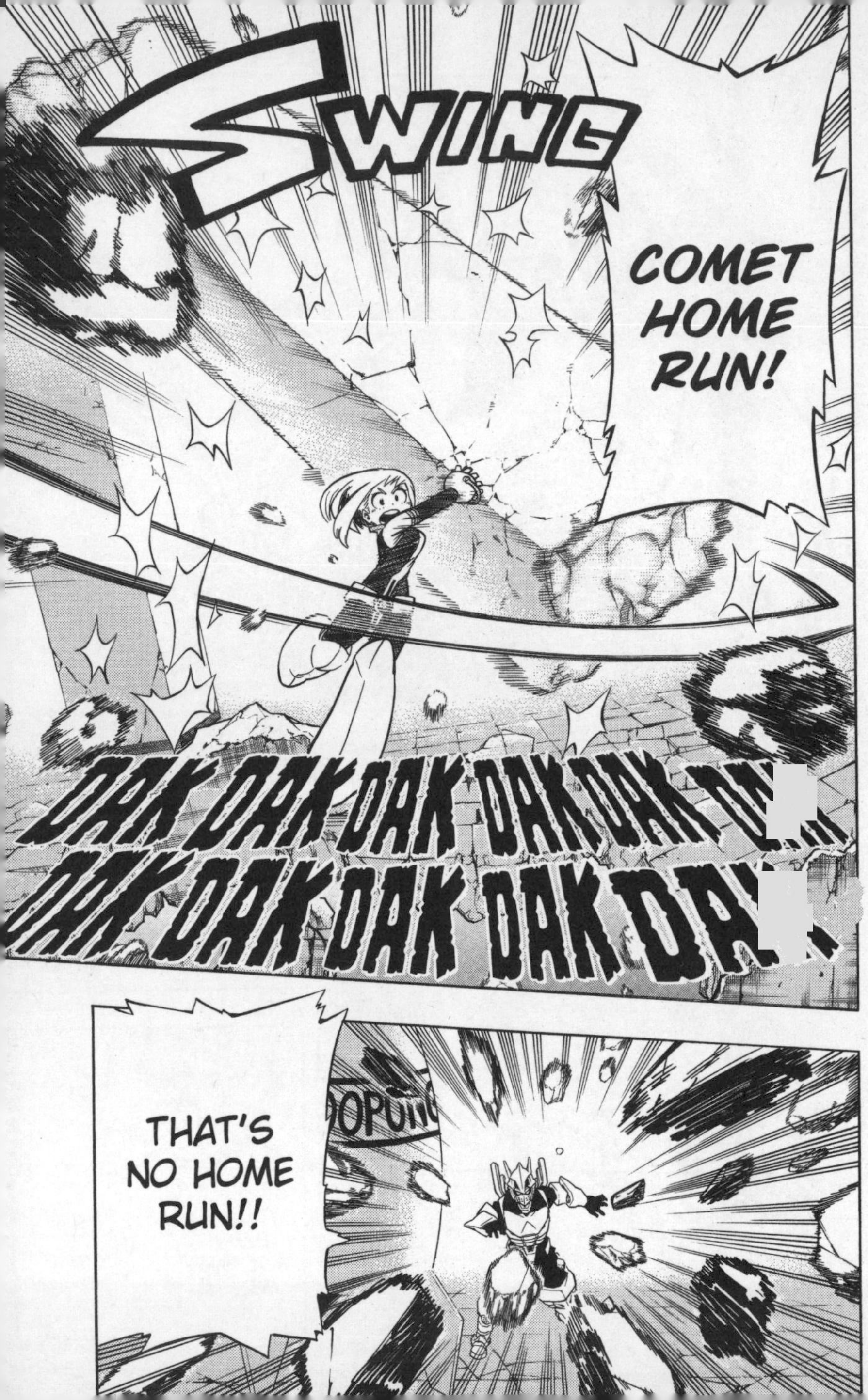
SWING
COMET HOME RUN!
DAK DAK DAK DAK DAK
DAK DAK DAK DAK
THAT'S NO HOME RUN!!

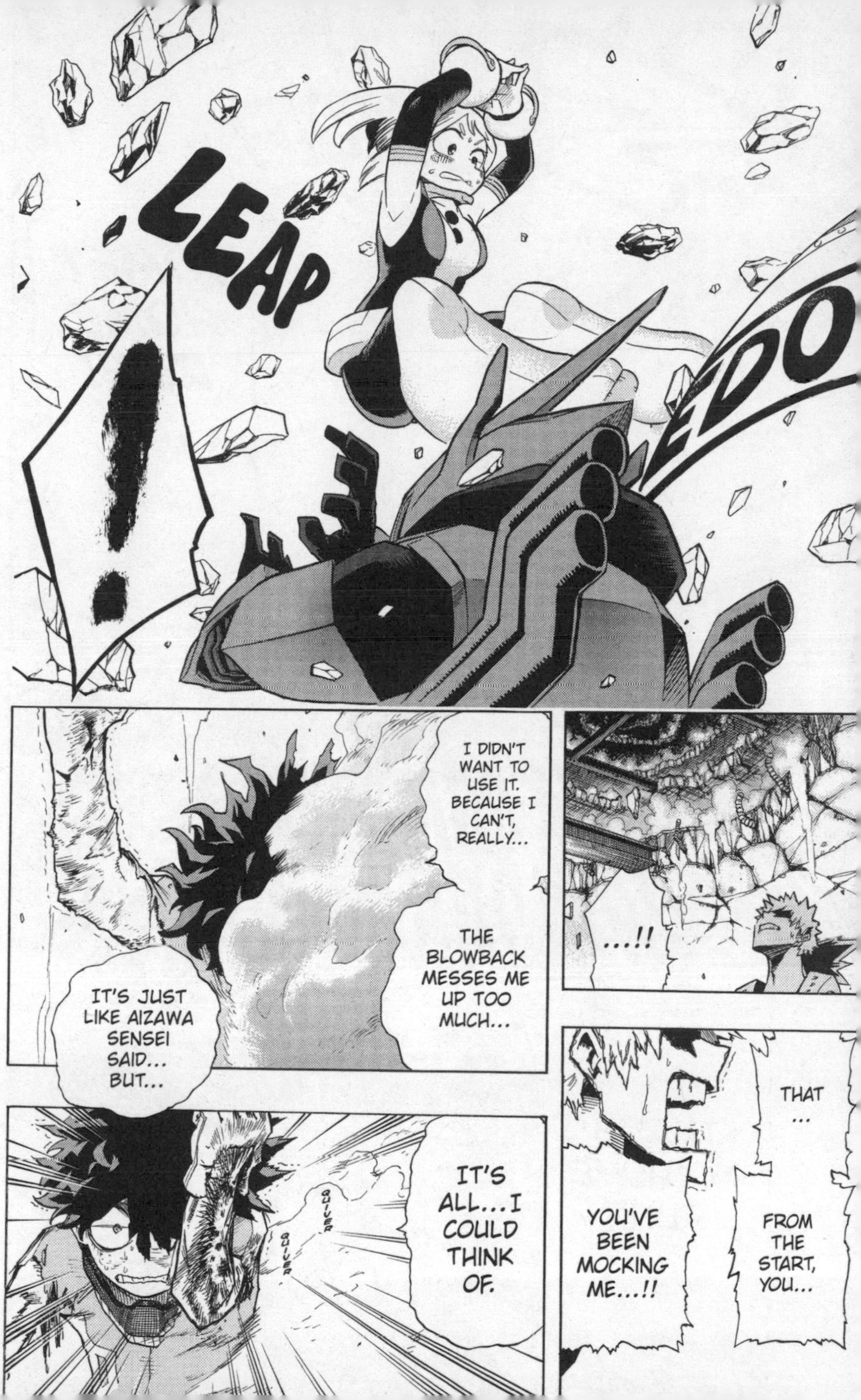
DO
LEAP
!
...!!
I DIDN'T WANT TO USE IT. BECAUSE I CAN'T, REALLY...
THE BLOWBACK MESSES ME UP TOO MUCH...
IT'S JUST LIKE AIZAWA SENSEI SAID... BUT...
THAT ...
FROM THE START, YOU...
YOU'VE BEEN MOCKING ME...!!
IT'S ALL...I COULD THINK OF.
QUIVER
QUIVER

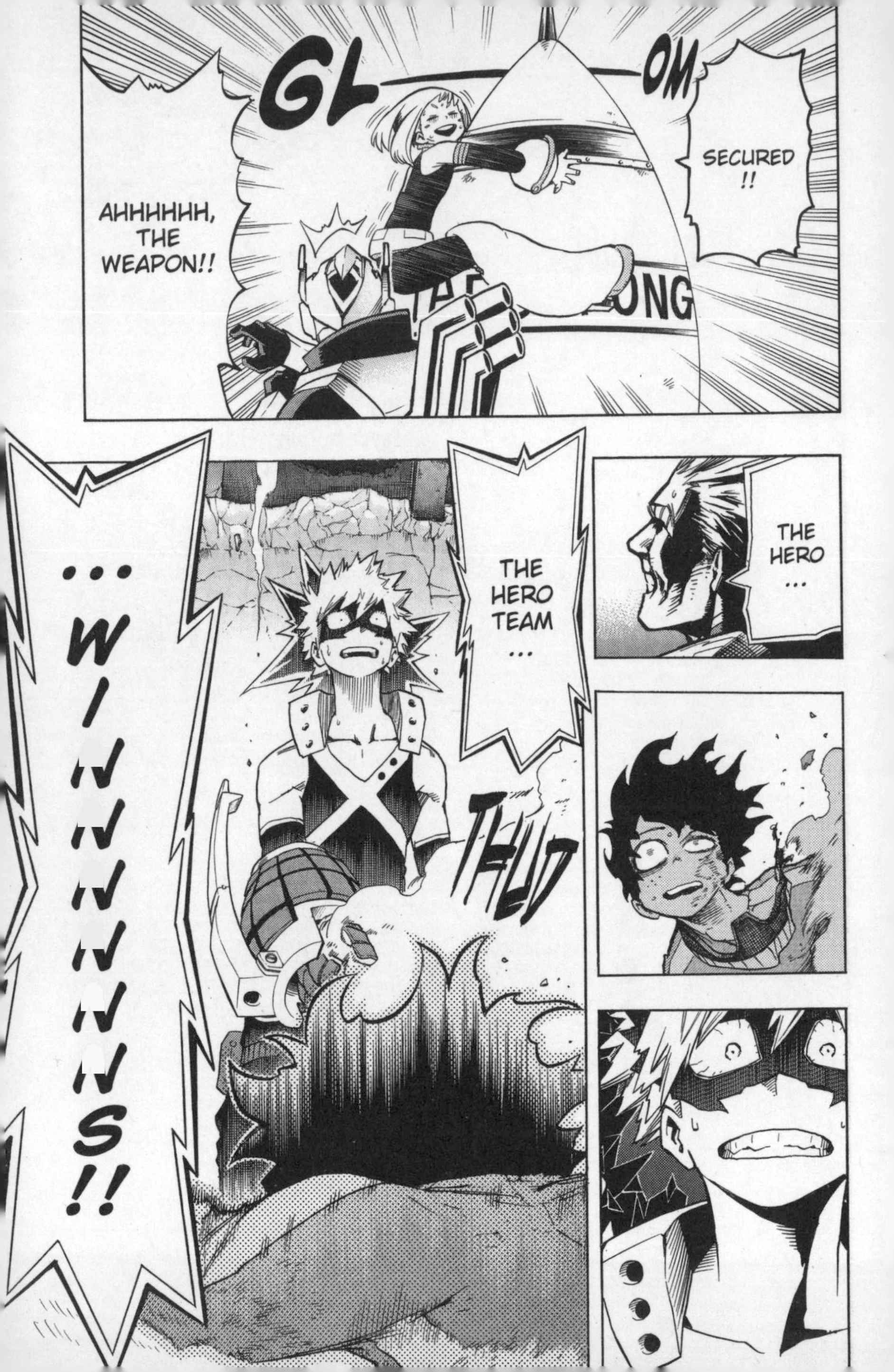
GLOM
SECURED!!
AHHHHHH, THE WEAPON!!
THE HERO ...
THE HERO TEAM ...
THUD
...WINNNNNNS!!

FULL NUDE

Birthday: 6/16
Height: 152 cm
Favorite Things: Caramel, hidden-camera shows

BEHIND THE SCENES

She started out as a dude, but at some point I realized she'd be a whole lot more fun as a girl. I keep wanting to properly introduce her Quirk, but the right opportunity hasn't presented itself. I'm working on it.

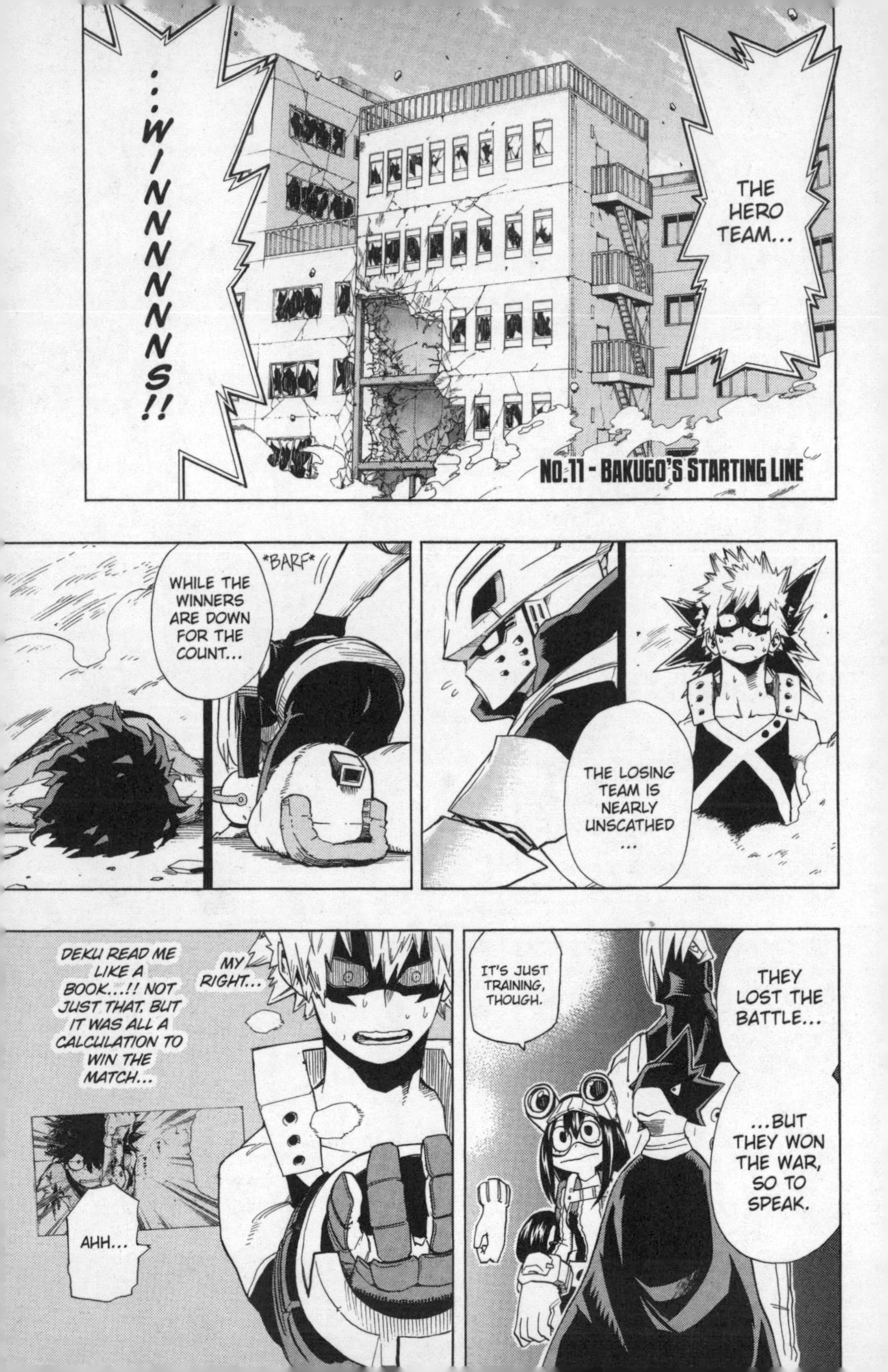
THE HERO TEAM...
...WINNNNNNNNS!!
NO.11 - BAKUGO'S STARTING LINE
THE LOSING TEAM IS NEARLY UNSCATHED ...
BARF
WHILE THE WINNERS ARE DOWN FOR THE COUNT...
THEY LOST THE BATTLE...
IT'S JUST TRAINING, THOUGH.
...BUT THEY WON THE WAR, SO TO SPEAK.
MY RIGHT...
DEKU READ ME LIKE A BOOK...!! NOT JUST THAT, BUT IT WAS ALL A CALCULATION TO WIN THE MATCH...
AHH...

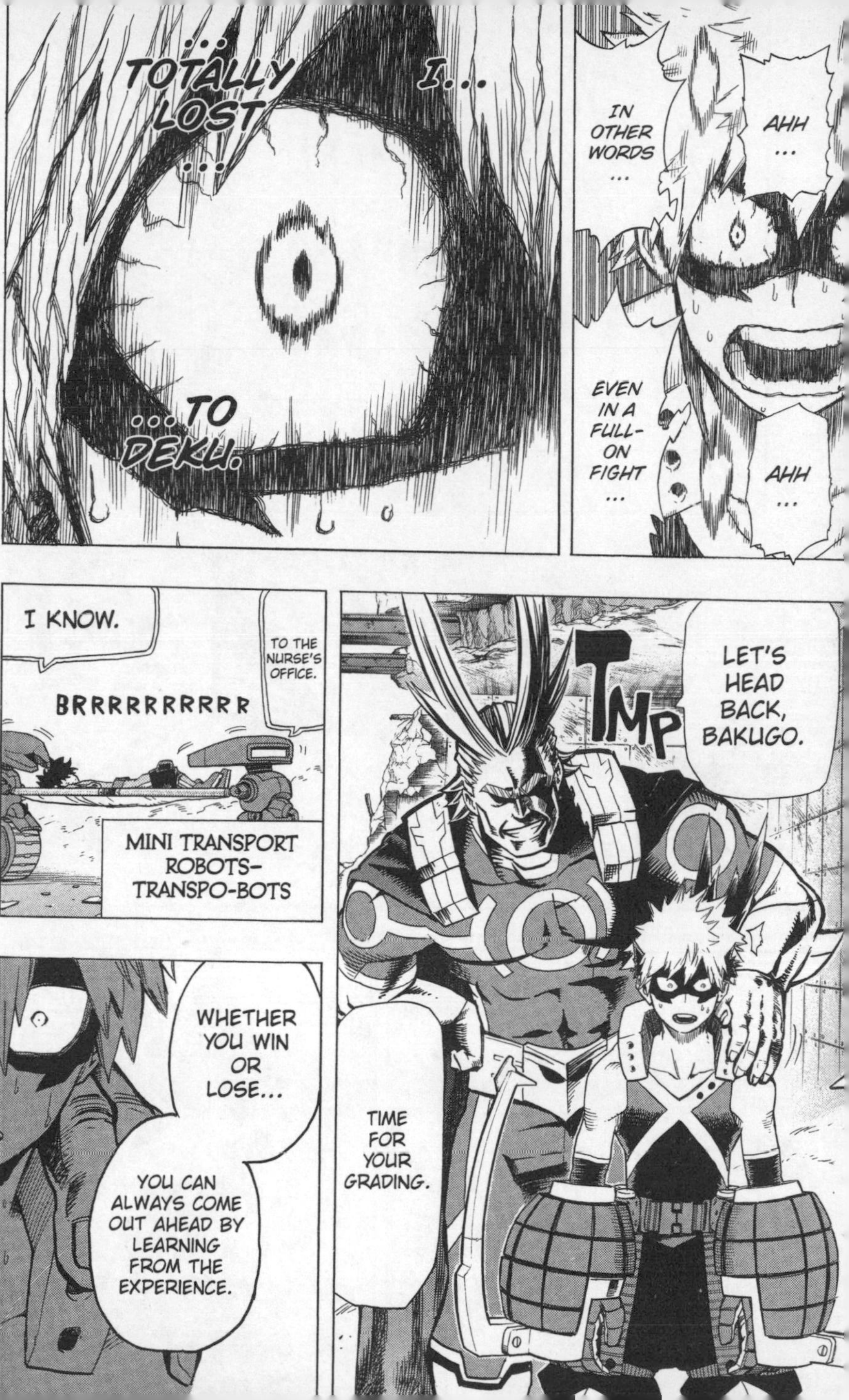
AHH ...
IN OTHER WORDS ...
AHH ...
EVEN IN A FULL-ON FIGHT ...
I...
...TOTALLY LOST...
...TO DEKU.
TMP
LET'S HEAD BACK, BAKUGO.
TIME FOR YOUR GRADING.
TO THE NURSE'S OFFICE.
I KNOW.
BRRRRRRRRRR
MINI TRANSPORT ROBOTS-TRANSPO-BOTS
WHETHER YOU WIN OR LOSE...
YOU CAN ALWAYS COME OUT AHEAD BY LEARNING FROM THE EXPERIENCE.

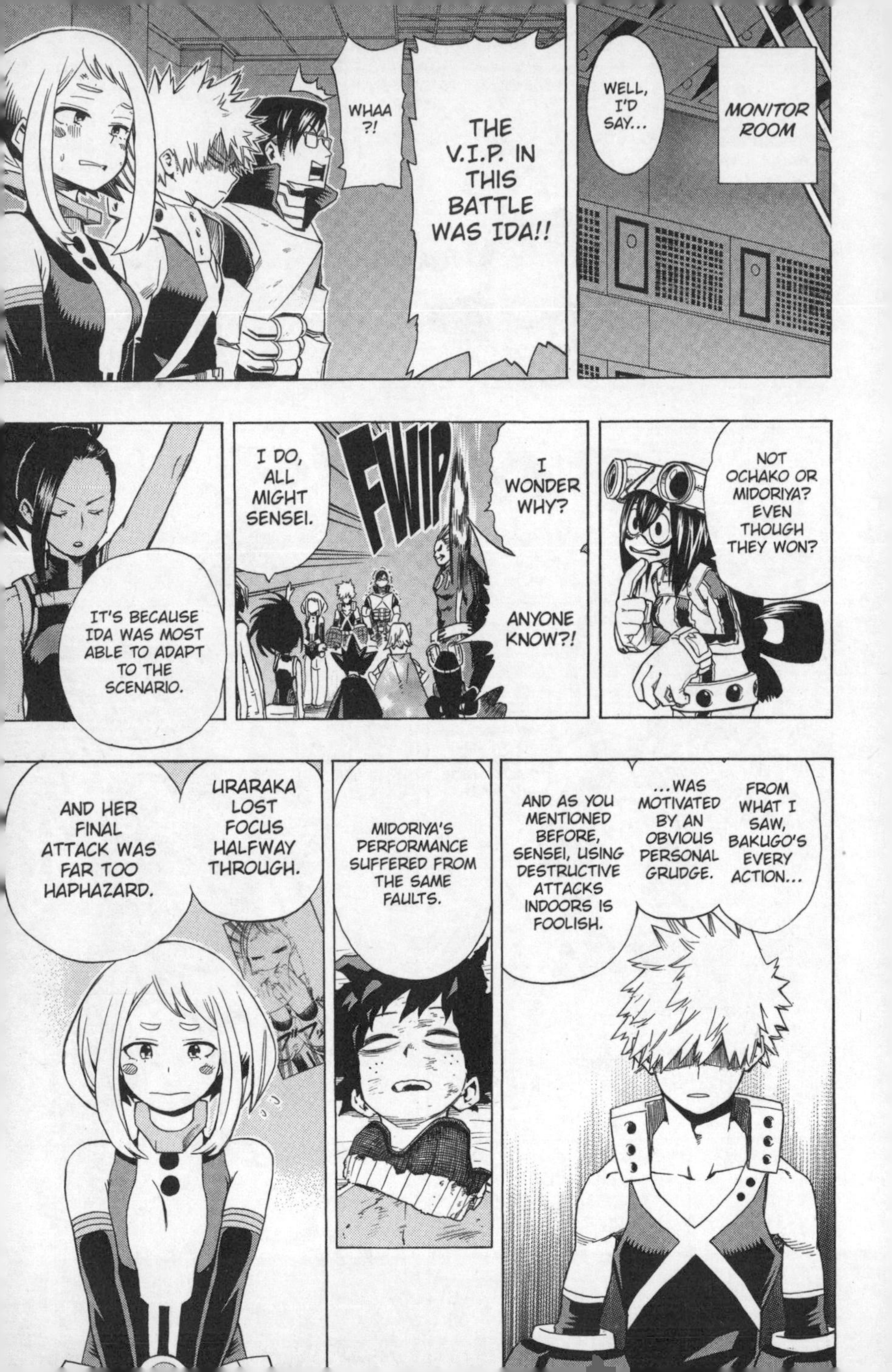
MONITOR ROOM
WELL, I'D SAY...
THE V.I.P. IN THIS BATTLE WAS IDA!!
WHAA?!
NOT OCHAKO OR MIDORIYA? EVEN THOUGH THEY WON?
I WONDER WHY?
ANYONE KNOW?!
FWIP
I DO, ALL MIGHT SENSEI.
IT'S BECAUSE IDA WAS MOST ABLE TO ADAPT TO THE SCENARIO.
FROM WHAT I SAW, BAKUGO'S EVERY ACTION...
...WAS MOTIVATED BY AN OBVIOUS PERSONAL GRUDGE.
AND AS YOU MENTIONED BEFORE, SENSEI, USING DESTRUCTIVE ATTACKS INDOORS IS FOOLISH.
MIDORIYA'S PERFORMANCE SUFFERED FROM THE SAME FAULTS.
URARAKA LOST FOCUS HALFWAY THROUGH.
AND HER FINAL ATTACK WAS FAR TOO HAPHAZARD.

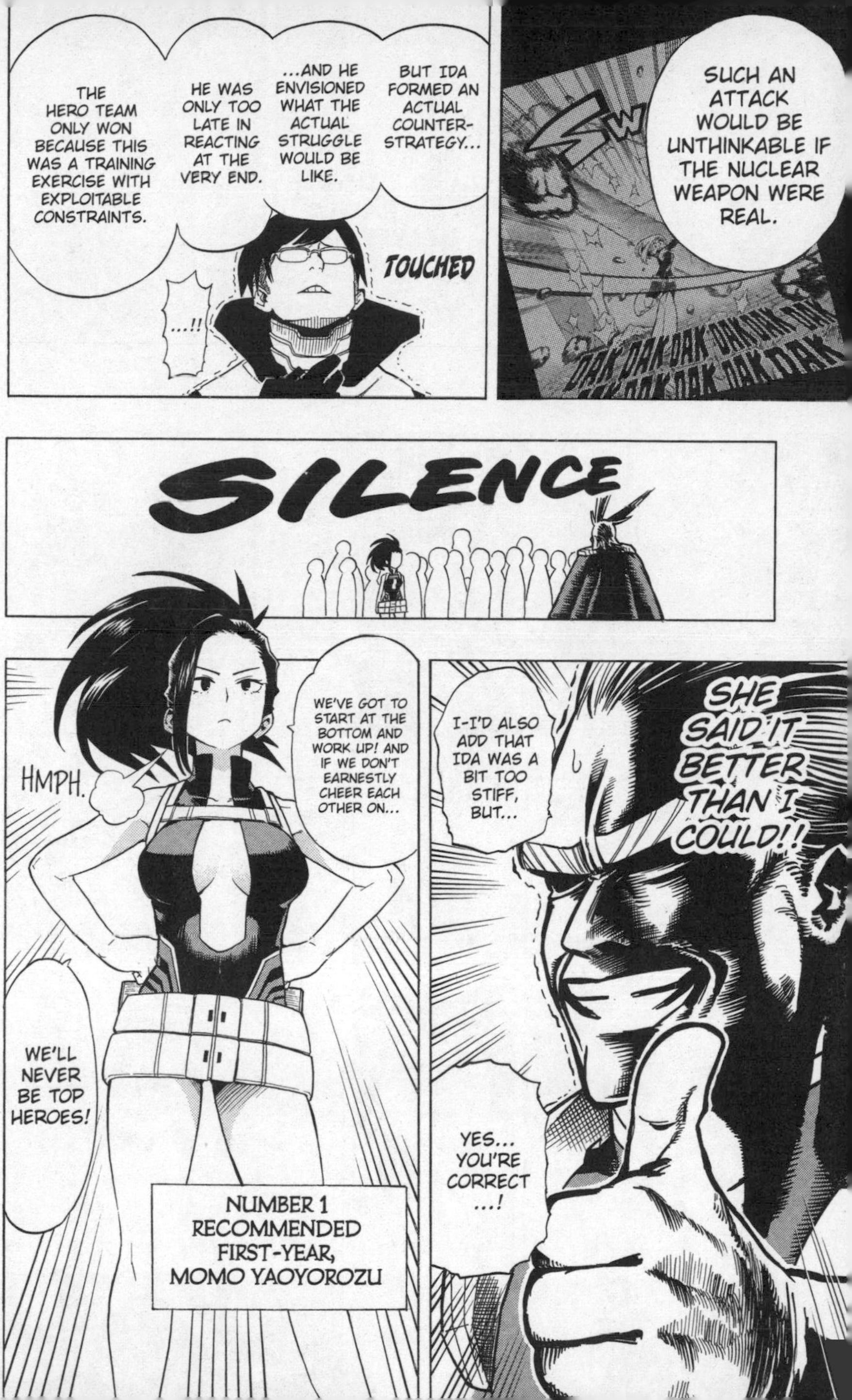
SUCH AN ATTACK WOULD BE UNTHINKABLE IF THE NUCLEAR WEAPON WERE REAL.
DAK DAK DAK DAK DAK
BUT IDA FORMED AN ACTUAL COUNTER-STRATEGY...
...AND HE ENVISIONED WHAT THE ACTUAL STRUGGLE WOULD BE LIKE.
HE WAS ONLY TOO LATE IN REACTING AT THE VERY END.
THE HERO TEAM ONLY WON BECAUSE THIS WAS A TRAINING EXERCISE WITH EXPLOITABLE CONSTRAINTS.
TOUCHED
...!!
SILENCE
SHE SAID IT BETTER THAN I COULD!!
I-I'D ALSO ADD THAT IDA WAS A BIT TOO STIFF, BUT...
YES... YOU'RE CORRECT ...!
WE'VE GOT TO START AT THE BOTTOM AND WORK UP! AND IF WE DON'T EARNESTLY CHEER EACH OTHER ON...
HMPH.
WE'LL NEVER BE TOP HEROES!
NUMBER 1 RECOMMENDED FIRST-YEAR, MOMO YAOYOROZU

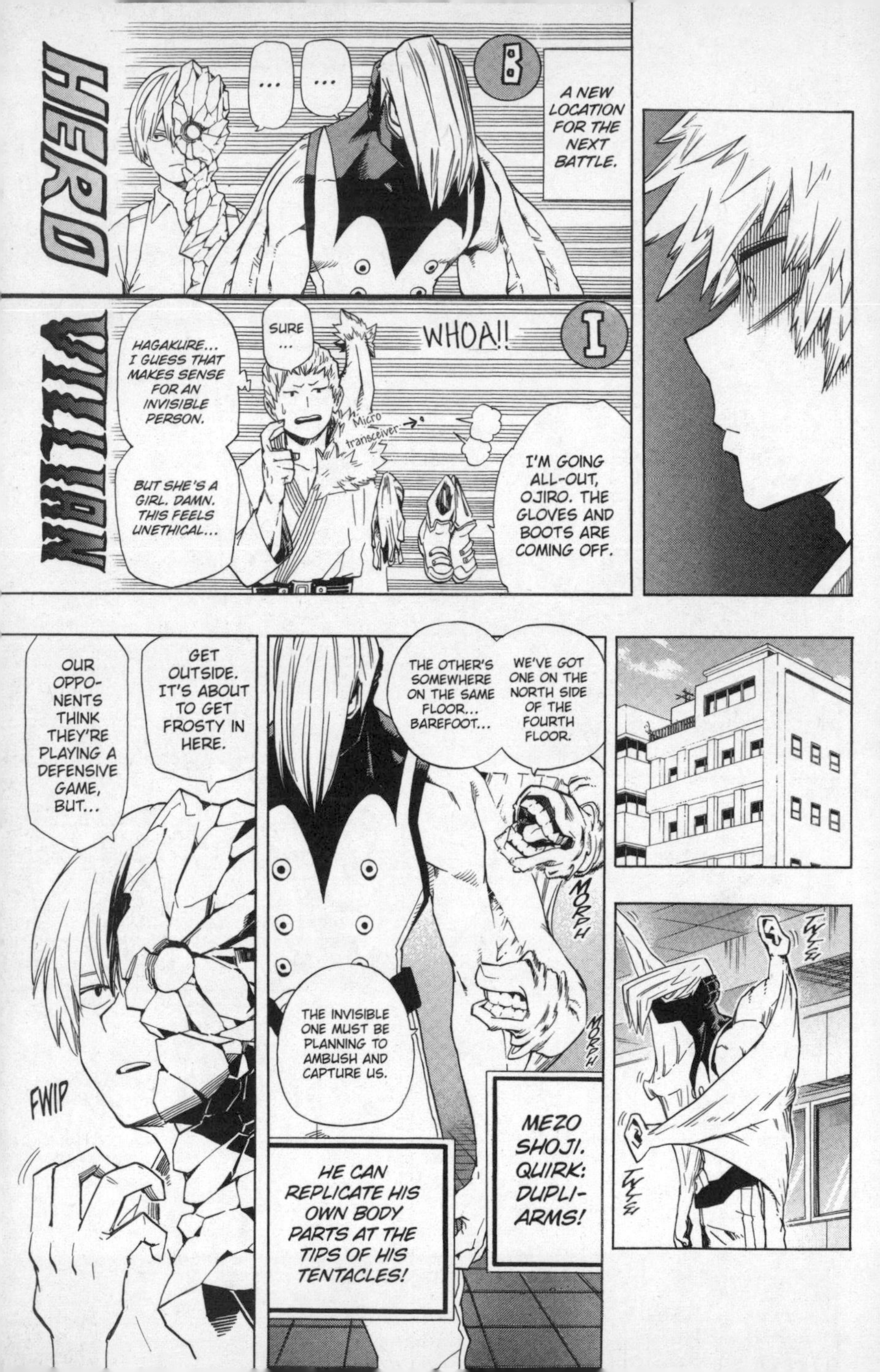
B
A NEW LOCATION FOR THE NEXT BATTLE.
...
...
HERO
I
WHOA!!
I'M GOING ALL-OUT, OJIRO. THE GLOVES AND BOOTS ARE COMING OFF.
SURE ...
HAGAKURE... I GUESS THAT MAKES SENSE FOR AN INVISIBLE PERSON.
Micro transceiver
BUT SHE'S A GIRL. DAMN. THIS FEELS UNETHICAL...
VILLAIN
WE'VE GOT ONE ON THE NORTH SIDE OF THE FOURTH FLOOR.
THE OTHER'S SOMEWHERE ON THE SAME FLOOR... BAREFOOT...
MORPH
MORPH
THE INVISIBLE ONE MUST BE PLANNING TO AMBUSH AND CAPTURE US.
MEZO SHOJI. QUIRK: DUPLI-ARMS!
HE CAN REPLICATE HIS OWN BODY PARTS AT THE TIPS OF HIS TENTACLES!
GET OUTSIDE. IT'S ABOUT TO GET FROSTY IN HERE.
OUR OPPONENTS THINK THEY'RE PLAYING A DEFENSIVE GAME, BUT...
FWIP

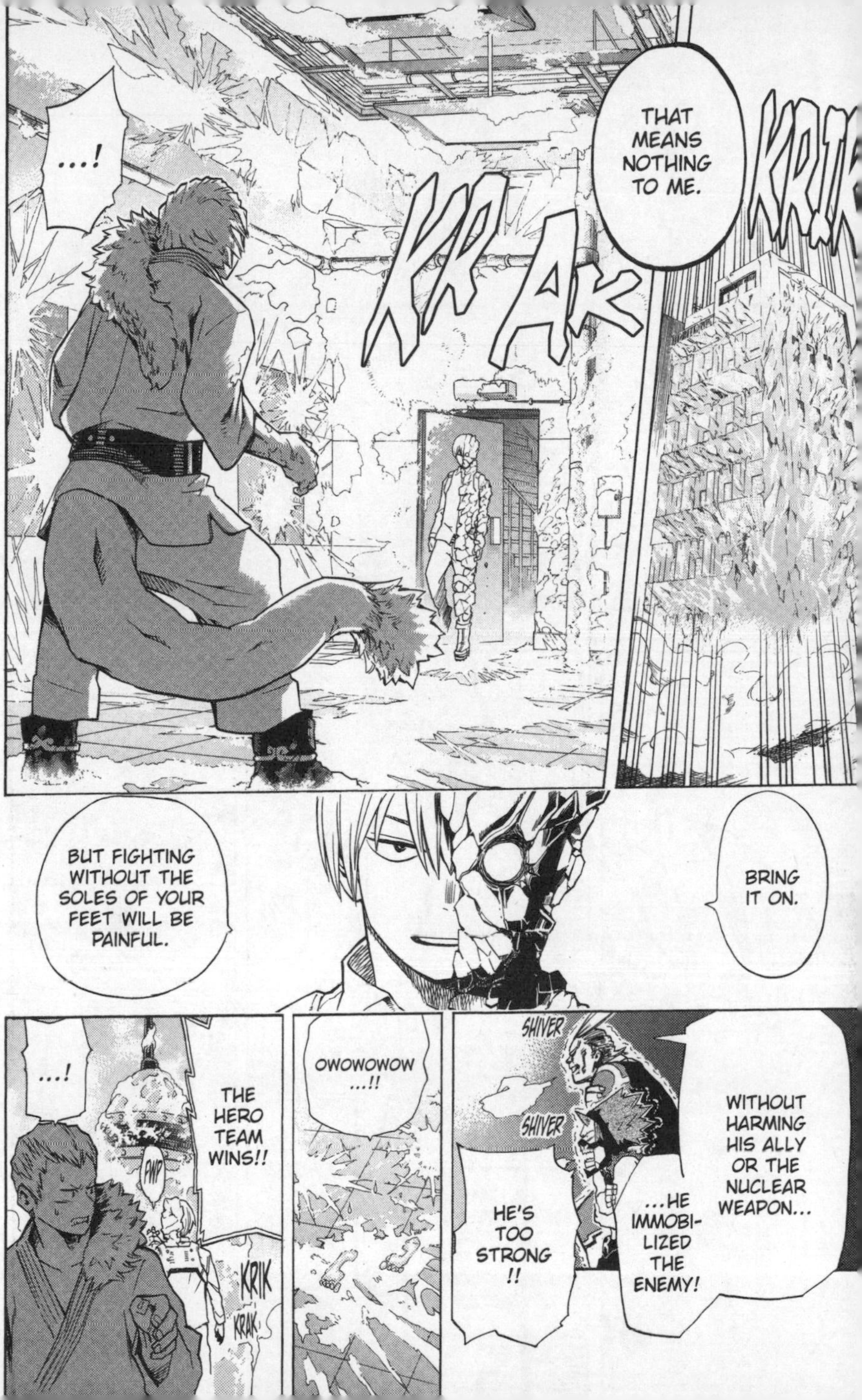
THAT MEANS NOTHING TO ME.
KRIK
KRAK
...!
BRING IT ON.
BUT FIGHTING WITHOUT THE SOLES OF YOUR FEET WILL BE PAINFUL.
SHIVER
SHIVER
WITHOUT HARMING HIS ALLY OR THE NUCLEAR WEAPON...
...HE IMMOBI-LIZED THE ENEMY!
HE'S TOO STRONG!!
OWOWOWOW...!!
...!
THE HERO TEAM WINS!!
FWP
KRIK
KRAK

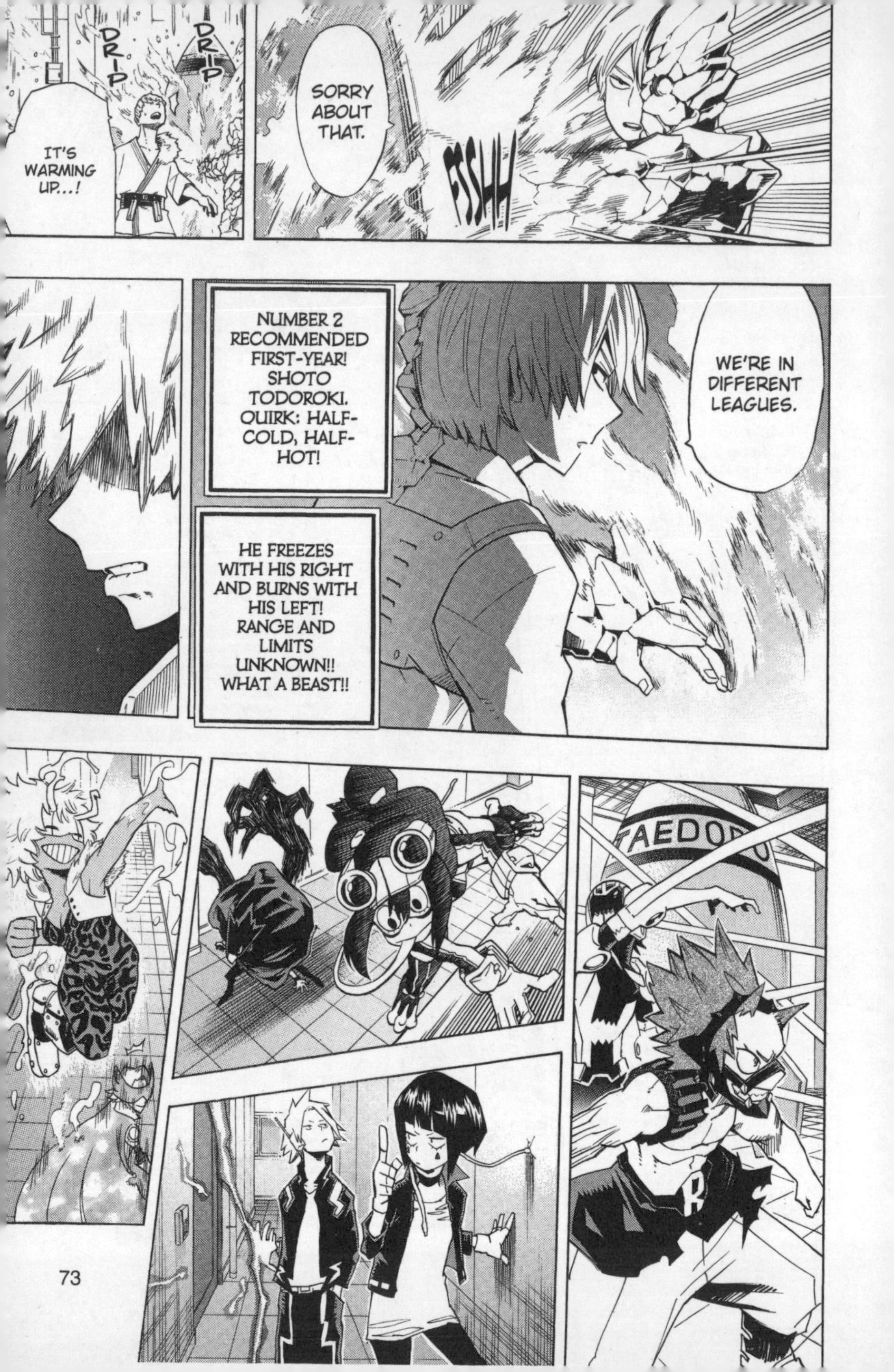
SORRY ABOUT THAT.
FSSHH
DRIP
DRIP
IT'S WARMING UP...!
WE'RE IN DIFFERENT LEAGUES.
NUMBER 2 RECOMMENDED FIRST-YEAR! SHOTO TODOROKI. QUIRK: HALF-COLD, HALF-HOT!
HE FREEZES WITH HIS RIGHT AND BURNS WITH HIS LEFT! RANGE AND LIMITS UNKNOWN!! WHAT A BEAST!!

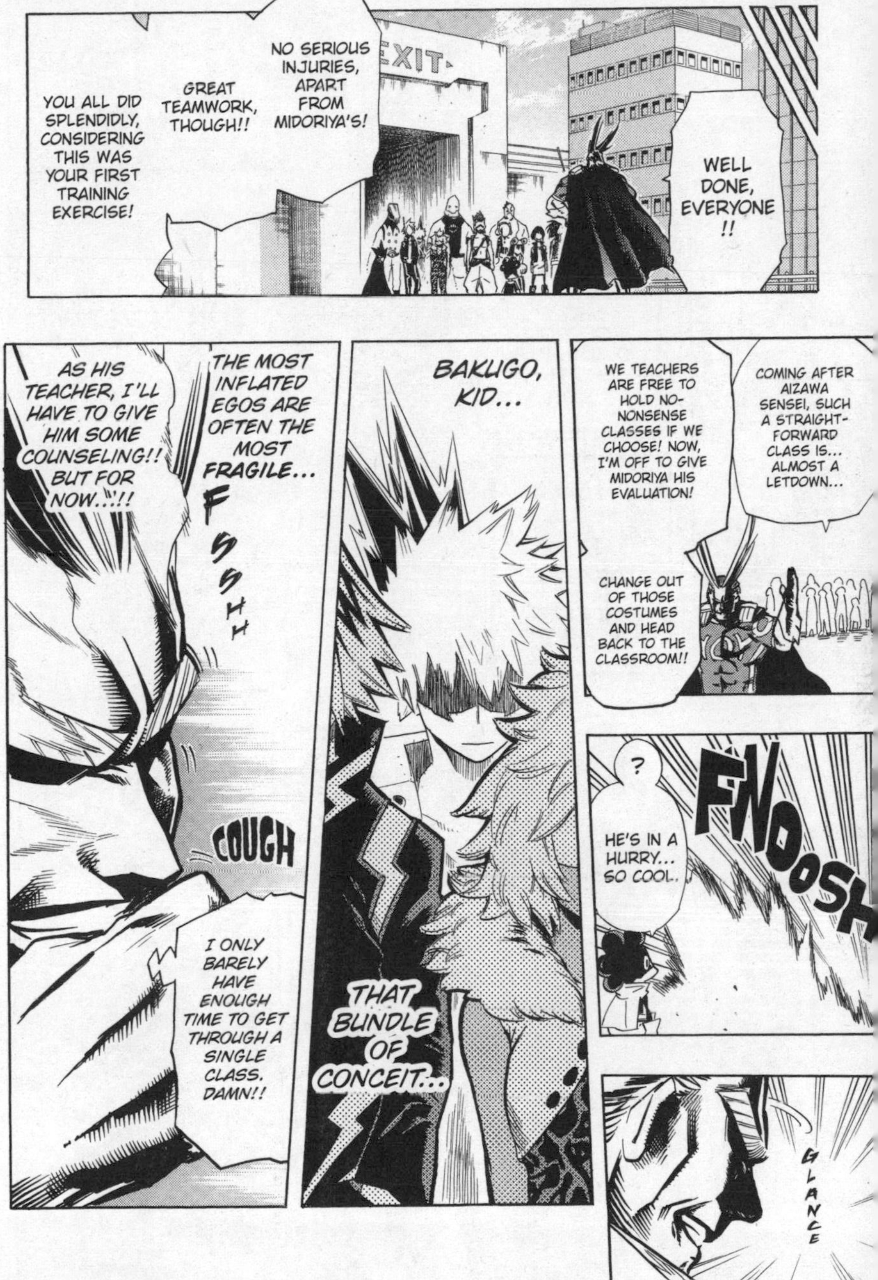
WELL DONE, EVERYONE!!
NO SERIOUS INJURIES, APART FROM MIDORIYA'S!
GREAT TEAMWORK, THOUGH!!
YOU ALL DID SPLENDIDLY, CONSIDERING THIS WAS YOUR FIRST TRAINING EXERCISE!
EXIT
COMING AFTER AIZAWA SENSEI, SUCH A STRAIGHT-FORWARD CLASS IS... ALMOST A LETDOWN...
WE TEACHERS ARE FREE TO HOLD NO-NONSENSE CLASSES IF WE CHOOSE! NOW, I'M OFF TO GIVE MIDORIYA HIS EVALUATION!
CHANGE OUT OF THOSE COSTUMES AND HEAD BACK TO THE CLASSROOM!!
FNOOSH
?
HE'S IN A HURRY... SO COOL..
GLANCE
BAKUGO, KID...
THAT BUNDLE OF CONCEIT...
THE MOST INFLATED EGOS ARE OFTEN THE MOST FRAGILE...
FSSHH
AS HIS TEACHER, I'LL HAVE TO GIVE HIM SOME COUNSELING!! BUT FOR NOW...!!
COUGH
I ONLY BARELY HAVE ENOUGH TIME TO GET THROUGH A SINGLE CLASS. DAMN!!

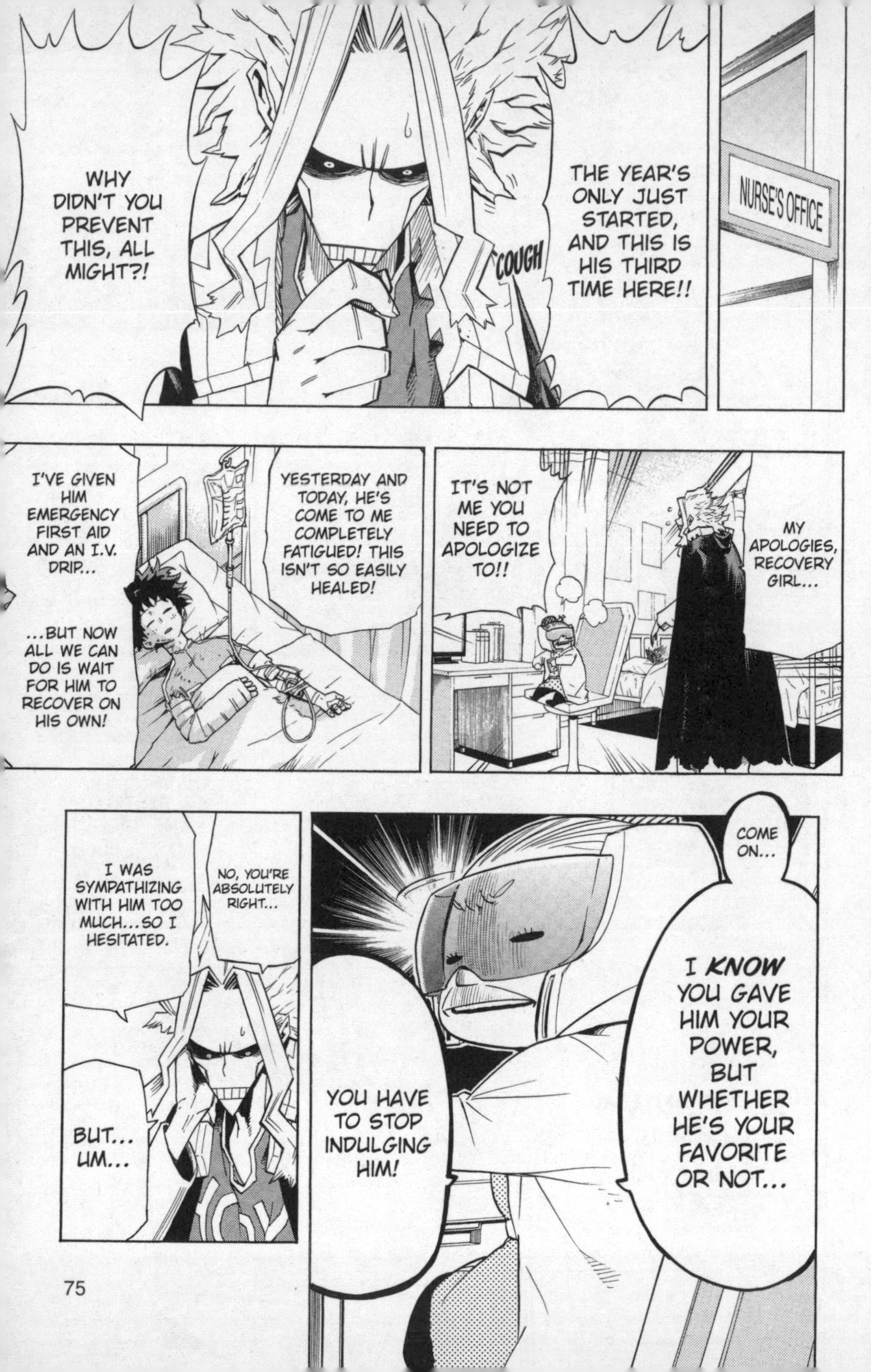
NURSE'S OFFICE
THE YEAR'S ONLY JUST STARTED, AND THIS IS HIS THIRD TIME HERE!!
COUGH
WHY DIDN'T YOU PREVENT THIS, ALL MIGHT?!
MY APOLOGIES, RECOVERY GIRL...
IT'S NOT ME YOU NEED TO APOLOGIZE TO!!
YESTERDAY AND TODAY, HE'S COME TO ME COMPLETELY FATIGUED! THIS ISN'T SO EASILY HEALED!
I'VE GIVEN HIM EMERGENCY FIRST AID AND AN I.V. DRIP...
...BUT NOW ALL WE CAN DO IS WAIT FOR HIM TO RECOVER ON HIS OWN!
COME ON...
I KNOW YOU GAVE HIM YOUR POWER, BUT WHETHER HE'S YOUR FAVORITE OR NOT...
YOU HAVE TO STOP INDULGING HIM!
NO, YOU'RE ABSOLUTELY RIGHT...
I WAS SYMPATHIZING WITH HIM TOO MUCH...SO I HESITATED.
BUT... UM...

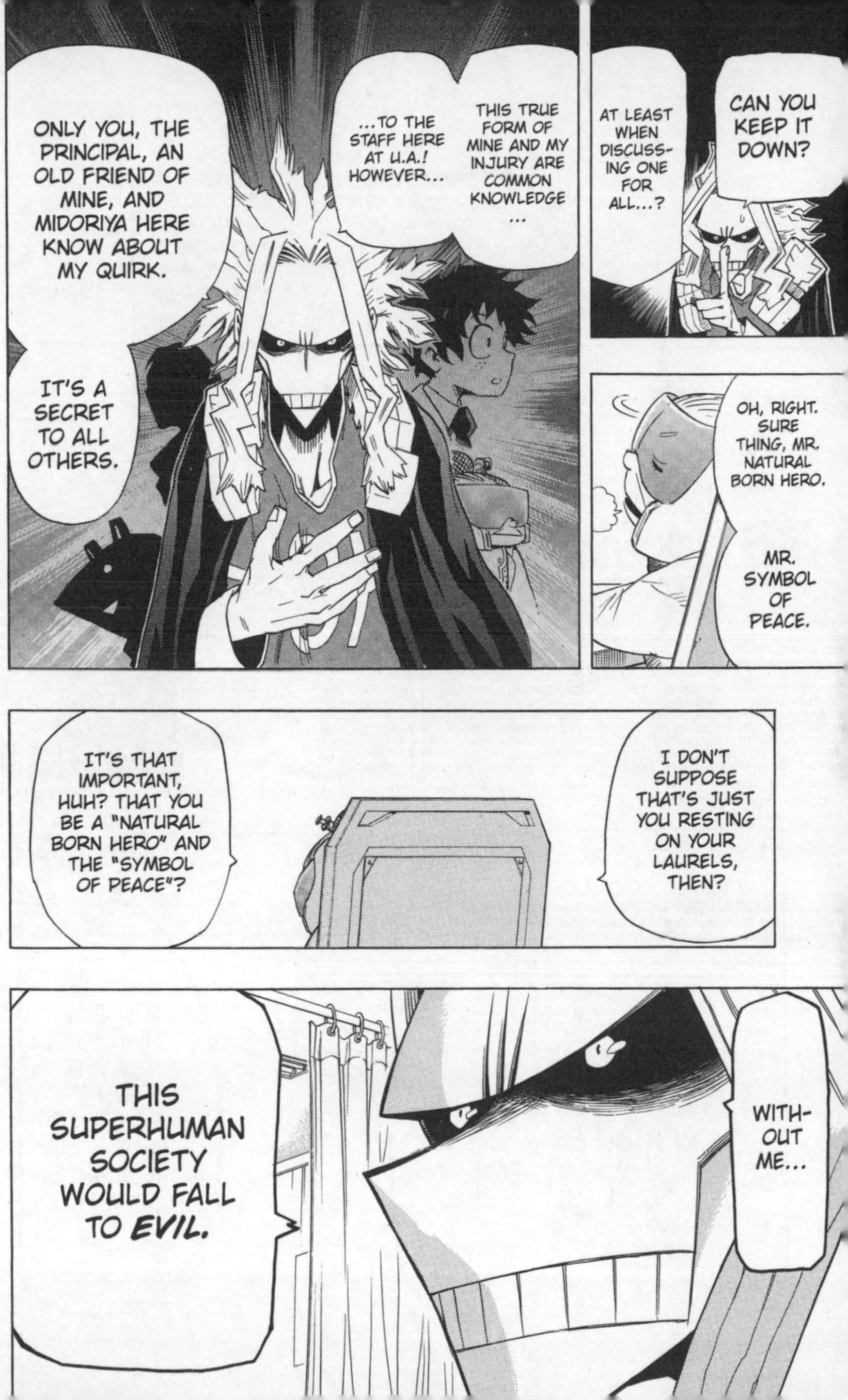
CAN YOU KEEP IT DOWN?
AT LEAST WHEN DISCUSS-ING ONE FOR ALL...?
OH, RIGHT. SURE THING, MR. NATURAL BORN HERO.
MR. SYMBOL OF PEACE.
THIS TRUE FORM OF MINE AND MY INJURY ARE COMMON KNOWLEDGE...
...TO THE STAFF HERE AT U.A.! HOWEVER...
ONLY YOU, THE PRINCIPAL, AN OLD FRIEND OF MINE, AND MIDORIYA HERE KNOW ABOUT MY QUIRK.
IT'S A SECRET TO ALL OTHERS.
I DON'T SUPPOSE THAT'S JUST YOU RESTING ON YOUR LAURELS, THEN?
IT'S THAT IMPORTANT, HUH? THAT YOU BE A "NATURAL BORN HERO" AND THE "SYMBOL OF PEACE"?
WITH-OUT ME...
THIS SUPERHUMAN SOCIETY WOULD FALL TO *EVIL.*

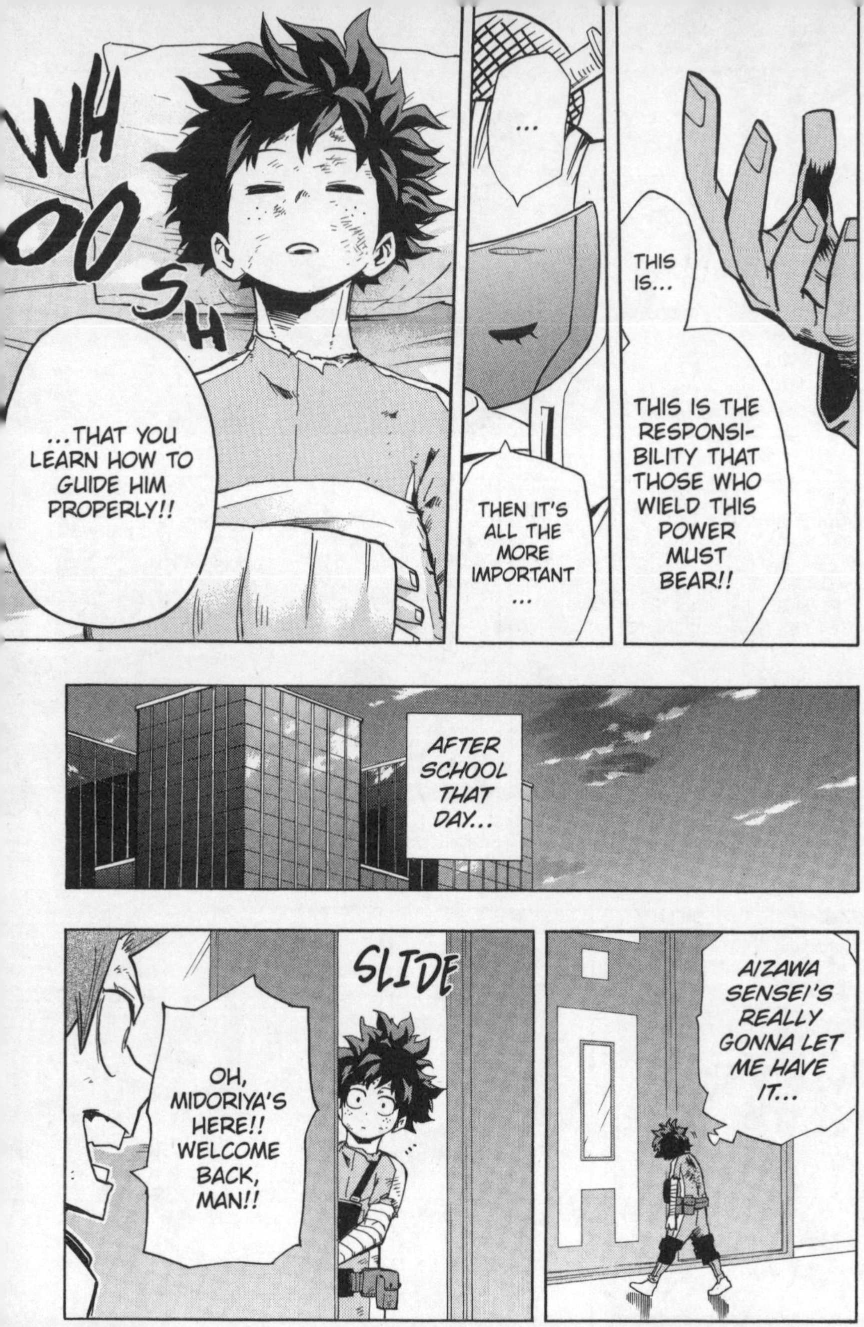
THIS IS...
THIS IS THE RESPONSIBILITY THAT THOSE WHO WIELD THIS POWER MUST BEAR!!
...
THEN IT'S ALL THE MORE IMPORTANT...
WHOOSH
...THAT YOU LEARN HOW TO GUIDE HIM PROPERLY!!
AFTER SCHOOL THAT DAY...
AIZAWA SENSEI'S REALLY GONNA LET ME HAVE IT...
SLIDE
OH, MIDORIYA'S HERE!! WELCOME BACK, MAN!!

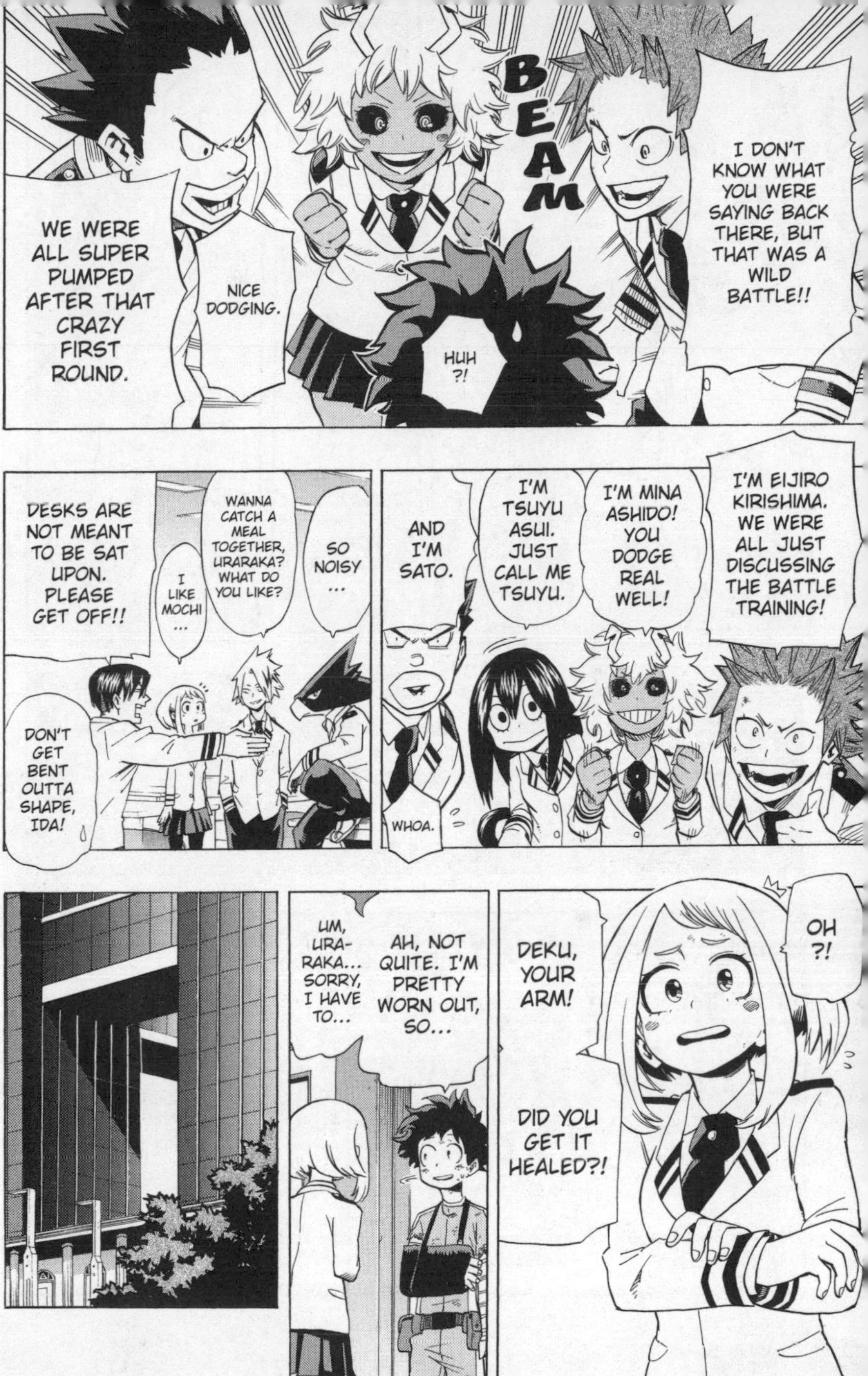
I DON'T KNOW WHAT YOU WERE SAYING BACK THERE, BUT THAT WAS A WILD BATTLE!!
BEAM
NICE DODGING.
HUH?!
WE WERE ALL SUPER PUMPED AFTER THAT CRAZY FIRST ROUND.
I'M EIJIRO KIRISHIMA. WE WERE ALL JUST DISCUSSING THE BATTLE TRAINING!
I'M MINA ASHIDO! YOU DODGE REAL WELL!
I'M TSUYU ASUI. JUST CALL ME TSUYU.
AND I'M SATO.
WHOA.
SO NOISY...
WANNA CATCH A MEAL TOGETHER, URARAKA? WHAT DO YOU LIKE?
I LIKE MOCHI...
DESKS ARE NOT MEANT TO BE SAT UPON. PLEASE GET OFF!!
DON'T GET BENT OUTTA SHAPE, IDA!
OH?!
DEKU, YOUR ARM!
DID YOU GET IT HEALED?!
AH, NOT QUITE. I'M PRETTY WORN OUT, SO...
UM, URA-RAKA... SORRY, I HAVE TO...

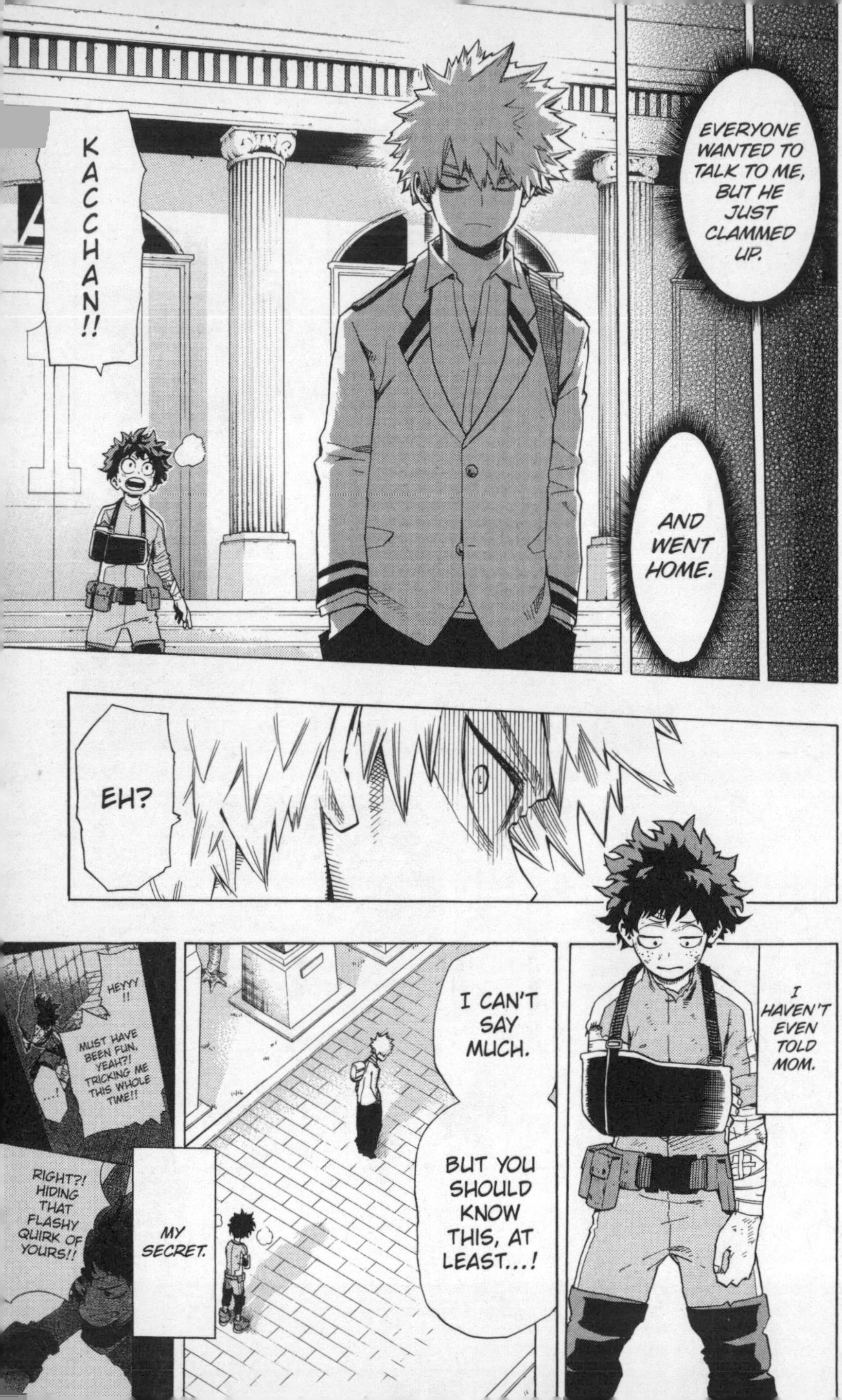
EVERYONE WANTED TO TALK TO ME, BUT HE JUST CLAMMED UP.
AND WENT HOME.
KACCHAN!!
EH?
I HAVEN'T EVEN TOLD MOM.
I CAN'T SAY MUCH.
BUT YOU SHOULD KNOW THIS, AT LEAST...!
MY SECRET.
HEYYY!!
MUST HAVE BEEN FUN, YEAH?! TRICKING ME THIS WHOLE TIME!!
...!
RIGHT?! HIDING THAT FLASHY QUIRK OF YOURS!!

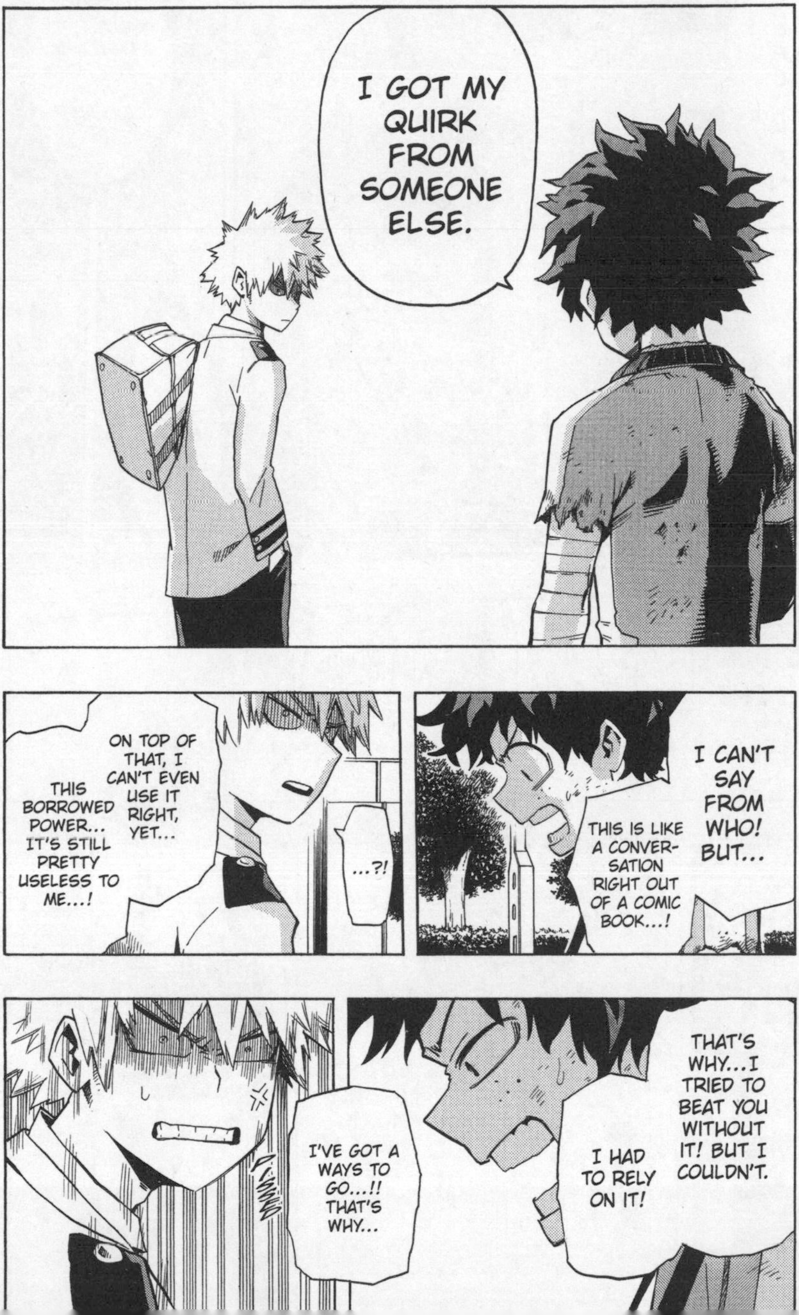

I GOT MY QUIRK FROM SOMEONE ELSE.
I CAN'T SAY FROM WHO! BUT...
THIS IS LIKE A CONVER-SATION RIGHT OUT OF A COMIC BOOK...!
...?!
THIS BORROWED POWER... IT'S STILL PRETTY USELESS TO ME...!
ON TOP OF THAT, I CAN'T EVEN USE IT RIGHT, YET...
THAT'S WHY...I TRIED TO BEAT YOU WITHOUT IT! BUT I COULDN'T.
I HAD TO RELY ON IT!
I'VE GOT A WAYS TO GO...!! THAT'S WHY...

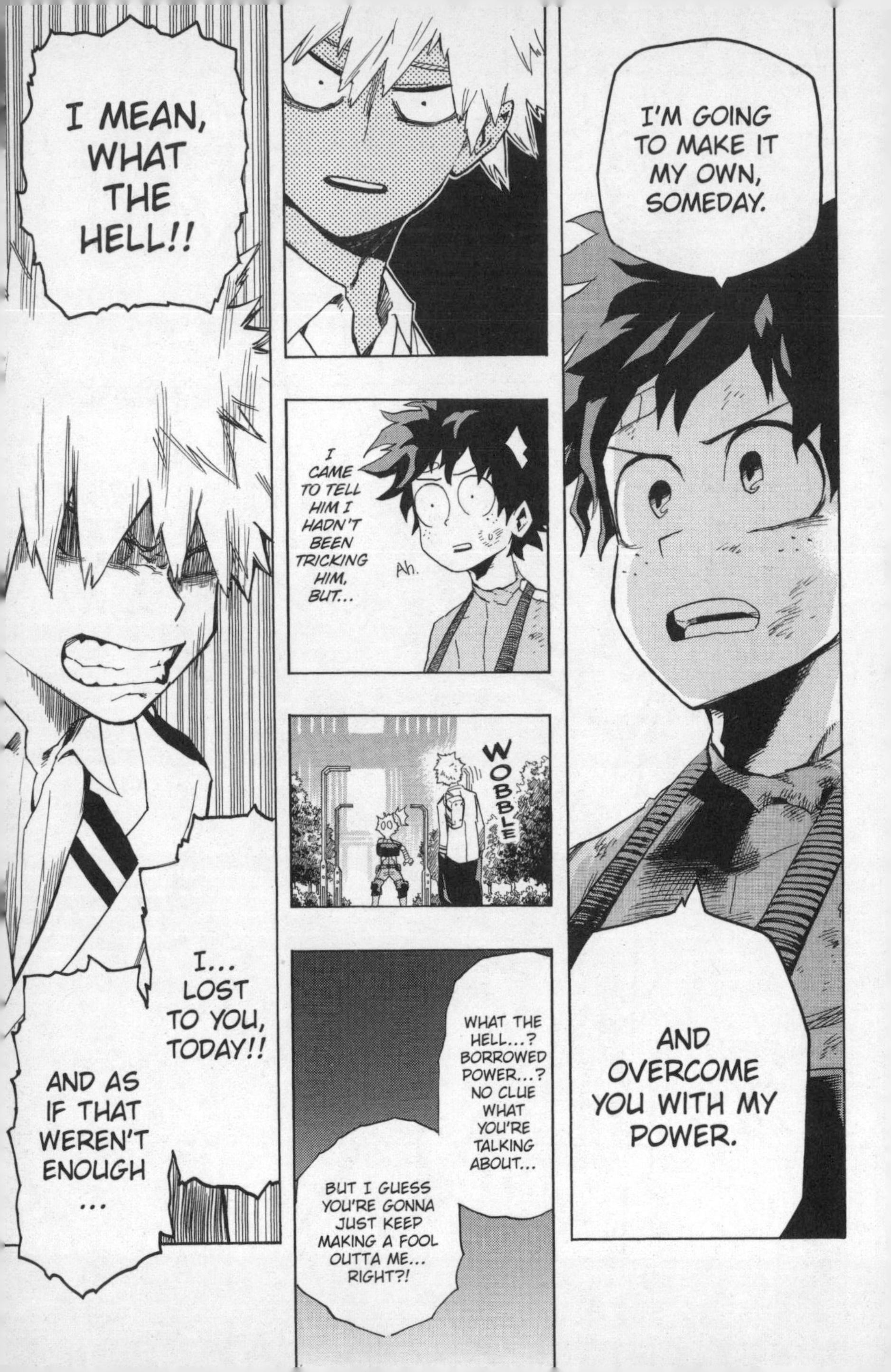
I'M GOING TO MAKE IT MY OWN, SOMEDAY.
AND OVERCOME YOU WITH MY POWER.
I CAME TO TELL HIM I HADN'T BEEN TRICKING HIM, BUT...
Ah.
WOBBLE
WHAT THE HELL...? BORROWED POWER...? NO CLUE WHAT YOU'RE TALKING ABOUT...
BUT I GUESS YOU'RE GONNA JUST KEEP MAKING A FOOL OUTTA ME... RIGHT?!
I MEAN, WHAT THE HELL!!
I... LOST TO YOU, TODAY!!
AND AS IF THAT WEREN'T ENOUGH ...

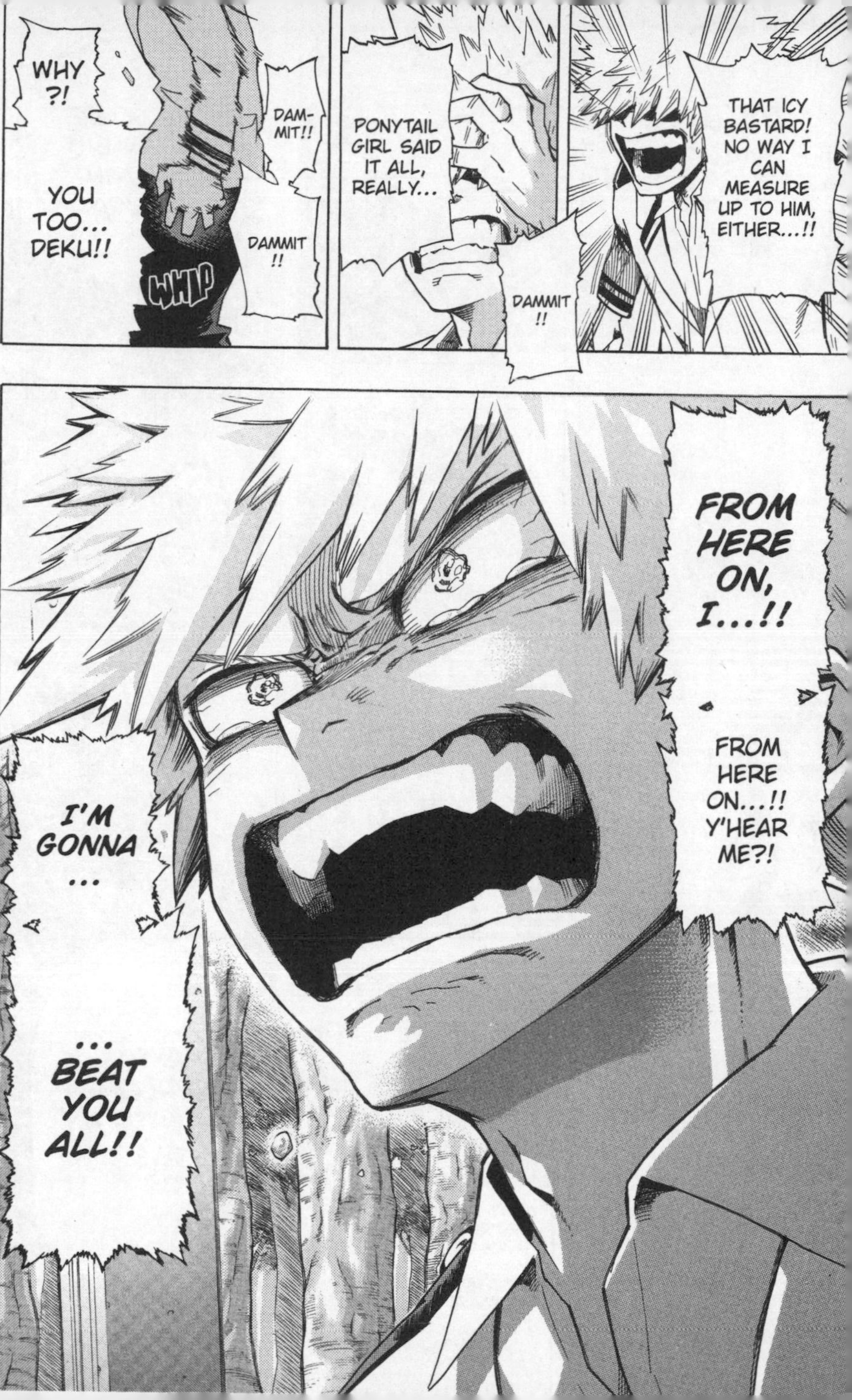
THAT ICY BASTARD! NO WAY I CAN MEASURE UP TO HIM, EITHER...!!
PONYTAIL GIRL SAID IT ALL, REALLY...
DAMMIT !!
DAM-MIT!!
WHY ?!
DAMMIT !!
YOU TOO... DEKU!!
WHIP
FROM HERE ON, I...!!
FROM HERE ON...!! Y'HEAR ME?!
I'M GONNA ...
... BEAT YOU ALL!!

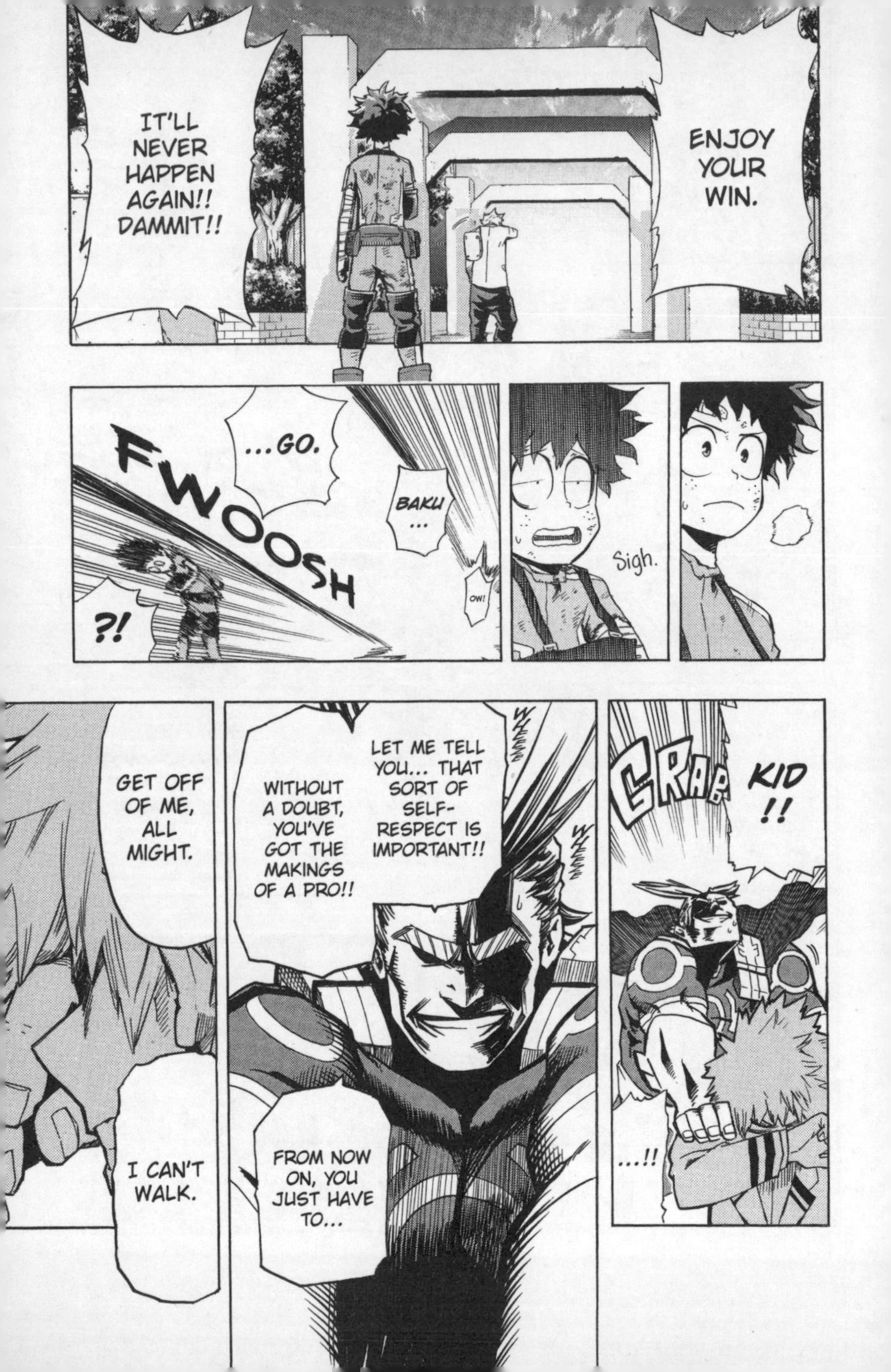
ENJOY YOUR WIN.
IT'LL NEVER HAPPEN AGAIN!! DAMMIT!!
Sigh.
BAKU ...
...GO.
OW!
FWOOSH
?!
KID !!
GRAB
...!!
LET ME TELL YOU... THAT SORT OF SELF-RESPECT IS IMPORTANT!!
WITHOUT A DOUBT, YOU'VE GOT THE MAKINGS OF A PRO!!
FROM NOW ON, YOU JUST HAVE TO...
GET OFF OF ME, ALL MIGHT.
I CAN'T WALK.

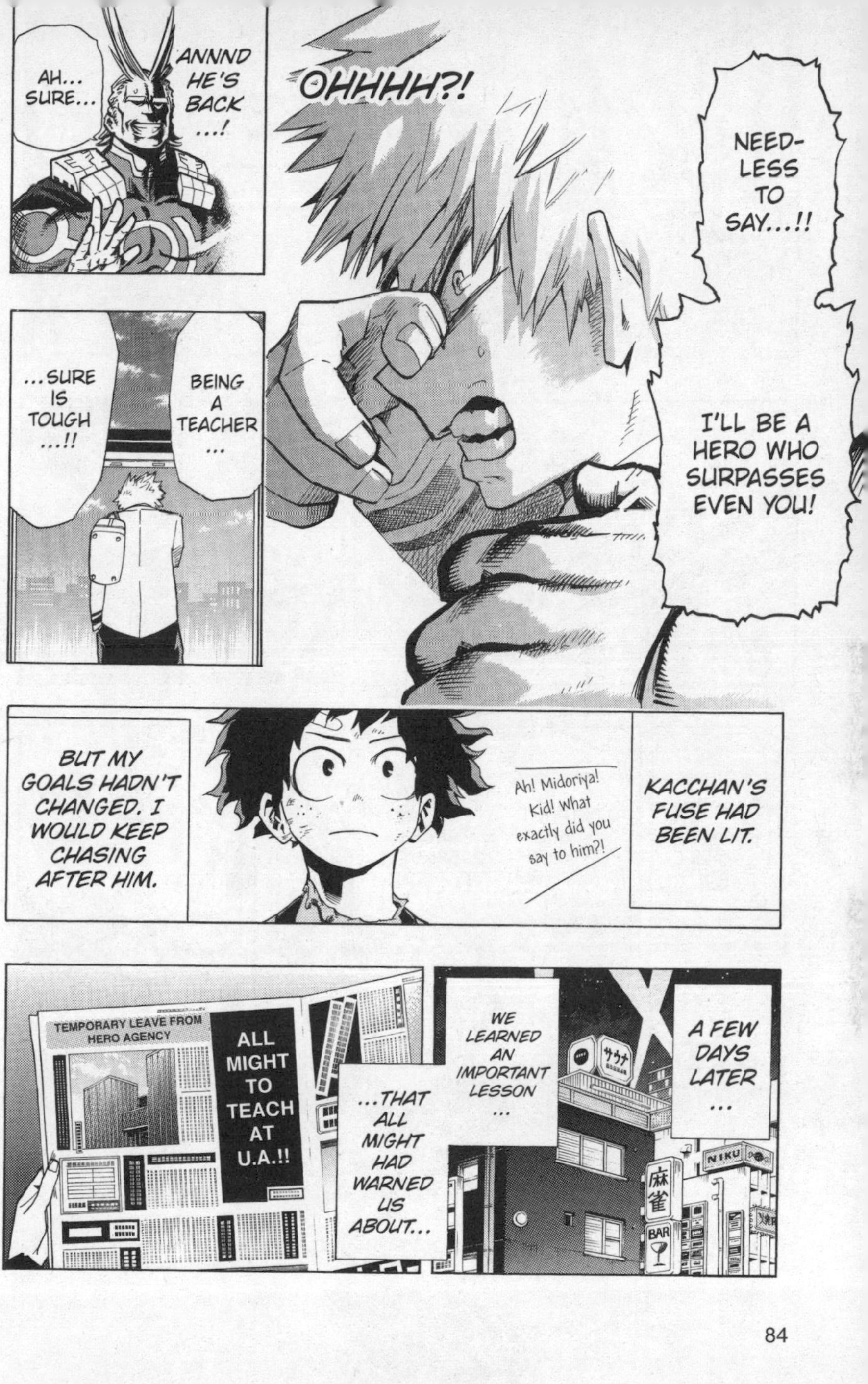
NEED-LESS TO SAY...!!
OHHHHH?!
I'LL BE A HERO WHO SURPASSES EVEN YOU!
ANNND HE'S BACK ...!
AH... SURE...
BEING A TEACHER ...
...SURE IS TOUGH ...!!
KACCHAN'S FUSE HAD BEEN LIT.
Ah! Midoriya! Kid! What exactly did you say to him?!
BUT MY GOALS HADN'T CHANGED. I WOULD KEEP CHASING AFTER HIM.
A FEW DAYS LATER ...
サウナ
NIKU
麻雀
BAR
WE LEARNED AN IMPORTANT LESSON ...
...THAT ALL MIGHT HAD WARNED US ABOUT...
TEMPORARY LEAVE FROM HERO AGENCY
ALL MIGHT TO TEACH AT U.A.!!

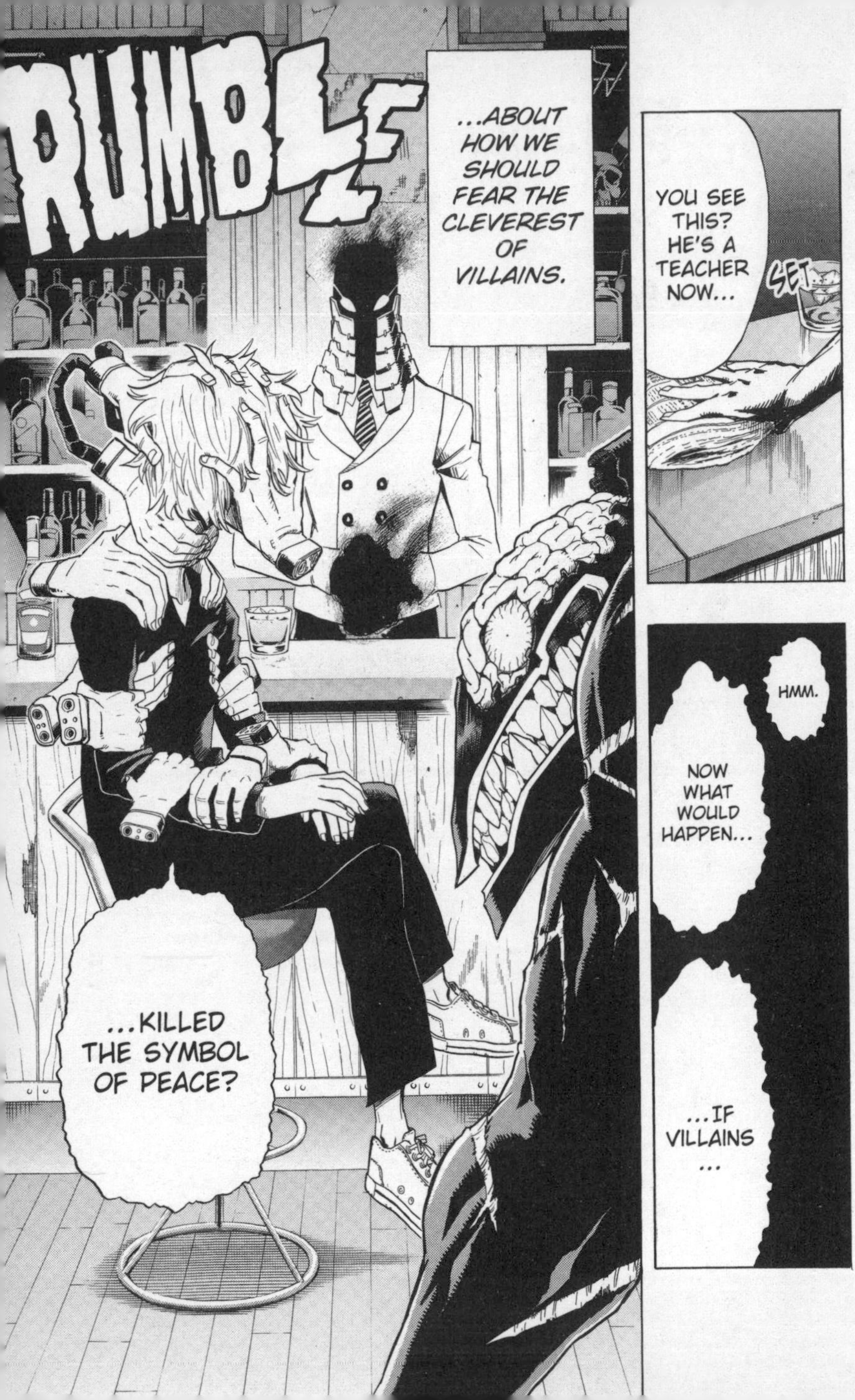
YOU SEE THIS? HE'S A TEACHER NOW...
SET
HMM.
NOW WHAT WOULD HAPPEN...
...IF VILLAINS ...
...ABOUT HOW WE SHOULD FEAR THE CLEVEREST OF VILLAINS.
RUMBLE
...KILLED THE SYMBOL OF PEACE?

SHOTO TODOROKI (15)

STREET CLOTHES

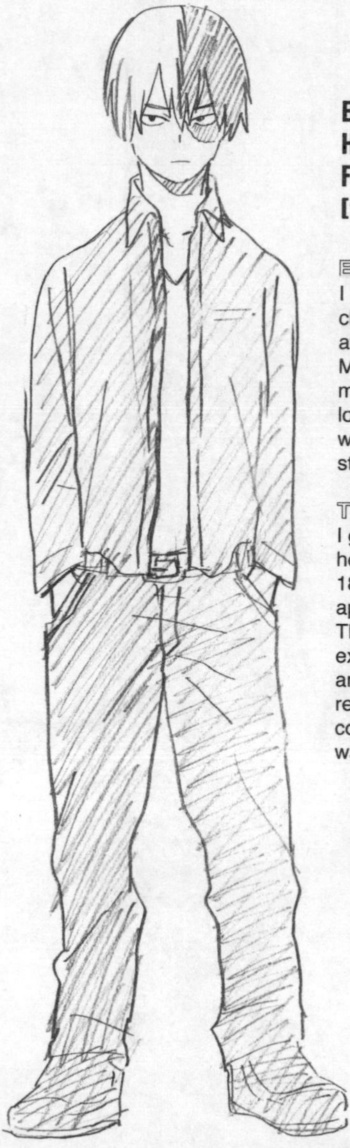

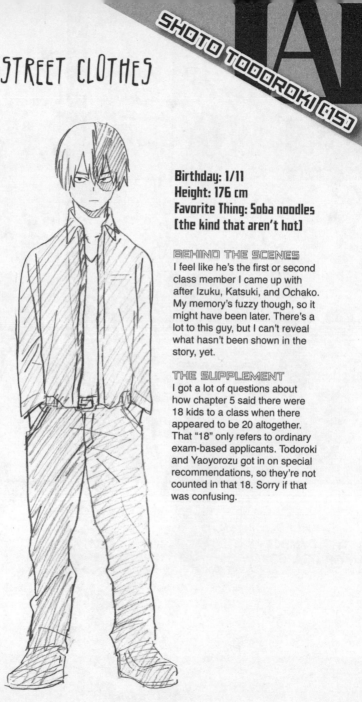

Birthday: 1/11
Height: 176 cm
Favorite Thing: Soba noodles [the kind that aren't hot]

BEHIND THE SCENES

I feel like he's the first or second class member I came up with after Izuku, Katsuki, and Ochako. My memory's fuzzy though, so it might have been later. There's a lot to this guy, but I can't reveal what hasn't been shown in the story, yet.

THE SUPPLEMENT

I got a lot of questions about how chapter 5 said there were 18 kids to a class when there appeared to be 20 altogether. That "18" only refers to ordinary exam-based applicants. Todoroki and Yaoyorozu got in on special recommendations, so they're not counted in that 18. Sorry if that was confusing.

NO.12 - YEAH, JUST DO YOUR BEST, IDA!

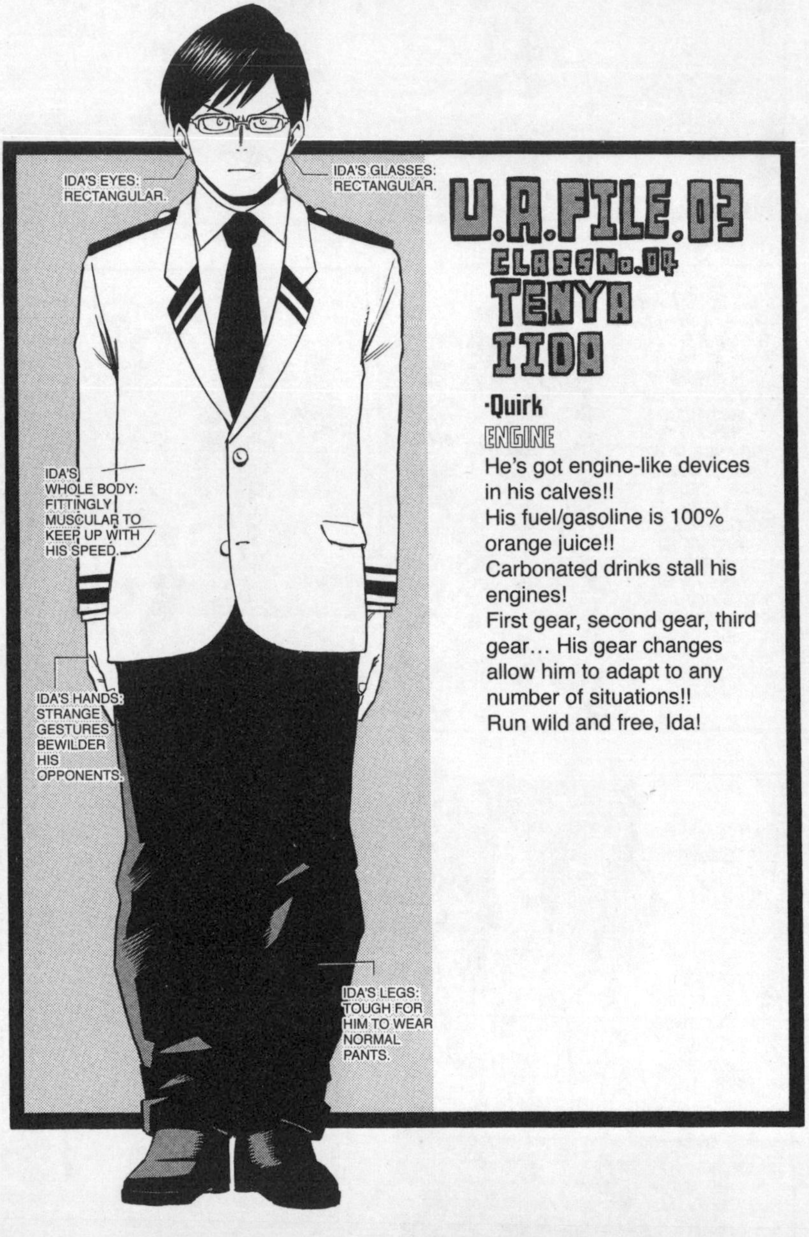
IDA'S EYES: RECTANGULAR.
IDA'S GLASSES: RECTANGULAR.
IDA'S WHOLE BODY: FITTINGLY MUSCULAR TO KEEP UP WITH HIS SPEED.
IDA'S HANDS: STRANGE GESTURES BEWILDER HIS OPPONENTS.
IDA'S LEGS: TOUGH FOR HIM TO WEAR NORMAL PANTS.

U.A. FILE.03

CLASS No.04

TENYA IIDA

·Quirk

ENGINE

He's got engine-like devices in his calves!!
His fuel/gasoline is 100% orange juice!!
Carbonated drinks stall his engines!
First gear, second gear, third gear… His gear changes allow him to adapt to any number of situations!!
Run wild and free, Ida!

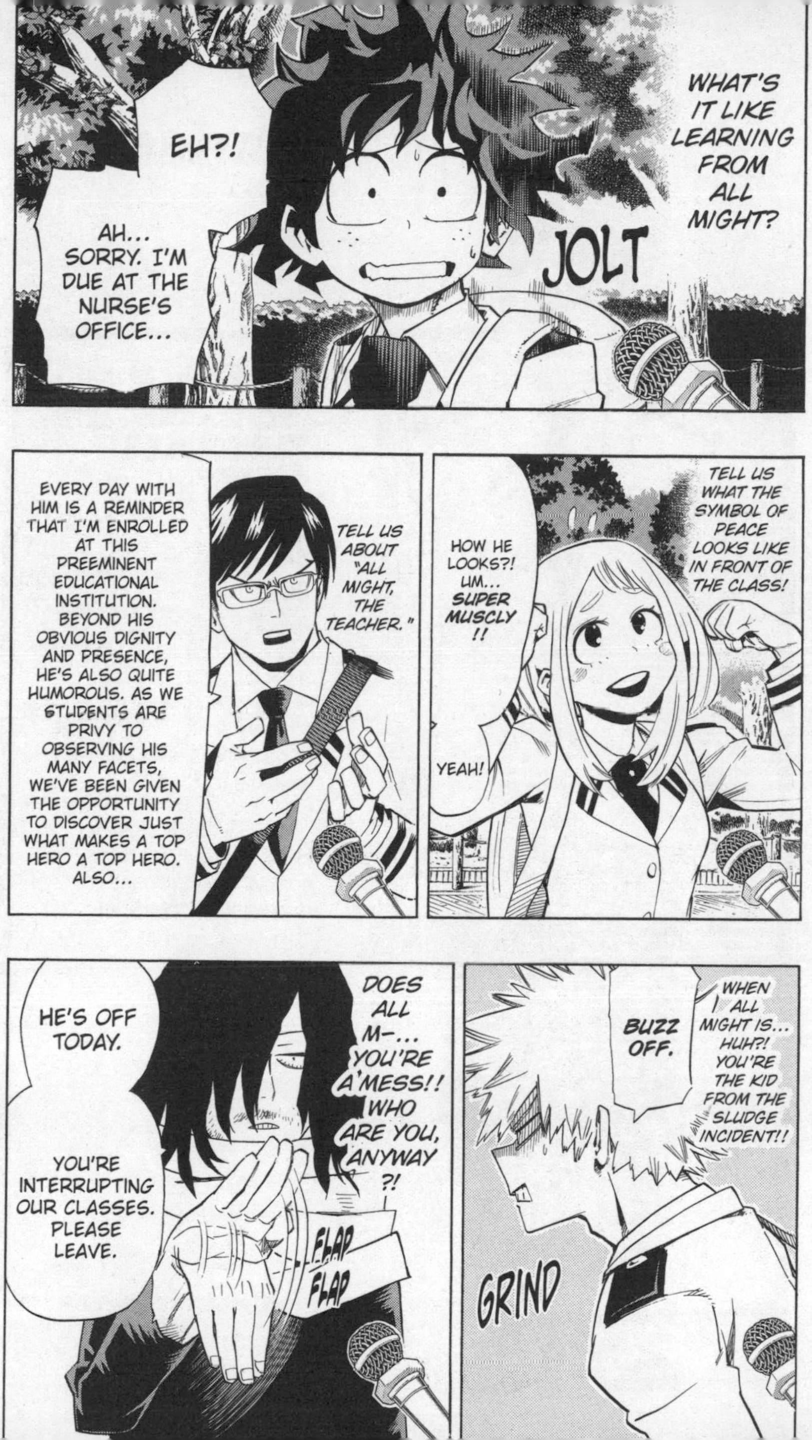
WHAT'S IT LIKE LEARNING FROM ALL MIGHT?
JOLT
EH?!
AH... SORRY. I'M DUE AT THE NURSE'S OFFICE...
TELL US WHAT THE SYMBOL OF PEACE LOOKS LIKE IN FRONT OF THE CLASS!
HOW HE LOOKS?! UM... SUPER MUSCLY!!
YEAH!
TELL US ABOUT "ALL MIGHT, THE TEACHER."
EVERY DAY WITH HIM IS A REMINDER THAT I'M ENROLLED AT THIS PREEMINENT EDUCATIONAL INSTITUTION. BEYOND HIS OBVIOUS DIGNITY AND PRESENCE, HE'S ALSO QUITE HUMOROUS. AS WE STUDENTS ARE PRIVY TO OBSERVING HIS MANY FACETS, WE'VE BEEN GIVEN THE OPPORTUNITY TO DISCOVER JUST WHAT MAKES A TOP HERO A TOP HERO. ALSO...
WHEN ALL MIGHT IS... HUH?! YOU'RE THE KID FROM THE SLUDGE INCIDENT!!
BUZZ OFF.
GRIND
DOES ALL M-... YOU'RE A MESS!! WHO ARE YOU, ANYWAY ?!
HE'S OFF TODAY.
YOU'RE INTERRUPTING OUR CLASSES. PLEASE LEAVE.
FLAP
FLAP

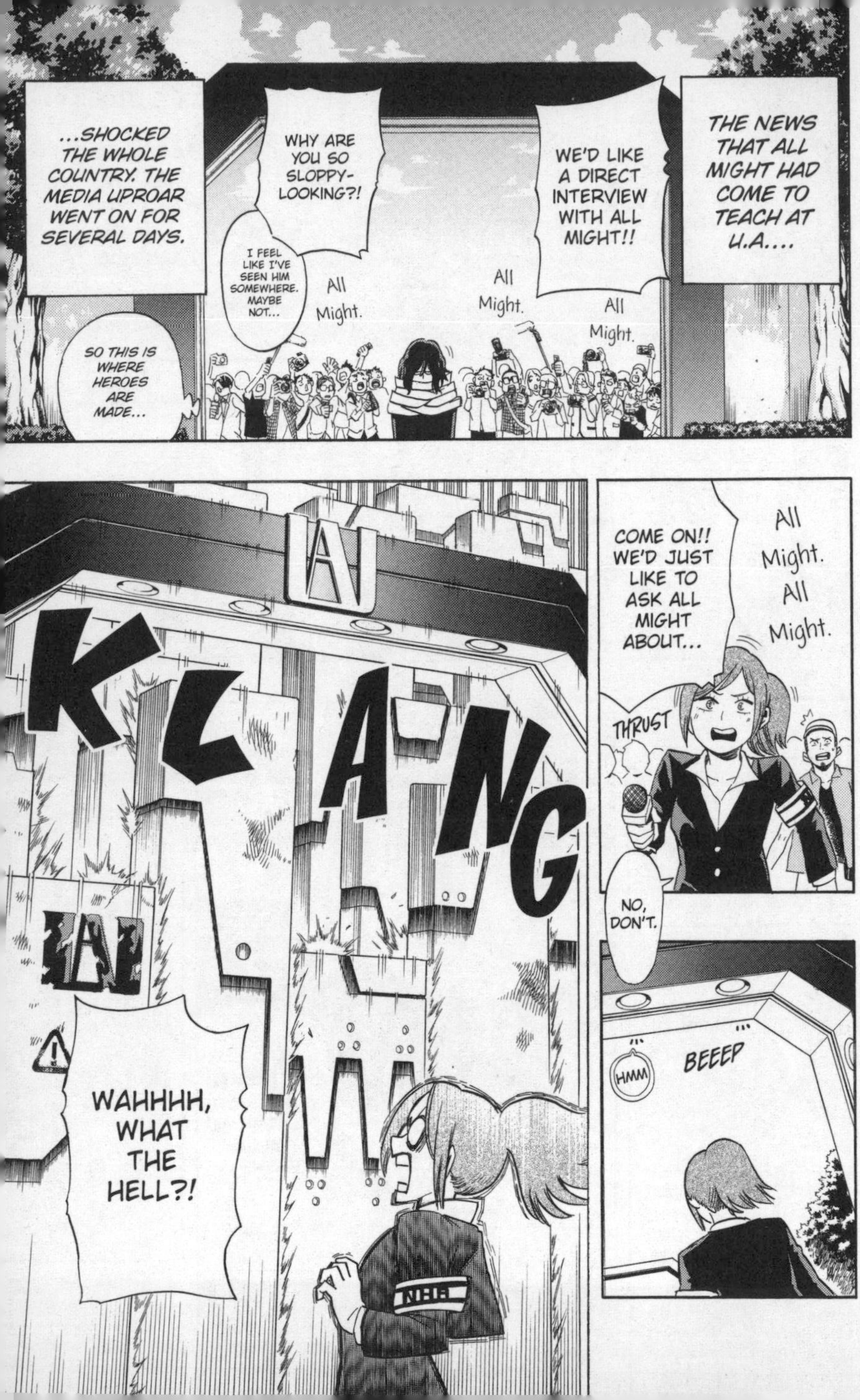
THE NEWS THAT ALL MIGHT HAD COME TO TEACH AT U.A....
WE'D LIKE A DIRECT INTERVIEW WITH ALL MIGHT!!
All Might.
All Might.
WHY ARE YOU SO SLOPPY-LOOKING?!
I FEEL LIKE I'VE SEEN HIM SOMEWHERE. MAYBE NOT...
All Might.
...SHOCKED THE WHOLE COUNTRY. THE MEDIA UPROAR WENT ON FOR SEVERAL DAYS.
SO THIS IS WHERE HEROES ARE MADE...
All Might. All Might.
COME ON!! WE'D JUST LIKE TO ASK ALL MIGHT ABOUT...
THRUST
NO, DON'T.
HMM
BEEEP
KLANG
WAHHHH, WHAT THE HELL?!

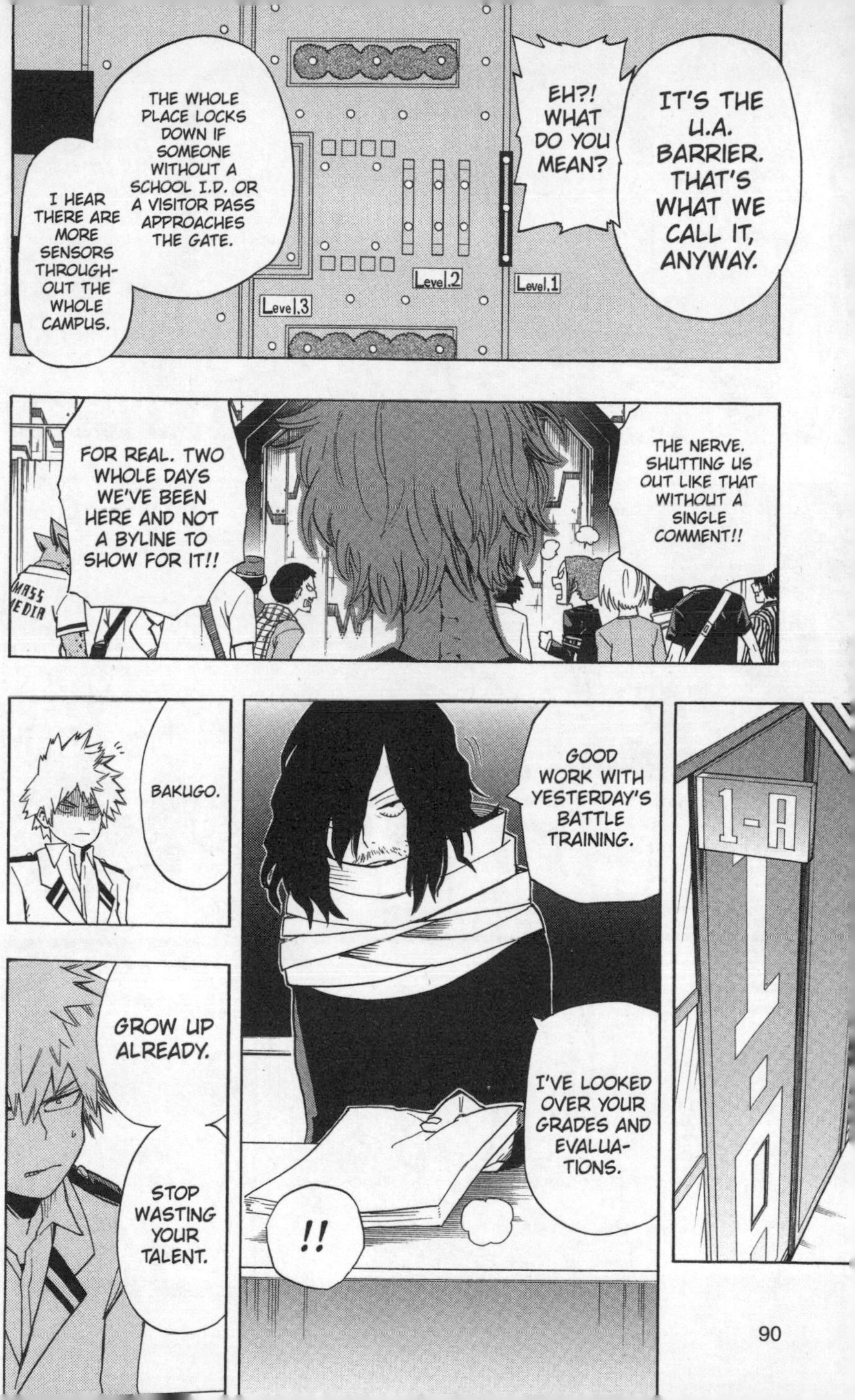
IT'S THE U.A. BARRIER. THAT'S WHAT WE CALL IT, ANYWAY.
EH?! WHAT DO YOU MEAN?
THE WHOLE PLACE LOCKS DOWN IF SOMEONE WITHOUT A SCHOOL I.D. OR A VISITOR PASS APPROACHES THE GATE.
I HEAR THERE ARE MORE SENSORS THROUGH-OUT THE WHOLE CAMPUS.
Level.1
Level.2
Level.3
THE NERVE. SHUTTING US OUT LIKE THAT WITHOUT A SINGLE COMMENT!!
FOR REAL. TWO WHOLE DAYS WE'VE BEEN HERE AND NOT A BYLINE TO SHOW FOR IT!!
MASS MEDIA
1-A
GOOD WORK WITH YESTERDAY'S BATTLE TRAINING.
I'VE LOOKED OVER YOUR GRADES AND EVALUA-TIONS.
!!
BAKUGO.
GROW UP ALREADY.
STOP WASTING YOUR TALENT.

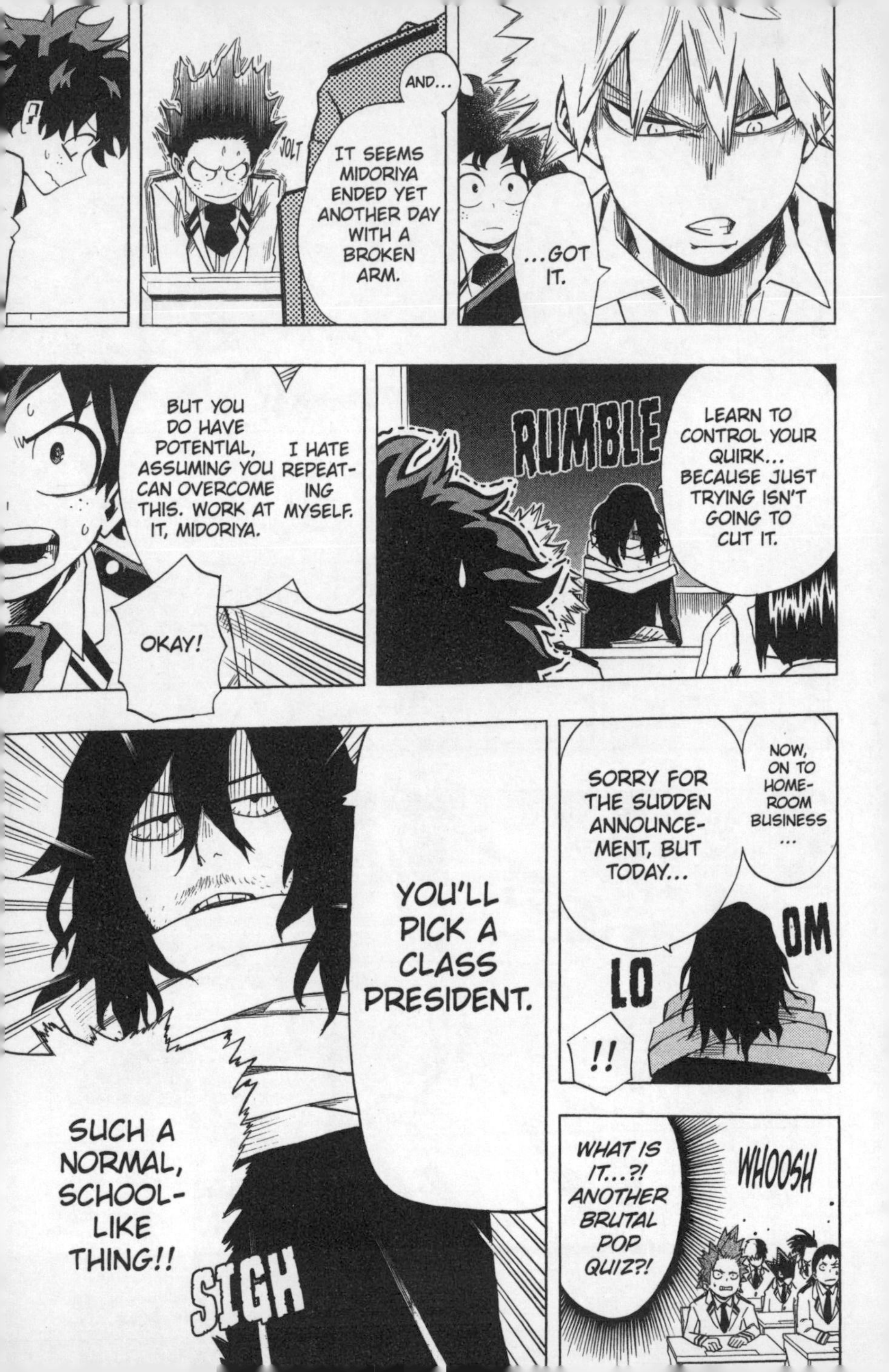
...GOT IT.
AND...
JOLT
IT SEEMS MIDORIYA ENDED YET ANOTHER DAY WITH A BROKEN ARM.
RUMBLE
LEARN TO CONTROL YOUR QUIRK... BECAUSE JUST TRYING ISN'T GOING TO CUT IT.
I HATE REPEATING MYSELF.
BUT YOU DO HAVE POTENTIAL, ASSUMING YOU CAN OVERCOME THIS. WORK AT IT, MIDORIYA.
OKAY!
NOW, ON TO HOME-ROOM BUSINESS...
SORRY FOR THE SUDDEN ANNOUNCE-MENT, BUT TODAY...
LOOM
!!
WHOOSH
WHAT IS IT...?! ANOTHER BRUTAL POP QUIZ?!
YOU'LL PICK A CLASS PRESIDENT.
SUCH A NORMAL, SCHOOL-LIKE THING!!
SIGH

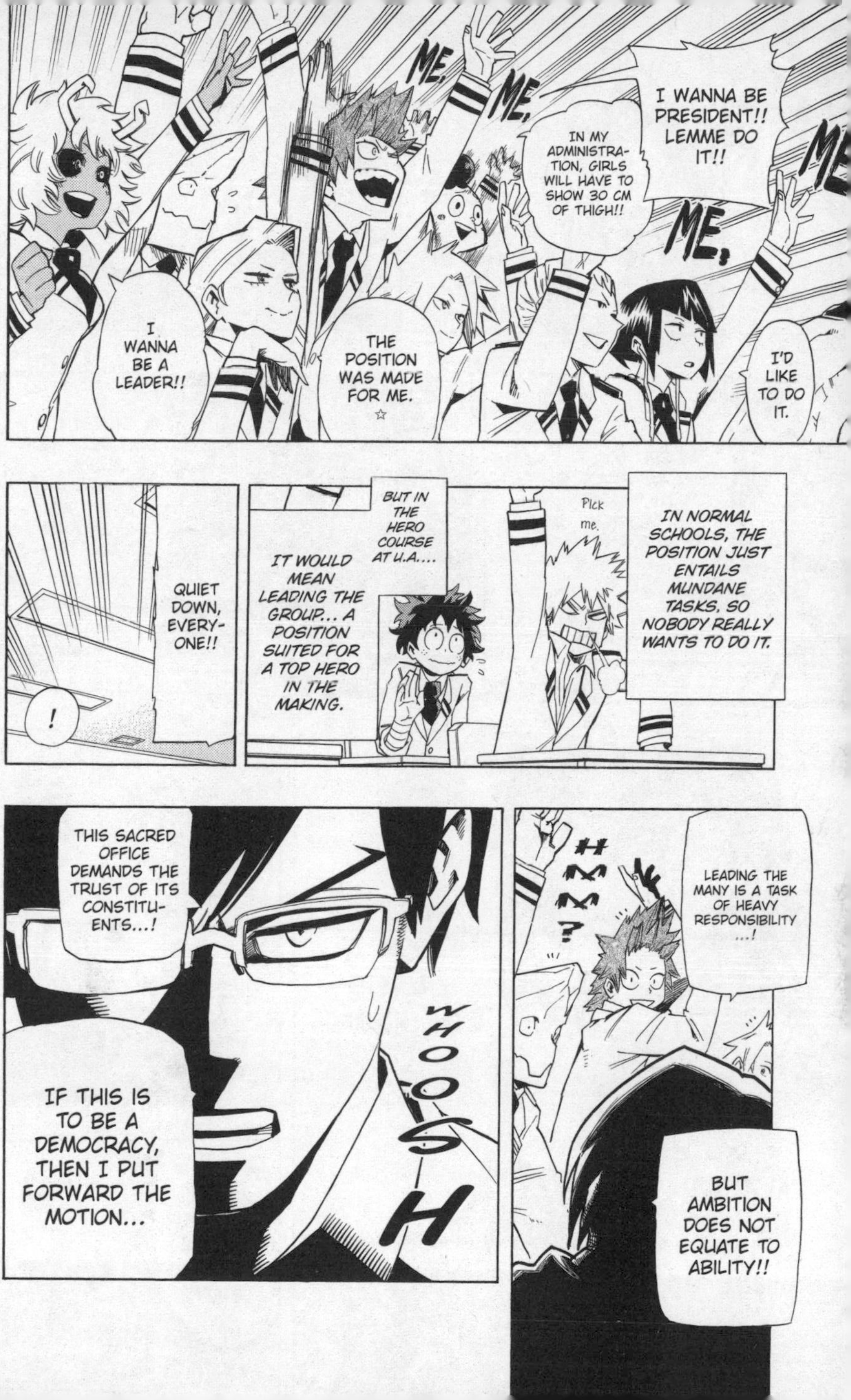
I WANNA BE PRESIDENT!! LEMME DO IT!!
ME,
ME,
IN MY ADMINISTRATION, GIRLS WILL HAVE TO SHOW 30 CM OF THIGH!!
ME,
ME,
I'D LIKE TO DO IT.
THE POSITION WAS MADE FOR ME. ☆
I WANNA BE A LEADER!!
IN NORMAL SCHOOLS, THE POSITION JUST ENTAILS MUNDANE TASKS, SO NOBODY REALLY WANTS TO DO IT.
Pick me.
BUT IN THE HERO COURSE AT U.A....
IT WOULD MEAN LEADING THE GROUP... A POSITION SUITED FOR A TOP HERO IN THE MAKING.
QUIET DOWN, EVERYONE!!
!
LEADING THE MANY IS A TASK OF HEAVY RESPONSIBILITY ...!
HMM?
BUT AMBITION DOES NOT EQUATE TO ABILITY!!
THIS SACRED OFFICE DEMANDS THE TRUST OF ITS CONSTITUENTS...!
WHOOSH
IF THIS IS TO BE A DEMOCRACY, THEN I PUT FORWARD THE MOTION...

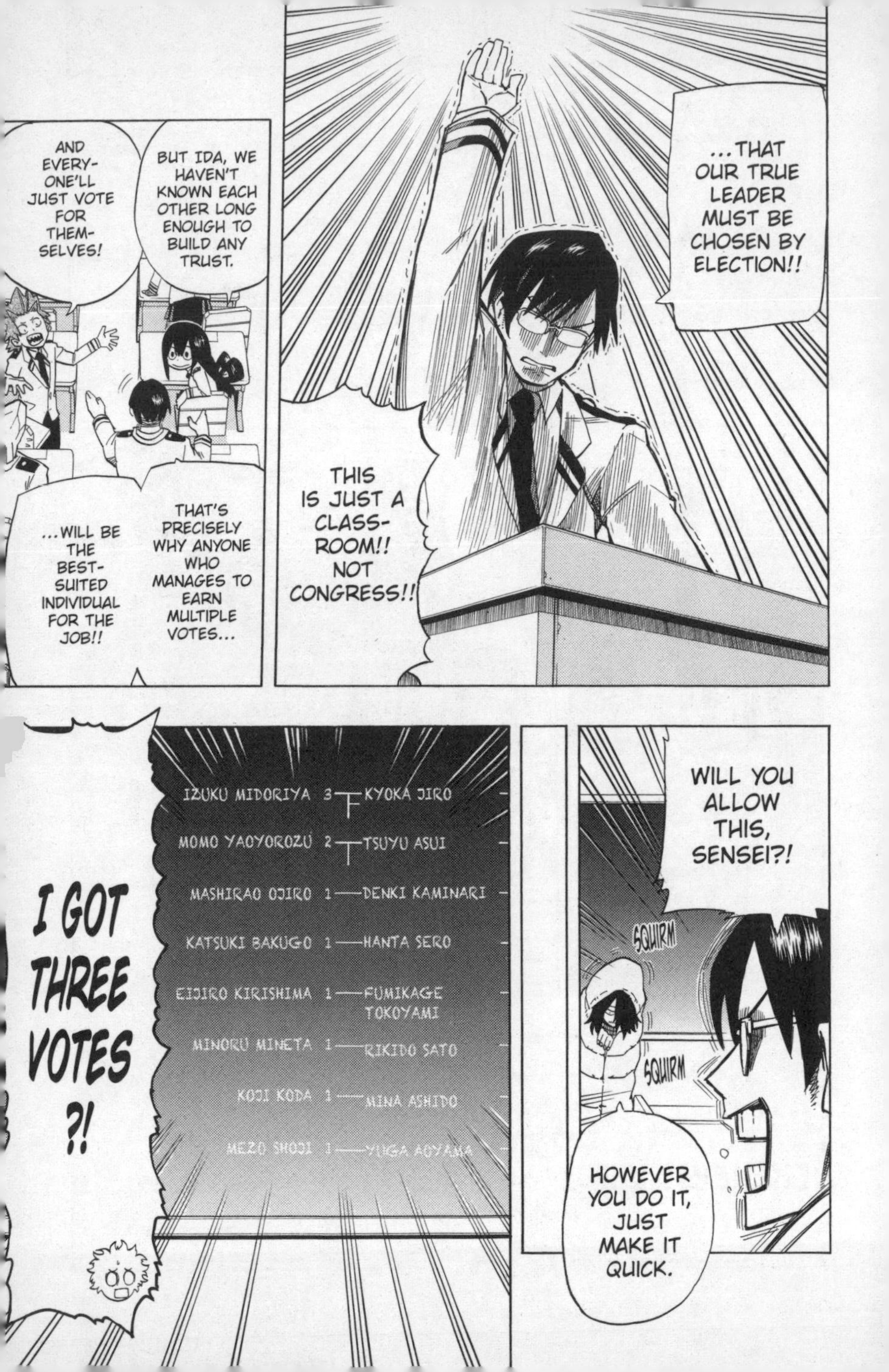
...THAT OUR TRUE LEADER MUST BE CHOSEN BY ELECTION!!
THIS IS JUST A CLASSROOM!! NOT CONGRESS!!
BUT IDA, WE HAVEN'T KNOWN EACH OTHER LONG ENOUGH TO BUILD ANY TRUST.
AND EVERYONE'LL JUST VOTE FOR THEMSELVES!
THAT'S PRECISELY WHY ANYONE WHO MANAGES TO EARN MULTIPLE VOTES...
...WILL BE THE BEST-SUITED INDIVIDUAL FOR THE JOB!!
WILL YOU ALLOW THIS, SENSEI?!
SQUIRM
SQUIRM
HOWEVER YOU DO IT, JUST MAKE IT QUICK.
IZUKU MIDORIYA 3 KYOKA JIRO
MOMO YAOYOROZU 2 TSUYU ASUI
MASHIRAO OJIRO 1 DENKI KAMINARI
KATSUKI BAKUGO 1 HANTA SERO
EIJIRO KIRISHIMA 1 FUMIKAGE TOKOYAMI
MINORU MINETA 1 RIKIDO SATO
KOJI KODA 1 MINA ASHIDO
MEZO SHOJI 1 YUGA AOYAMA
I GOT THREE VOTES ?!

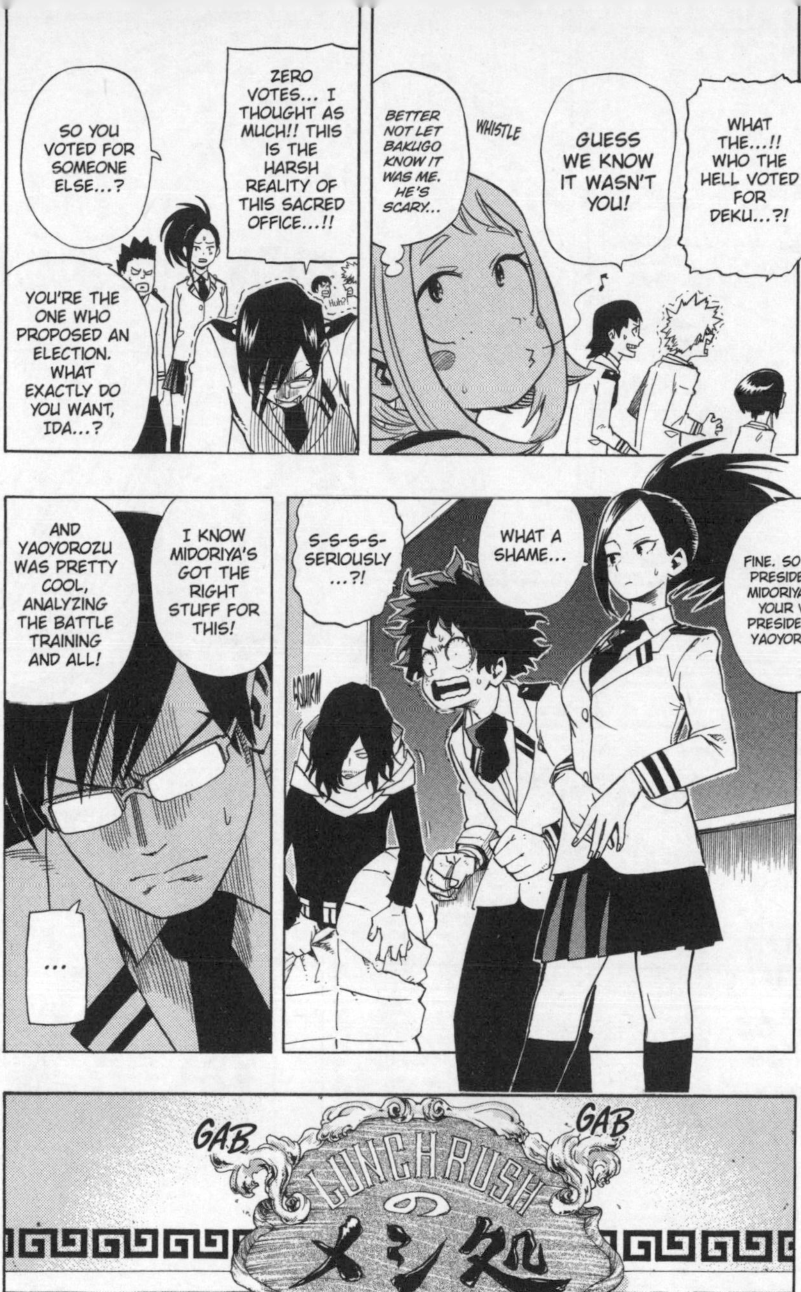
WHAT THE...!! WHO THE HELL VOTED FOR DEKU...?!
GUESS WE KNOW IT WASN'T YOU!
WHISTLE
BETTER NOT LET BAKUGO KNOW IT WAS ME. HE'S SCARY...
ZERO VOTES... I THOUGHT AS MUCH!! THIS IS THE HARSH REALITY OF THIS SACRED OFFICE...!!
SO YOU VOTED FOR SOMEONE ELSE...?
Huh?
YOU'RE THE ONE WHO PROPOSED AN ELECTION. WHAT EXACTLY DO YOU WANT, IDA...?
FINE. SO YOUR PRESIDENT'S MIDORIYA AND YOUR VICE PRESIDENT IS YAOYOROZU.
WHAT A SHAME...
S-S-S-S-SERIOUSLY...?!
I KNOW MIDORIYA'S GOT THE RIGHT STUFF FOR THIS!
AND YAOYOROZU WAS PRETTY COOL, ANALYZING THE BATTLE TRAINING AND ALL!
...
GAB
GAB
LUNCH RUSH のメシ処

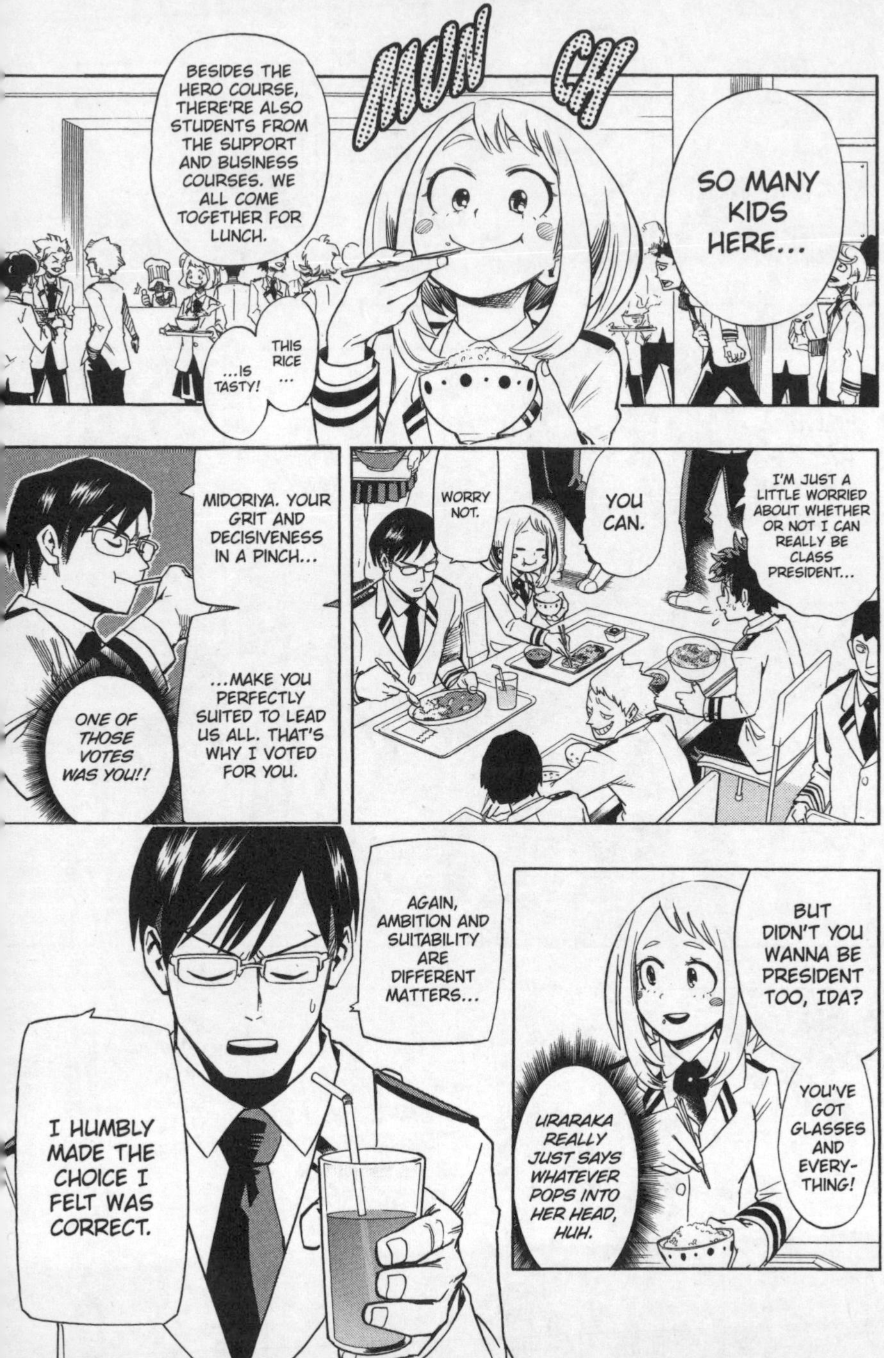
MUN CH
SO MANY KIDS HERE...
BESIDES THE HERO COURSE, THERE'RE ALSO STUDENTS FROM THE SUPPORT AND BUSINESS COURSES. WE ALL COME TOGETHER FOR LUNCH.
THIS RICE ...
...IS TASTY!
I'M JUST A LITTLE WORRIED ABOUT WHETHER OR NOT I CAN REALLY BE CLASS PRESIDENT...
YOU CAN.
WORRY NOT.
MIDORIYA. YOUR GRIT AND DECISIVENESS IN A PINCH...
...MAKE YOU PERFECTLY SUITED TO LEAD US ALL. THAT'S WHY I VOTED FOR YOU.
ONE OF THOSE VOTES WAS YOU!!
BUT DIDN'T YOU WANNA BE PRESIDENT TOO, IDA?
YOU'VE GOT GLASSES AND EVERY-THING!
URARAKA REALLY JUST SAYS WHATEVER POPS INTO HER HEAD, HUH.
AGAIN, AMBITION AND SUITABILITY ARE DIFFERENT MATTERS...
I HUMBLY MADE THE CHOICE I FELT WAS CORRECT.

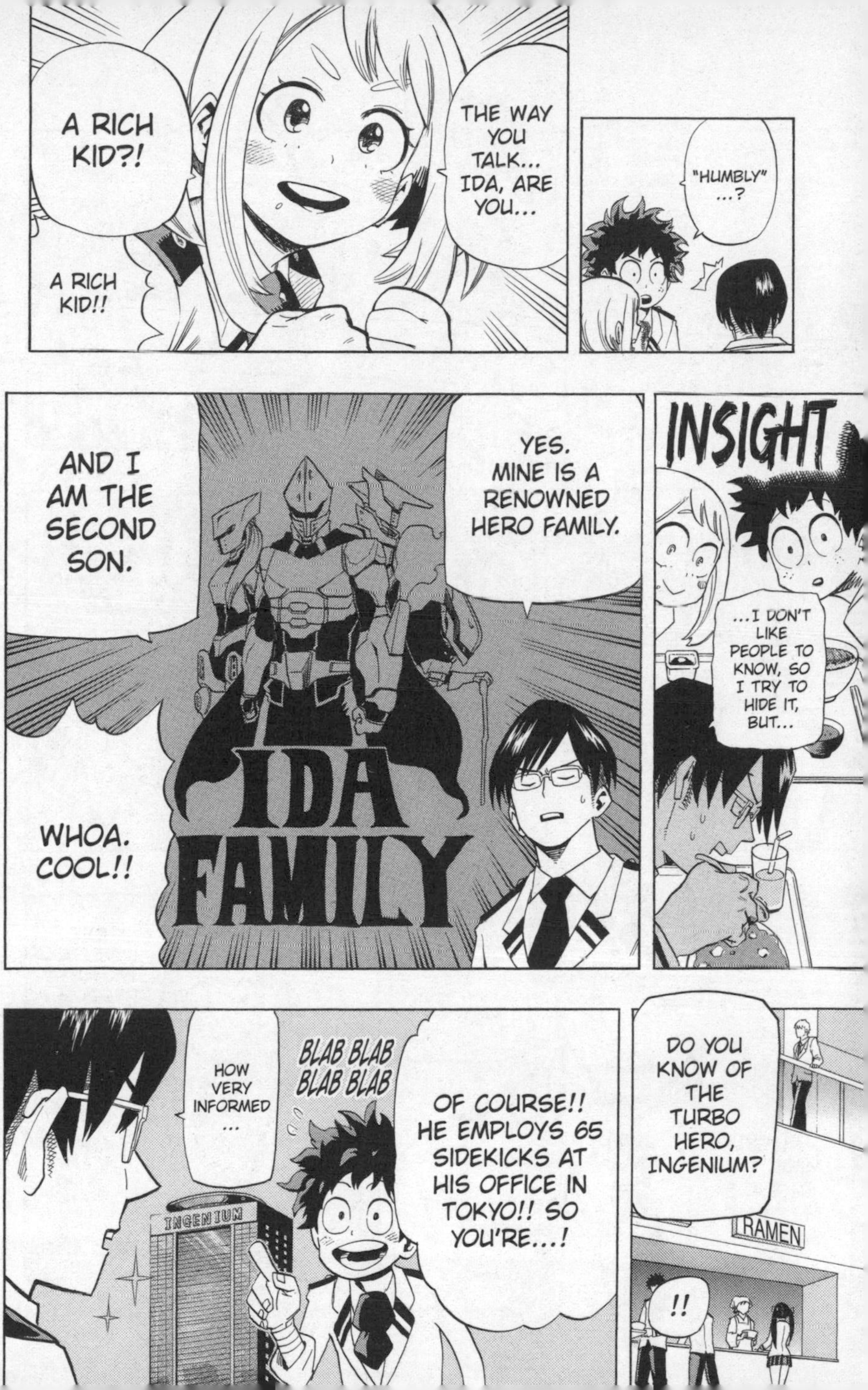
"HUMBLY" ...?
THE WAY YOU TALK... IDA, ARE YOU...
A RICH KID?!
A RICH KID!!
INSIGHT
...I DON'T LIKE PEOPLE TO KNOW, SO I TRY TO HIDE IT, BUT...
YES. MINE IS A RENOWNED HERO FAMILY.
AND I AM THE SECOND SON.
IDA FAMILY
WHOA. COOL!!
DO YOU KNOW OF THE TURBO HERO, INGENIUM?
RAMEN
!!
OF COURSE!! HE EMPLOYS 65 SIDEKICKS AT HIS OFFICE IN TOKYO!! SO YOU'RE...!
BLAB BLAB BLAB BLAB
HOW VERY INFORMED ...
INGENIUM

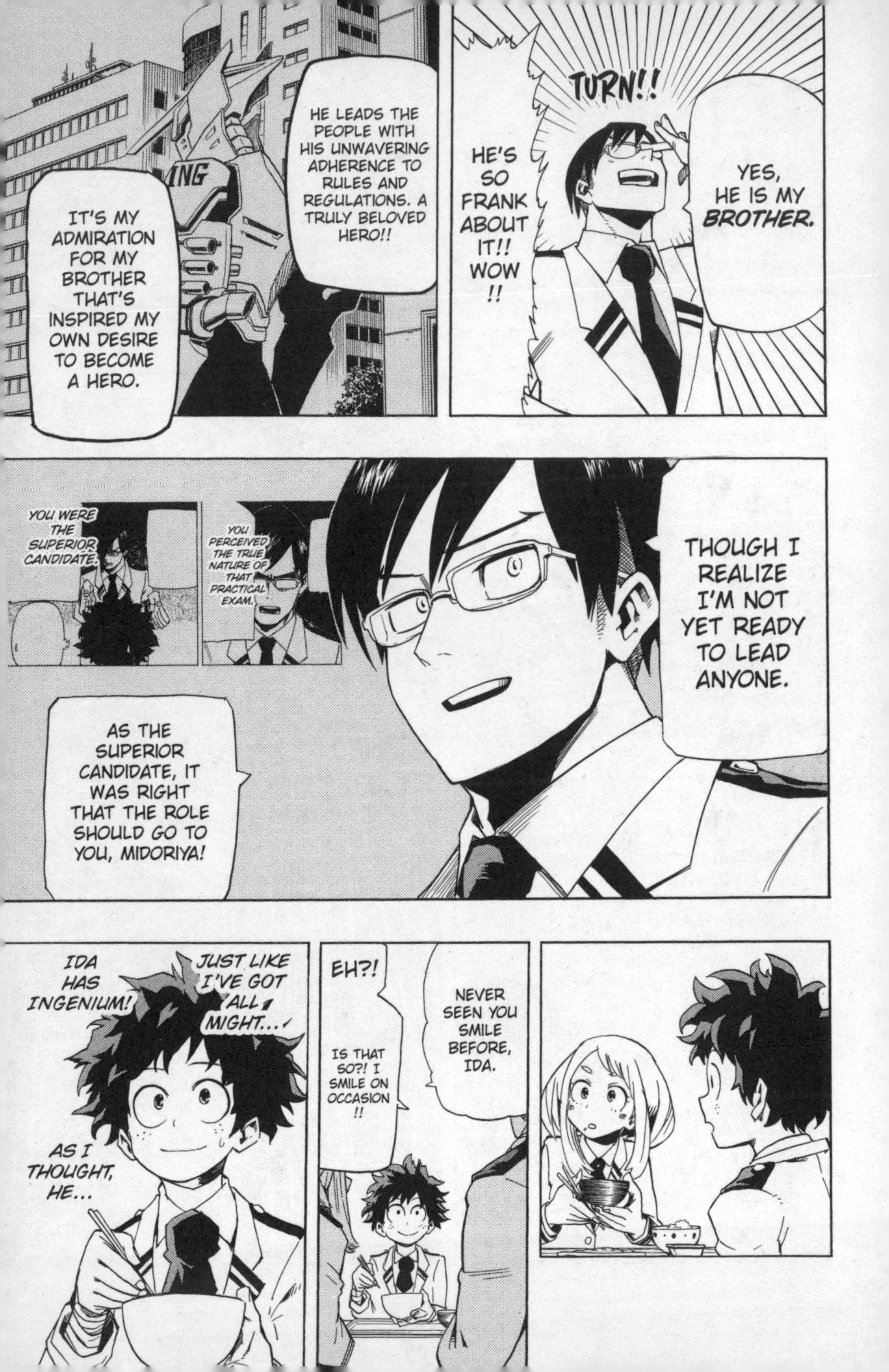
TURN!!
YES, HE IS MY BROTHER.
HE'S SO FRANK ABOUT IT!! WOW!!
HE LEADS THE PEOPLE WITH HIS UNWAVERING ADHERENCE TO RULES AND REGULATIONS. A TRULY BELOVED HERO!!
IT'S MY ADMIRATION FOR MY BROTHER THAT'S INSPIRED MY OWN DESIRE TO BECOME A HERO.
THOUGH I REALIZE I'M NOT YET READY TO LEAD ANYONE.
YOU PERCEIVED THE TRUE NATURE OF THAT PRACTICAL EXAM.
YOU WERE THE SUPERIOR CANDIDATE.
AS THE SUPERIOR CANDIDATE, IT WAS RIGHT THAT THE ROLE SHOULD GO TO YOU, MIDORIYA!
NEVER SEEN YOU SMILE BEFORE, IDA.
EH?!
IS THAT SO?! I SMILE ON OCCASION!!
JUST LIKE I'VE GOT ALL MIGHT...
IDA HAS INGENIUM!
AS I THOUGHT, HE...

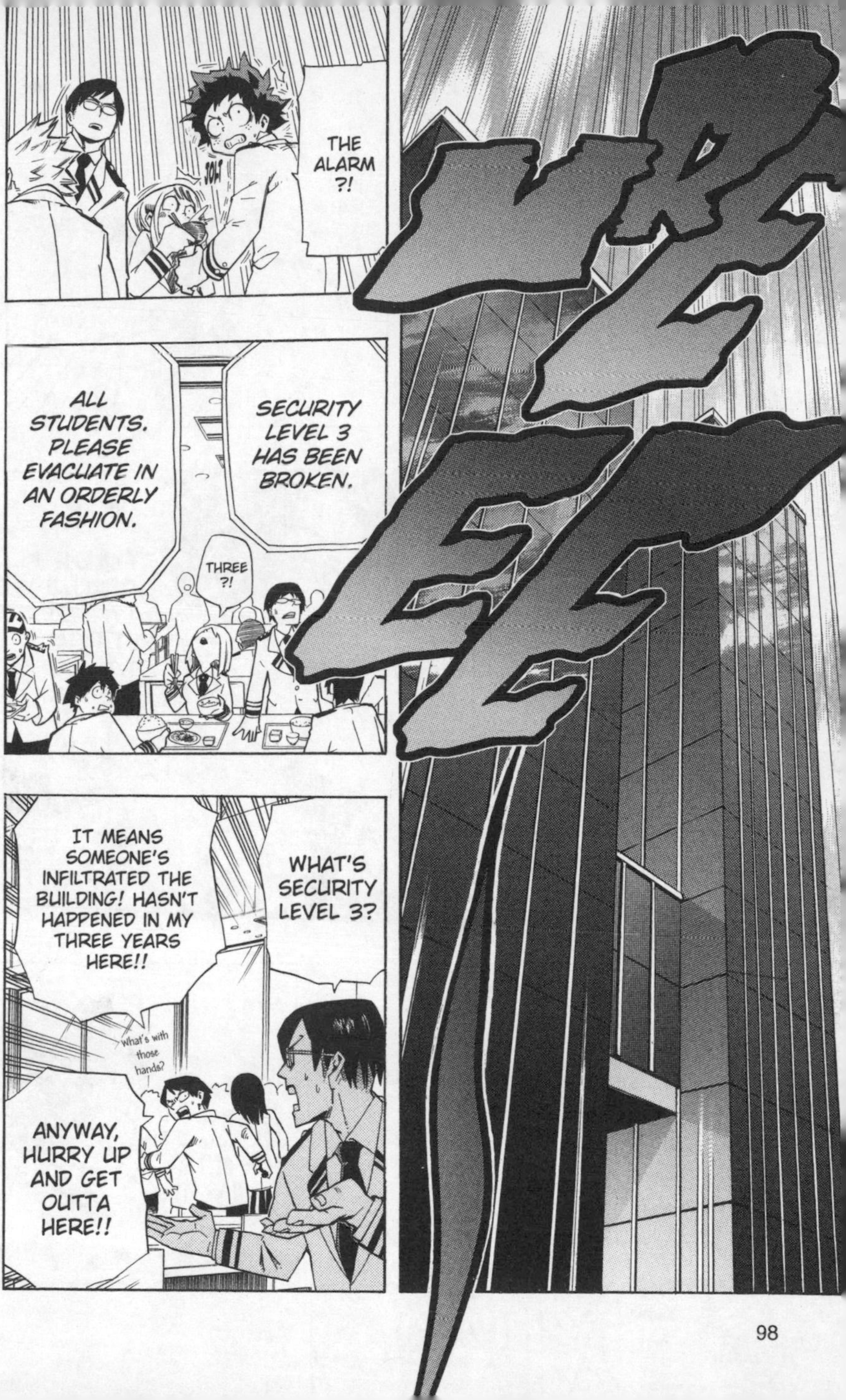
JOLT
THE ALARM ?!
SECURITY LEVEL 3 HAS BEEN BROKEN.
ALL STUDENTS. PLEASE EVACUATE IN AN ORDERLY FASHION.
THREE ?!
WHAT'S SECURITY LEVEL 3?
IT MEANS SOMEONE'S INFILTRATED THE BUILDING! HASN'T HAPPENED IN MY THREE YEARS HERE!!
What's with those hands?
ANYWAY, HURRY UP AND GET OUTTA HERE!!

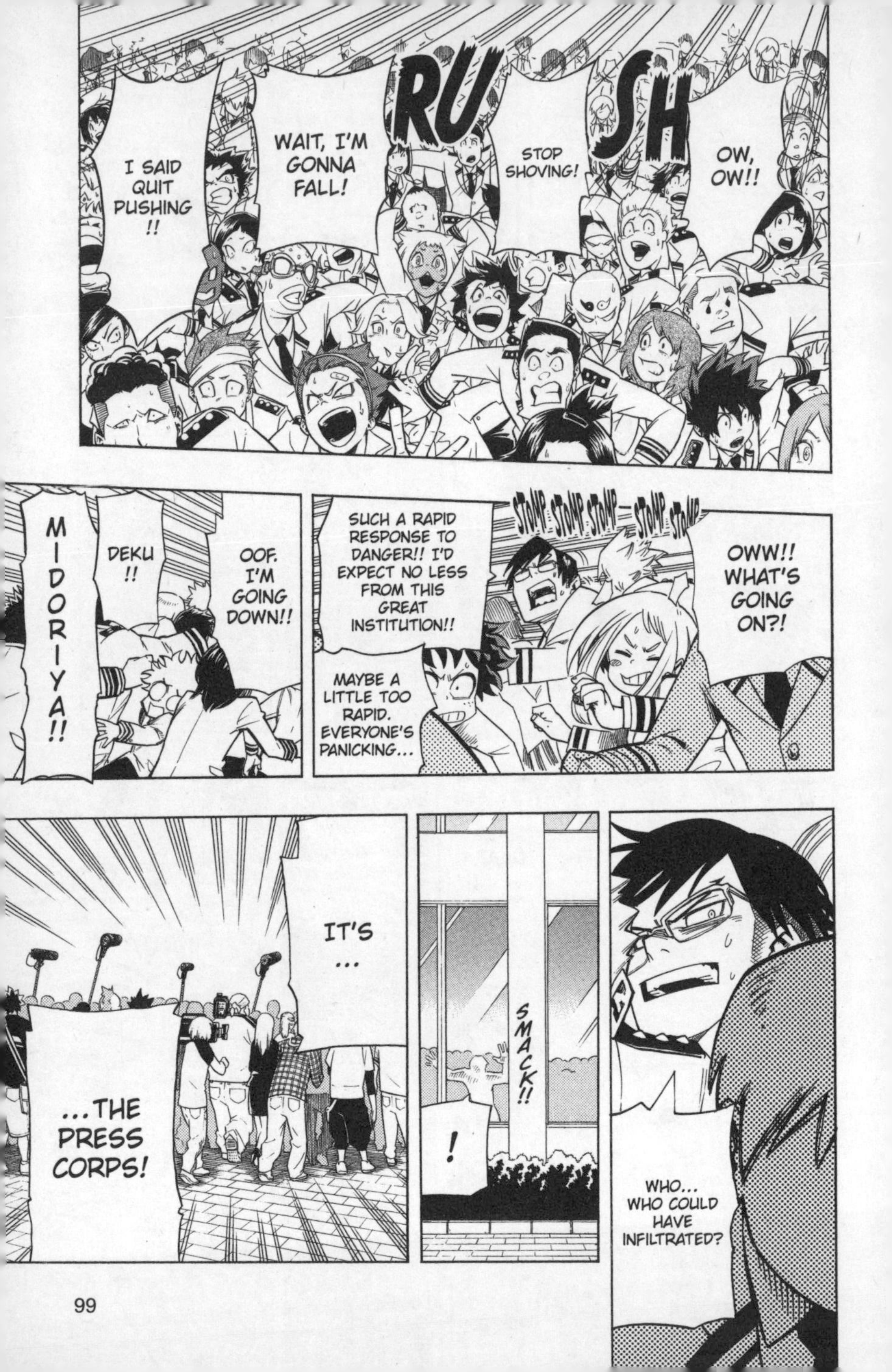
OW, OW!!
STOP SHOVING!
RUSH
WAIT, I'M GONNA FALL!
I SAID QUIT PUSHING!!
STOMP STOMP STOMP STOMP STOMP
OWW!! WHAT'S GOING ON?!
SUCH A RAPID RESPONSE TO DANGER!! I'D EXPECT NO LESS FROM THIS GREAT INSTITUTION!!
MAYBE A LITTLE TOO RAPID. EVERYONE'S PANICKING...
OOF. I'M GOING DOWN!!
DEKU!!
MIDORIYA!!
WHO... WHO COULD HAVE INFILTRATED?
SMACK!!
!
IT'S...
...THE PRESS CORPS!

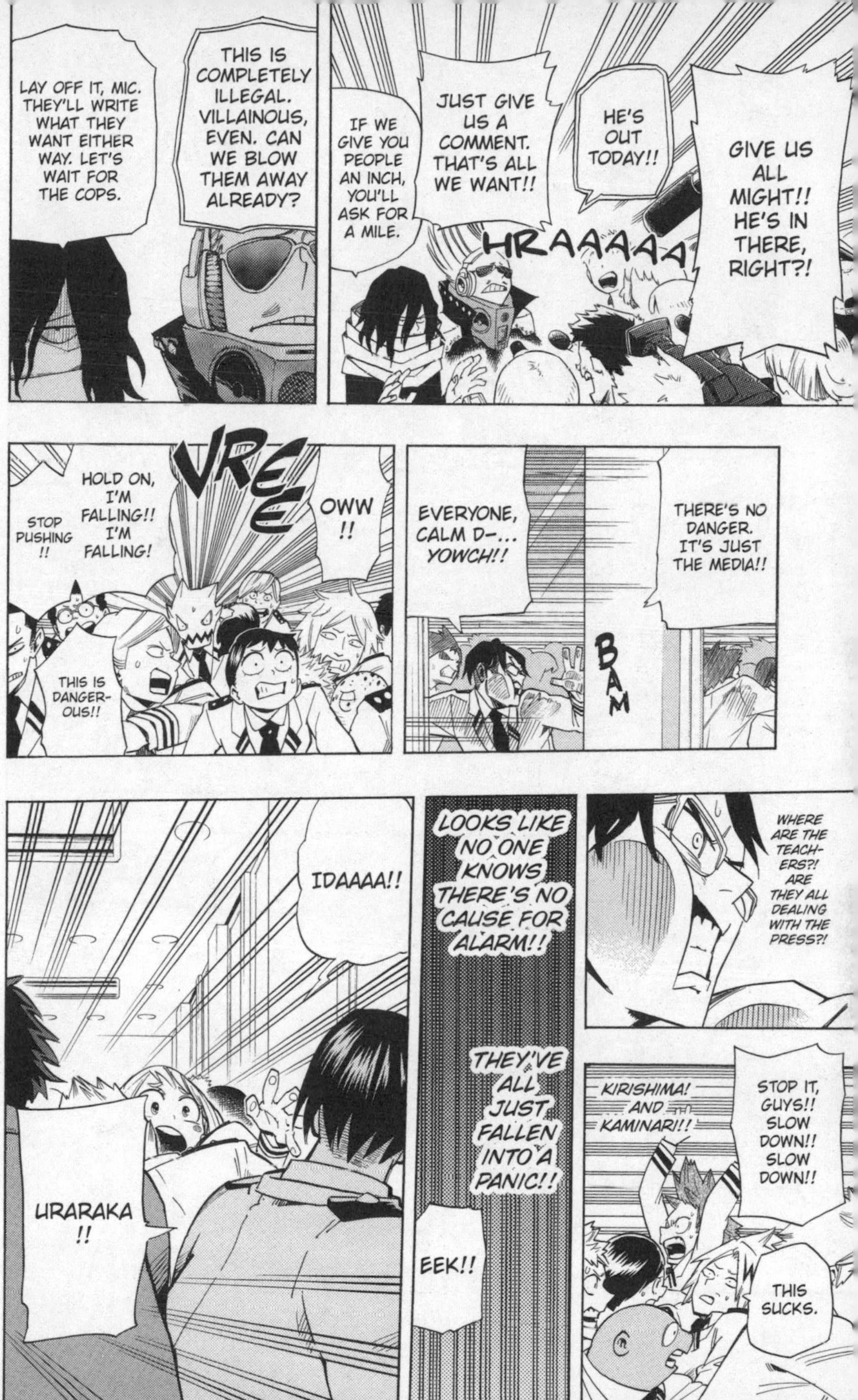
GIVE US ALL MIGHT!! HE'S IN THERE, RIGHT?!
HE'S OUT TODAY!!
JUST GIVE US A COMMENT. THAT'S ALL WE WANT!!
IF WE GIVE YOU PEOPLE AN INCH, YOU'LL ASK FOR A MILE.
HRAAAAAA
THIS IS COMPLETELY ILLEGAL. VILLAINOUS, EVEN. CAN WE BLOW THEM AWAY ALREADY?
LAY OFF IT, MIC. THEY'LL WRITE WHAT THEY WANT EITHER WAY. LET'S WAIT FOR THE COPS.
THERE'S NO DANGER. IT'S JUST THE MEDIA!!
EVERYONE, CALM D-... YOWCH!!
BAM
OWW!!
VREE
HOLD ON, I'M FALLING!! I'M FALLING!
STOP PUSHING!!
THIS IS DANGER-OUS!!
WHERE ARE THE TEACH-ERS?! ARE THEY ALL DEALING WITH THE PRESS?!
STOP IT, GUYS!! SLOW DOWN!! SLOW DOWN!!
KIRISHIMA! AND KAMINARI!!
THIS SUCKS.
LOOKS LIKE NO ONE KNOWS THERE'S NO CAUSE FOR ALARM!!
THEY'VE ALL JUST FALLEN INTO A PANIC!!
EEK!!
IDAAAA!!
URARAKA!!

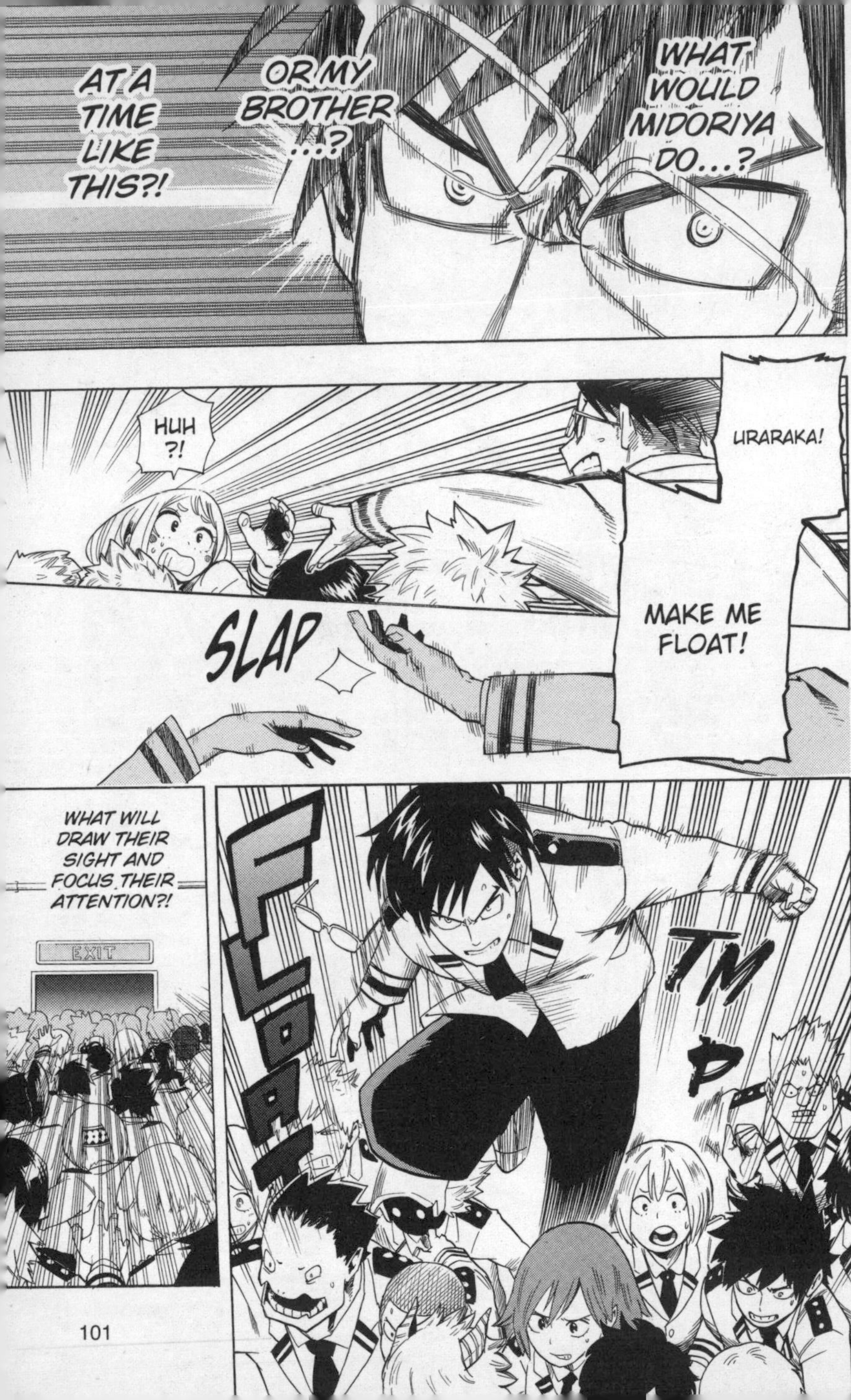
WHAT WOULD MIDORIYA DO...?
OR MY BROTHER...?
AT A TIME LIKE THIS?!
URARAKA!
HUH?!
MAKE ME FLOAT!
SLAP
TMP
WHAT WILL DRAW THEIR SIGHT AND FOCUS THEIR ATTENTION?!
EXIT

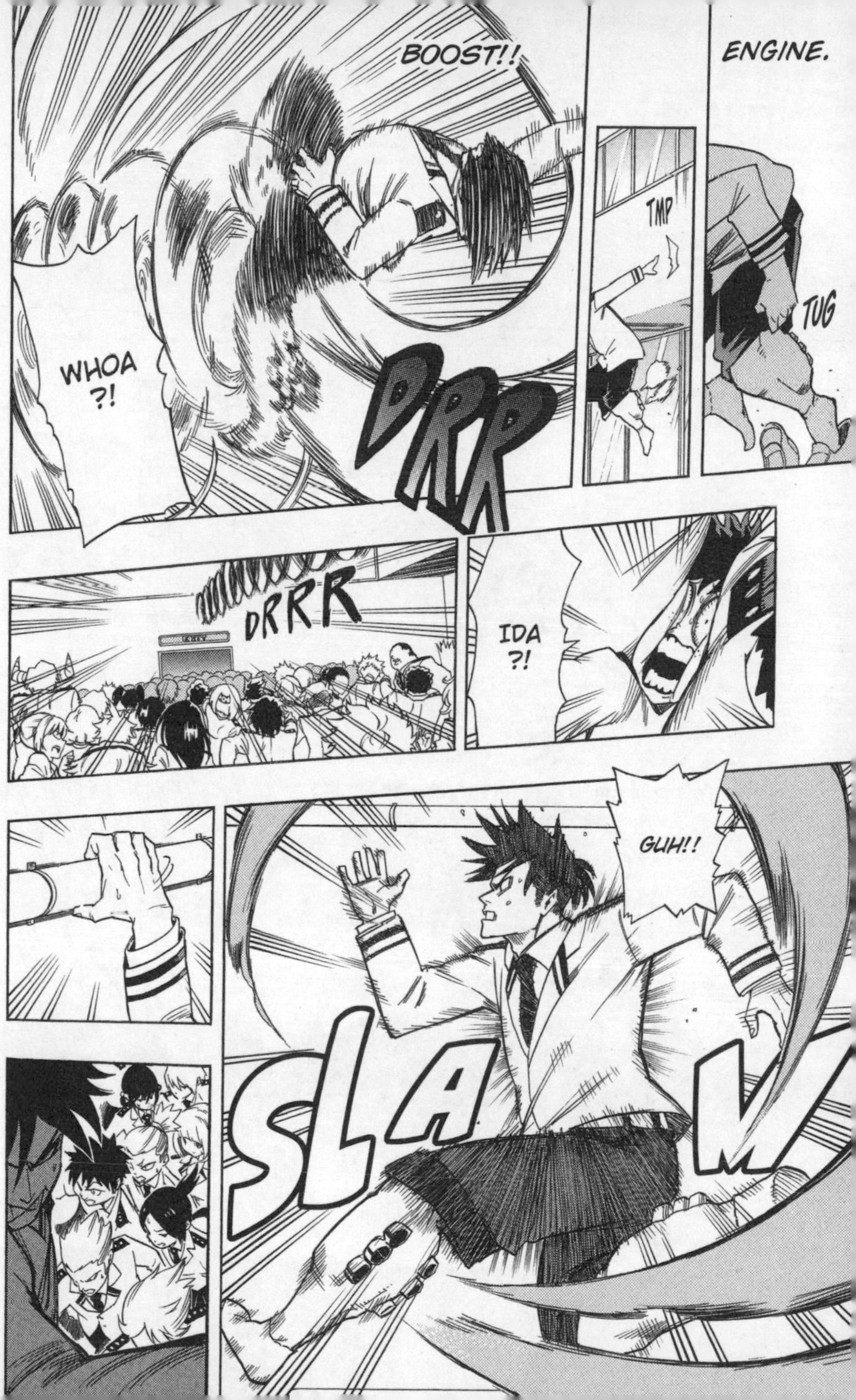
ENGINE.
TUG
TMP
BOOST!!
DRRR
WHOA ?!
IDA ?!
DRRR
GUH!!
SLAM

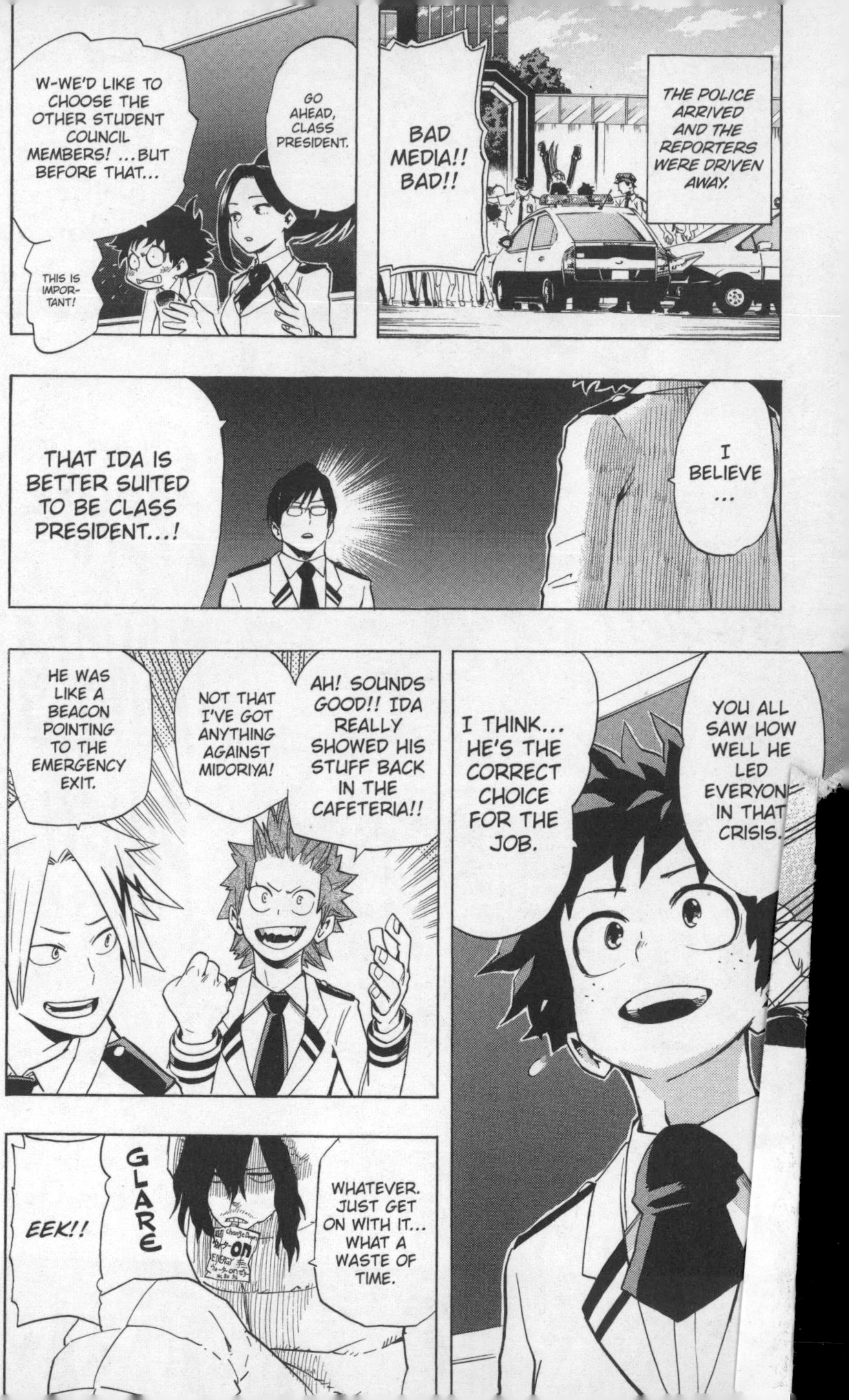
THE POLICE ARRIVED AND THE REPORTERS WERE DRIVEN AWAY.
BAD MEDIA!! BAD!!
GO AHEAD, CLASS PRESIDENT.
W-WE'D LIKE TO CHOOSE THE OTHER STUDENT COUNCIL MEMBERS! ...BUT BEFORE THAT...
THIS IS IMPORTANT!
I BELIEVE...
THAT IDA IS BETTER SUITED TO BE CLASS PRESIDENT...!
YOU ALL SAW HOW WELL HE LED EVERYONE IN THAT CRISIS.
I THINK... HE'S THE CORRECT CHOICE FOR THE JOB.
AH! SOUNDS GOOD!! IDA REALLY SHOWED HIS STUFF BACK IN THE CAFETERIA!!
NOT THAT I'VE GOT ANYTHING AGAINST MIDORIYA!
HE WAS LIKE A BEACON POINTING TO THE EMERGENCY EXIT.
WHATEVER. JUST GET ON WITH IT... WHAT A WASTE OF TIME.
GLARE
EEK!!

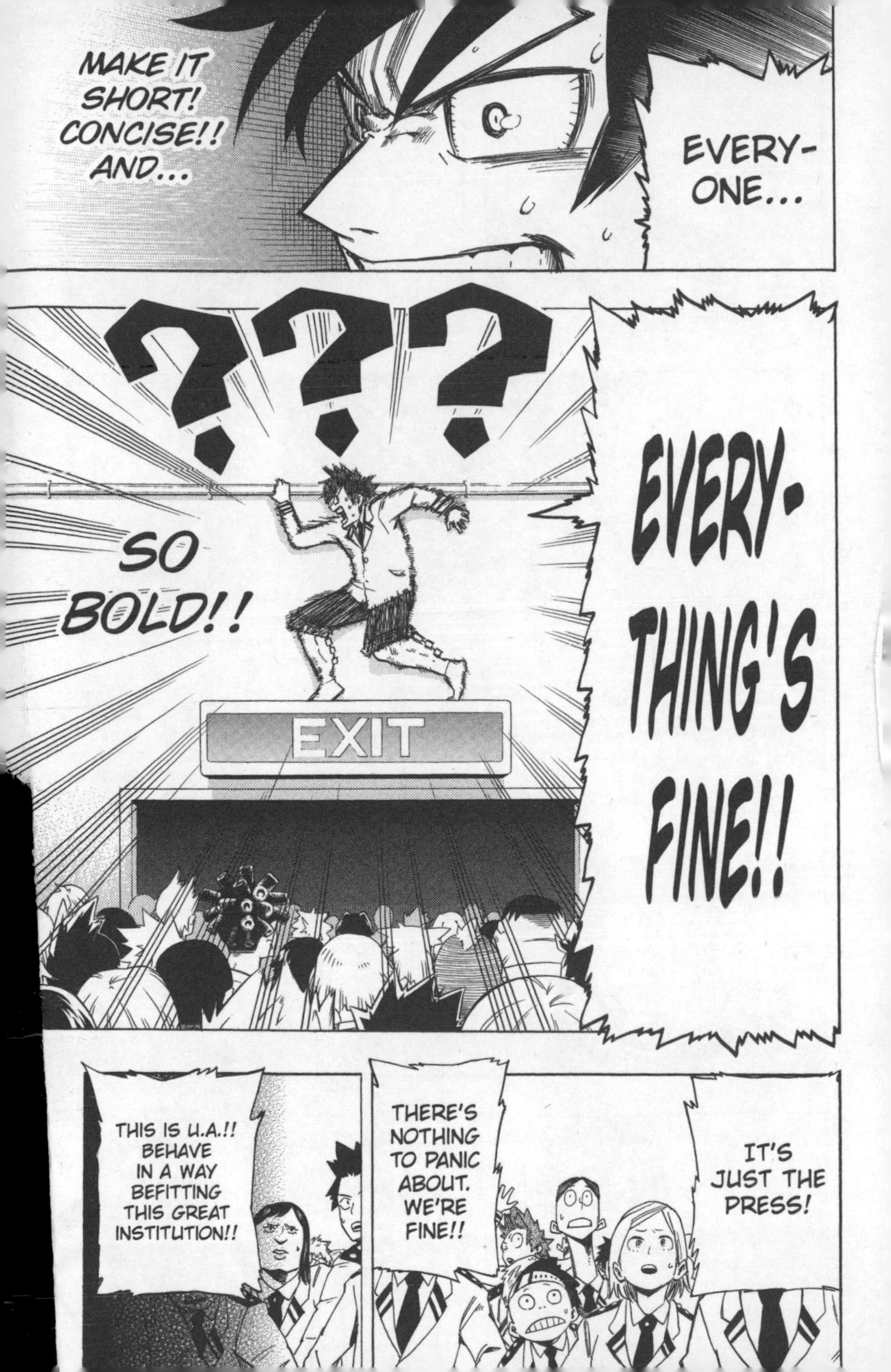
MAKE IT SHORT! CONCISE!! AND...
EVERY-ONE...
EVERY-THING'S FINE!!
???
SO BOLD!!
EXIT
IT'S JUST THE PRESS!
THERE'S NOTHING TO PANIC ABOUT. WE'RE FINE!!
THIS IS U.A.!! BEHAVE IN A WAY BEFITTING THIS GREAT INSTITUTION!!

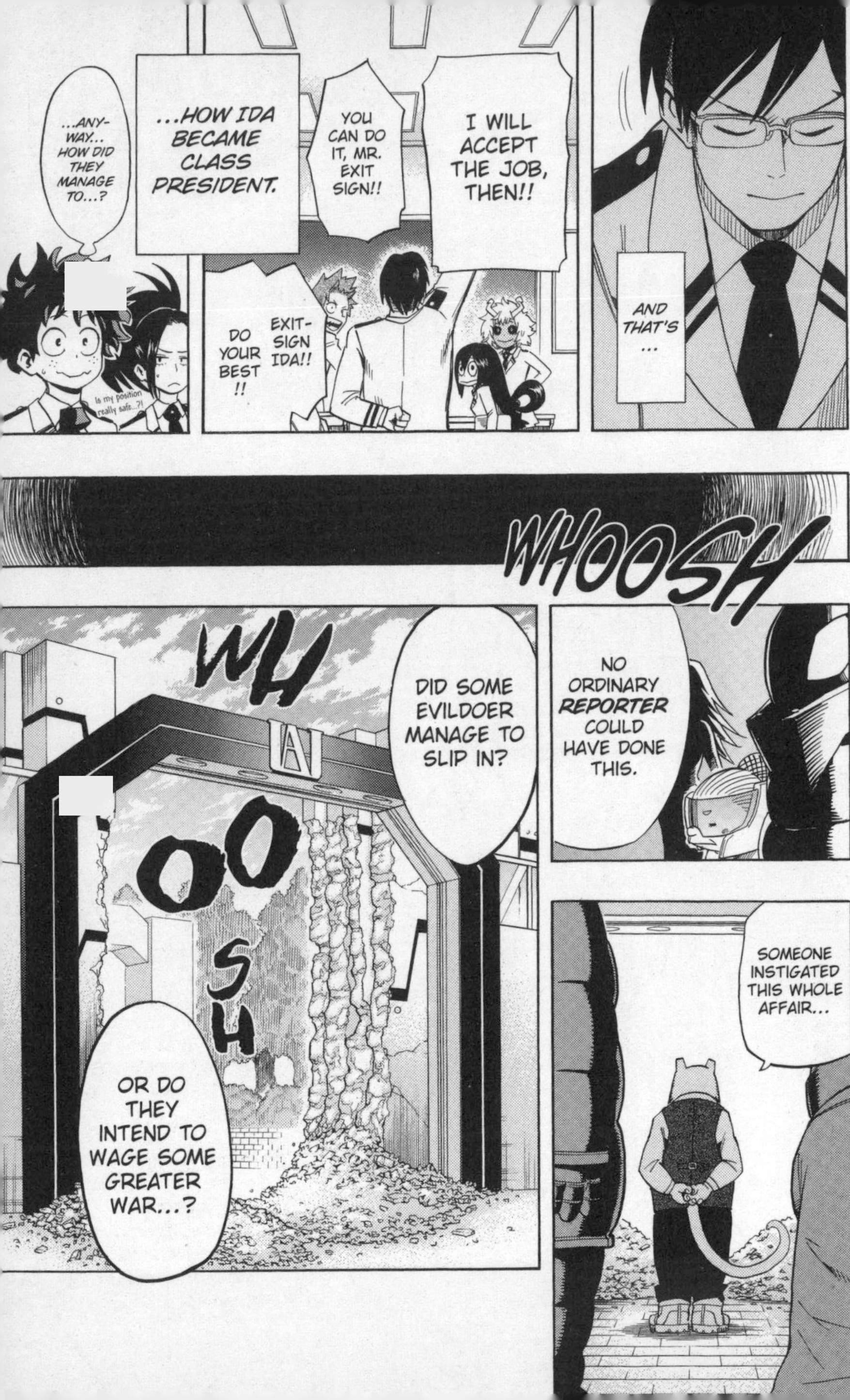
AND THAT'S ...
I WILL ACCEPT THE JOB, THEN!!
YOU CAN DO IT, MR. EXIT SIGN!!
EXIT-SIGN IDA!!
DO YOUR BEST!!
...HOW IDA BECAME CLASS PRESIDENT.
...ANY-WAY... HOW DID THEY MANAGE TO...?
Is my position really safe...?!
WHOOSH
NO ORDINARY REPORTER COULD HAVE DONE THIS.
SOMEONE INSTIGATED THIS WHOLE AFFAIR...
WHOOSH
DID SOME EVILDOER MANAGE TO SLIP IN?
OR DO THEY INTEND TO WAGE SOME GREATER WAR...?

MASHIRAO OJIRO (15)

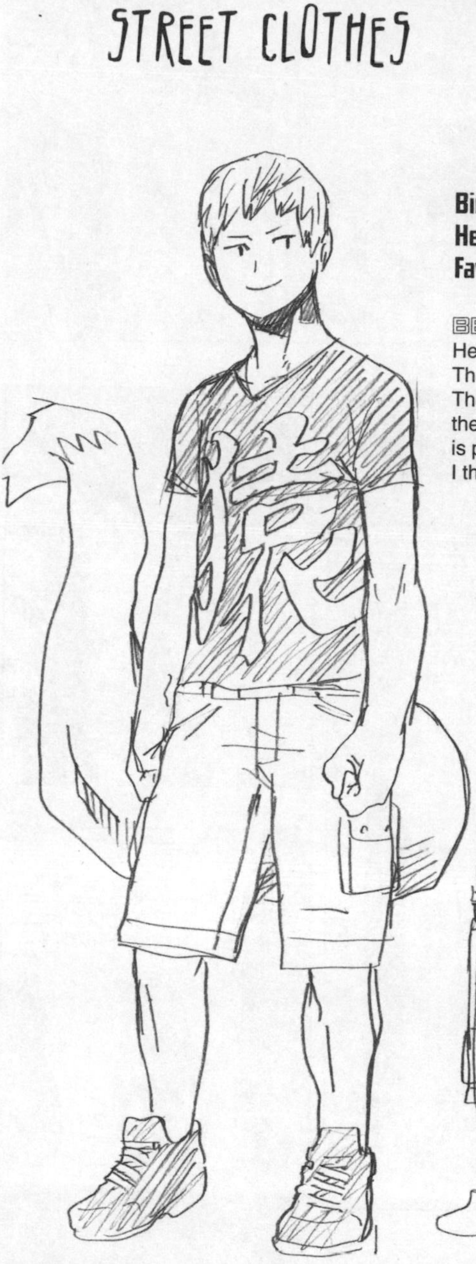
STREET CLOTHES

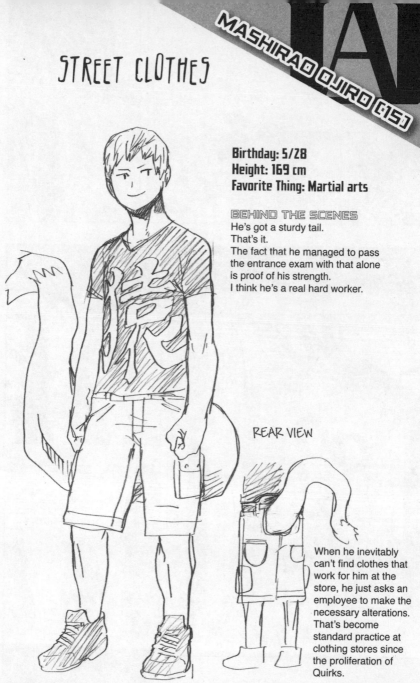

Birthday: 5/28
Height: 169 cm
Favorite Thing: Martial arts

BEHIND THE SCENES

He's got a sturdy tail.
That's it.
The fact that he managed to pass the entrance exam with that alone is proof of his strength.
I think he's a real hard worker.

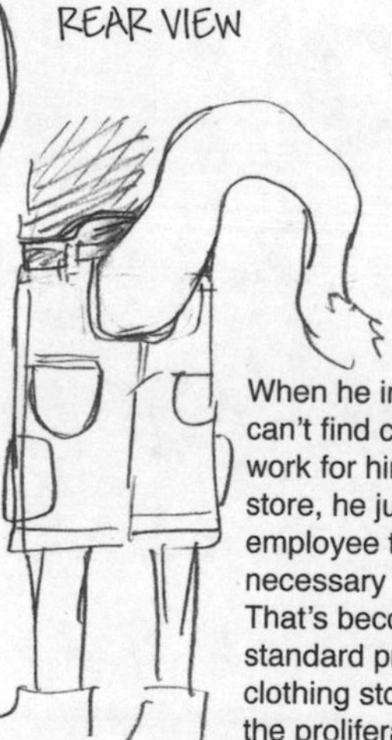
REAR VIEW

When he inevitably can't find clothes that work for him at the store, he just asks an employee to make the necessary alterations. That's become standard practice at clothing stores since the proliferation of Quirks.

No.13 - Rescue Training

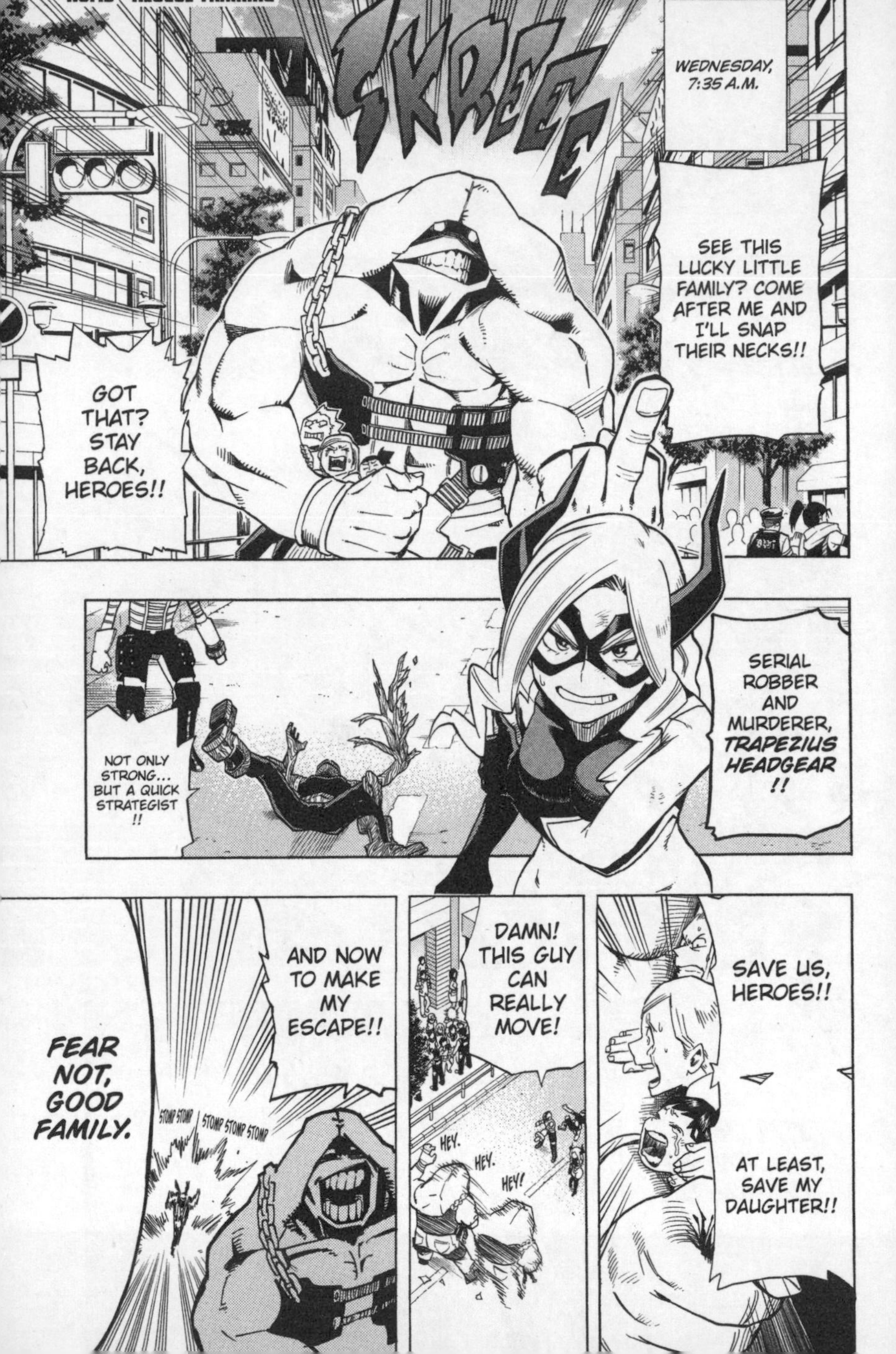
WEDNESDAY, 7:35 A.M.
SEE THIS LUCKY LITTLE FAMILY? COME AFTER ME AND I'LL SNAP THEIR NECKS!!
GOT THAT? STAY BACK, HEROES!!
SERIAL ROBBER AND MURDERER, TRAPEZIUS HEADGEAR!!
NOT ONLY STRONG... BUT A QUICK STRATEGIST!!
SAVE US, HEROES!!
AT LEAST, SAVE MY DAUGHTER!!
DAMN! THIS GUY CAN REALLY MOVE!
HEY.
HEY.
HEY!
AND NOW TO MAKE MY ESCAPE!!
STOMP STOMP STOMP
STOMP STOMP
FEAR NOT, GOOD FAMILY.

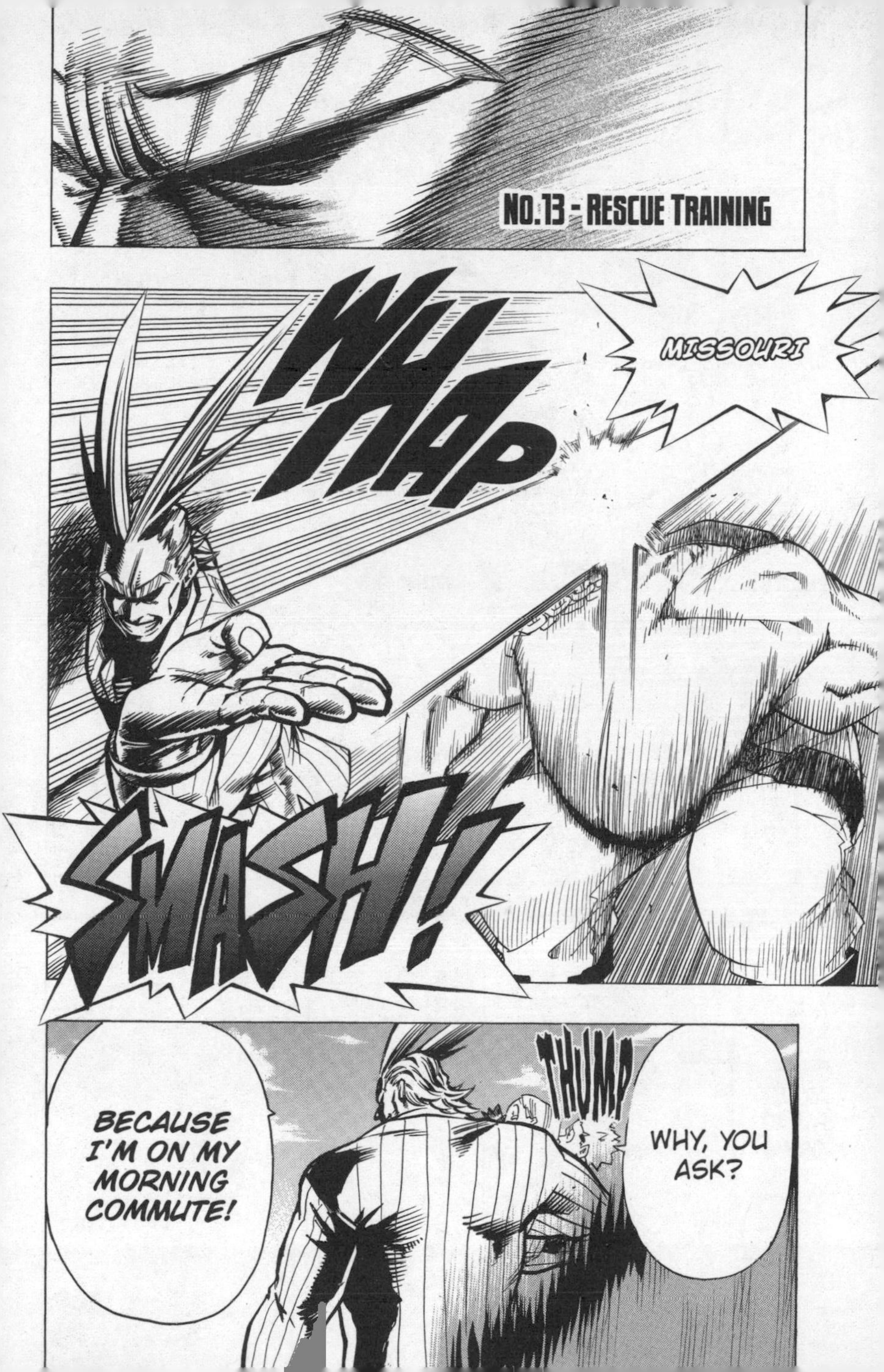
No.13 - Rescue Training
MISSOURI
WHAP
SMASH!
WHY, YOU ASK?
THUMP
BECAUSE I'M ON MY MORNING COMMUTE!

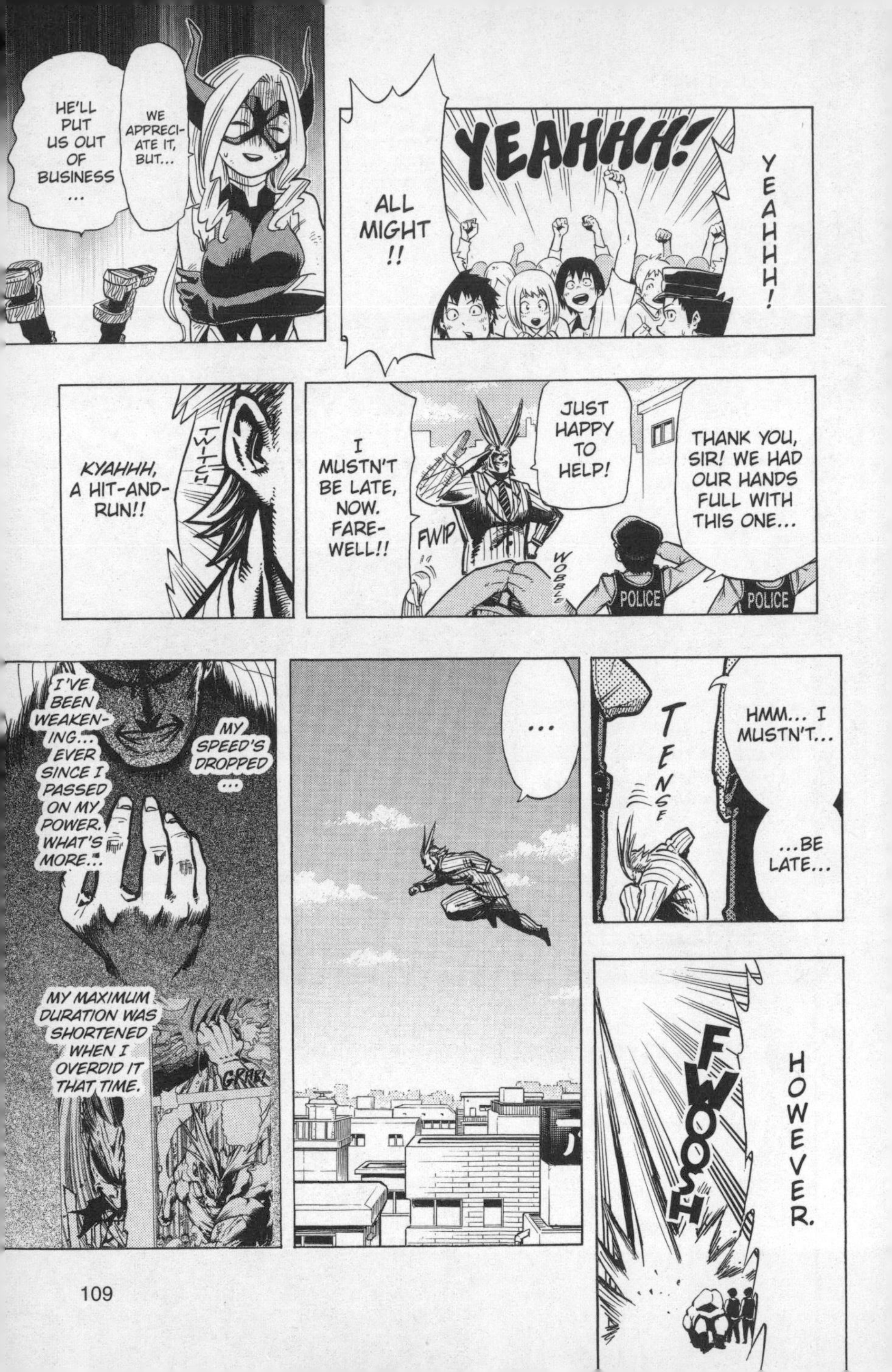
YEAHHH!
YEAHHH!
ALL MIGHT!!
WE APPRECIATE IT, BUT...
HE'LL PUT US OUT OF BUSINESS...
THANK YOU, SIR! WE HAD OUR HANDS FULL WITH THIS ONE...
JUST HAPPY TO HELP!
I MUSTN'T BE LATE, NOW. FAREWELL!!
FWIP
WOBBLE
POLICE
POLICE
TWITCH
KYAHHH, A HIT-AND-RUN!!
HMM... I MUSTN'T...
TENSE
...BE LATE...
HOWEVER.
FWOOSH
...
MY SPEED'S DROPPED...
I'VE BEEN WEAKENING... EVER SINCE I PASSED ON MY POWER. WHAT'S MORE...
MY MAXIMUM DURATION WAS SHORTENED WHEN I OVERDID IT THAT TIME.
GRAH!

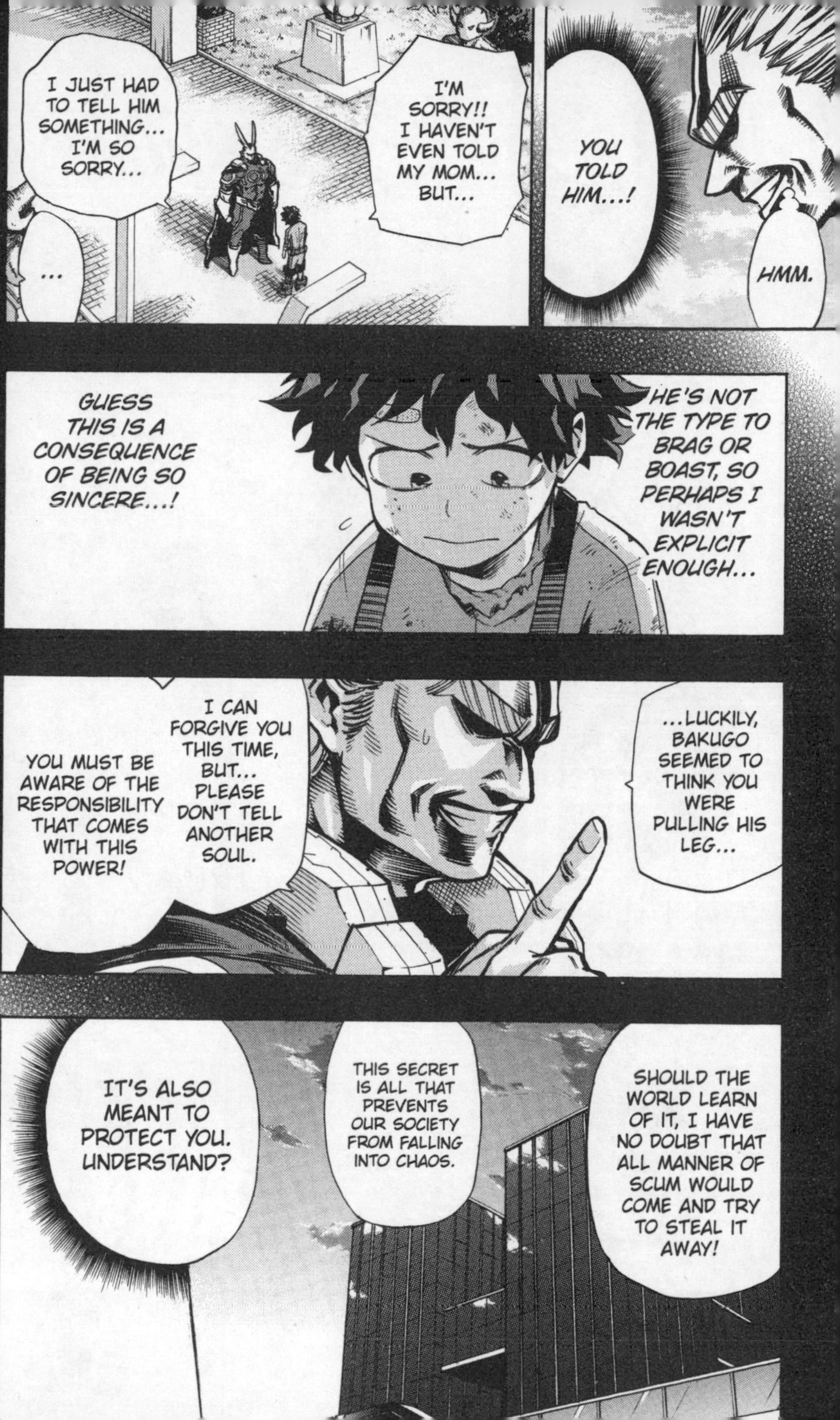
YOU TOLD HIM...!
HMM.
I'M SORRY!! I HAVEN'T EVEN TOLD MY MOM... BUT...
I JUST HAD TO TELL HIM SOMETHING... I'M SO SORRY...
...
HE'S NOT THE TYPE TO BRAG OR BOAST, SO PERHAPS I WASN'T EXPLICIT ENOUGH...
GUESS THIS IS A CONSEQUENCE OF BEING SO SINCERE...!
...LUCKILY, BAKUGO SEEMED TO THINK YOU WERE PULLING HIS LEG...
I CAN FORGIVE YOU THIS TIME, BUT... PLEASE DON'T TELL ANOTHER SOUL.
YOU MUST BE AWARE OF THE RESPONSIBILITY THAT COMES WITH THIS POWER!
SHOULD THE WORLD LEARN OF IT, I HAVE NO DOUBT THAT ALL MANNER OF SCUM WOULD COME AND TRY TO STEAL IT AWAY!
THIS SECRET IS ALL THAT PREVENTS OUR SOCIETY FROM FALLING INTO CHAOS.
IT'S ALSO MEANT TO PROTECT YOU. UNDERSTAND?

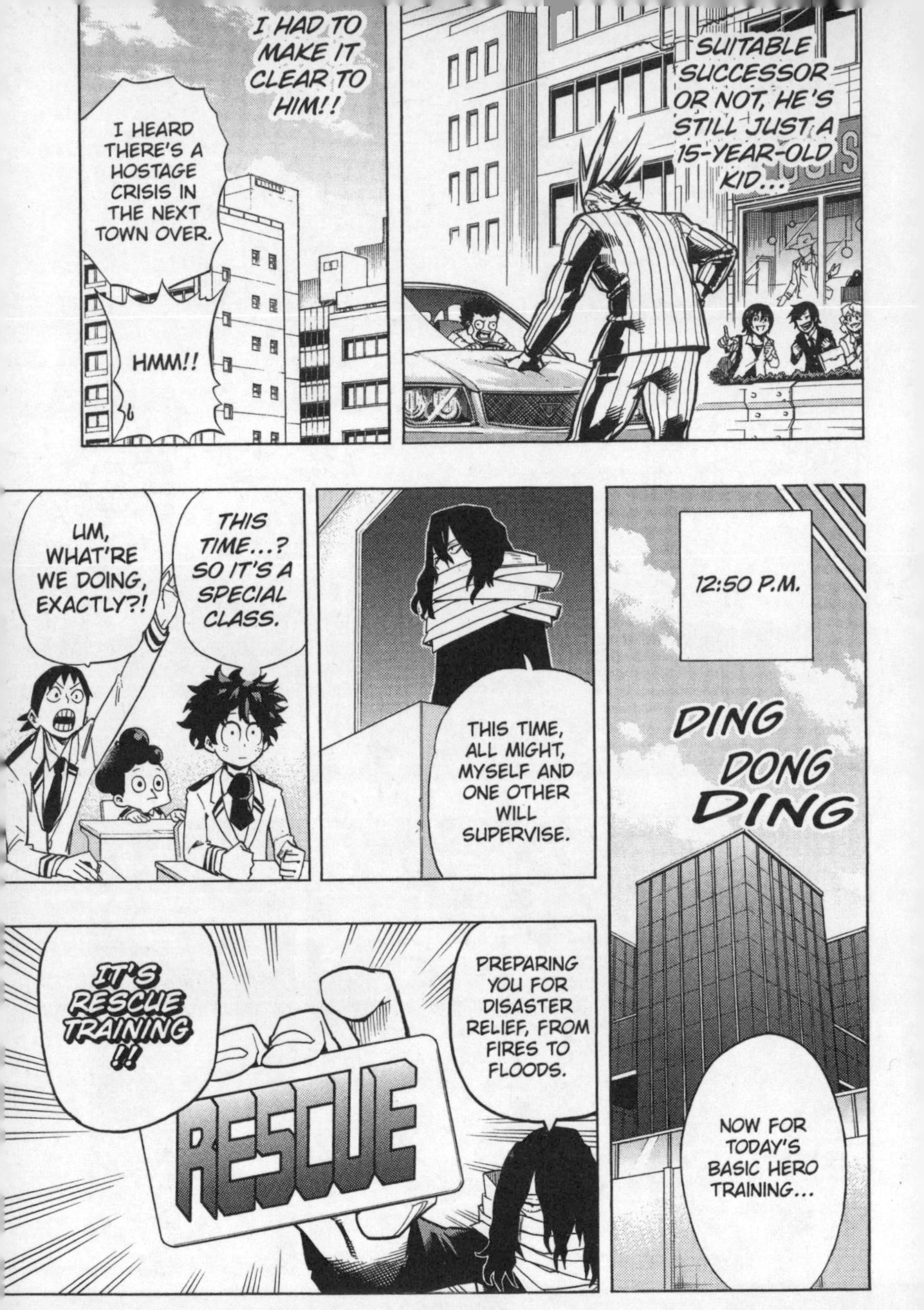
SUITABLE SUCCESSOR OR NOT, HE'S STILL JUST A 15-YEAR-OLD KID...
I HAD TO MAKE IT CLEAR TO HIM!!
I HEARD THERE'S A HOSTAGE CRISIS IN THE NEXT TOWN OVER.
HMM!!
12:50 P.M.
DING DONG DING
NOW FOR TODAY'S BASIC HERO TRAINING...
THIS TIME, ALL MIGHT, MYSELF AND ONE OTHER WILL SUPERVISE.
THIS TIME...? SO IT'S A SPECIAL CLASS.
UM, WHAT'RE WE DOING, EXACTLY?!
PREPARING YOU FOR DISASTER RELIEF, FROM FIRES TO FLOODS.
IT'S RESCUE TRAINING!!
RESCUE

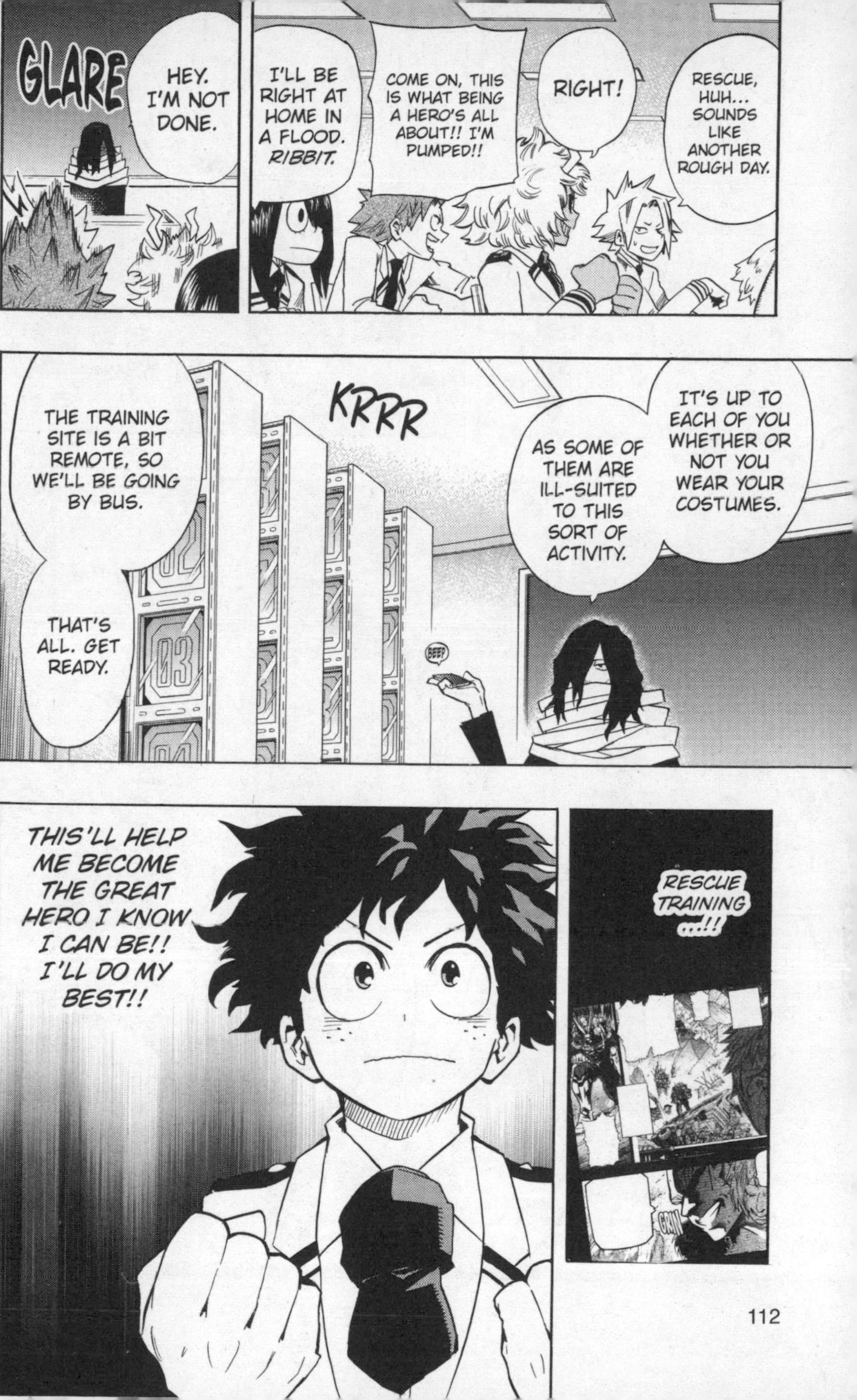
RESCUE, HUH... SOUNDS LIKE ANOTHER ROUGH DAY.
RIGHT!
COME ON, THIS IS WHAT BEING A HERO'S ALL ABOUT!! I'M PUMPED!!
I'LL BE RIGHT AT HOME IN A FLOOD. *RIBBIT.*
HEY. I'M NOT DONE.
GLARE
IT'S UP TO EACH OF YOU WHETHER OR NOT YOU WEAR YOUR COSTUMES.
AS SOME OF THEM ARE ILL-SUITED TO THIS SORT OF ACTIVITY.
KRRR
THE TRAINING SITE IS A BIT REMOTE, SO WE'LL BE GOING BY BUS.
BEEP
THAT'S ALL. GET READY.
RESCUE TRAINING ...!!!
THIS'LL HELP ME BECOME THE GREAT HERO I KNOW I CAN BE!! I'LL DO MY BEST!!

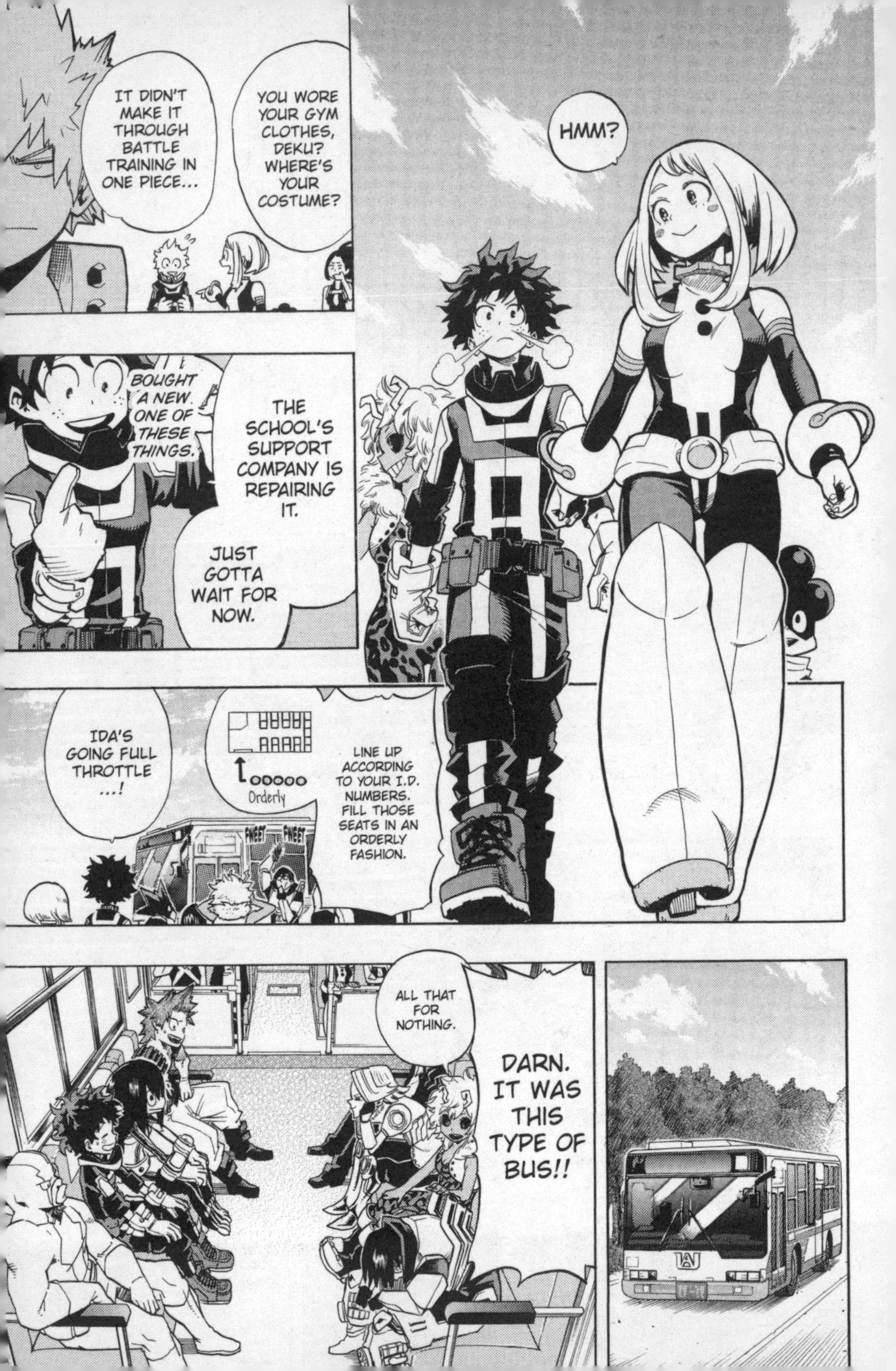
HMM?
YOU WORE YOUR GYM CLOTHES, DEKU? WHERE'S YOUR COSTUME?
IT DIDN'T MAKE IT THROUGH BATTLE TRAINING IN ONE PIECE...
THE SCHOOL'S SUPPORT COMPANY IS REPAIRING IT.
JUST GOTTA WAIT FOR NOW.
BOUGHT A NEW ONE OF THESE THINGS.
Orderly
LINE UP ACCORDING TO YOUR I.D. NUMBERS. FILL THOSE SEATS IN AN ORDERLY FASHION.
FWEET
FWEET
IDA'S GOING FULL THROTTLE ...!
DARN. IT WAS THIS TYPE OF BUS!!
ALL THAT FOR NOTHING.

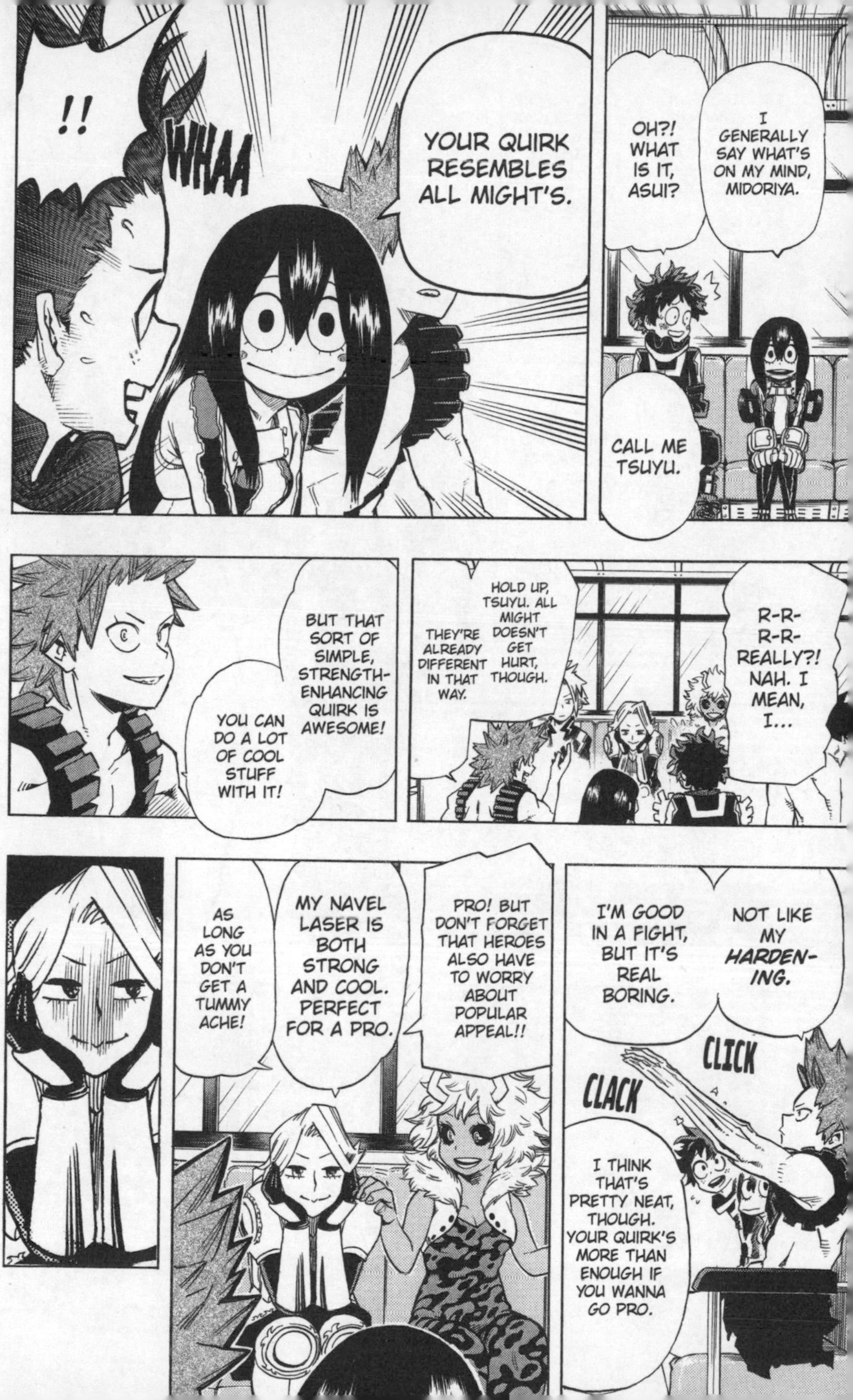
I GENERALLY SAY WHAT'S ON MY MIND, MIDORIYA.
OH?! WHAT IS IT, ASUI?
CALL ME TSUYU.
YOUR QUIRK RESEMBLES ALL MIGHT'S.
WHAA
!!
R-R-R-R-REALLY?! NAH. I MEAN, I...
HOLD UP, TSUYU. ALL MIGHT DOESN'T GET HURT, THOUGH.
THEY'RE ALREADY DIFFERENT IN THAT WAY.
BUT THAT SORT OF SIMPLE, STRENGTH-ENHANCING QUIRK IS AWESOME!
YOU CAN DO A LOT OF COOL STUFF WITH IT!
NOT LIKE MY *HARDENING.*
I'M GOOD IN A FIGHT, BUT IT'S REAL BORING.
CLICK
CLACK
I THINK THAT'S PRETTY NEAT, THOUGH. YOUR QUIRK'S MORE THAN ENOUGH IF YOU WANNA GO PRO.
PRO! BUT DON'T FORGET THAT HEROES ALSO HAVE TO WORRY ABOUT POPULAR APPEAL!!
MY NAVEL LASER IS BOTH STRONG AND COOL. PERFECT FOR A PRO.
AS LONG AS YOU DON'T GET A TUMMY ACHE!

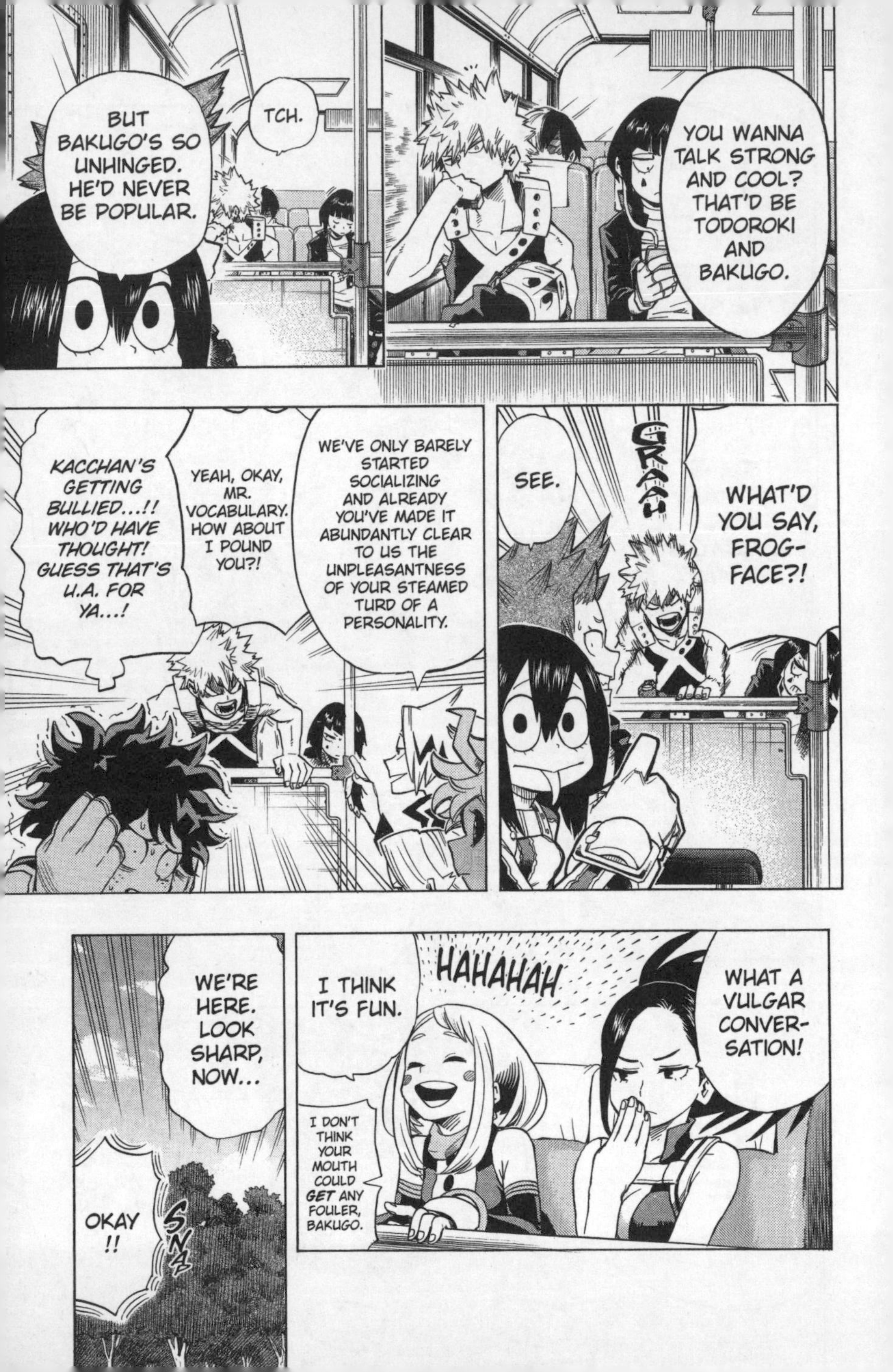
YOU WANNA TALK STRONG AND COOL? THAT'D BE TODOROKI AND BAKUGO.
BUT BAKUGO'S SO UNHINGED. HE'D NEVER BE POPULAR.
TCH.
WHAT'D YOU SAY, FROG-FACE?!
GRAAH
SEE.
WE'VE ONLY BARELY STARTED SOCIALIZING AND ALREADY YOU'VE MADE IT ABUNDANTLY CLEAR TO US THE UNPLEASANTNESS OF YOUR STEAMED TURD OF A PERSONALITY.
YEAH, OKAY, MR. VOCABULARY. HOW ABOUT I POUND YOU?!
KACCHAN'S GETTING BULLIED...!! WHO'D HAVE THOUGHT! GUESS THAT'S U.A. FOR YA...!
WHAT A VULGAR CONVER-SATION!
HAHAHAH
I THINK IT'S FUN.
I DON'T THINK YOUR MOUTH COULD GET ANY FOULER, BAKUGO.
WE'RE HERE. LOOK SHARP, NOW...
OKAY !!
SNAP

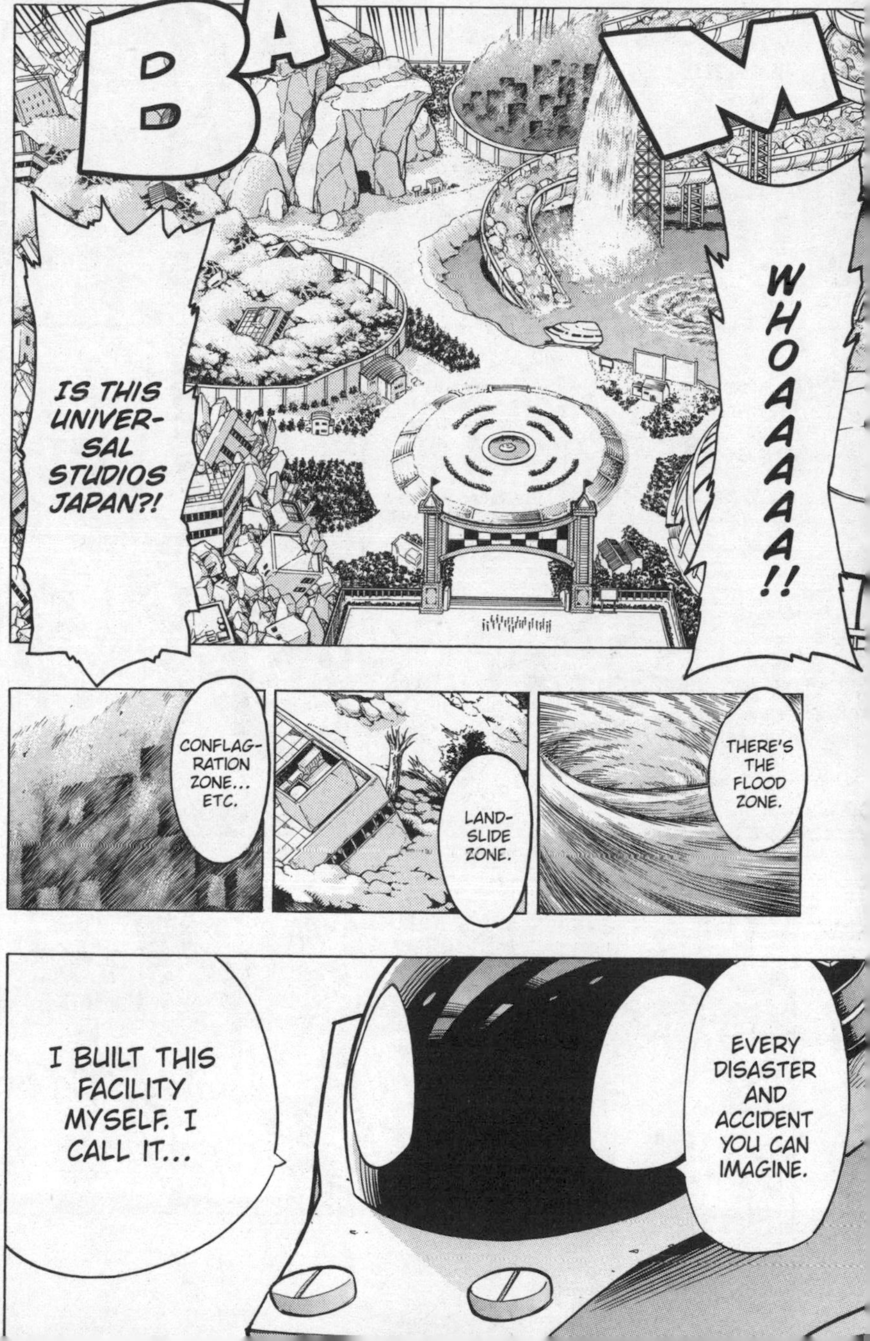
BAM
WHOAAAAAAA!!
IS THIS UNIVERSAL STUDIOS JAPAN?!
THERE'S THE FLOOD ZONE.
LANDSLIDE ZONE.
CONFLAGRATION ZONE... ETC.
EVERY DISASTER AND ACCIDENT YOU CAN IMAGINE.
I BUILT THIS FACILITY MYSELF. I CALL IT...

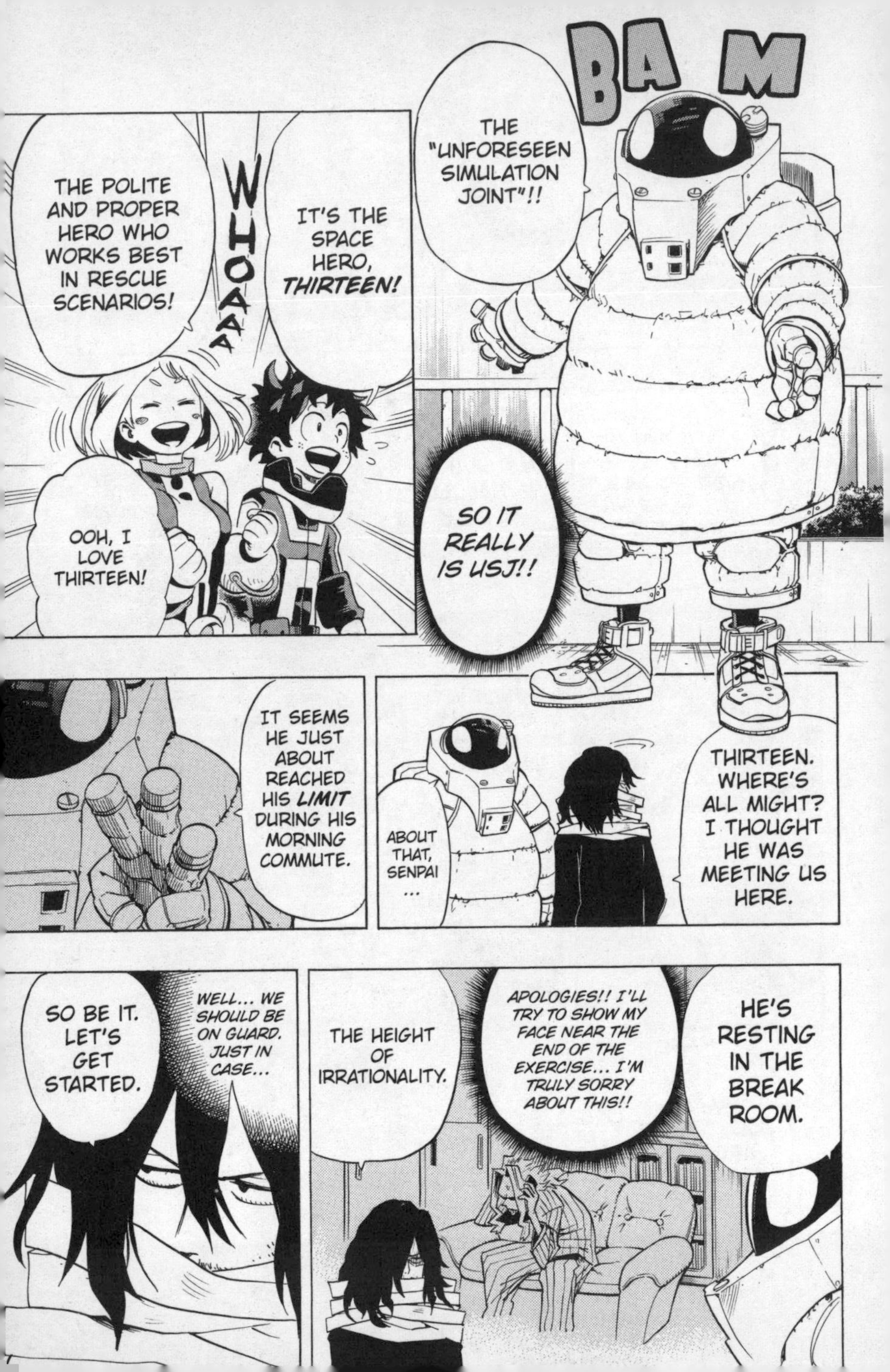
BAM
THE "UNFORESEEN SIMULATION JOINT"!!
SO IT REALLY IS USJ!!
IT'S THE SPACE HERO, THIRTEEN!
WHOAAA
THE POLITE AND PROPER HERO WHO WORKS BEST IN RESCUE SCENARIOS!
OOH, I LOVE THIRTEEN!
THIRTEEN. WHERE'S ALL MIGHT? I THOUGHT HE WAS MEETING US HERE.
ABOUT THAT, SENPAI...
IT SEEMS HE JUST ABOUT REACHED HIS LIMIT DURING HIS MORNING COMMUTE.
HE'S RESTING IN THE BREAK ROOM.
APOLOGIES!! I'LL TRY TO SHOW MY FACE NEAR THE END OF THE EXERCISE... I'M TRULY SORRY ABOUT THIS!!
THE HEIGHT OF IRRATIONALITY.
WELL... WE SHOULD BE ON GUARD. JUST IN CASE...
SO BE IT. LET'S GET STARTED.

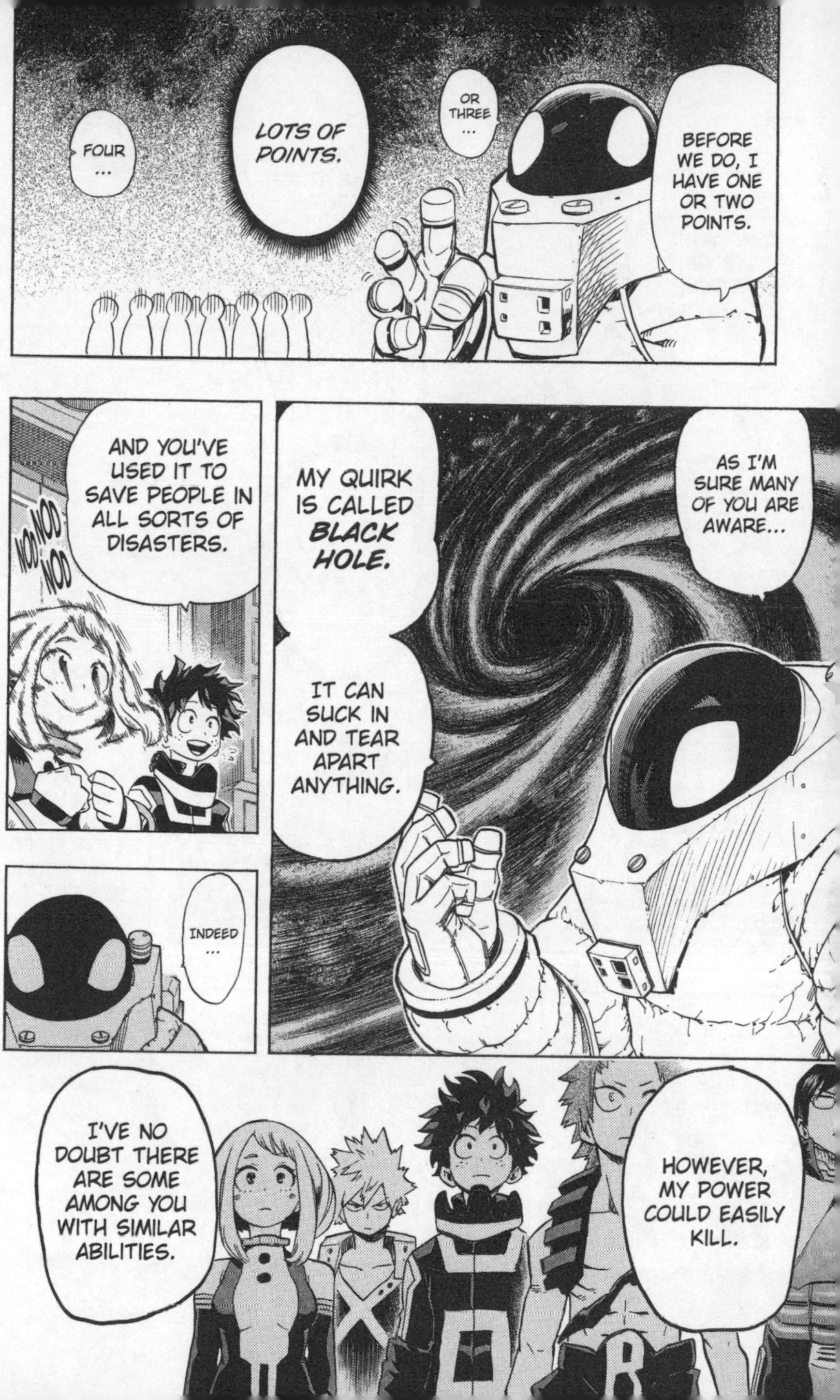
BEFORE WE DO, I HAVE ONE OR TWO POINTS.
OR THREE ...
LOTS OF POINTS.
FOUR ...
AS I'M SURE MANY OF YOU ARE AWARE...
MY QUIRK IS CALLED BLACK HOLE.
IT CAN SUCK IN AND TEAR APART ANYTHING.
AND YOU'VE USED IT TO SAVE PEOPLE IN ALL SORTS OF DISASTERS.
NOD NOD NOD
INDEED ...
HOWEVER, MY POWER COULD EASILY KILL.
I'VE NO DOUBT THERE ARE SOME AMONG YOU WITH SIMILAR ABILITIES.

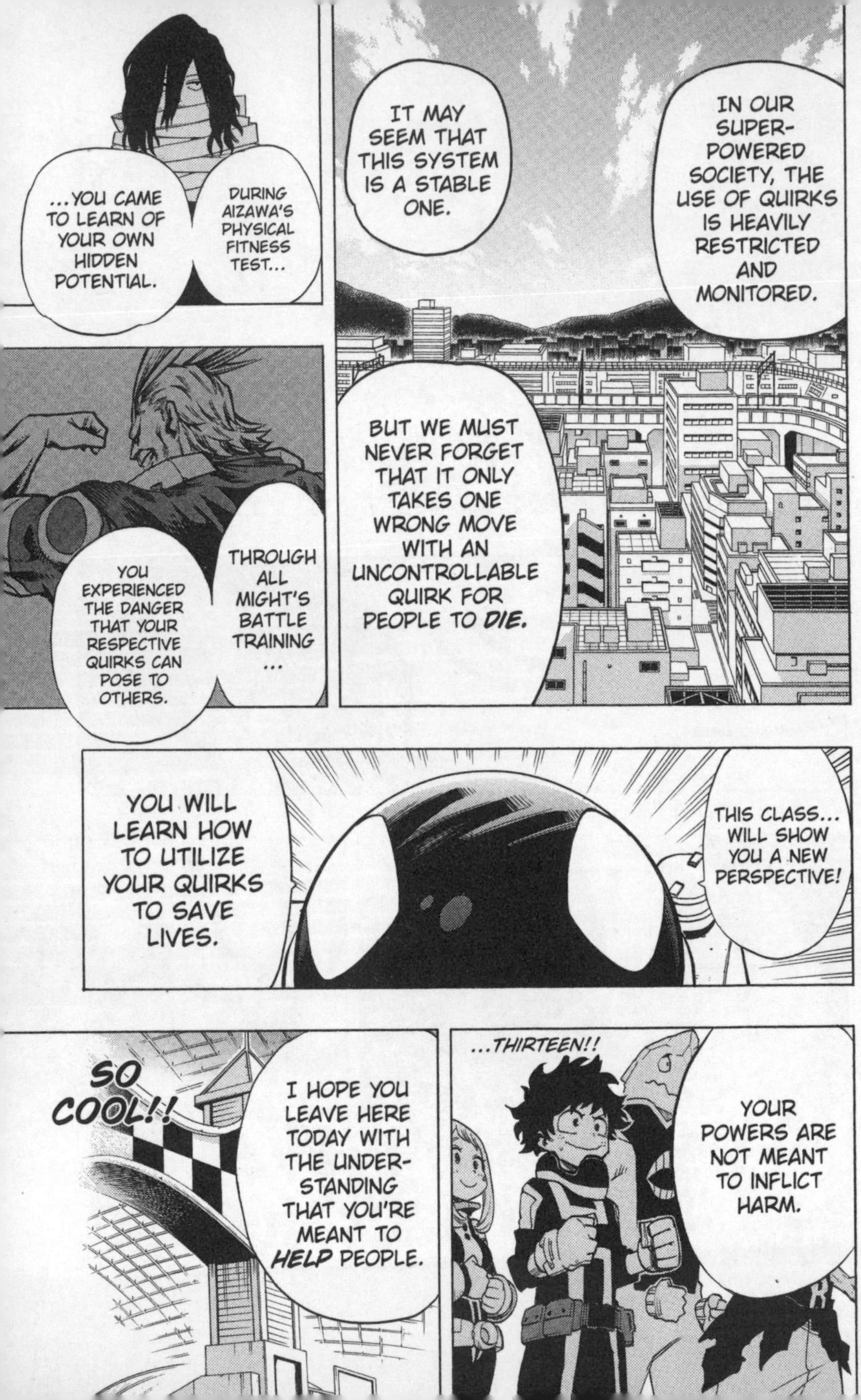
IN OUR SUPER-POWERED SOCIETY, THE USE OF QUIRKS IS HEAVILY RESTRICTED AND MONITORED.
IT MAY SEEM THAT THIS SYSTEM IS A STABLE ONE.
BUT WE MUST NEVER FORGET THAT IT ONLY TAKES ONE WRONG MOVE WITH AN UNCONTROLLABLE QUIRK FOR PEOPLE TO *DIE.*
DURING AIZAWA'S PHYSICAL FITNESS TEST...
...YOU CAME TO LEARN OF YOUR OWN HIDDEN POTENTIAL.
THROUGH ALL MIGHT'S BATTLE TRAINING...
YOU EXPERIENCED THE DANGER THAT YOUR RESPECTIVE QUIRKS CAN POSE TO OTHERS.
THIS CLASS... WILL SHOW YOU A NEW PERSPECTIVE!
YOU WILL LEARN HOW TO UTILIZE YOUR QUIRKS TO SAVE LIVES.
YOUR POWERS ARE NOT MEANT TO INFLICT HARM.
...THIRTEEN!!
I HOPE YOU LEAVE HERE TODAY WITH THE UNDER-STANDING THAT YOU'RE MEANT TO ***HELP*** PEOPLE.
SO COOL!!

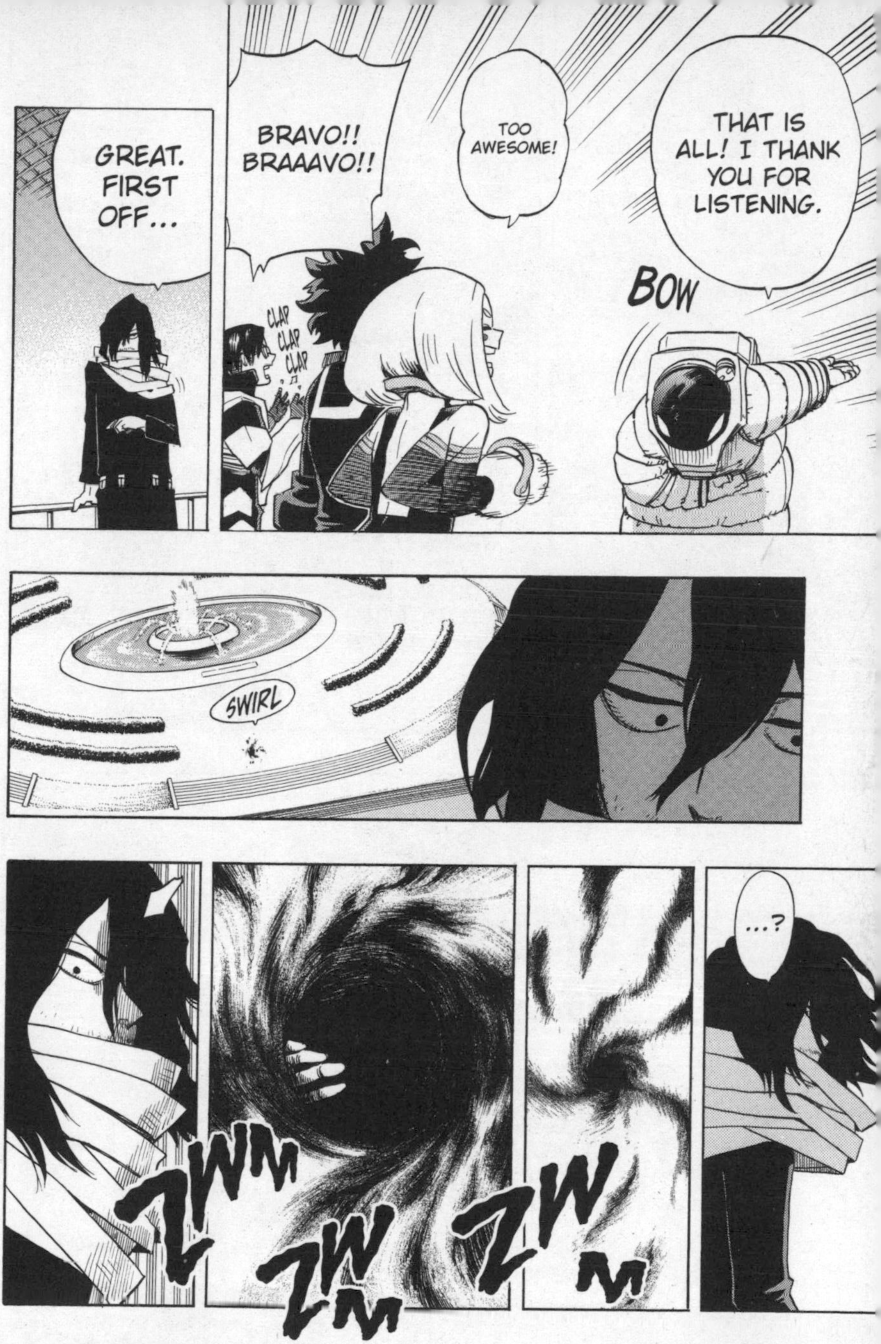
THAT IS ALL! I THANK YOU FOR LISTENING.
BOW
TOO AWESOME!
BRAVO!! BRAAAVO!!
CLAP CLAP CLAP
GREAT. FIRST OFF...
SWIRL
...?
ZWM
ZWM
ZWM

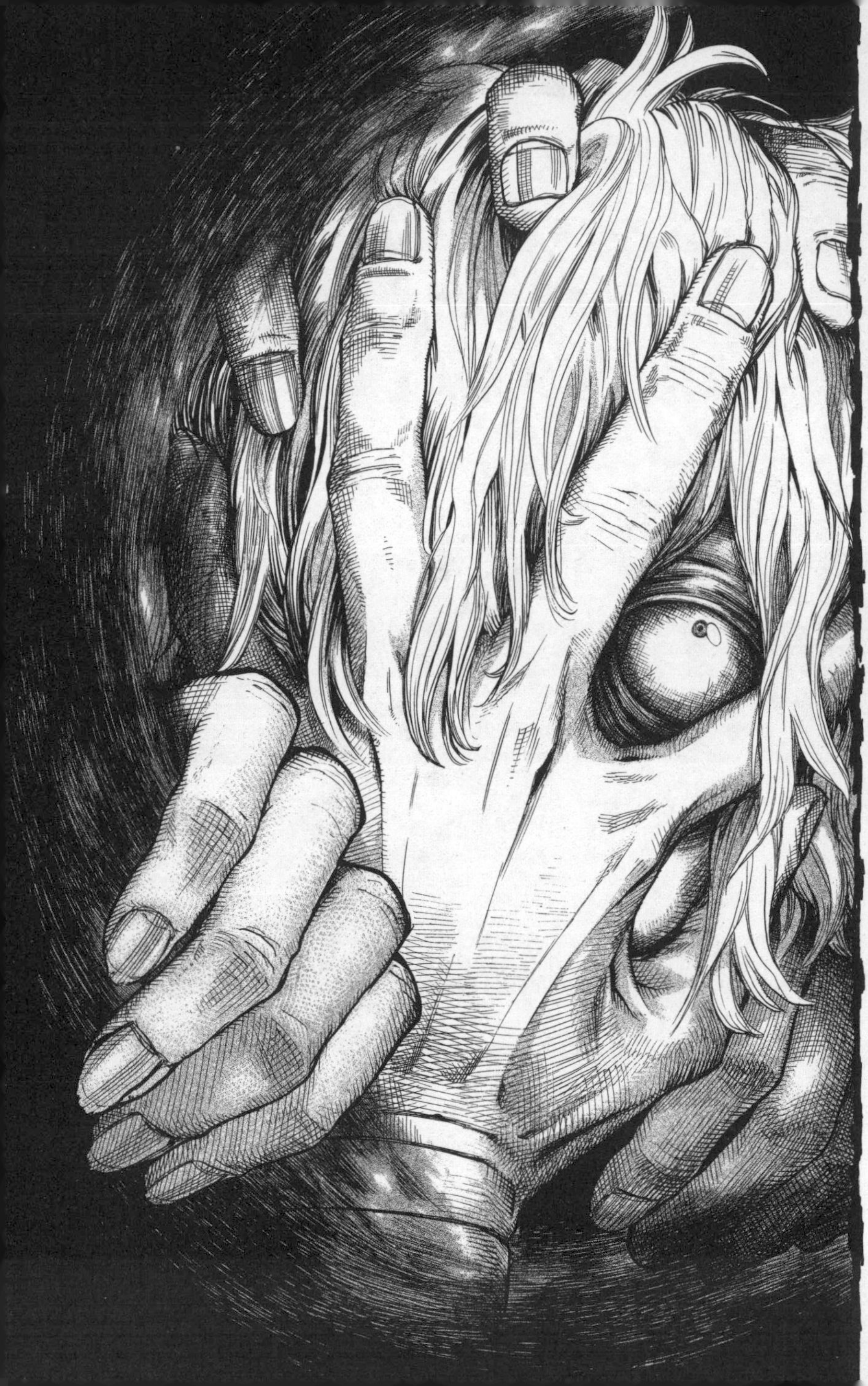

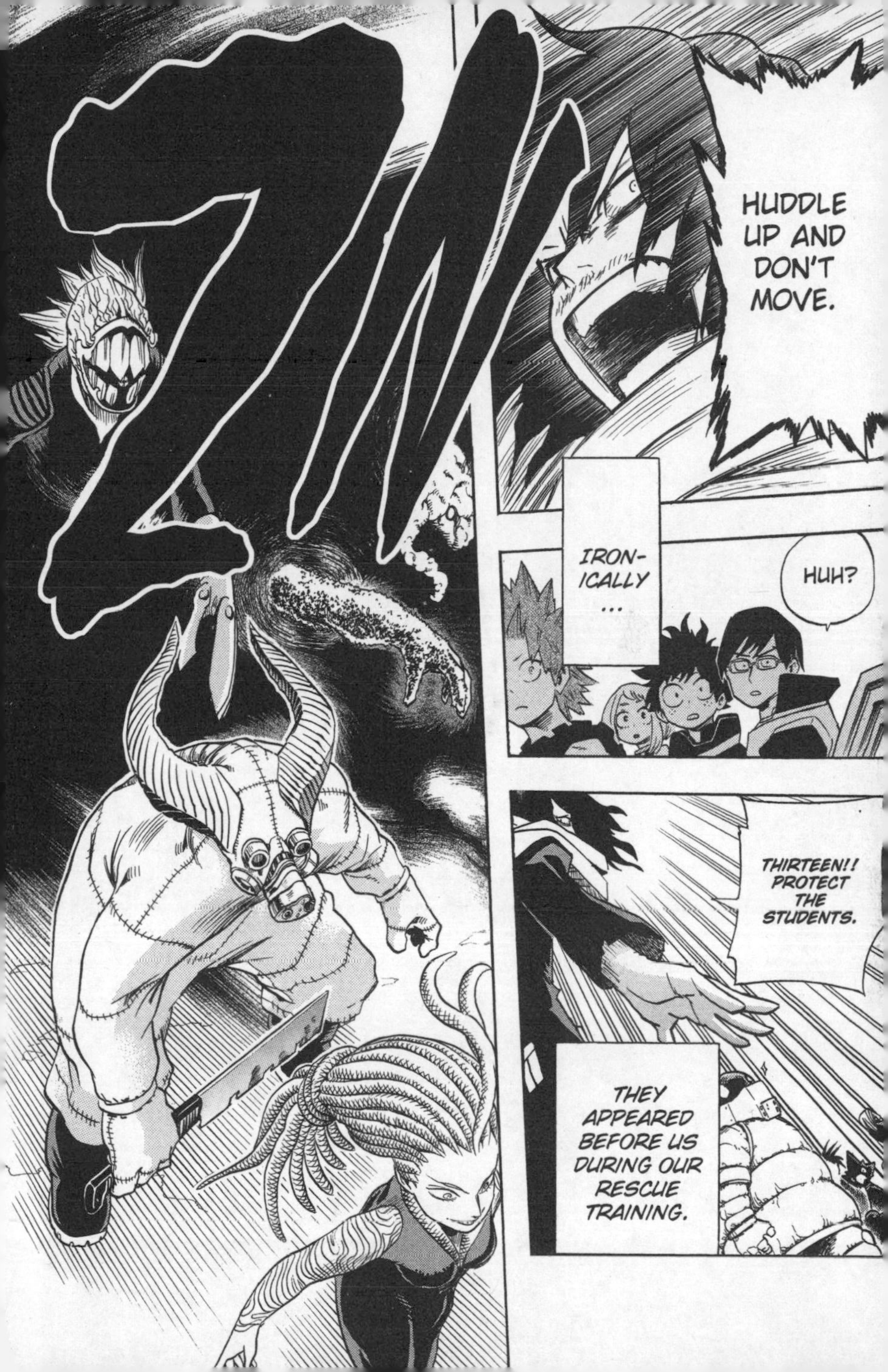
HUDDLE UP AND DON'T MOVE.
IRON-ICALLY...
HUH?
THIRTEEN!! PROTECT THE STUDENTS.
THEY APPEARED BEFORE US DURING OUR RESCUE TRAINING.

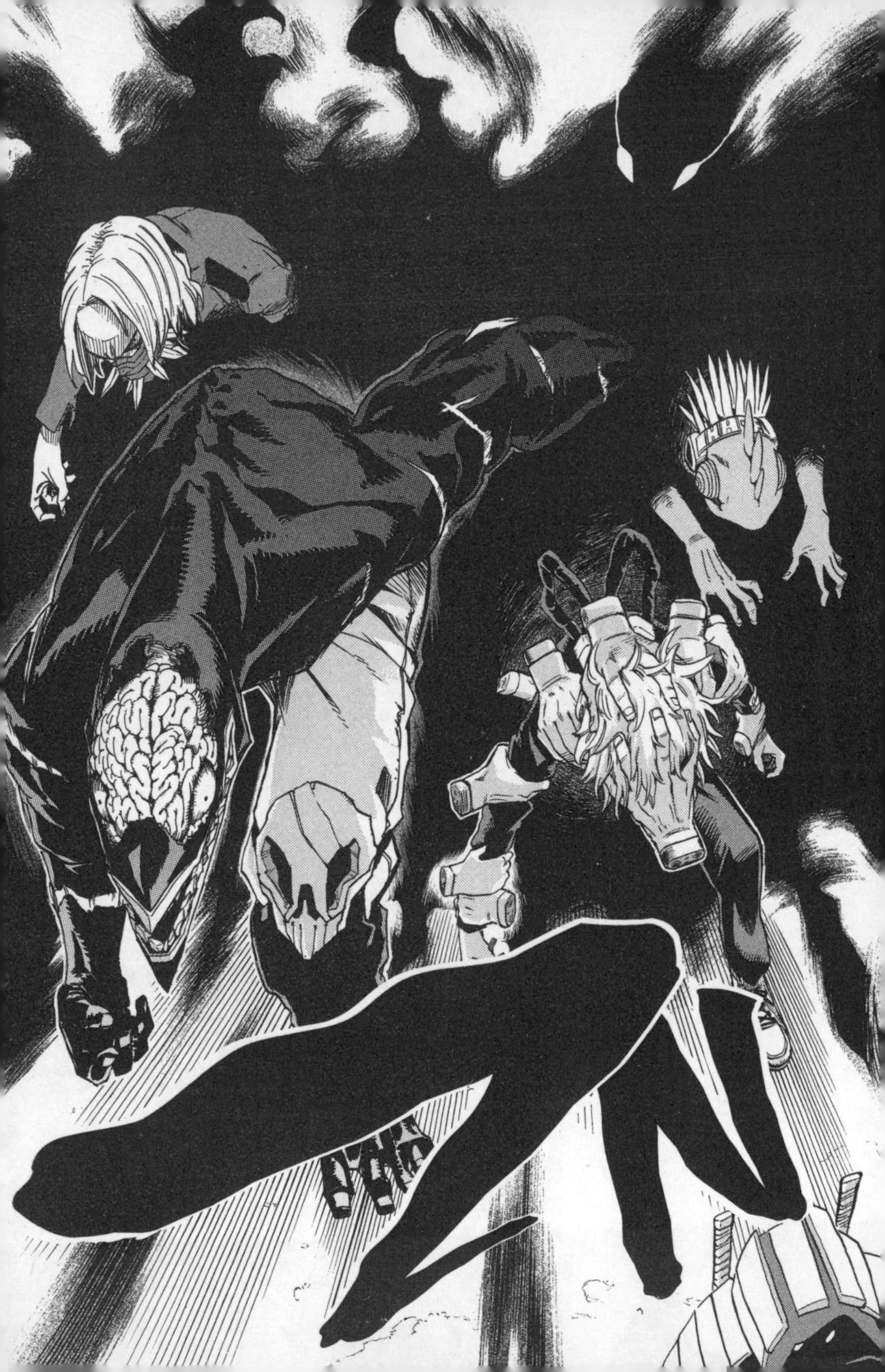

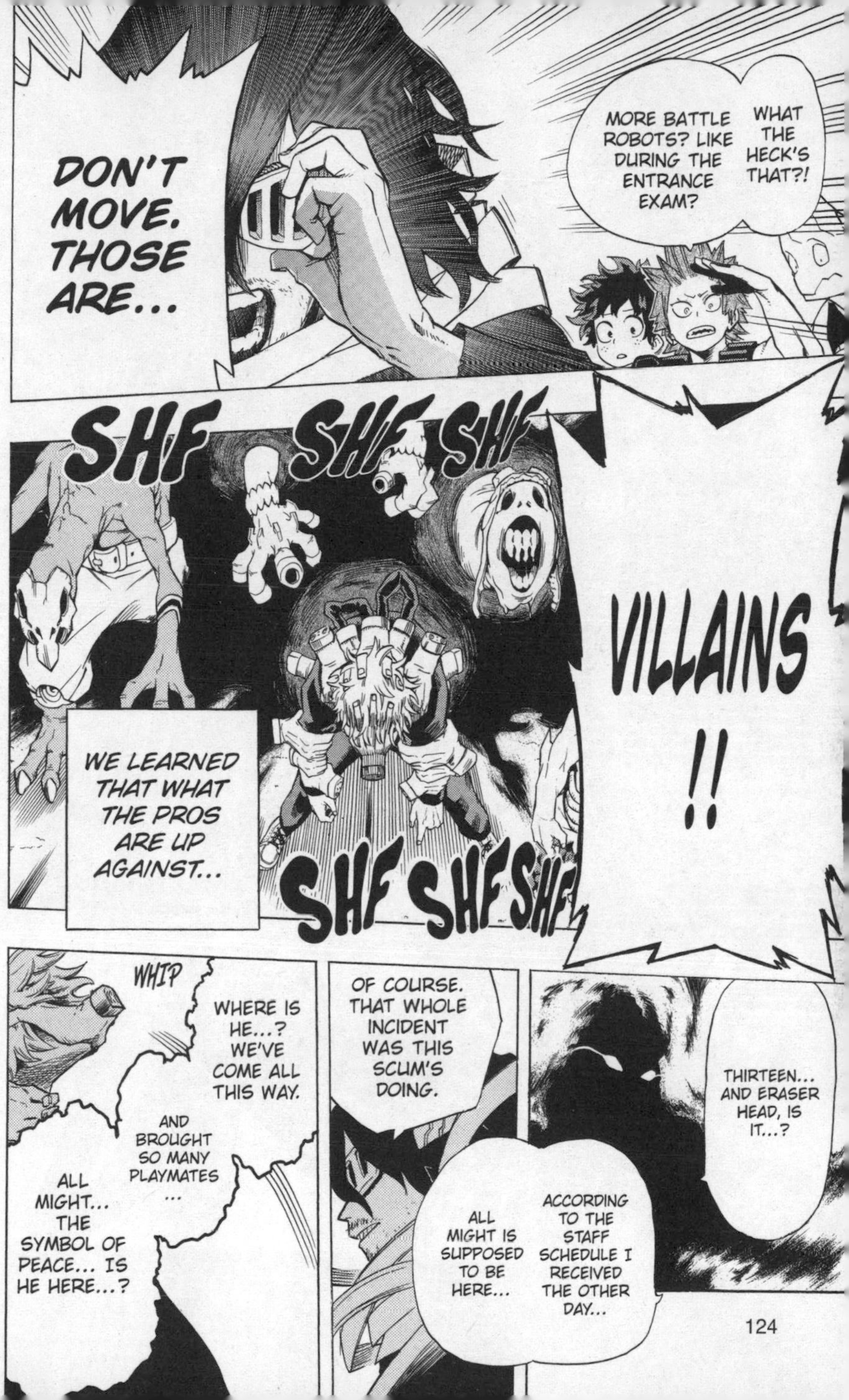
WHAT THE HECK'S THAT?!
MORE BATTLE ROBOTS? LIKE DURING THE ENTRANCE EXAM?
DON'T MOVE. THOSE ARE...
VILLAINS!!
SHF SHF SHF
WE LEARNED THAT WHAT THE PROS ARE UP AGAINST...
SHF SHF SHF
THIRTEEN... AND ERASER HEAD, IS IT...?
OF COURSE. THAT WHOLE INCIDENT WAS THIS SCUM'S DOING.
ACCORDING TO THE STAFF SCHEDULE I RECEIVED THE OTHER DAY...
ALL MIGHT IS SUPPOSED TO BE HERE...
WHIP
WHERE IS HE...? WE'VE COME ALL THIS WAY.
AND BROUGHT SO MANY PLAYMATES...
ALL MIGHT... THE SYMBOL OF PEACE... IS HE HERE...?

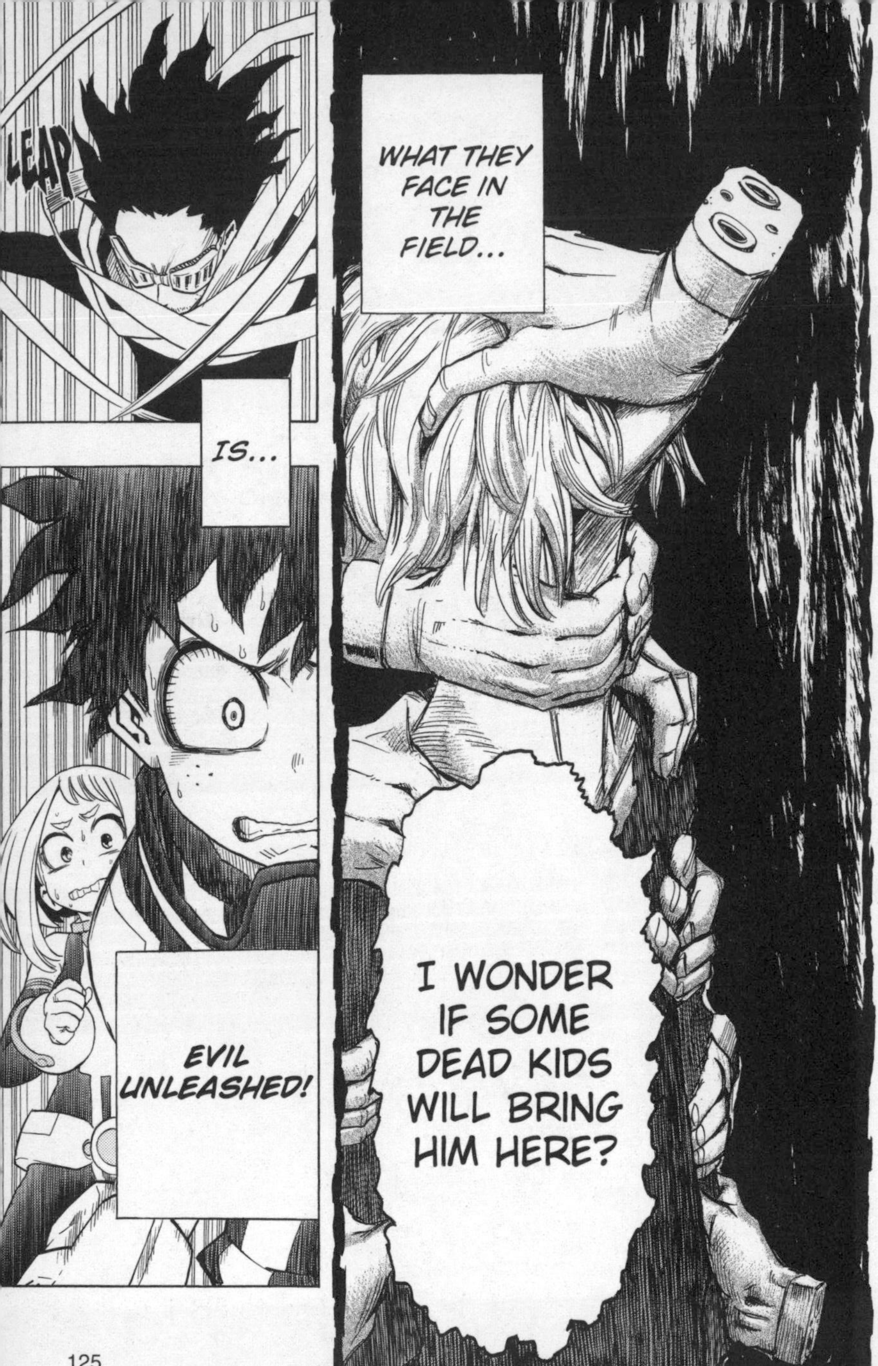
WHAT THEY FACE IN THE FIELD...
I WONDER IF SOME DEAD KIDS WILL BRING HIM HERE?
LEAP
IS...
EVIL UNLEASHED!

THIRTEEN [28]

THE HERO

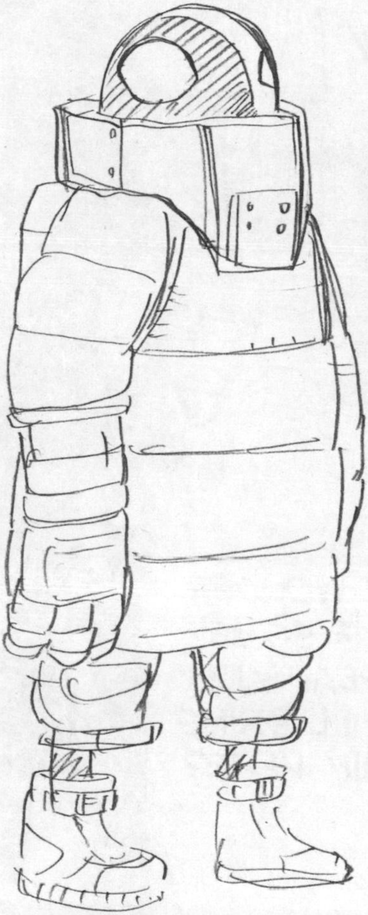

Birthday: 2/3
Height: 180 cm
Favorite Things: Museums, nature documentaries

BEHIND THE SCENES

Meant to be someone who demonstrates that being a hero isn't just about fighting. I really like this design.
But what about under the helmet?!
If I get the chance to remove the suit, I will. If not, I won't.

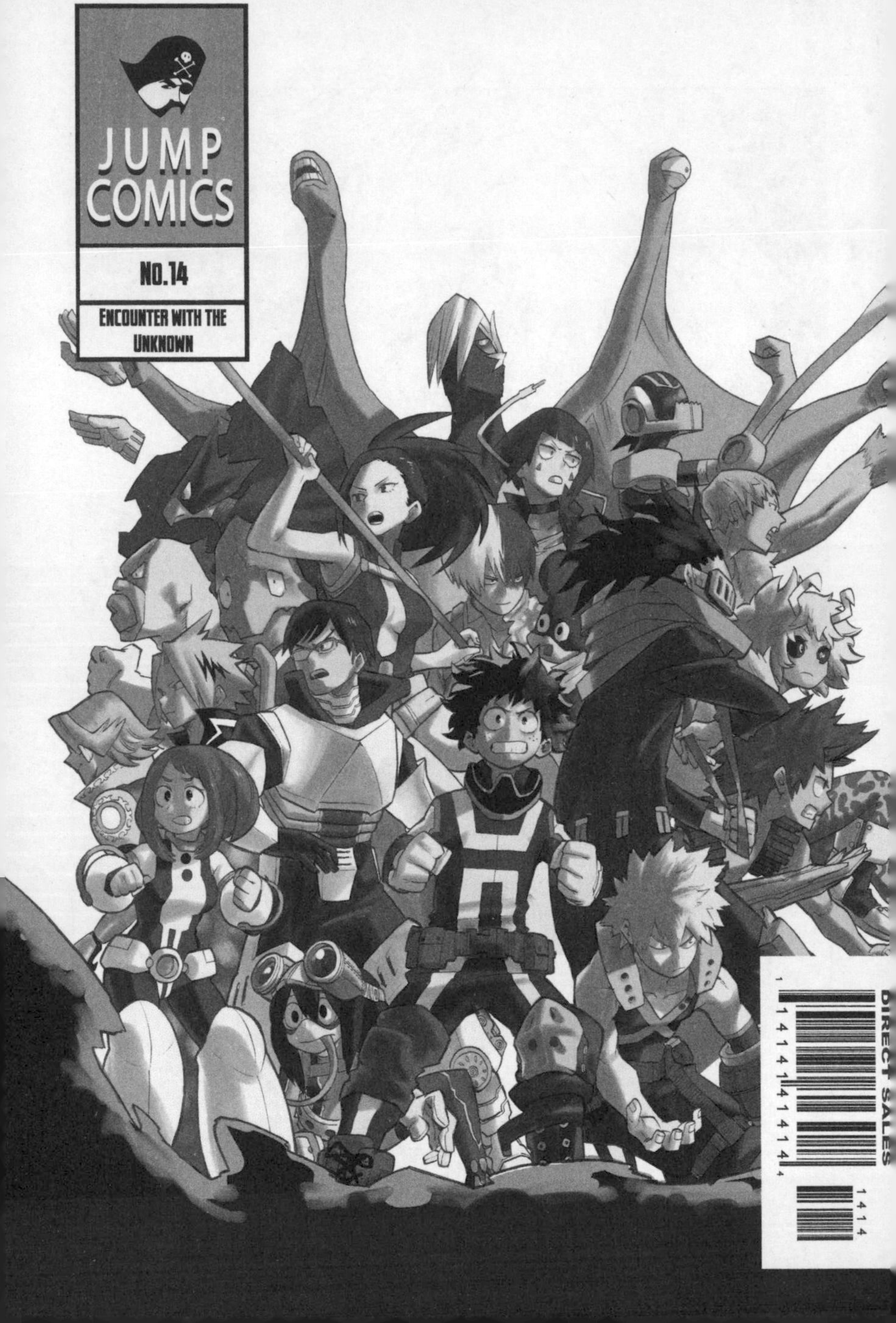
JUMP COMICS
No.14
ENCOUNTER WITH THE UNKNOWN
DIRECT SALES

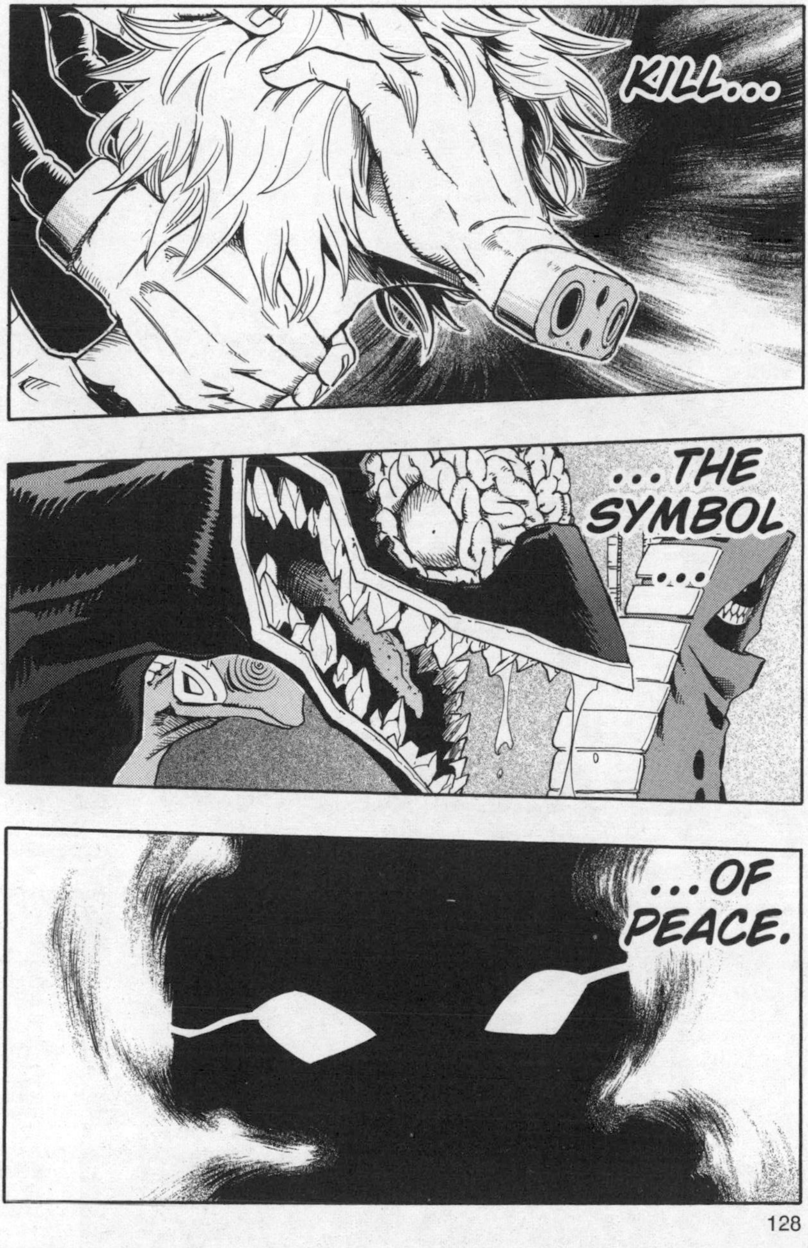
KILL...
...THE SYMBOL
...
...OF PEACE.

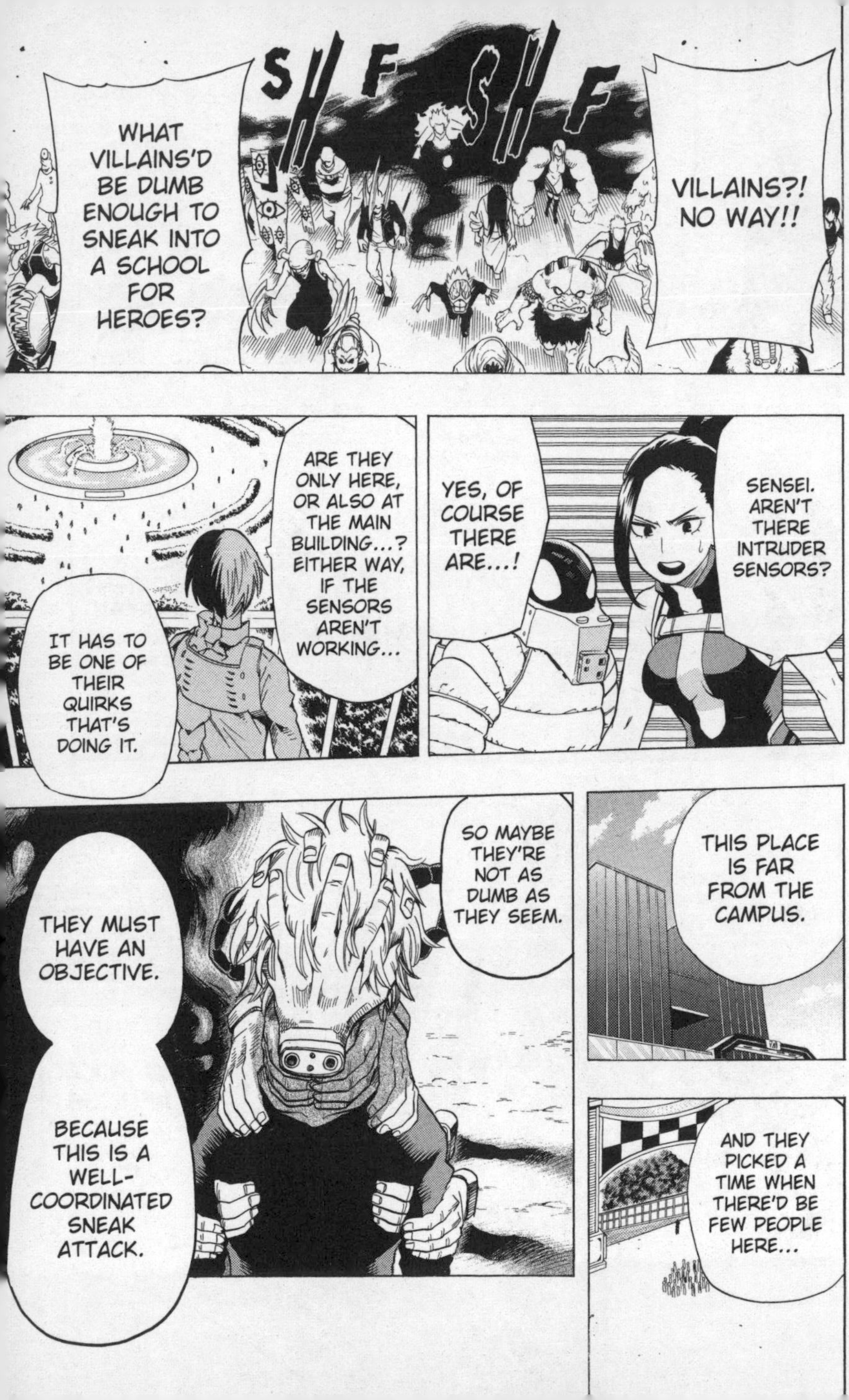
VILLAINS?! NO WAY!!
SHF SHF
WHAT VILLAINS'D BE DUMB ENOUGH TO SNEAK INTO A SCHOOL FOR HEROES?
SENSEI. AREN'T THERE INTRUDER SENSORS?
YES, OF COURSE THERE ARE...!
ARE THEY ONLY HERE, OR ALSO AT THE MAIN BUILDING...? EITHER WAY, IF THE SENSORS AREN'T WORKING...
IT HAS TO BE ONE OF THEIR QUIRKS THAT'S DOING IT.
THIS PLACE IS FAR FROM THE CAMPUS.
AND THEY PICKED A TIME WHEN THERE'D BE FEW PEOPLE HERE...
SO MAYBE THEY'RE NOT AS DUMB AS THEY SEEM.
THEY MUST HAVE AN OBJECTIVE.
BECAUSE THIS IS A WELL-COORDINATED SNEAK ATTACK.

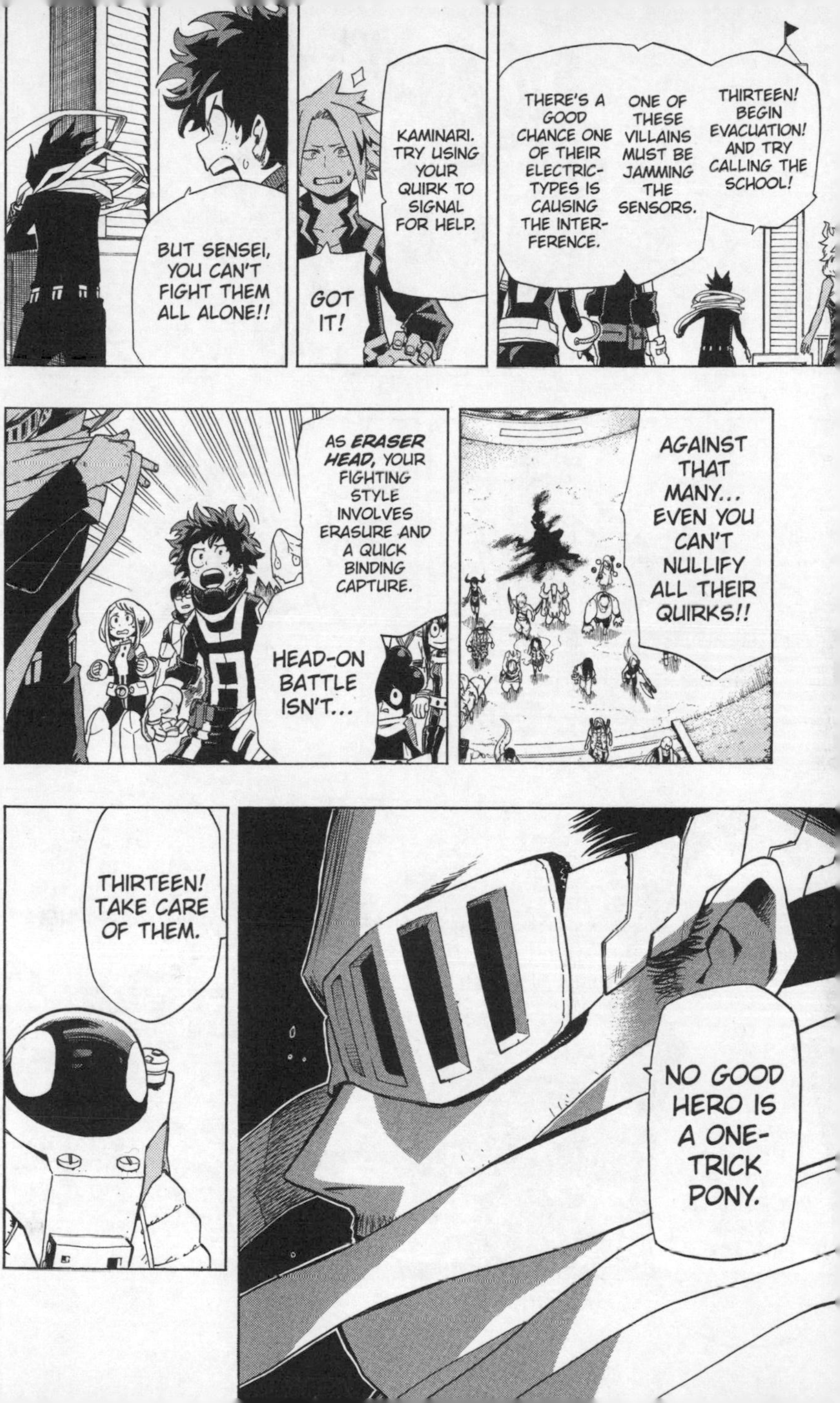
THIRTEEN! BEGIN EVACUATION! AND TRY CALLING THE SCHOOL!
ONE OF THESE VILLAINS MUST BE JAMMING THE SENSORS.
THERE'S A GOOD CHANCE ONE OF THEIR ELECTRIC-TYPES IS CAUSING THE INTERFERENCE.
KAMINARI. TRY USING YOUR QUIRK TO SIGNAL FOR HELP.
GOT IT!
BUT SENSEI, YOU CAN'T FIGHT THEM ALL ALONE!!
AGAINST THAT MANY... EVEN YOU CAN'T NULLIFY ALL THEIR QUIRKS!!
AS *ERASER HEAD*, YOUR FIGHTING STYLE INVOLVES ERASURE AND A QUICK BINDING CAPTURE.
HEAD-ON BATTLE ISN'T...
NO GOOD HERO IS A ONE-TRICK PONY.
THIRTEEN! TAKE CARE OF THEM.

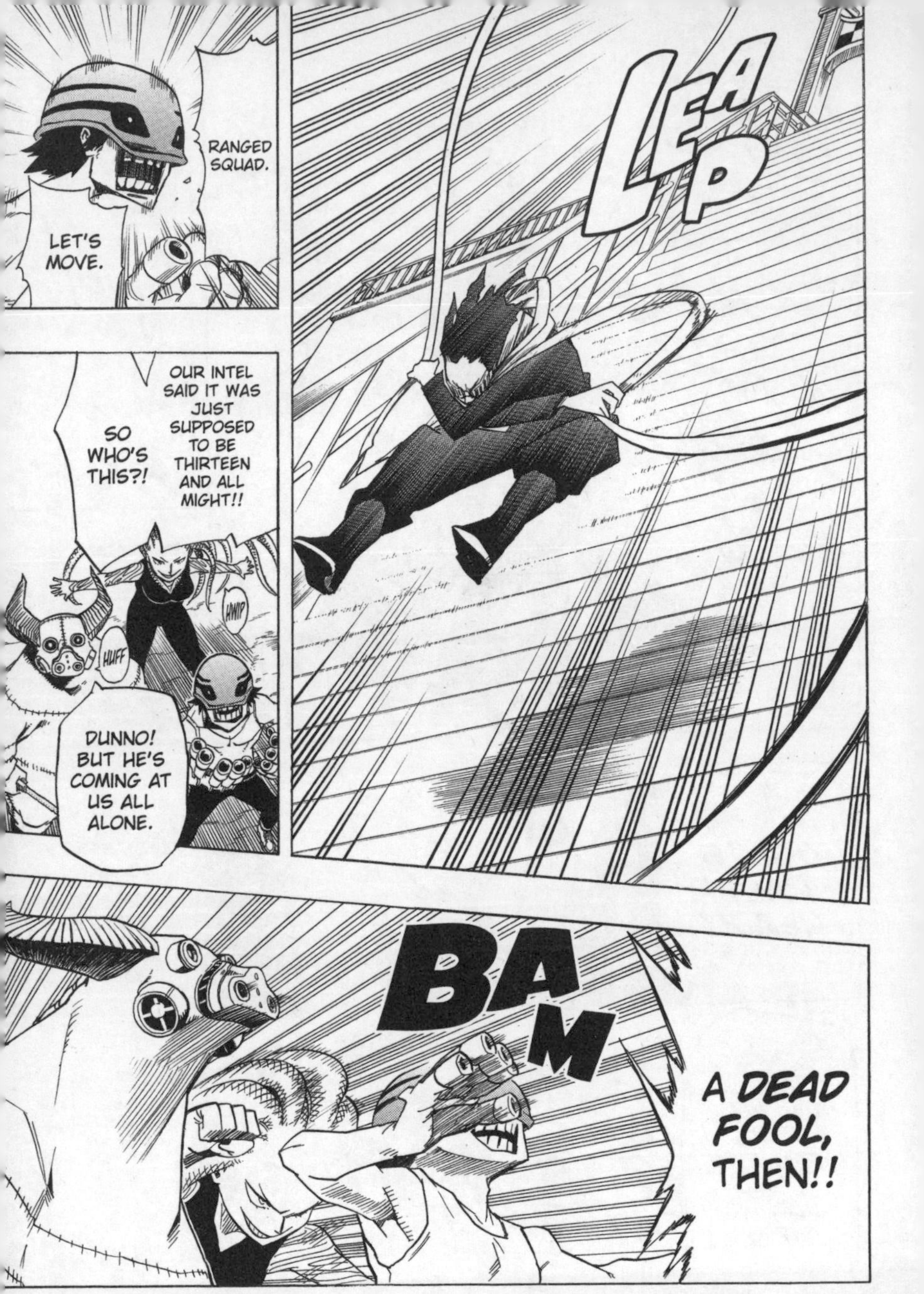
LEAP
RANGED SQUAD.
LET'S MOVE.
OUR INTEL SAID IT WAS JUST SUPPOSED TO BE THIRTEEN AND ALL MIGHT!!
SO WHO'S THIS?!
WHIP
HUFF
DUNNO! BUT HE'S COMING AT US ALL ALONE.
BAM
A DEAD FOOL, THEN!!

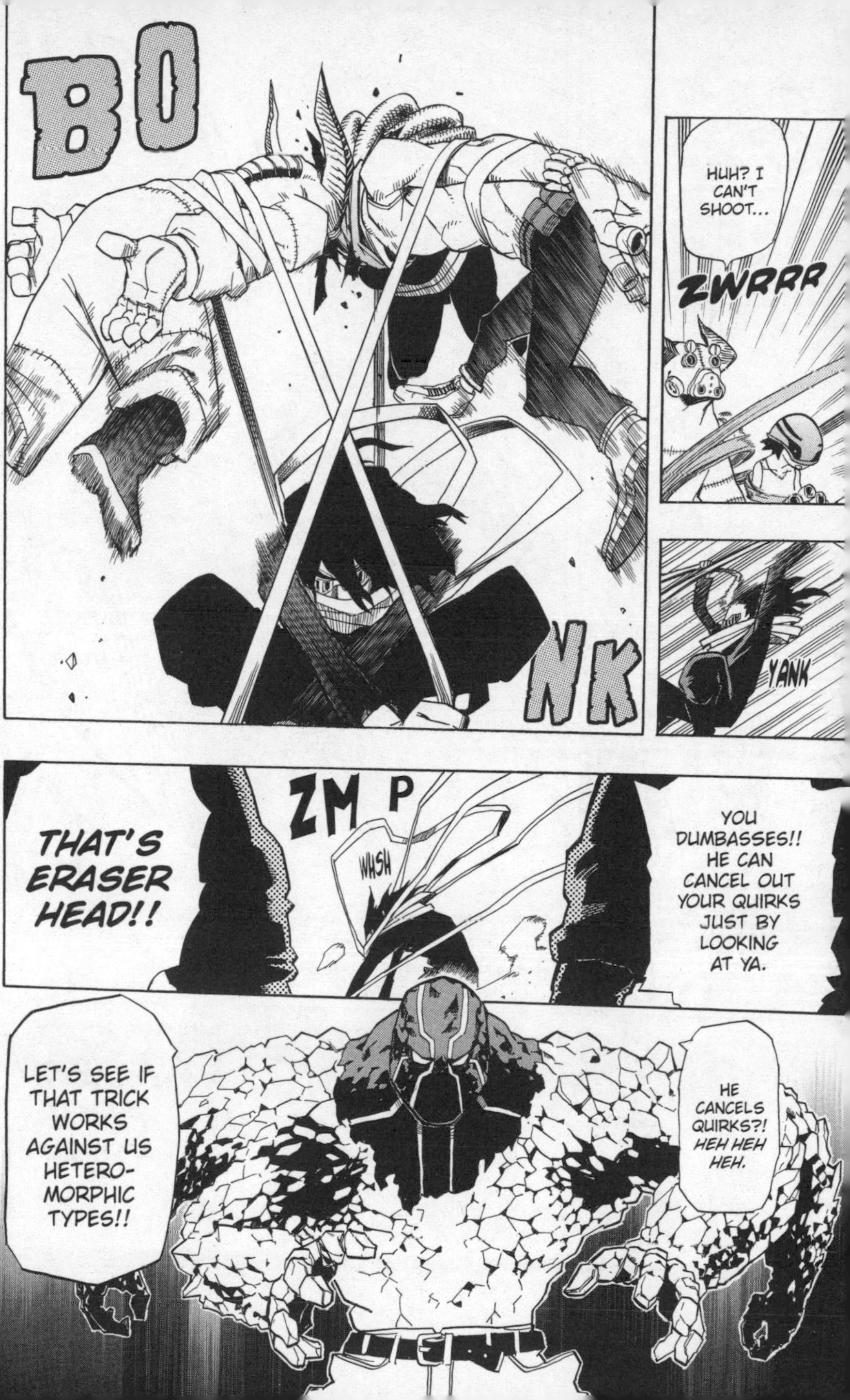
HUH? I CAN'T SHOOT...
ZWRRR
YANK
BO
NK
YOU DUMBASSES!! HE CAN CANCEL OUT YOUR QUIRKS JUST BY LOOKING AT YA.
ZM P
WHSH
THAT'S ERASER HEAD!!
HE CANCELS QUIRKS?! HEH HEH HEH.
LET'S SEE IF THAT TRICK WORKS AGAINST US HETERO-MORPHIC TYPES!!

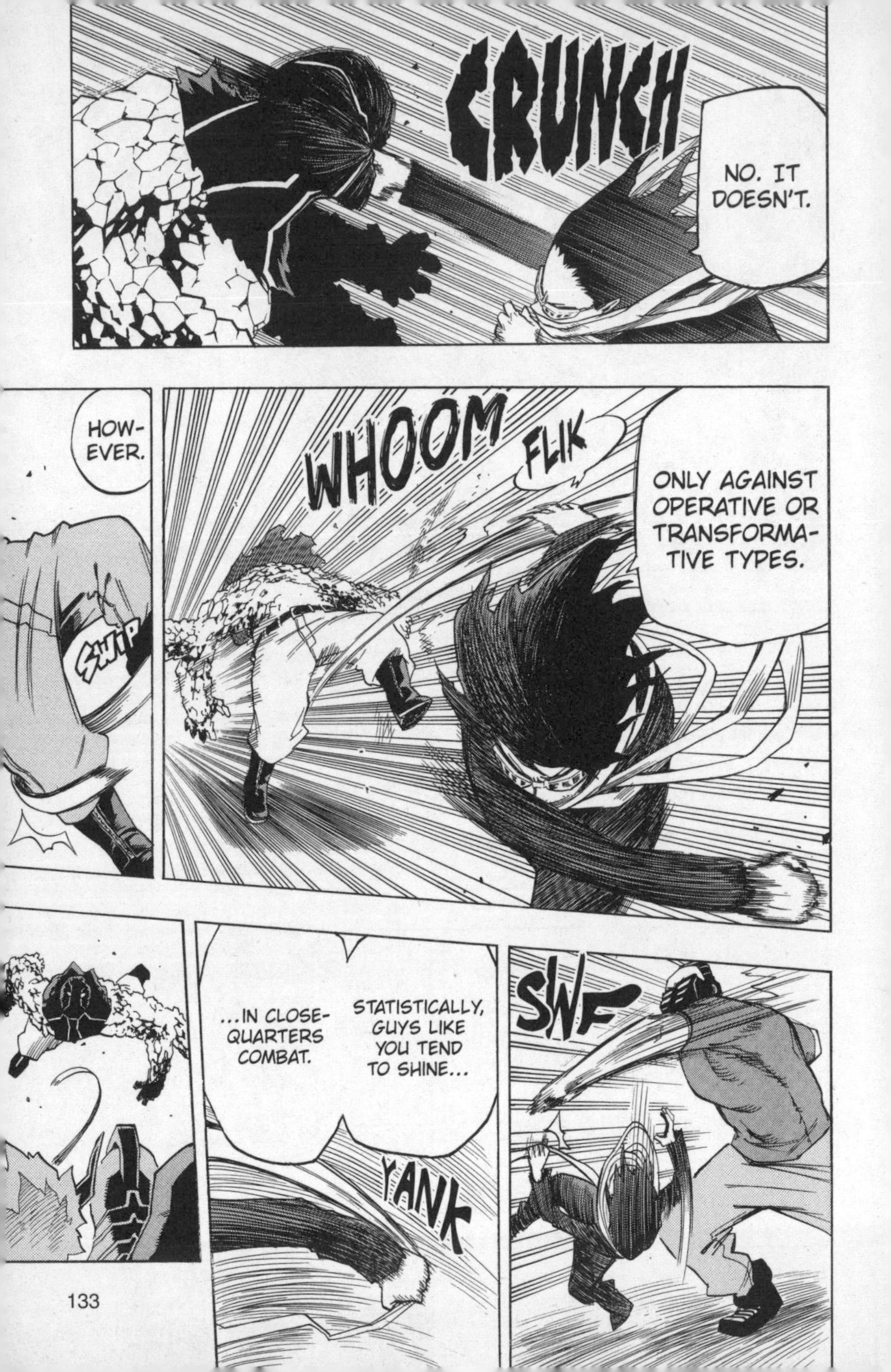
CRUNCH
NO. IT DOESN'T.
ONLY AGAINST OPERATIVE OR TRANSFORMATIVE TYPES.
FLIK
WHOOM
HOW-EVER.
SWIP
SWF
STATISTICALLY, GUYS LIKE YOU TEND TO SHINE...
...IN CLOSE-QUARTERS COMBAT.
YANK

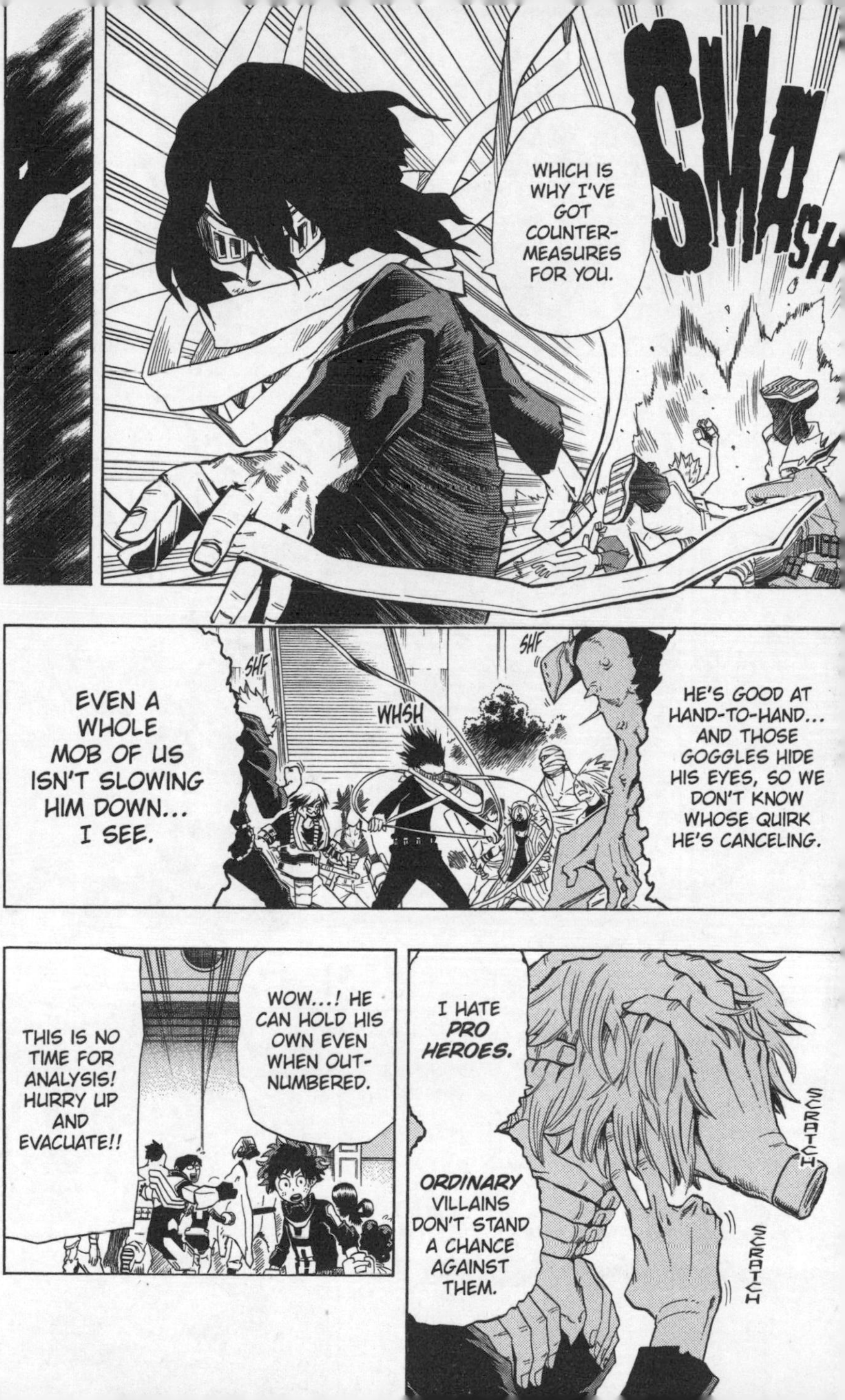
SMASH
WHICH IS WHY I'VE GOT COUNTER-MEASURES FOR YOU.
HE'S GOOD AT HAND-TO-HAND... AND THOSE GOGGLES HIDE HIS EYES, SO WE DON'T KNOW WHOSE QUIRK HE'S CANCELING.
SHF
WHSH
SHF
EVEN A WHOLE MOB OF US ISN'T SLOWING HIM DOWN... I SEE.
I HATE ***PRO HEROES.***
SCRATCH
SCRATCH
ORDINARY VILLAINS DON'T STAND A CHANCE AGAINST THEM.
WOW...! HE CAN HOLD HIS OWN EVEN WHEN OUT-NUMBERED.
THIS IS NO TIME FOR ANALYSIS! HURRY UP AND EVACUATE!!

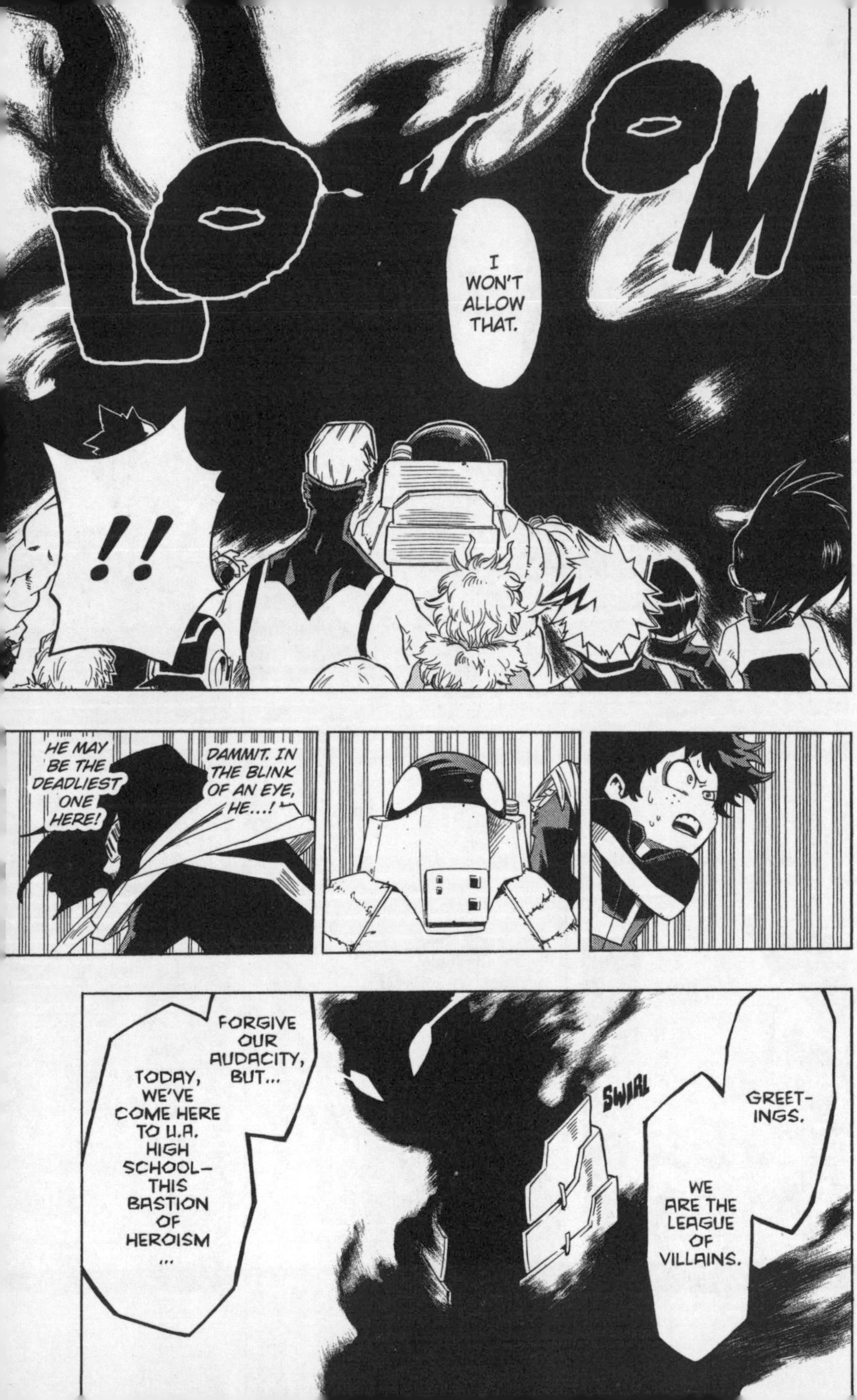

LOOM
I WON'T ALLOW THAT.
!!
DAMMIT. IN THE BLINK OF AN EYE, HE...!
HE MAY BE THE DEADLIEST ONE HERE!
GREET-INGS.
WE ARE THE LEAGUE OF VILLAINS.
SWIRL
FORGIVE OUR AUDACITY, BUT...
TODAY, WE'VE COME HERE TO U.A. HIGH SCHOOL—THIS BASTION OF HEROISM ...

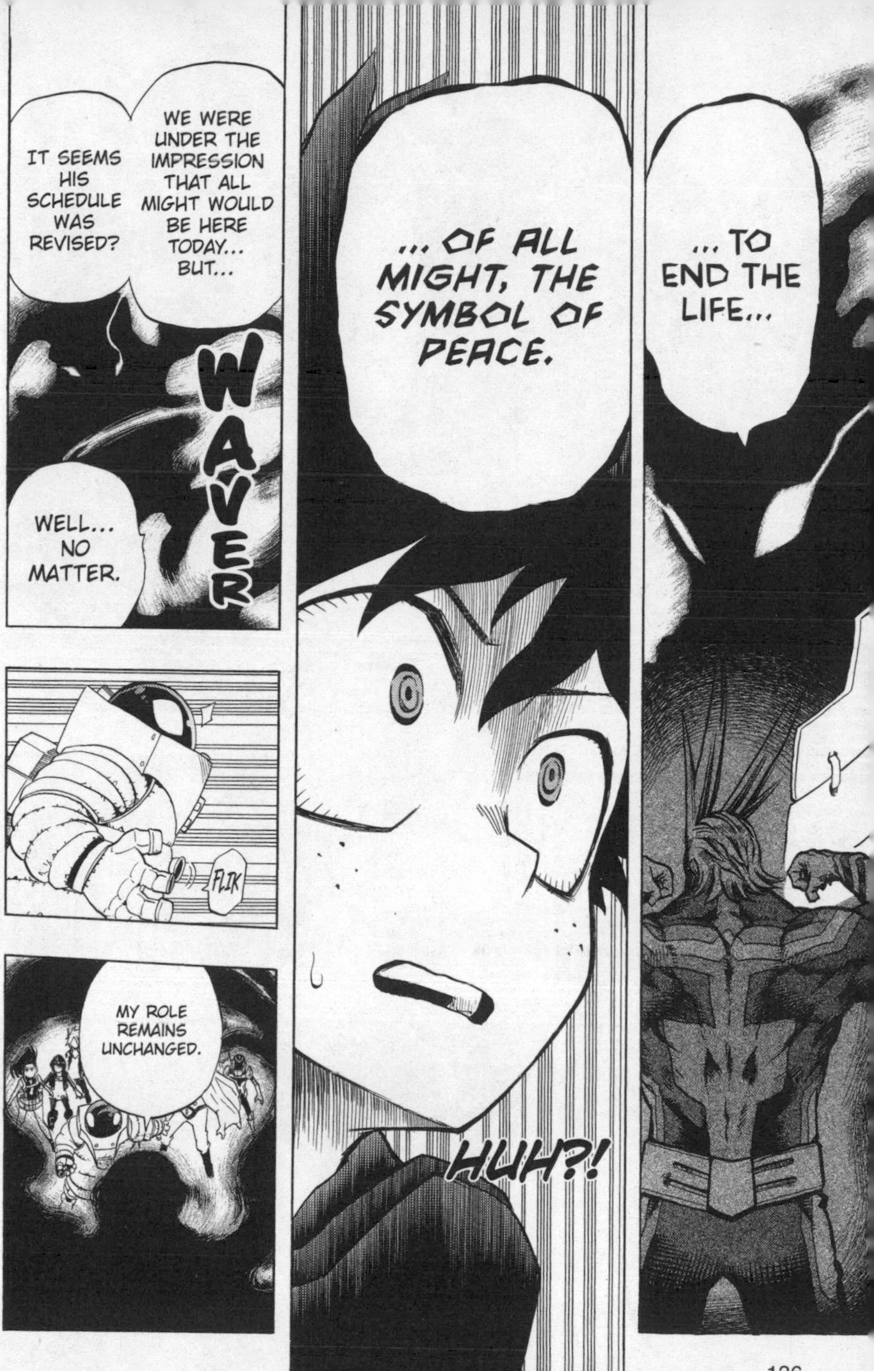
... TO END THE LIFE...
... OF ALL MIGHT, THE SYMBOL OF PEACE.
HUH?!
WE WERE UNDER THE IMPRESSION THAT ALL MIGHT WOULD BE HERE TODAY... BUT...
IT SEEMS HIS SCHEDULE WAS REVISED?
WAVER
WELL... NO MATTER.
FLIK
MY ROLE REMAINS UNCHANGED.

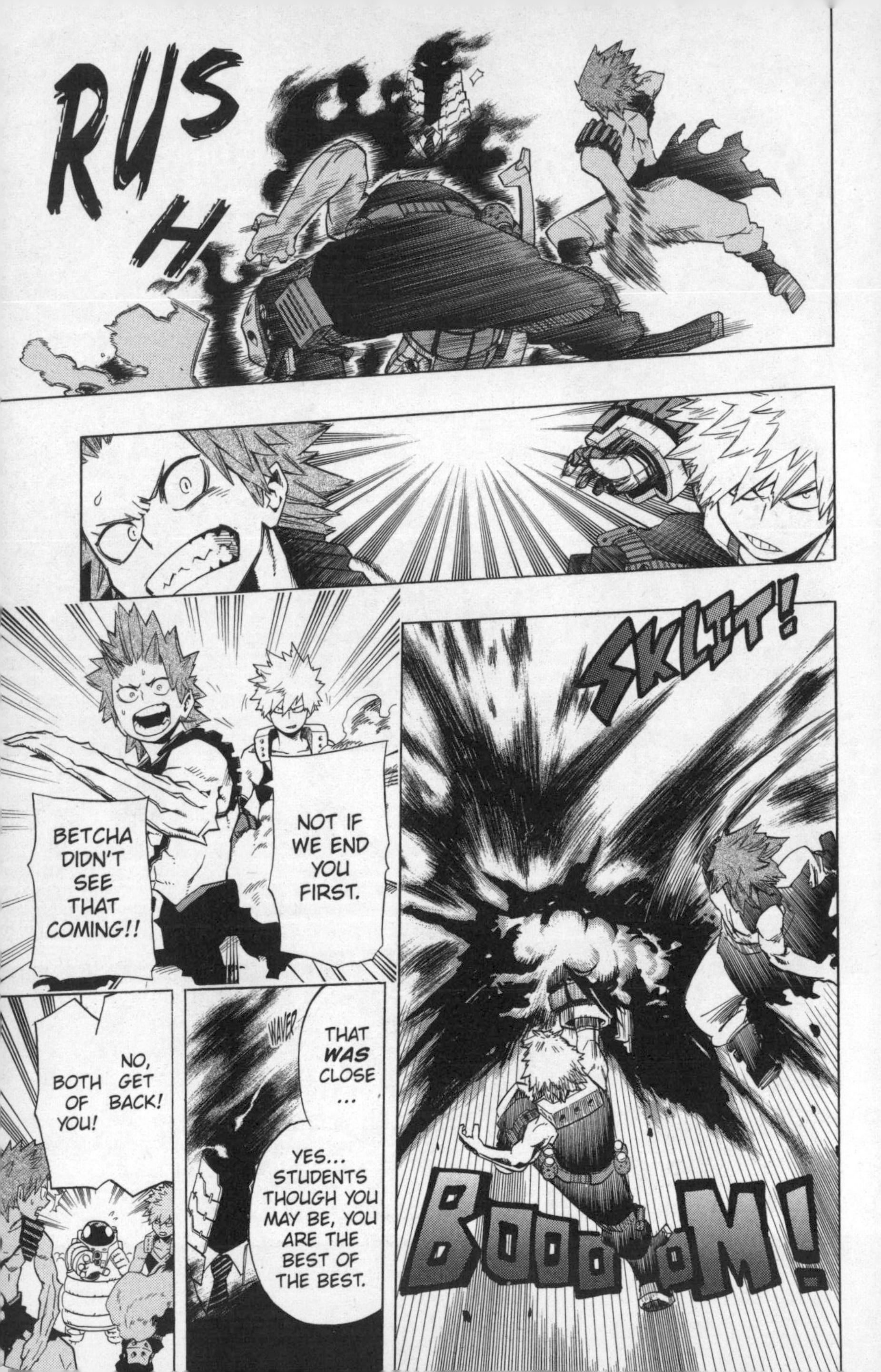
RUSH
SKLIT!
BOOOOM!
NOT IF WE END YOU FIRST.
BETCHA DIDN'T SEE THAT COMING!!
WAVER
THAT WAS CLOSE ...
YES... STUDENTS THOUGH YOU MAY BE, YOU ARE THE BEST OF THE BEST.
NO, GET BACK! BOTH OF YOU!

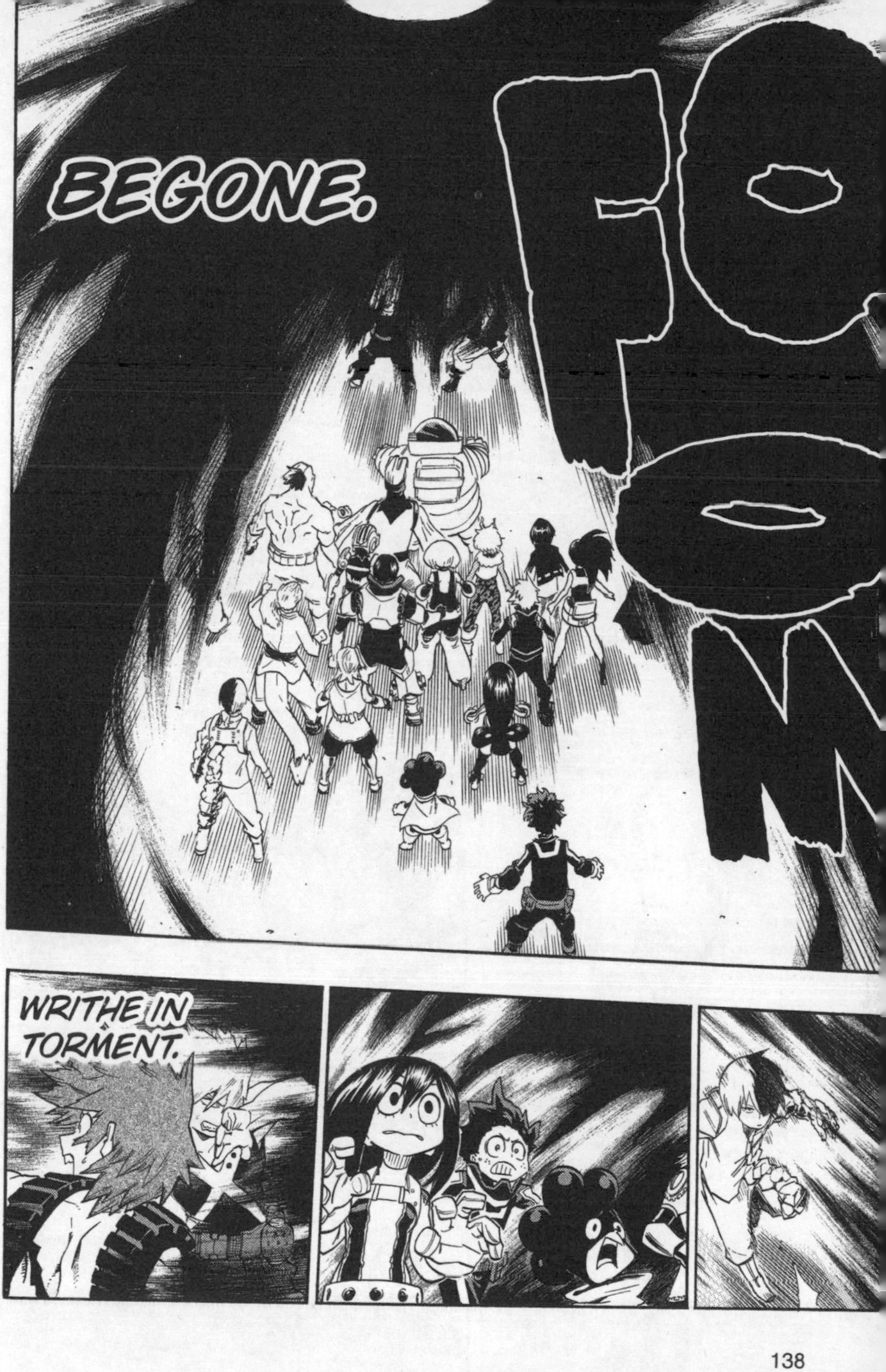
BEGONE.
FOOM
WRITHE IN TORMENT.

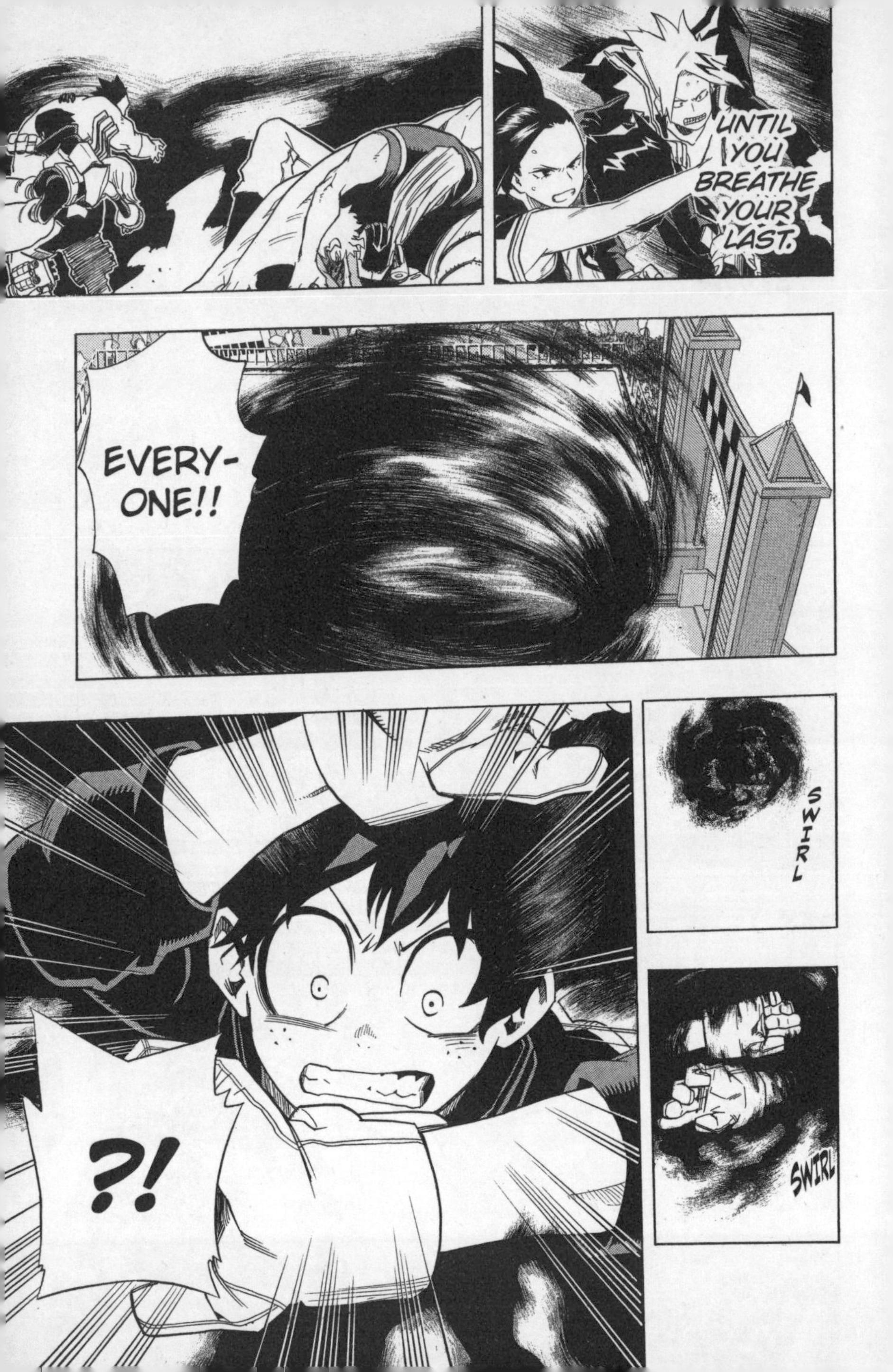
UNTIL YOU BREATHE YOUR LAST.
EVERY-ONE!!
SWIRL
SWIRL
?!

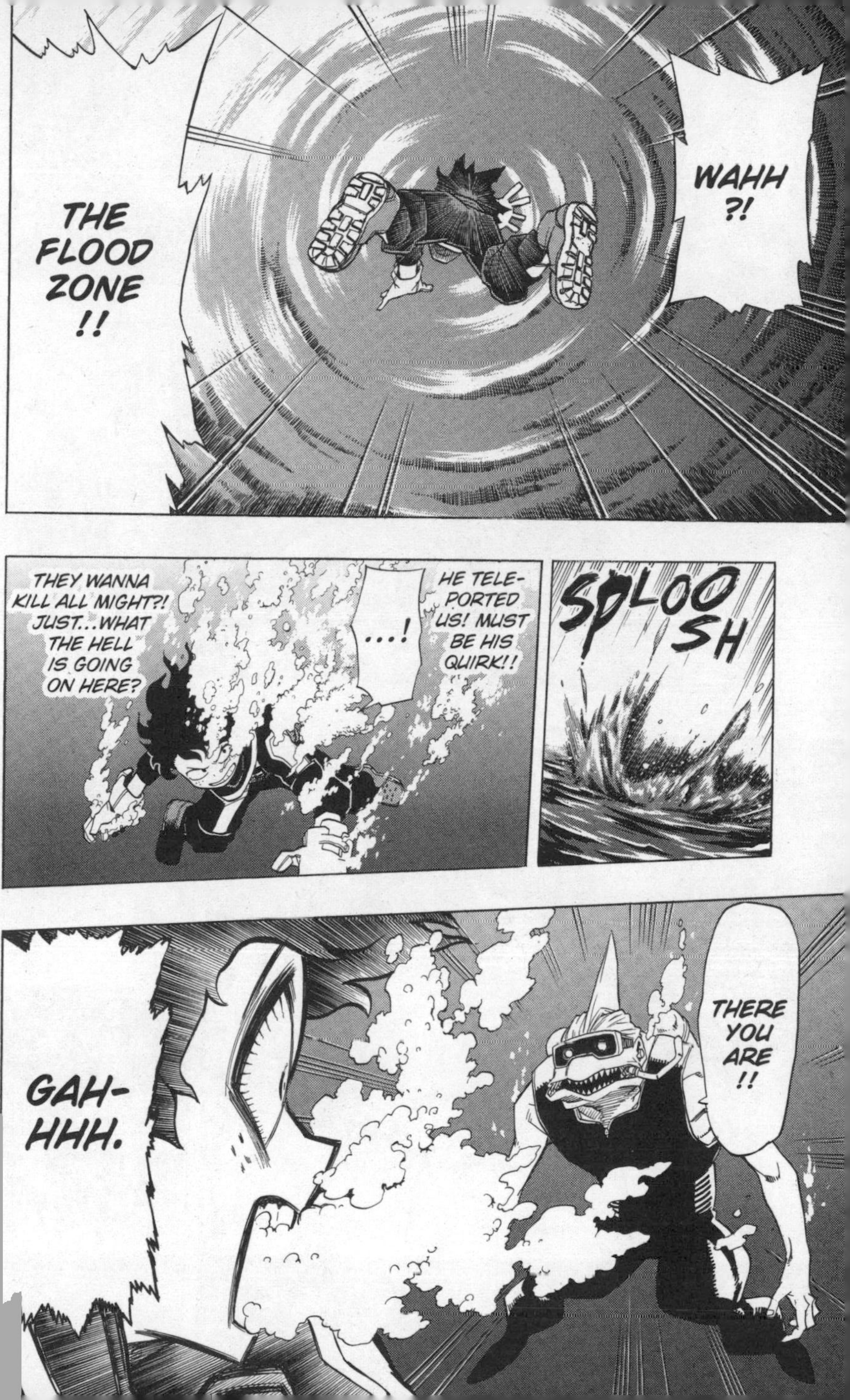
WAHH ?!
THE FLOOD ZONE !!
SPLOOSH
HE TELE-PORTED US! MUST BE HIS QUIRK!!
...!
THEY WANNA KILL ALL MIGHT?! JUST...WHAT THE HELL IS GOING ON HERE?
THERE YOU ARE !!
GAH-HHH.

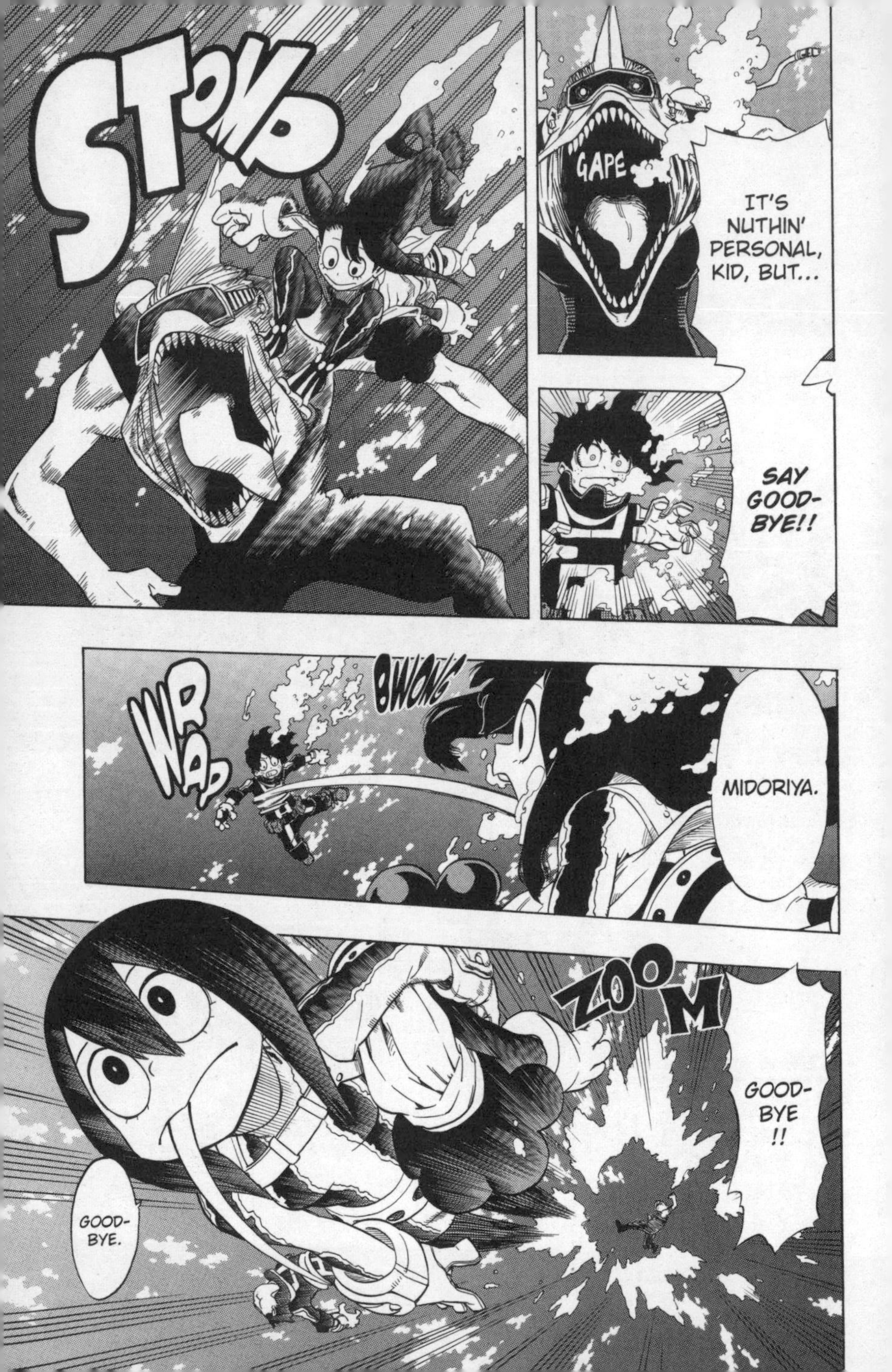
GAPE
IT'S NUTHIN' PERSONAL, KID, BUT...
SAY GOOD-BYE!!
STOMP
MIDORIYA.
BWONG
WRAP
GOOD-BYE !!
ZOOM
GOOD-BYE.

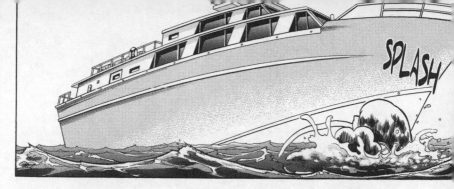

SPLASH

FOR A FROG, SHE'S GOT...

...PRETTY NICE BOOBS... TCH.

SPLAT

BUT WE SEEM TO BE IN TROUBLE, HERE.

CALL ME TSUYU.

THANKS, ASUI...

GAH!!

PCH PCH PCH

SLAM!!

TSUYU ASUI.
QUIRK: FROG.
CAN DO
WHATEVER A
FROG CAN—
OF COURSE!!

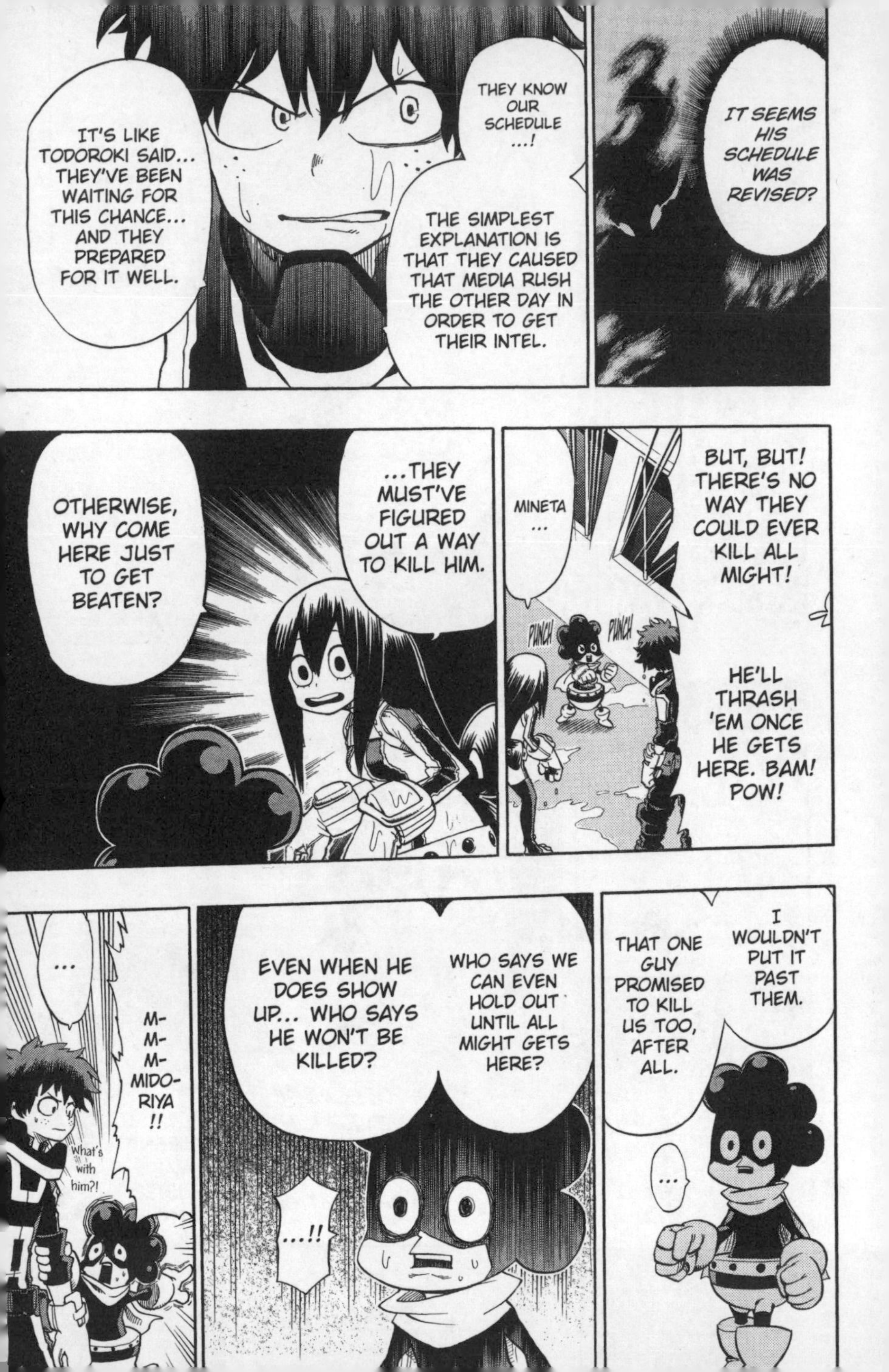
IT SEEMS HIS SCHEDULE WAS REVISED?
THEY KNOW OUR SCHEDULE ...!
THE SIMPLEST EXPLANATION IS THAT THEY CAUSED THAT MEDIA RUSH THE OTHER DAY IN ORDER TO GET THEIR INTEL.
IT'S LIKE TODOROKI SAID... THEY'VE BEEN WAITING FOR THIS CHANCE... AND THEY PREPARED FOR IT WELL.
BUT, BUT! THERE'S NO WAY THEY COULD EVER KILL ALL MIGHT!
MINETA ...
PUNCH
PUNCH
HE'LL THRASH 'EM ONCE HE GETS HERE. BAM! POW!
...THEY MUST'VE FIGURED OUT A WAY TO KILL HIM.
OTHERWISE, WHY COME HERE JUST TO GET BEATEN?
I WOULDN'T PUT IT PAST THEM.
THAT ONE GUY PROMISED TO KILL US TOO, AFTER ALL.
...
WHO SAYS WE CAN EVEN HOLD OUT UNTIL ALL MIGHT GETS HERE?
EVEN WHEN HE DOES SHOW UP... WHO SAYS HE WON'T BE KILLED?
...!!
...
M-M-M-MIDORIYA !!
What's with him?!

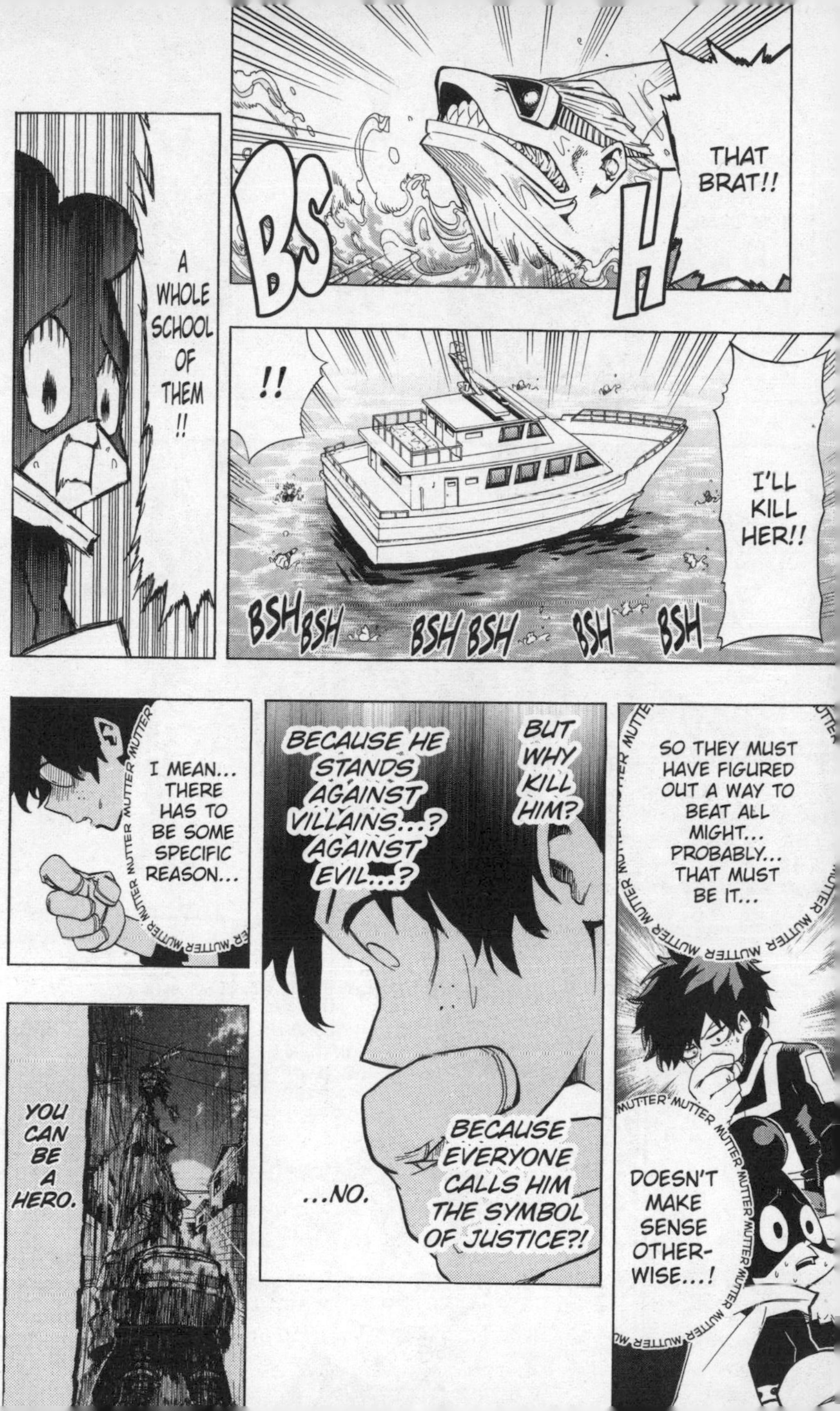

THAT BRAT!!
BSSH
!!
I'LL KILL HER!!
BSH BSH BSH BSH BSH BSH
A WHOLE SCHOOL OF THEM!!
MUTTER MUTTER MUTTER MUTTER
SO THEY MUST HAVE FIGURED OUT A WAY TO BEAT ALL MIGHT... PROBABLY... THAT MUST BE IT...
DOESN'T MAKE SENSE OTHER-WISE...!
MUTTER MUTTER MUTTER MUTTER MUTTER
BUT WHY KILL HIM?
BECAUSE HE STANDS AGAINST VILLAINS...? AGAINST EVIL...?
...NO.
BECAUSE EVERYONE CALLS HIM THE SYMBOL OF JUSTICE?!
I MEAN... THERE HAS TO BE SOME SPECIFIC REASON...
MUTTER MUTTER MUTTER MUTTER
YOU CAN BE A HERO.

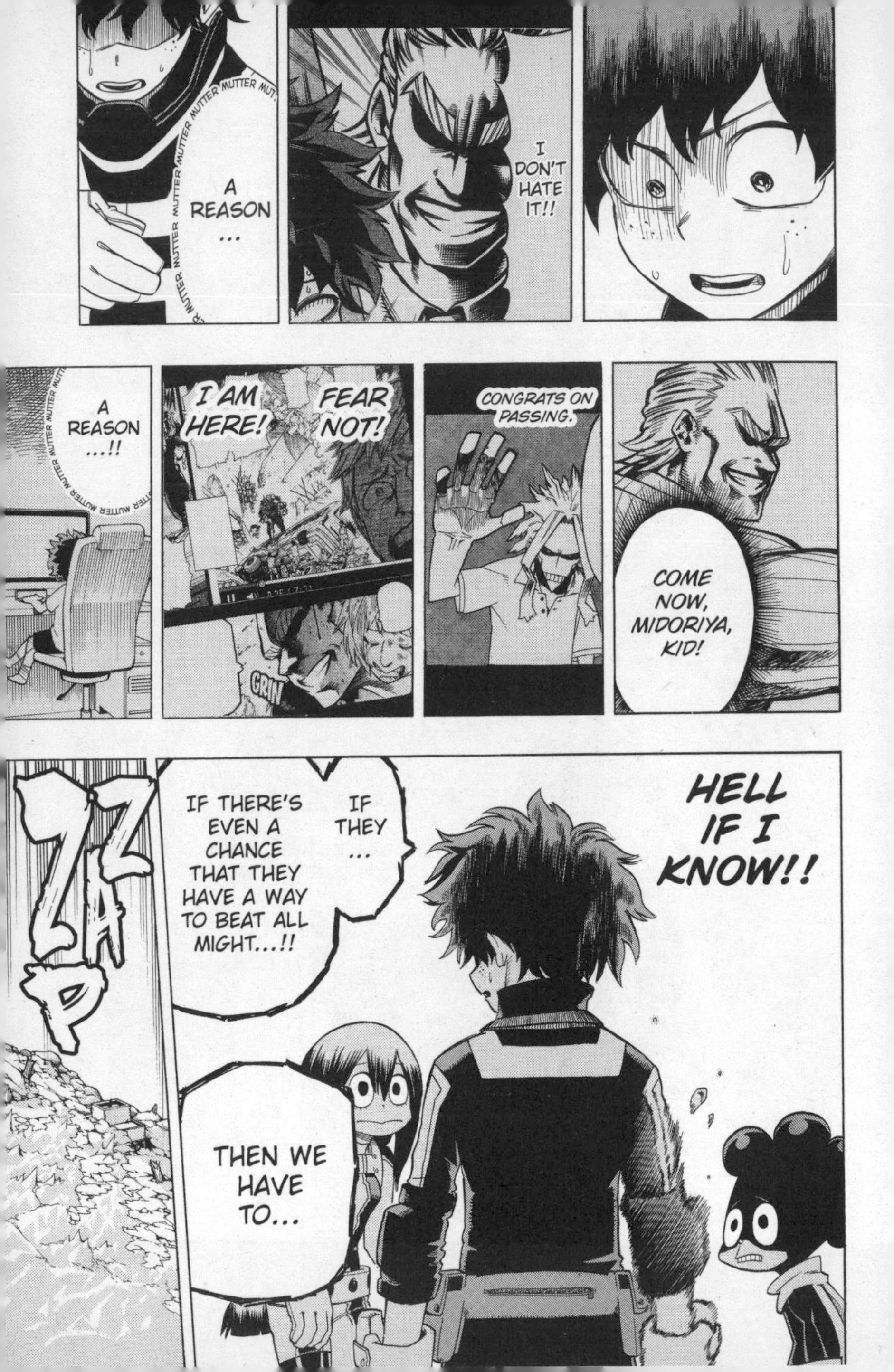
I DON'T HATE IT!!
A REASON ...
MUTTER MUTTER MUTTER
COME NOW, MIDORIYA, KID!
CONGRATS ON PASSING.
FEAR NOT!
I AM HERE!
GRIN
A REASON ...!!
MUTTER MUTTER MUTTER
HELL IF I KNOW!!
IF THEY ...
IF THERE'S EVEN A CHANCE THAT THEY HAVE A WAY TO BEAT ALL MIGHT...!!
THEN WE HAVE TO...
ZZAP

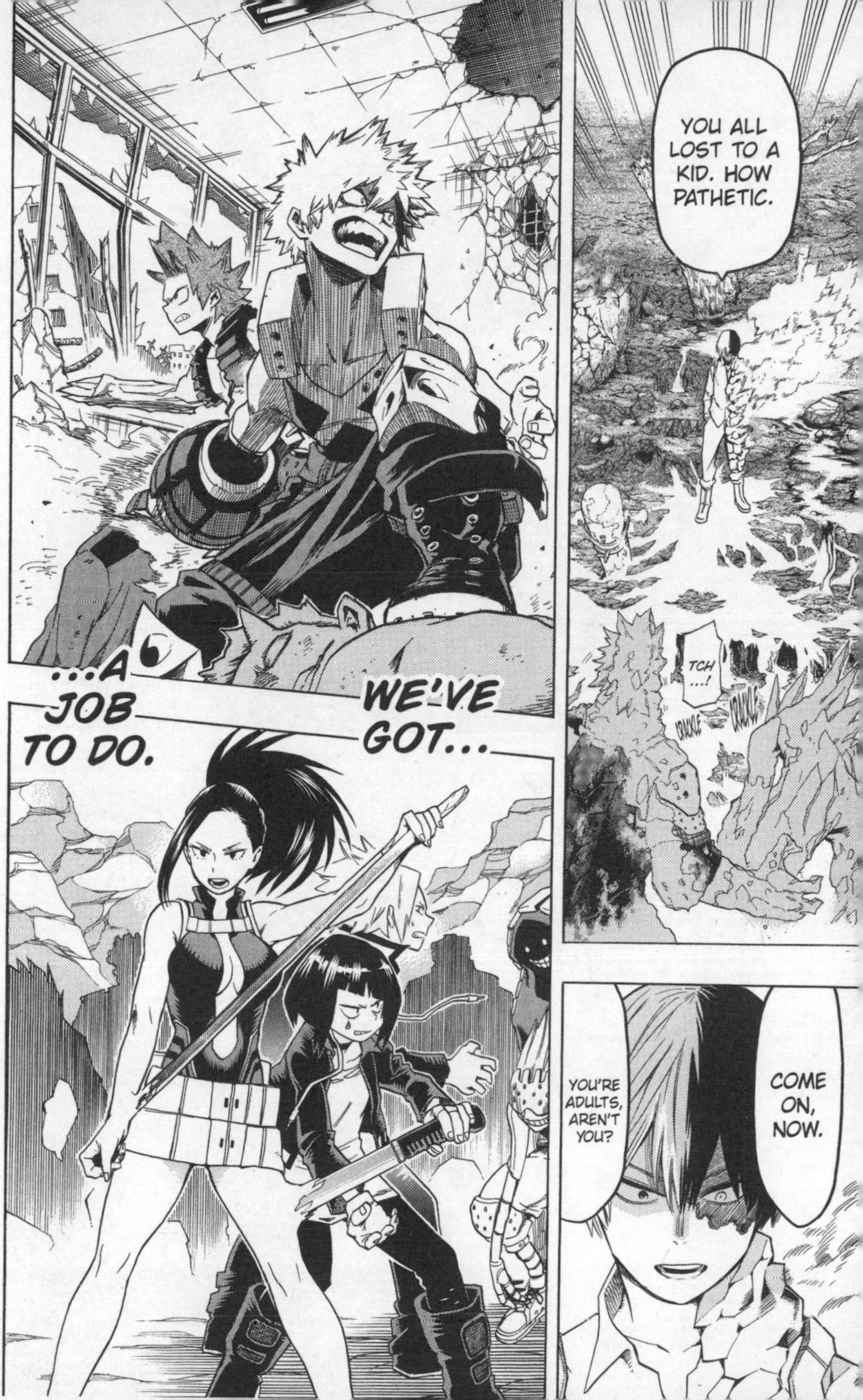
YOU ALL LOST TO A KID. HOW PATHETIC.
TCH ...!
CRACKLE
CRACKLE
COME ON, NOW.
YOU'RE ADULTS, AREN'T YOU?
WE'VE GOT...
...A JOB TO DO.

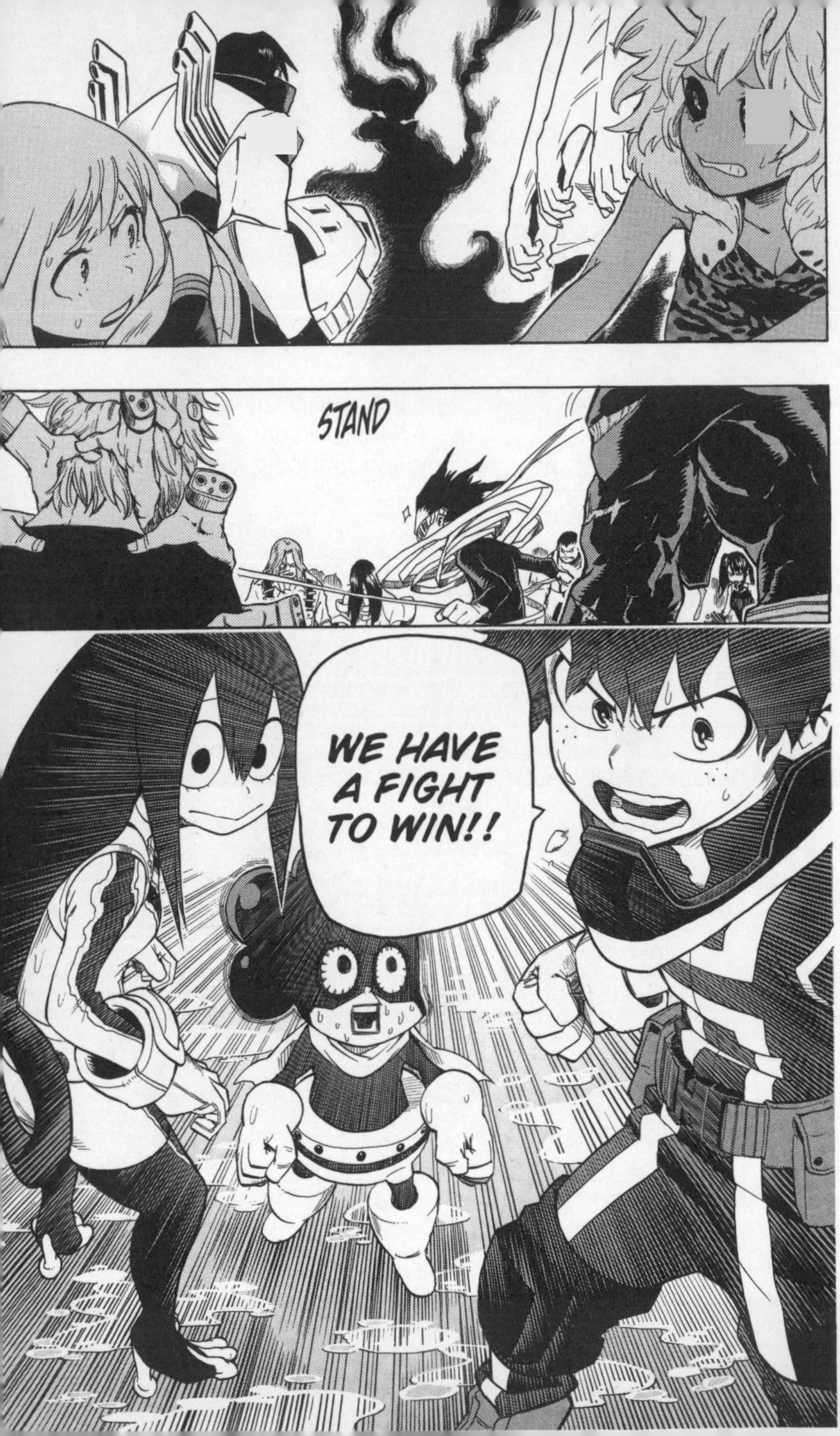
STAND
WE HAVE A FIGHT TO WIN!!

TSUYU ASUI (15)

WINTER CLOTHES

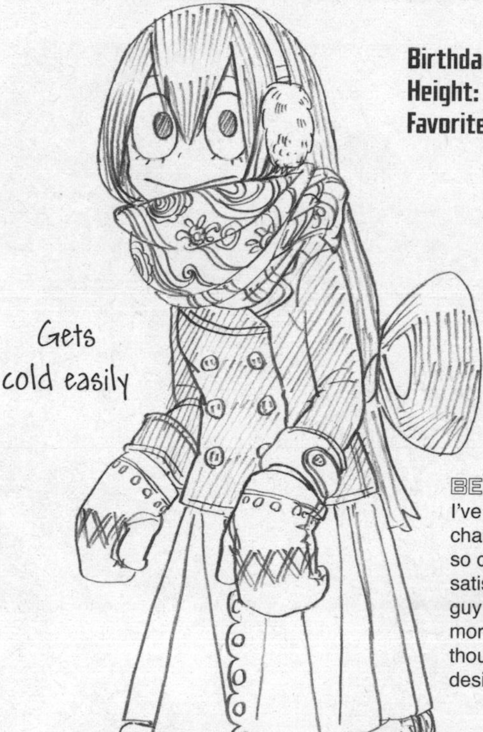
Gets
cold easily

Birthday: 2/12
Height: 150 cm
Favorite Things: Rain, jello

BEHIND THE SCENES

I've wanted to include a froggy character for quite a while now, so creating Tsuyu was really satisfying. She was meant to be a guy at first, but the class needed more girls. I'm glad she swapped, though, and I really like her design, overall.

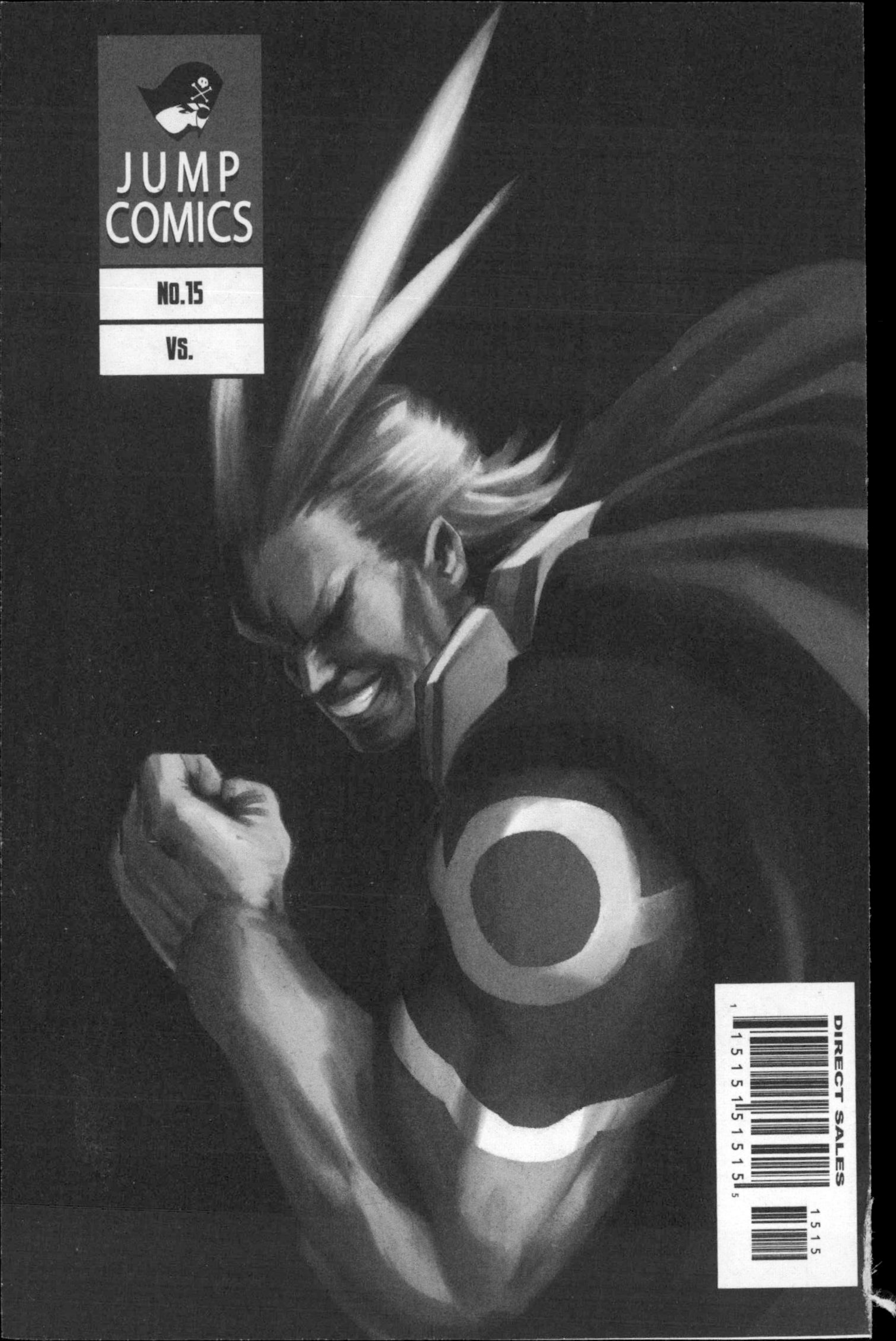
JUMP
COMICS
NO.15
VS.
DIRECT SALES

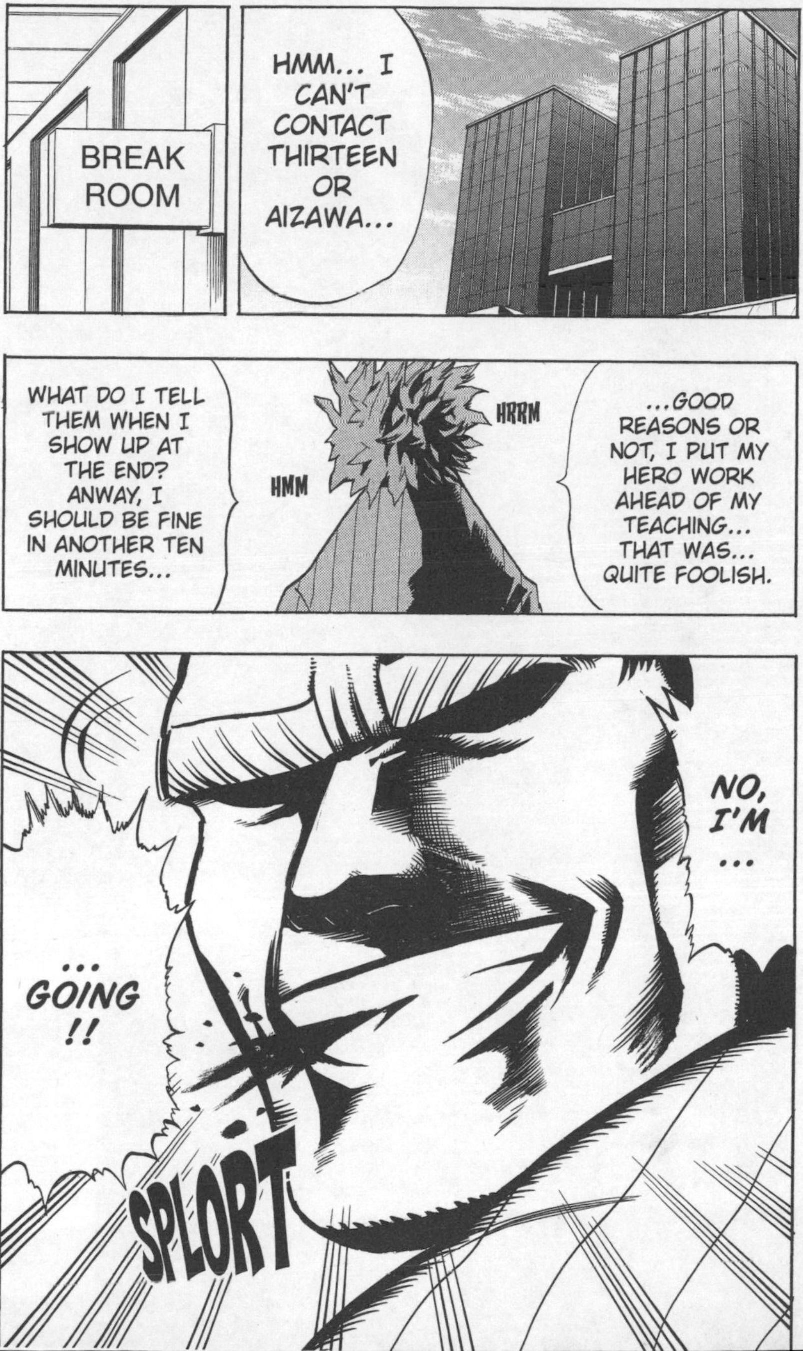
HMM... I CAN'T CONTACT THIRTEEN OR AIZAWA...
BREAK ROOM
...GOOD REASONS OR NOT, I PUT MY HERO WORK AHEAD OF MY TEACHING... THAT WAS... QUITE FOOLISH.
HRRM
HMM
WHAT DO I TELL THEM WHEN I SHOW UP AT THE END? ANWAY, I SHOULD BE FINE IN ANOTHER TEN MINUTES...
NO, I'M ...
... GOING !!
SPLORT

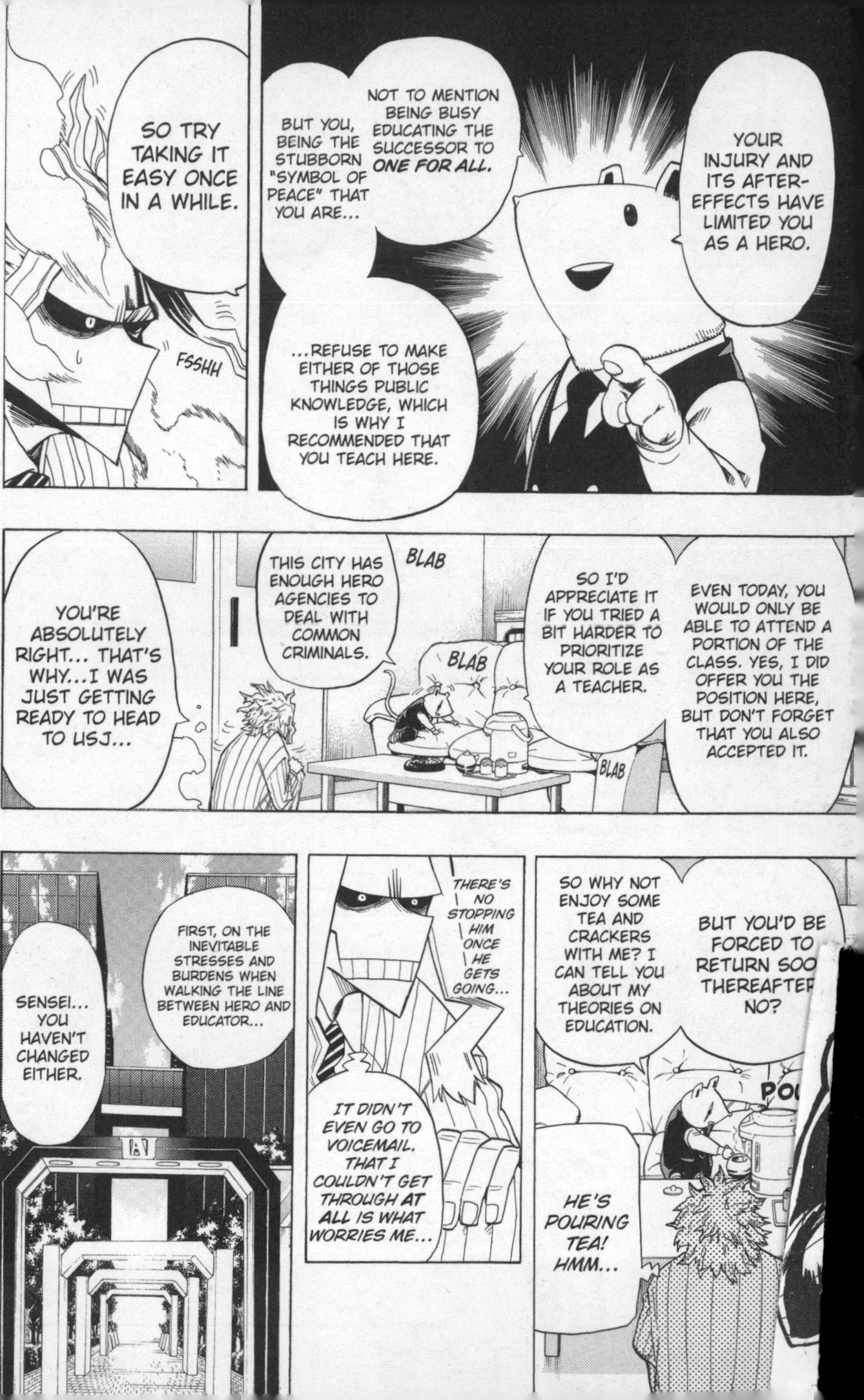
YOUR INJURY AND ITS AFTER-EFFECTS HAVE LIMITED YOU AS A HERO.
NOT TO MENTION BEING BUSY EDUCATING THE SUCCESSOR TO ONE FOR ALL.
BUT YOU, BEING THE STUBBORN "SYMBOL OF PEACE" THAT YOU ARE...
...REFUSE TO MAKE EITHER OF THOSE THINGS PUBLIC KNOWLEDGE, WHICH IS WHY I RECOMMENDED THAT YOU TEACH HERE.
SO TRY TAKING IT EASY ONCE IN A WHILE.
FSSHH
EVEN TODAY, YOU WOULD ONLY BE ABLE TO ATTEND A PORTION OF THE CLASS. YES, I DID OFFER YOU THE POSITION HERE, BUT DON'T FORGET THAT YOU ALSO ACCEPTED IT.
SO I'D APPRECIATE IT IF YOU TRIED A BIT HARDER TO PRIORITIZE YOUR ROLE AS A TEACHER.
BLAB
BLAB
THIS CITY HAS ENOUGH HERO AGENCIES TO DEAL WITH COMMON CRIMINALS.
BLAB
YOU'RE ABSOLUTELY RIGHT... THAT'S WHY...I WAS JUST GETTING READY TO HEAD TO USJ...
BUT YOU'D BE FORCED TO RETURN SOO THEREAFTE NO?
SO WHY NOT ENJOY SOME TEA AND CRACKERS WITH ME? I CAN TELL YOU ABOUT MY THEORIES ON EDUCATION.
POU
HE'S POURING TEA! HMM...
THERE'S NO STOPPING HIM ONCE HE GETS GOING...
IT DIDN'T EVEN GO TO VOICEMAIL. THAT I COULDN'T GET THROUGH AT ALL IS WHAT WORRIES ME...
FIRST, ON THE INEVITABLE STRESSES AND BURDENS WHEN WALKING THE LINE BETWEEN HERO AND EDUCATOR...
SENSEI... YOU HAVEN'T CHANGED EITHER.

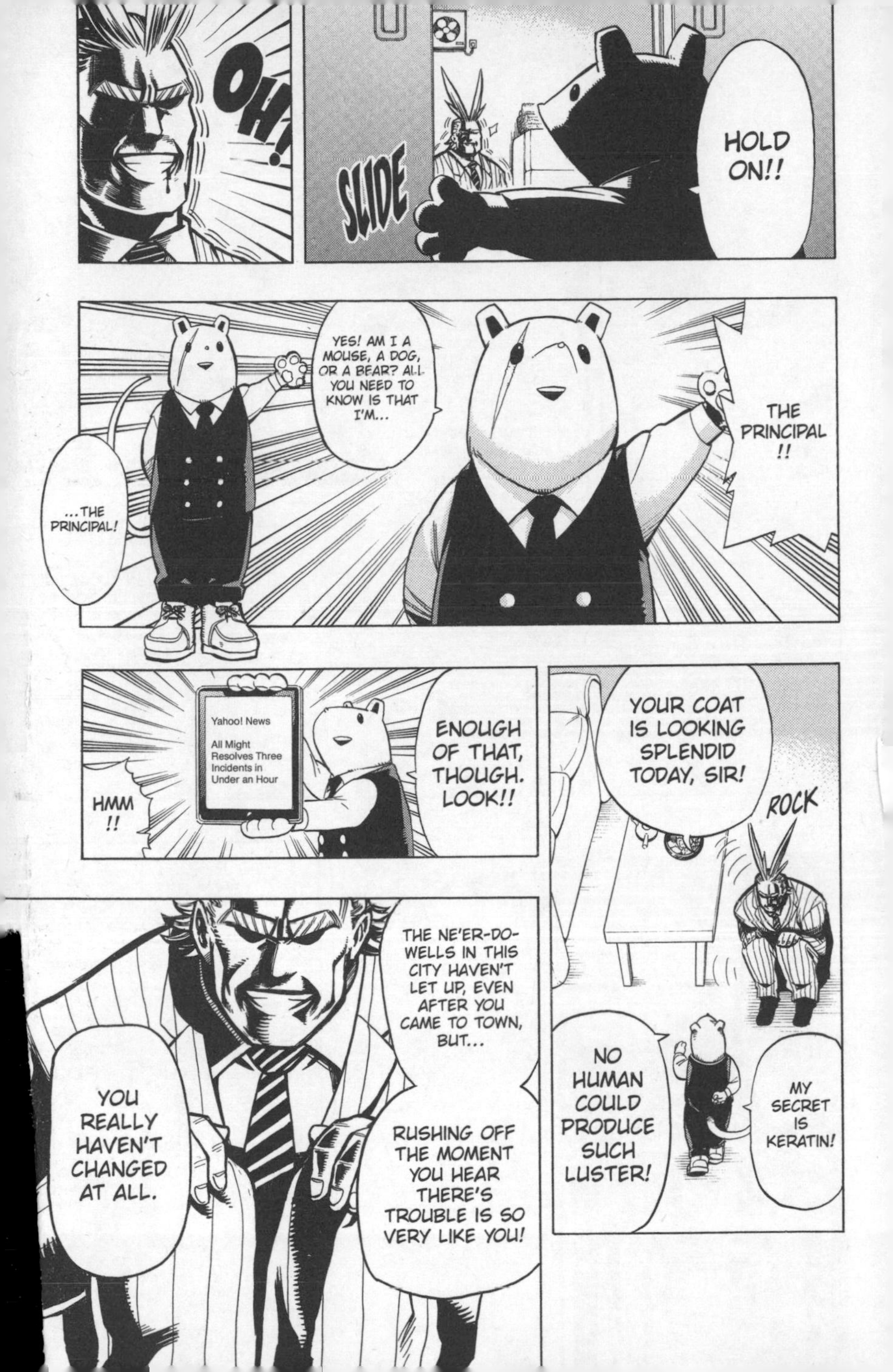
HOLD ON!!
SLIDE
OH!
YES! AM I A MOUSE, A DOG, OR A BEAR? ALL YOU NEED TO KNOW IS THAT I'M...
THE PRINCIPAL !!
...THE PRINCIPAL!
YOUR COAT IS LOOKING SPLENDID TODAY, SIR!
ROCK
NO HUMAN COULD PRODUCE SUCH LUSTER!
MY SECRET IS KERATIN!
ENOUGH OF THAT, THOUGH. LOOK!!
Yahoo! News
All Might Resolves Three Incidents in Under an Hour
HMM !!
THE NE'ER-DO-WELLS IN THIS CITY HAVEN'T LET UP, EVEN AFTER YOU CAME TO TOWN, BUT...
RUSHING OFF THE MOMENT YOU HEAR THERE'S TROUBLE IS SO VERY LIKE YOU!
YOU REALLY HAVEN'T CHANGED AT ALL.

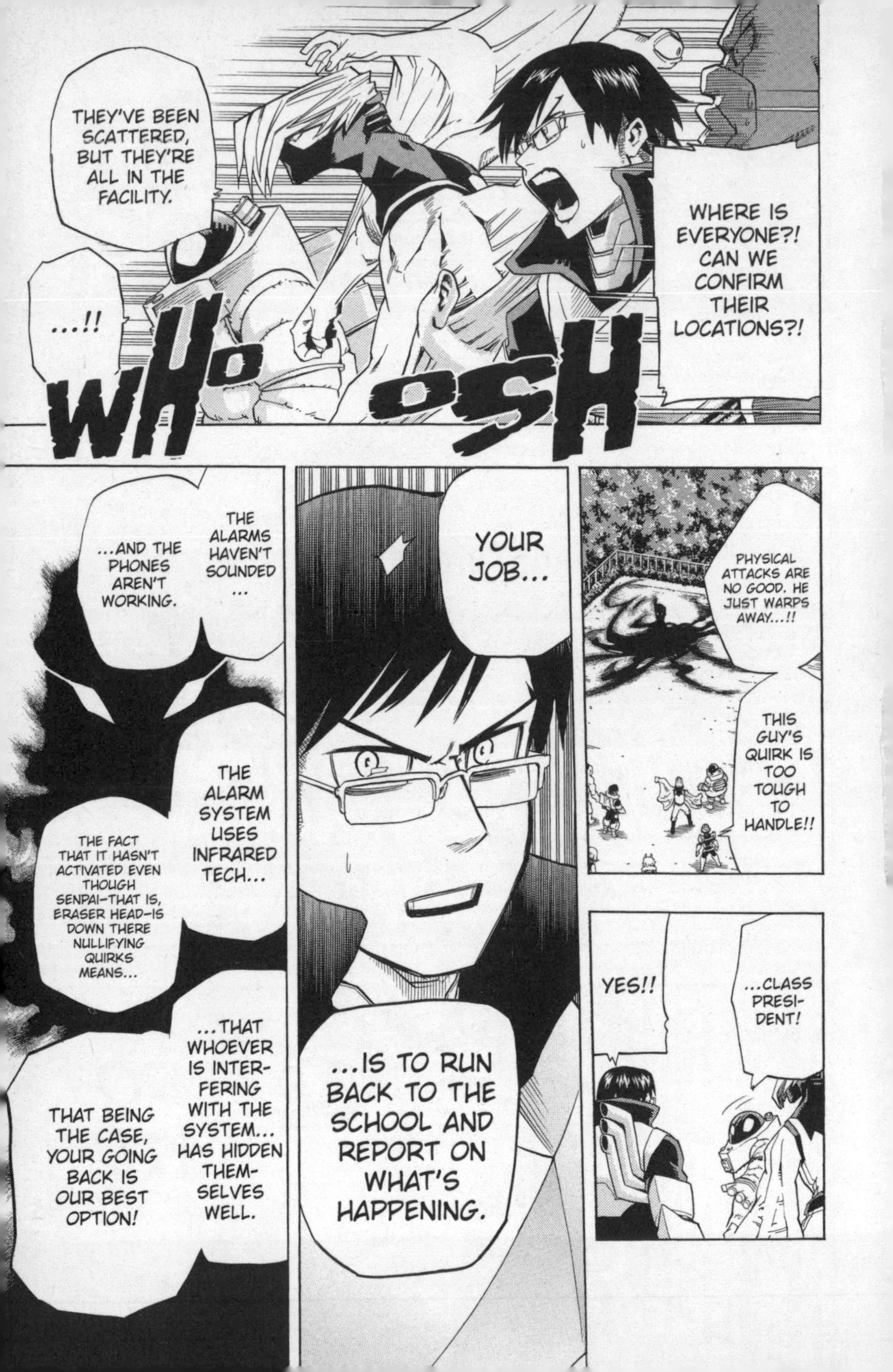
WHERE IS EVERYONE?! CAN WE CONFIRM THEIR LOCATIONS?!
THEY'VE BEEN SCATTERED, BUT THEY'RE ALL IN THE FACILITY.
...!!
WHOOSH
PHYSICAL ATTACKS ARE NO GOOD. HE JUST WARPS AWAY...!!
THIS GUY'S QUIRK IS TOO TOUGH TO HANDLE!!
...CLASS PRESI-DENT!
YES!!
YOUR JOB...
...IS TO RUN BACK TO THE SCHOOL AND REPORT ON WHAT'S HAPPENING.
THE ALARMS HAVEN'T SOUNDED ...
...AND THE PHONES AREN'T WORKING.
THE ALARM SYSTEM USES INFRARED TECH...
THE FACT THAT IT HASN'T ACTIVATED EVEN THOUGH SENPAI–THAT IS, ERASER HEAD–IS DOWN THERE NULLIFYING QUIRKS MEANS...
...THAT WHOEVER IS INTER-FERING WITH THE SYSTEM... HAS HIDDEN THEM-SELVES WELL.
THAT BEING THE CASE, YOUR GOING BACK IS OUR BEST OPTION!

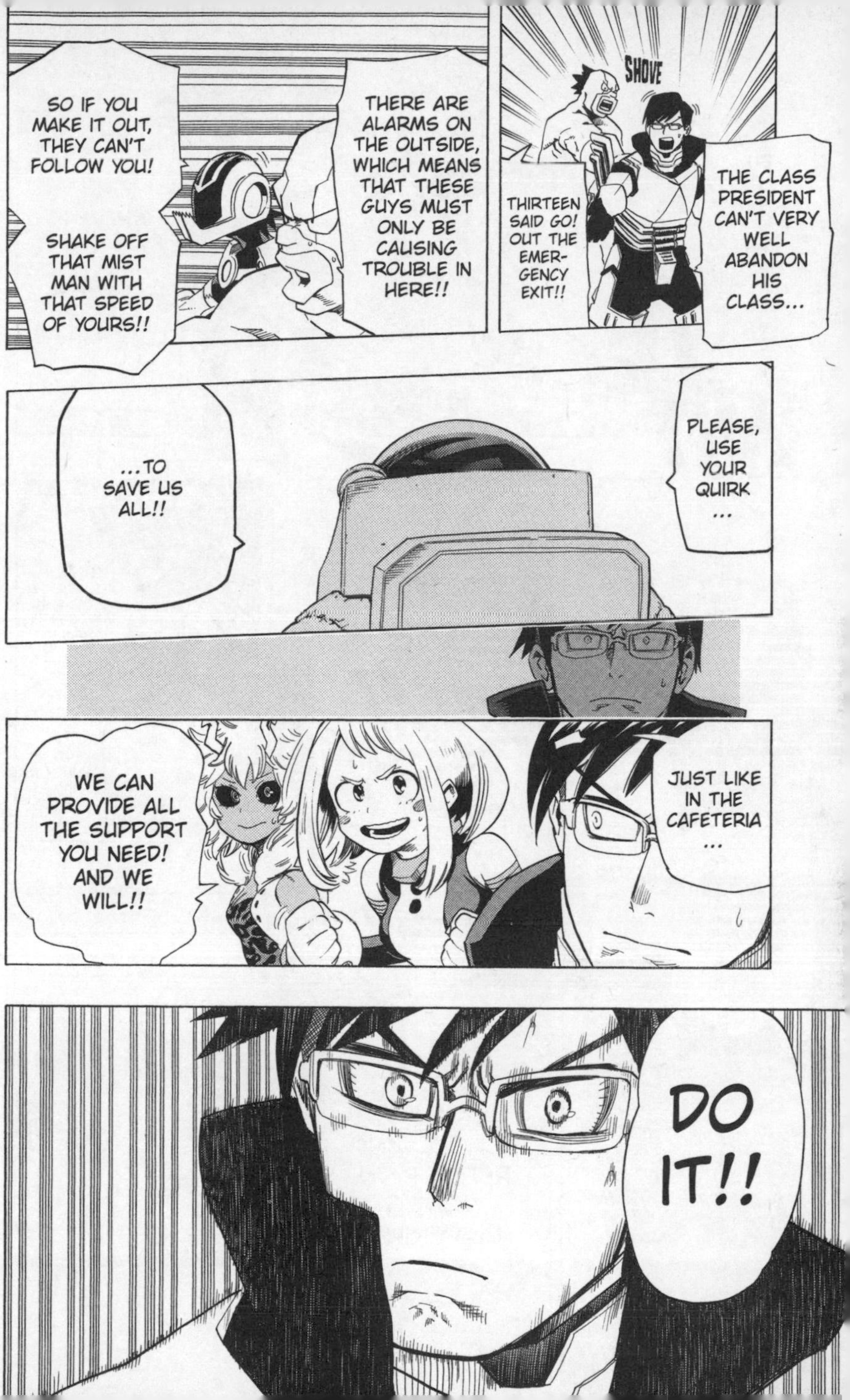
SHOVE
THIRTEEN SAID GO! OUT THE EMERGENCY EXIT!!
THE CLASS PRESIDENT CAN'T VERY WELL ABANDON HIS CLASS...
THERE ARE ALARMS ON THE OUTSIDE, WHICH MEANS THAT THESE GUYS MUST ONLY BE CAUSING TROUBLE IN HERE!!
SO IF YOU MAKE IT OUT, THEY CAN'T FOLLOW YOU!
SHAKE OFF THAT MIST MAN WITH THAT SPEED OF YOURS!!
PLEASE, USE YOUR QUIRK...
...TO SAVE US ALL!!
JUST LIKE IN THE CAFETERIA...
WE CAN PROVIDE ALL THE SUPPORT YOU NEED! AND WE WILL!!
DO IT!!

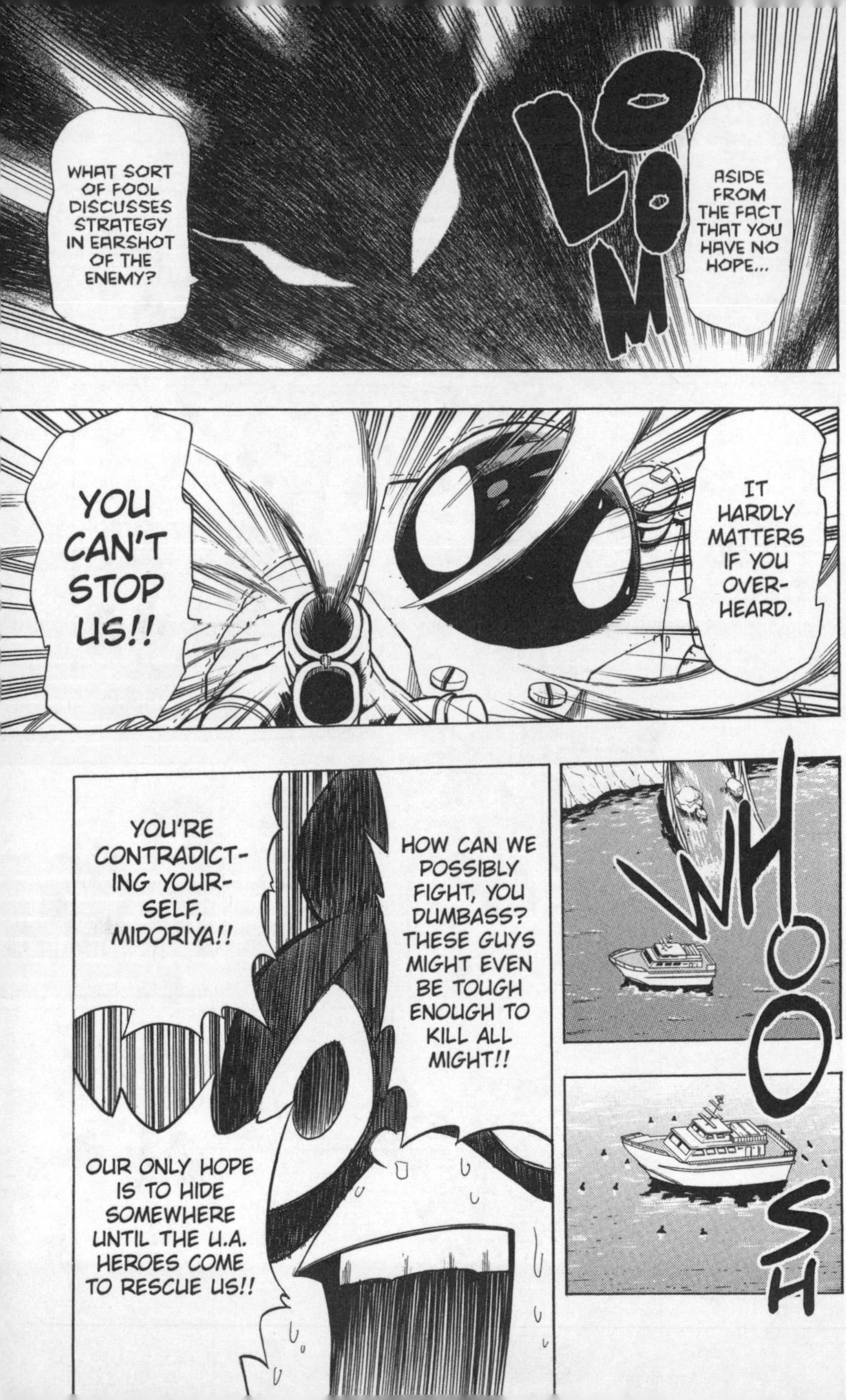

ASIDE FROM THE FACT THAT YOU HAVE NO HOPE...
LOOM
WHAT SORT OF FOOL DISCUSSES STRATEGY IN EARSHOT OF THE ENEMY?
IT HARDLY MATTERS IF YOU OVER-HEARD.
YOU CAN'T STOP US!!
WHOOSH
HOW CAN WE POSSIBLY FIGHT, YOU DUMBASS? THESE GUYS MIGHT EVEN BE TOUGH ENOUGH TO KILL ALL MIGHT!!
YOU'RE CONTRADICT-ING YOUR-SELF, MIDORIYA!!
OUR ONLY HOPE IS TO HIDE SOMEWHERE UNTIL THE U.A. HEROES COME TO RESCUE US!!

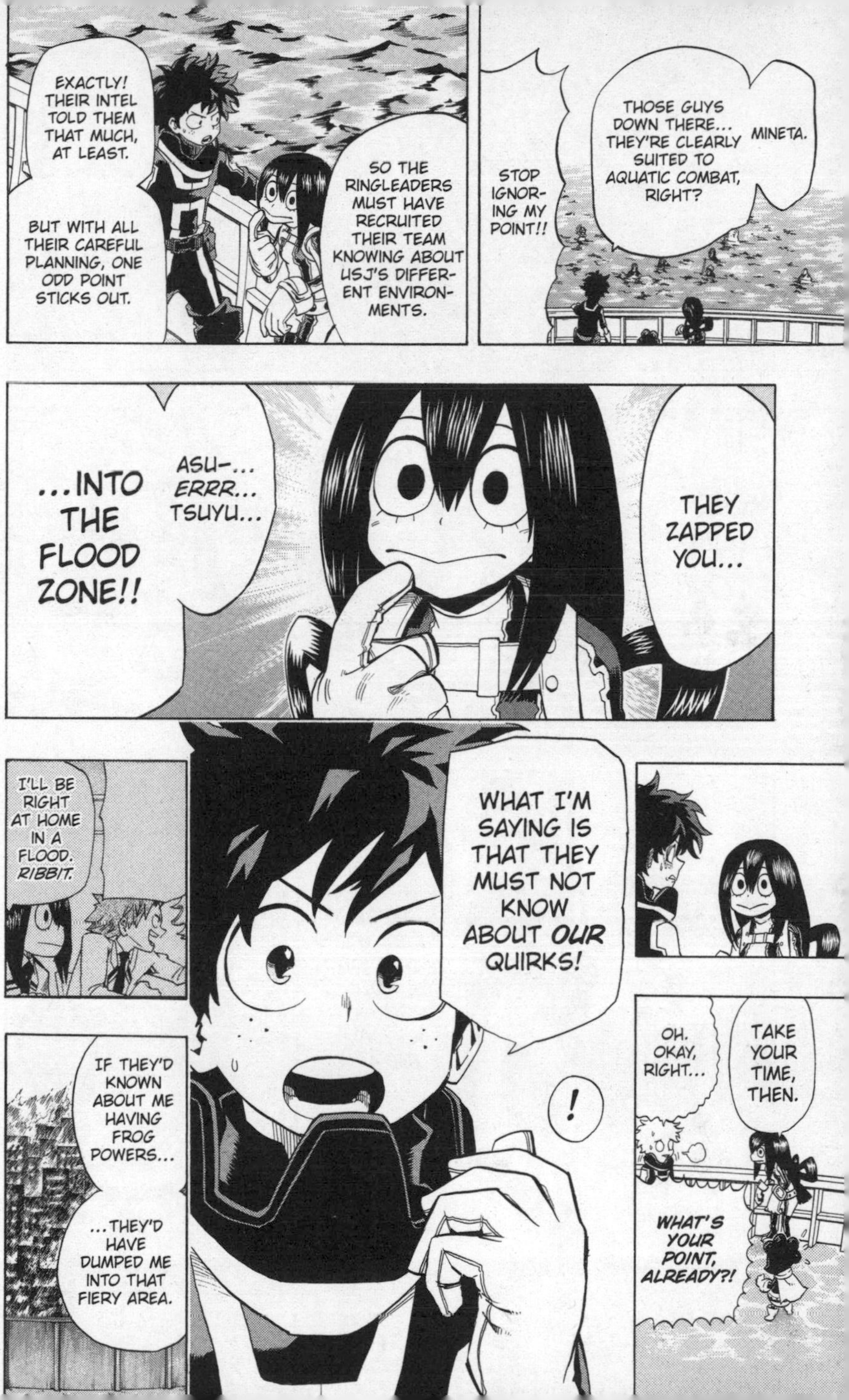
MINETA.
THOSE GUYS DOWN THERE... THEY'RE CLEARLY SUITED TO AQUATIC COMBAT, RIGHT?
STOP IGNORING MY POINT!!
SO THE RINGLEADERS MUST HAVE RECRUITED THEIR TEAM KNOWING ABOUT USJ'S DIFFERENT ENVIRONMENTS.
EXACTLY! THEIR INTEL TOLD THEM THAT MUCH, AT LEAST.
BUT WITH ALL THEIR CAREFUL PLANNING, ONE ODD POINT STICKS OUT.
THEY ZAPPED YOU...
ASU-... ERRR... TSUYU...
...INTO THE FLOOD ZONE!!
TAKE YOUR TIME, THEN.
OH. OKAY, RIGHT...
WHAT'S YOUR POINT, ALREADY?!
WHAT I'M SAYING IS THAT THEY MUST NOT KNOW ABOUT OUR QUIRKS!
!
I'LL BE RIGHT AT HOME IN A FLOOD. RIBBIT.
IF THEY'D KNOWN ABOUT ME HAVING FROG POWERS...
...THEY'D HAVE DUMPED ME INTO THAT FIERY AREA.

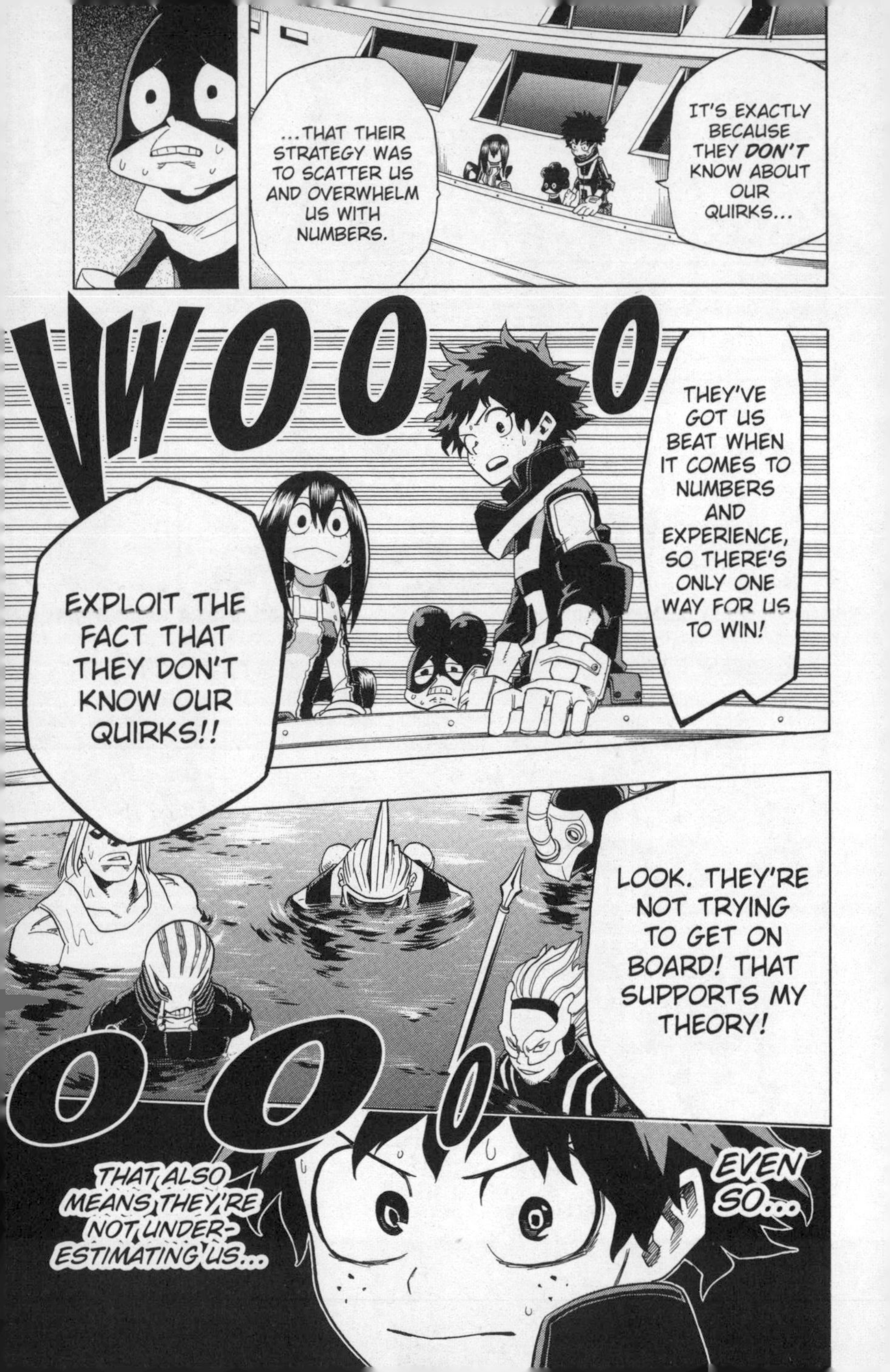
IT'S EXACTLY BECAUSE THEY DON'T KNOW ABOUT OUR QUIRKS...
...THAT THEIR STRATEGY WAS TO SCATTER US AND OVERWHELM US WITH NUMBERS.
VWOOO
THEY'VE GOT US BEAT WHEN IT COMES TO NUMBERS AND EXPERIENCE, SO THERE'S ONLY ONE WAY FOR US TO WIN!
EXPLOIT THE FACT THAT THEY DON'T KNOW OUR QUIRKS!!
LOOK. THEY'RE NOT TRYING TO GET ON BOARD! THAT SUPPORTS MY THEORY!
OOO
EVEN SO...
THAT ALSO MEANS THEY'RE NOT UNDER-ESTIMATING US...

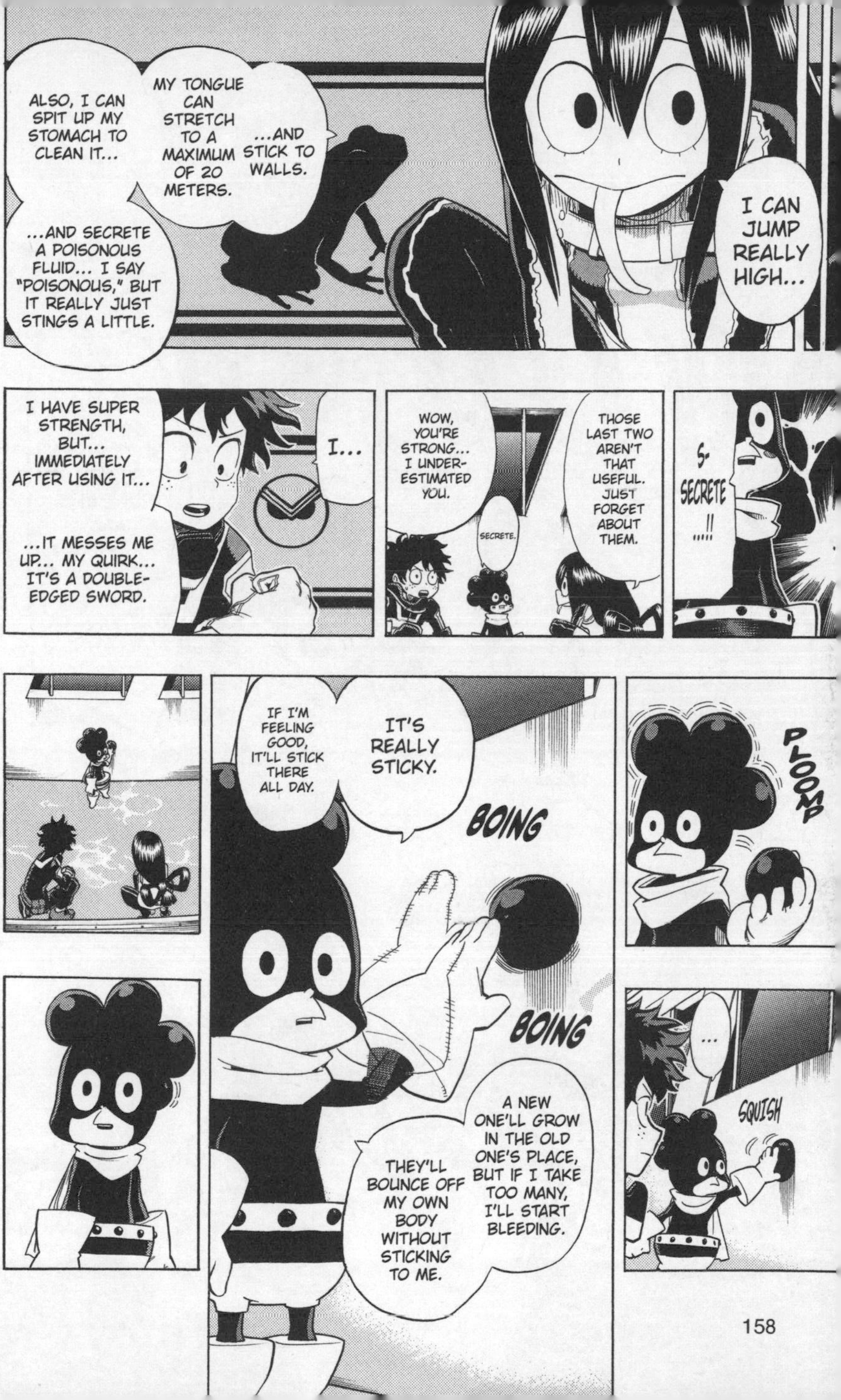
I CAN JUMP REALLY HIGH...
...AND STICK TO WALLS.
MY TONGUE CAN STRETCH TO A MAXIMUM OF 20 METERS.
ALSO, I CAN SPIT UP MY STOMACH TO CLEAN IT...
...AND SECRETE A POISONOUS FLUID... I SAY "POISONOUS," BUT IT REALLY JUST STINGS A LITTLE.
S-SECRETE ...!!
THOSE LAST TWO AREN'T THAT USEFUL. JUST FORGET ABOUT THEM.
WOW, YOU'RE STRONG... I UNDER-ESTIMATED YOU.
SECRETE.
I...
I HAVE SUPER STRENGTH, BUT... IMMEDIATELY AFTER USING IT...
...IT MESSES ME UP... MY QUIRK... IT'S A DOUBLE-EDGED SWORD.
PLOOMP
...
SQUISH
IT'S REALLY STICKY.
IF I'M FEELING GOOD, IT'LL STICK THERE ALL DAY.
BOING
BOING
A NEW ONE'LL GROW IN THE OLD ONE'S PLACE, BUT IF I TAKE TOO MANY, I'LL START BLEEDING.
THEY'LL BOUNCE OFF MY OWN BODY WITHOUT STICKING TO ME.

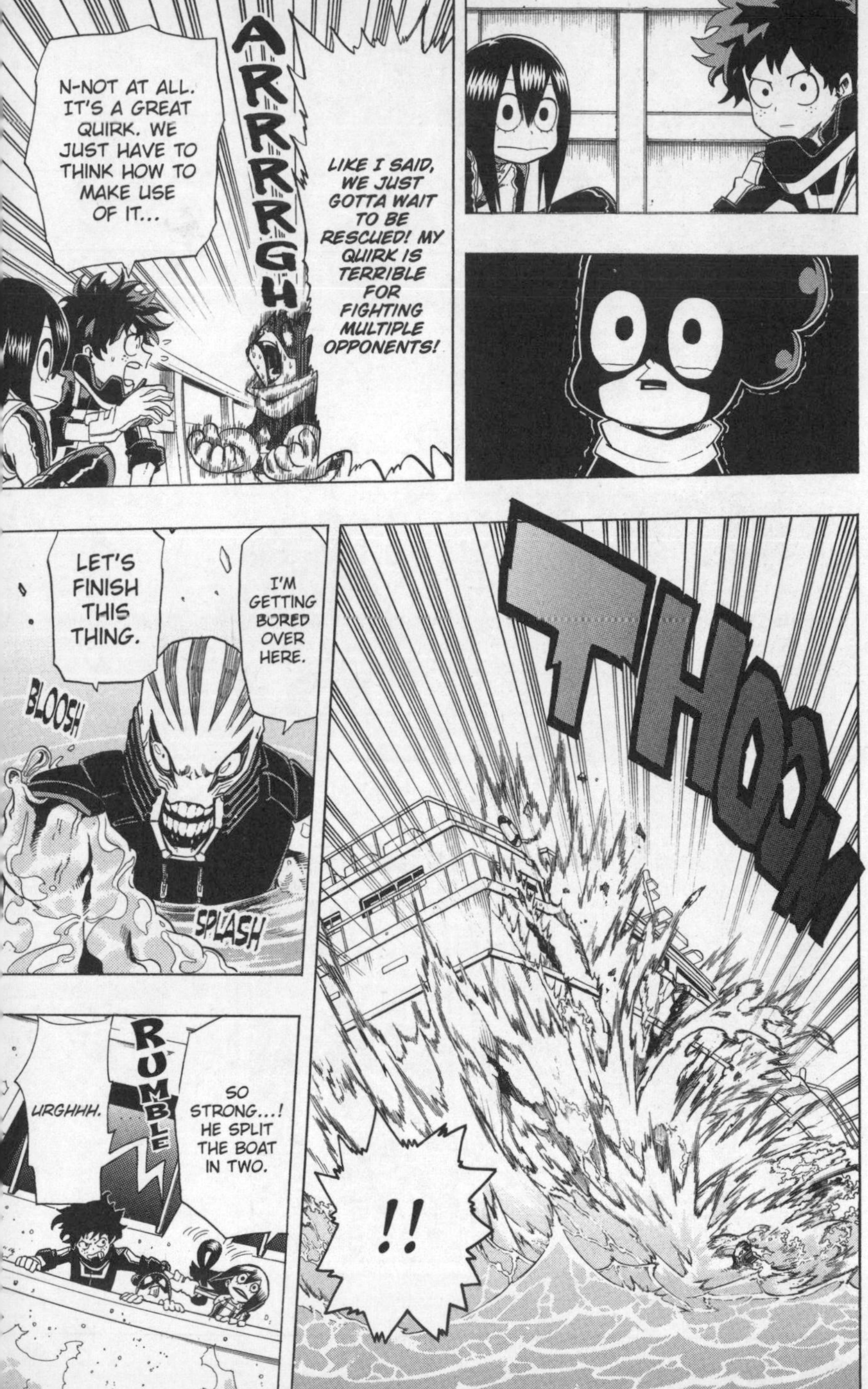
ARRRRGH
LIKE I SAID, WE JUST GOTTA WAIT TO BE RESCUED! MY QUIRK IS TERRIBLE FOR FIGHTING MULTIPLE OPPONENTS!
N-NOT AT ALL. IT'S A GREAT QUIRK. WE JUST HAVE TO THINK HOW TO MAKE USE OF IT...
THOOM
!!
I'M GETTING BORED OVER HERE.
LET'S FINISH THIS THING.
BLOOSH
SPLASH
RUMBLE
SO STRONG...! HE SPLIT THE BOAT IN TWO.
URGHHH.

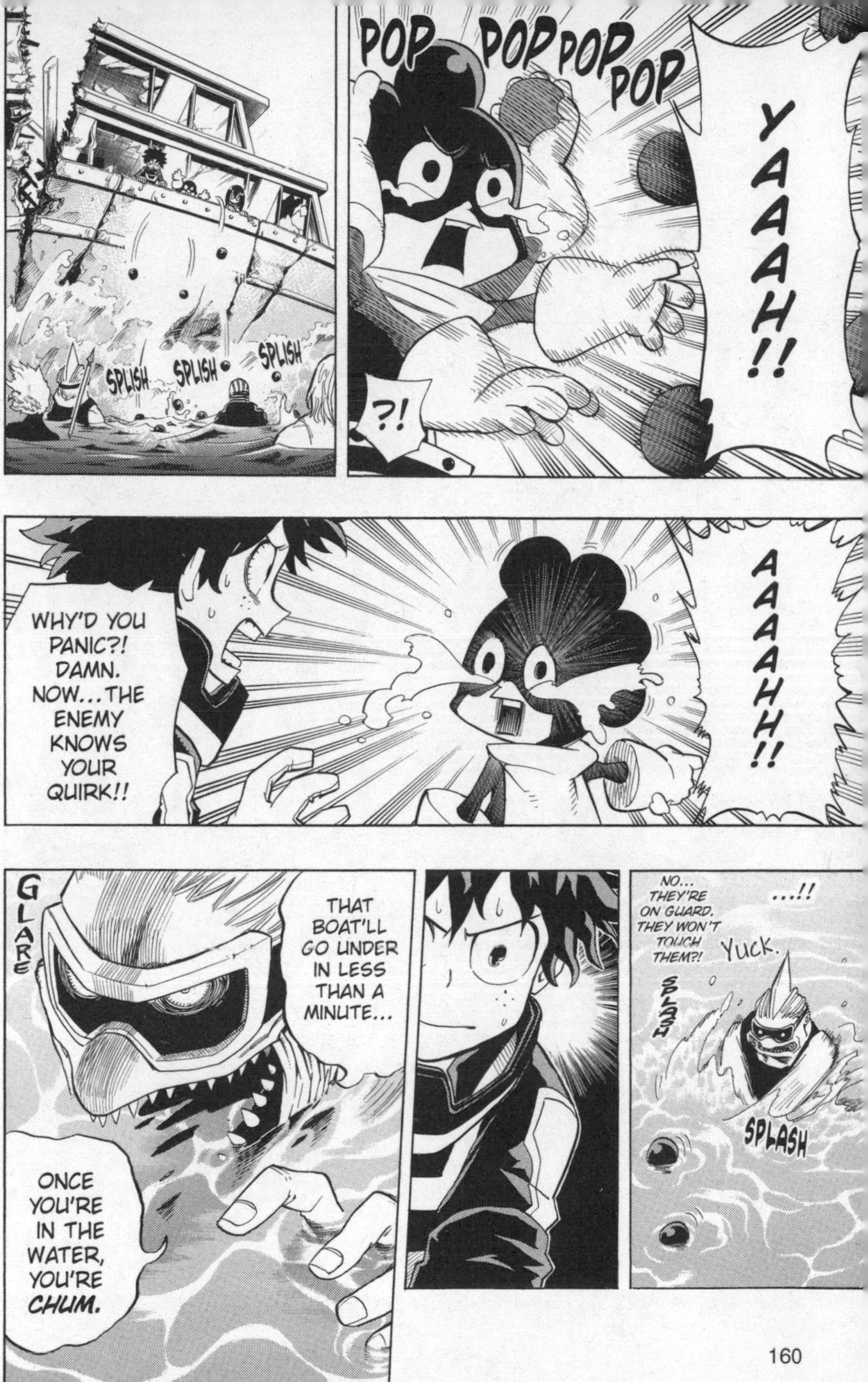

POP POP POP POP POP
YAAAAH!!
?!
SPLISH SPLISH SPLISH
AAAAAHH!!
WHY'D YOU PANIC?! DAMN. NOW... THE ENEMY KNOWS YOUR QUIRK!!
...!!
NO... THEY'RE ON GUARD. THEY WON'T TOUCH THEM?!
YUCK.
SPLASH
SPLASH
THAT BOAT'LL GO UNDER IN LESS THAN A MINUTE...
GLARE
ONCE YOU'RE IN THE WATER, YOU'RE CHUM.

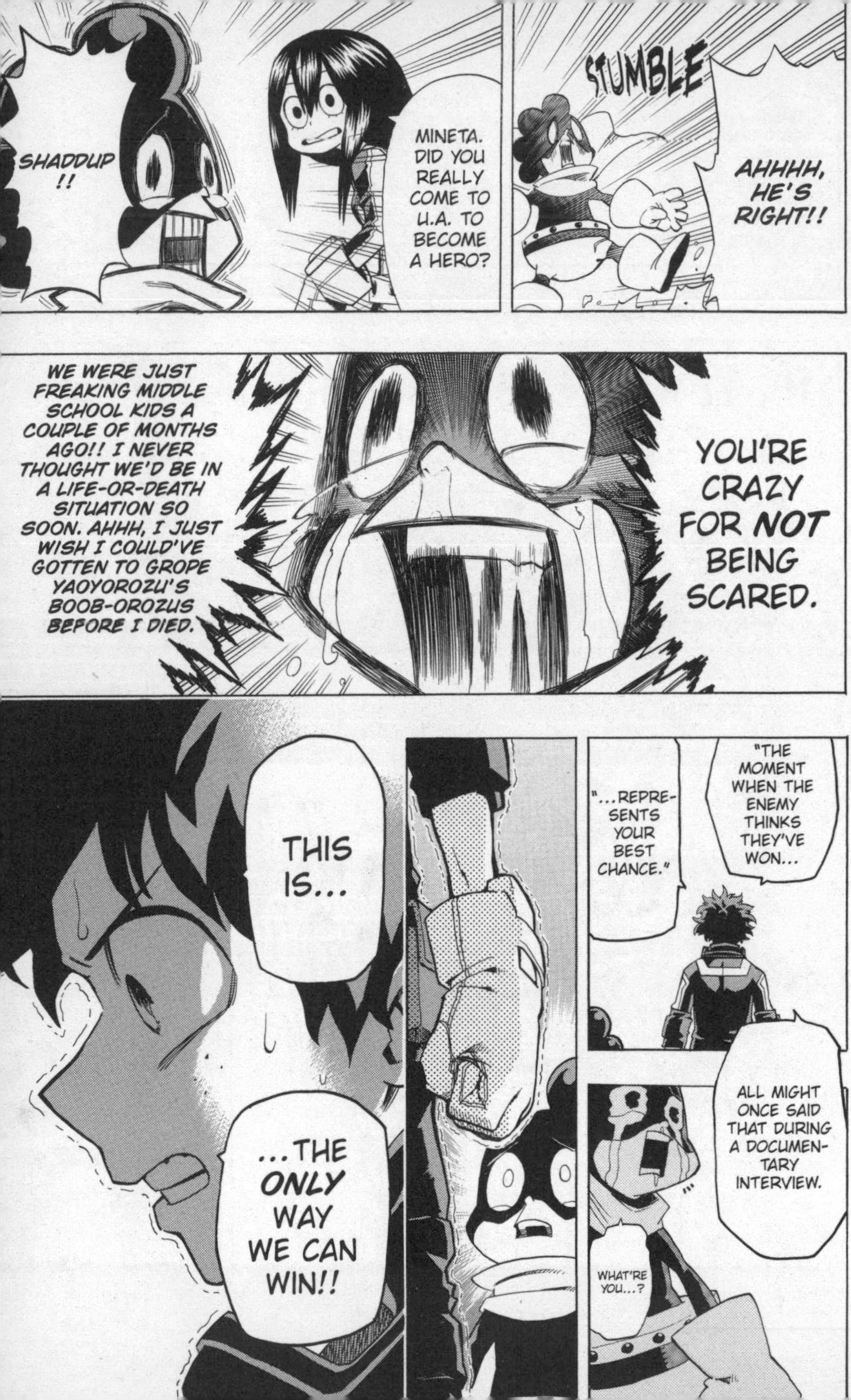
STUMBLE
AHHHH, HE'S RIGHT!!
MINETA. DID YOU REALLY COME TO U.A. TO BECOME A HERO?
SHADDUP!!
YOU'RE CRAZY FOR NOT BEING SCARED.
WE WERE JUST FREAKING MIDDLE SCHOOL KIDS A COUPLE OF MONTHS AGO!! I NEVER THOUGHT WE'D BE IN A LIFE-OR-DEATH SITUATION SO SOON. AHHH, I JUST WISH I COULD'VE GOTTEN TO GROPE YAOYOROZU'S BOOB-OROZUS BEFORE I DIED.
"THE MOMENT WHEN THE ENEMY THINKS THEY'VE WON...
"...REPRESENTS YOUR BEST CHANCE."
ALL MIGHT ONCE SAID THAT DURING A DOCUMENTARY INTERVIEW.
WHAT'RE YOU...?
THIS IS...
...THE ONLY WAY WE CAN WIN!!

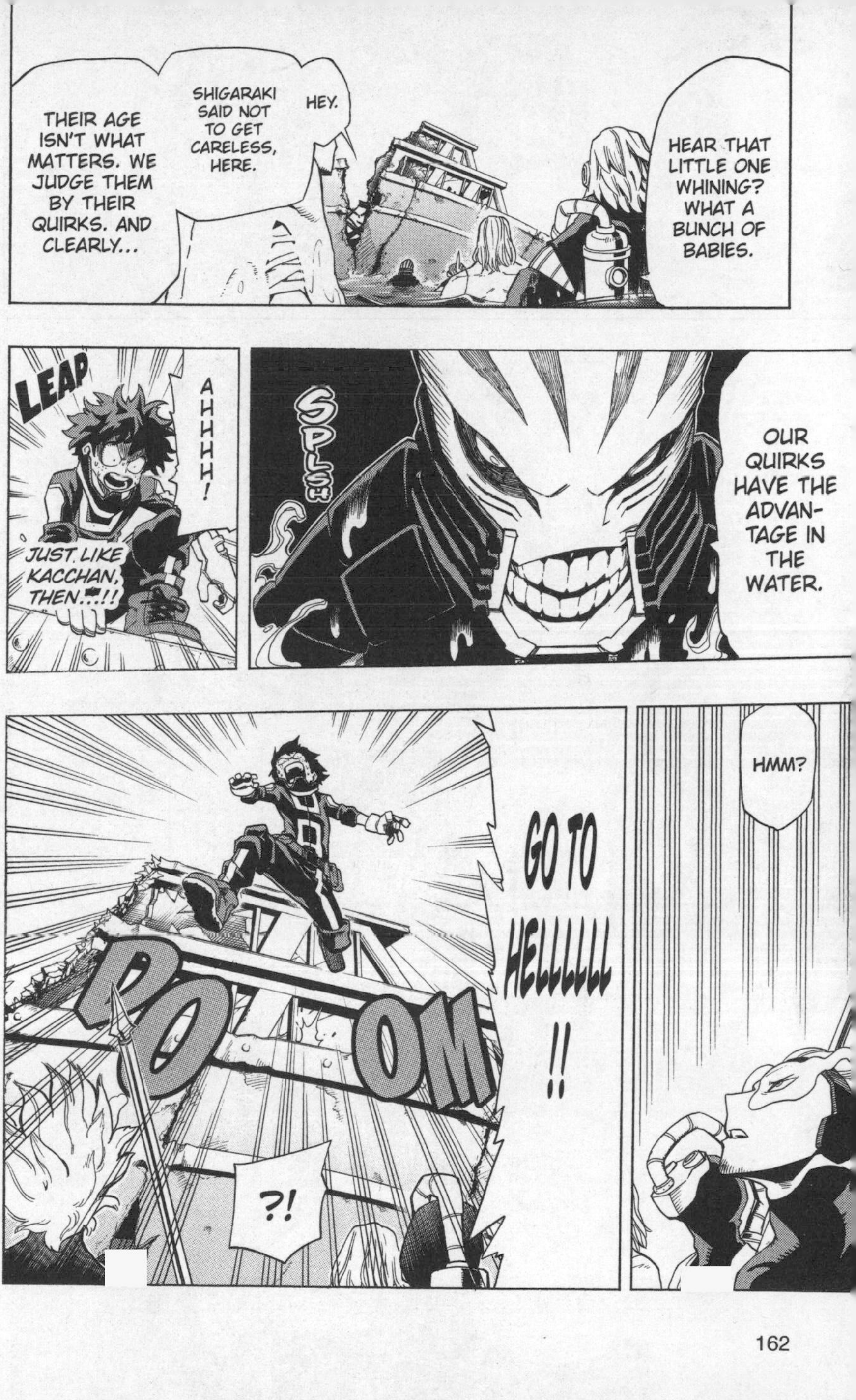
HEAR THAT LITTLE ONE WHINING? WHAT A BUNCH OF BABIES.
HEY.
SHIGARAKI SAID NOT TO GET CARELESS, HERE.
THEIR AGE ISN'T WHAT MATTERS. WE JUDGE THEM BY THEIR QUIRKS. AND CLEARLY...
OUR QUIRKS HAVE THE ADVANTAGE IN THE WATER.
SPLSH
LEAP
AHHHH!
JUST LIKE KACCHAN, THEN...!!
HMM?
GO TO HELLLLLL!!
BOOM
?!

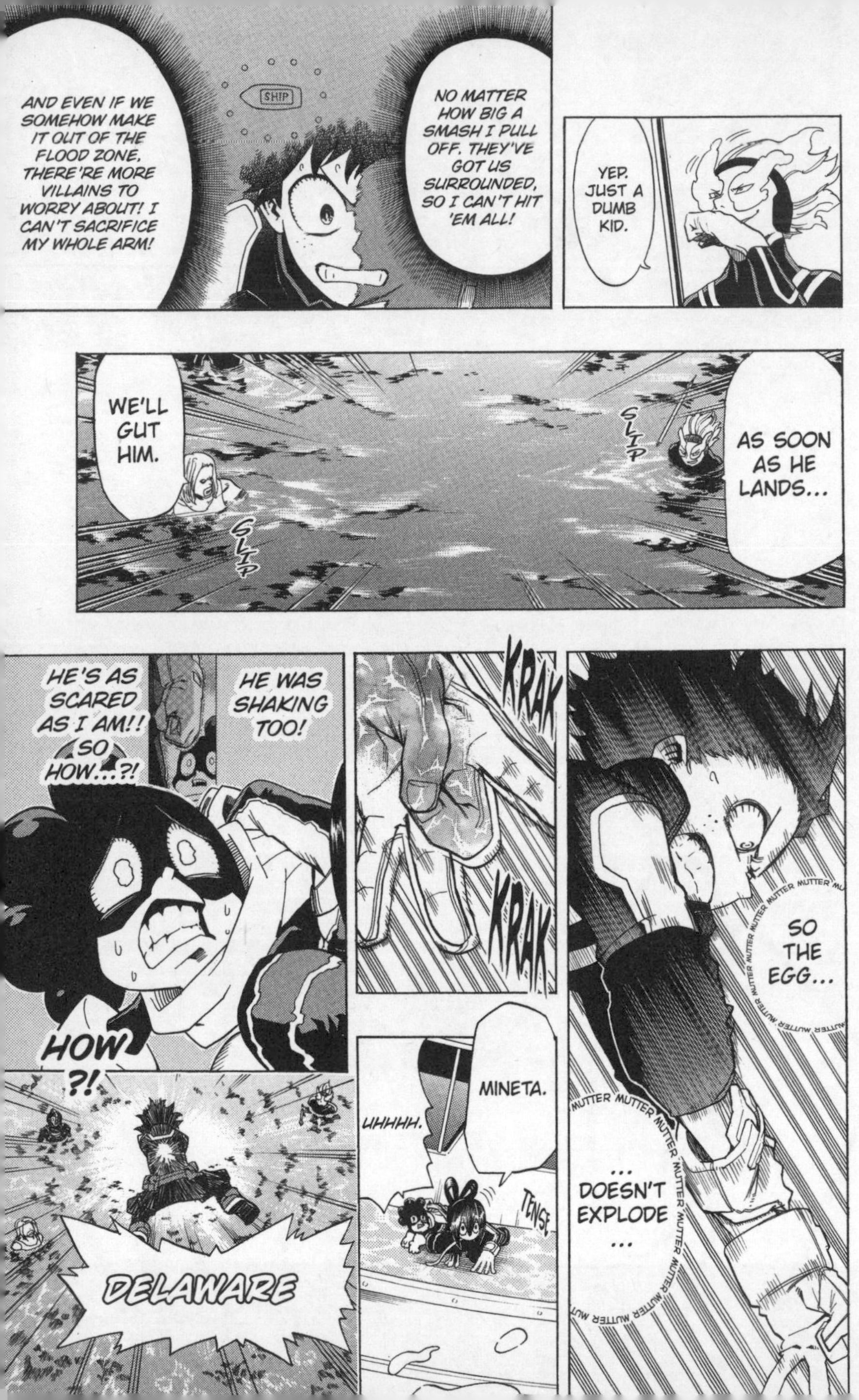
YEP. JUST A DUMB KID.
NO MATTER HOW BIG A SMASH I PULL OFF. THEY'VE GOT US SURROUNDED, SO I CAN'T HIT 'EM ALL!
SHIP
AND EVEN IF WE SOMEHOW MAKE IT OUT OF THE FLOOD ZONE, THERE'RE MORE VILLAINS TO WORRY ABOUT! I CAN'T SACRIFICE MY WHOLE ARM!
AS SOON AS HE LANDS...
SLIP
WE'LL GUT HIM.
SLIP
MUTTER MUTTER MUTTER MUTTER
SO THE EGG...
MUTTER MUTTER MUTTER MUTTER MUTTER MUTTER MUTT
... DOESN'T EXPLODE ...
KRAK
KRAK
MINETA.
UHHHH.
TENSE
HE WAS SHAKING TOO!
HE'S AS SCARED AS I AM!! SO HOW...?!
HOW ?!
DELAWARE

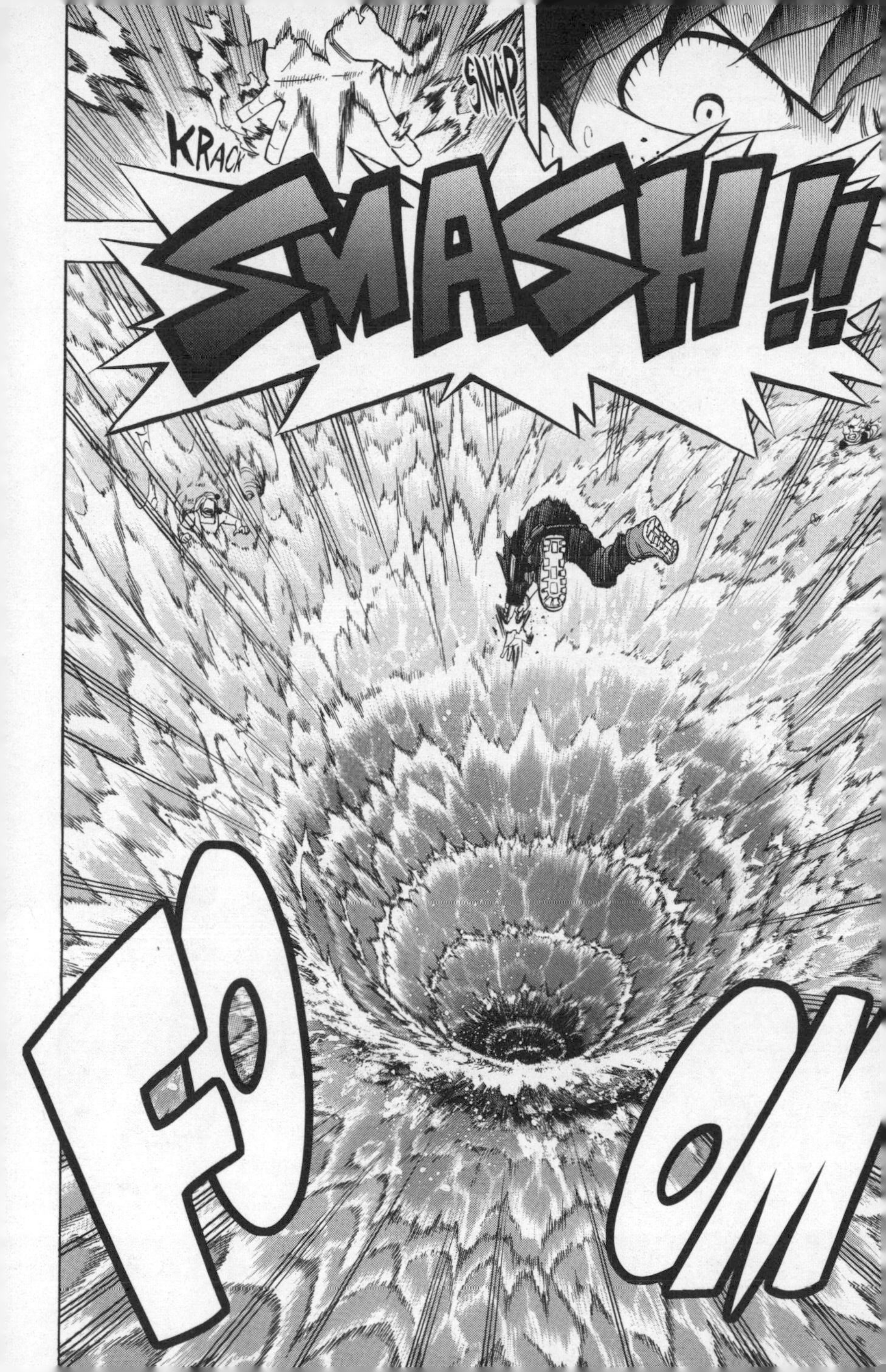
SNAP
KRACK
SMASH!!
FOOM

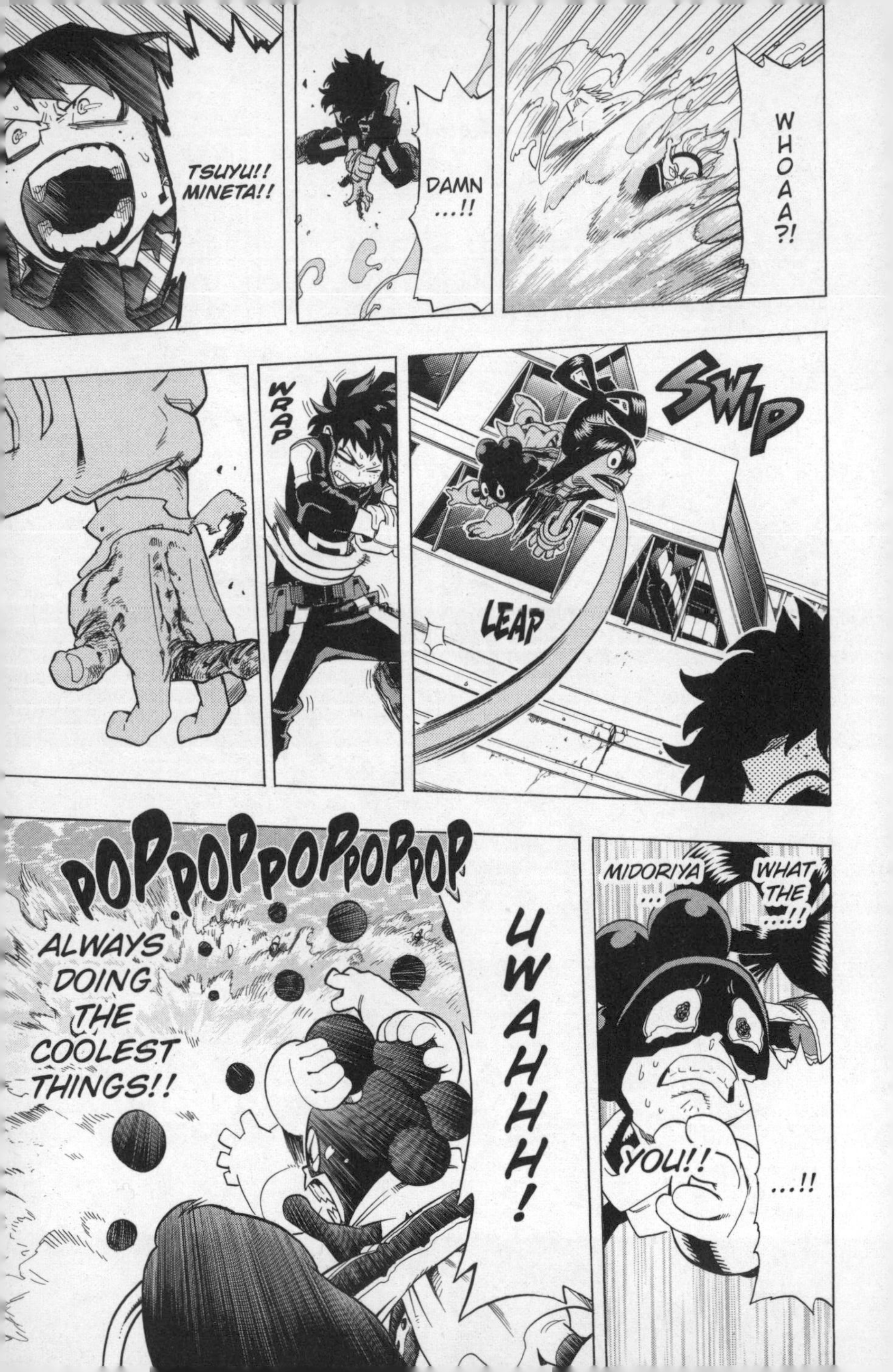
WHOAAA?!
DAMN ...!!
TSUYU!! MINETA!!
SWIP
LEAP
WRAP
WHAT THE ...!!
MIDORIYA ...
...!!
YOU!!
UWAHHH!
POPPOPPOPPOPPOP
ALWAYS DOING THE COOLEST THINGS!!

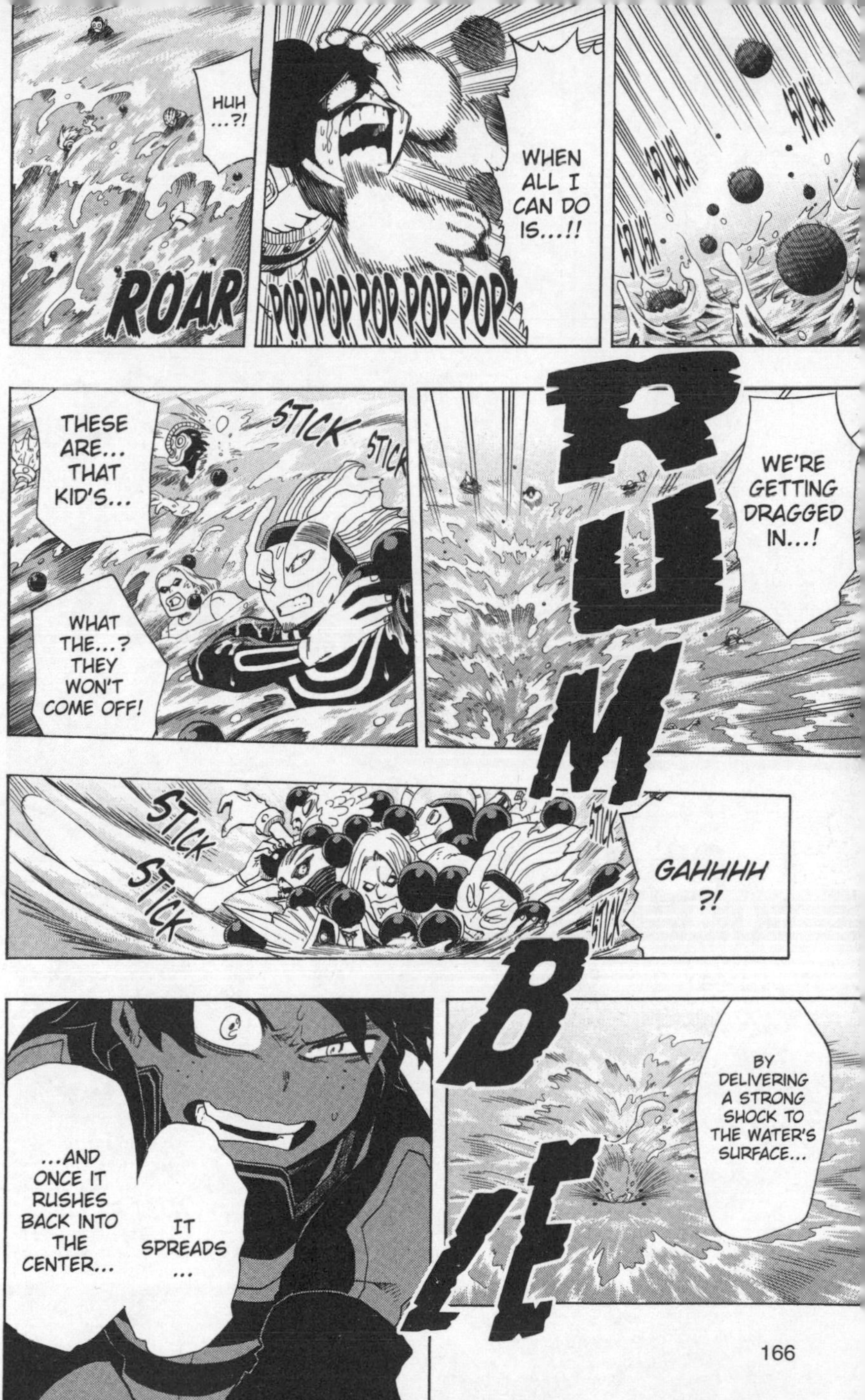
SPLISH
SPLISH
SPLISH
WHEN ALL I CAN DO IS...!!
POP POP POP POP POP
HUH ...?!
ROAR
WE'RE GETTING DRAGGED IN...!
RUMBLE
THESE ARE... THAT KID'S...
STICK
STICK
WHAT THE...? THEY WON'T COME OFF!
GAHHHH ?!
STICK
STICK
STICK
STICK
BY DELIVERING A STRONG SHOCK TO THE WATER'S SURFACE...
...AND ONCE IT RUSHES BACK INTO THE CENTER...
IT SPREADS ...

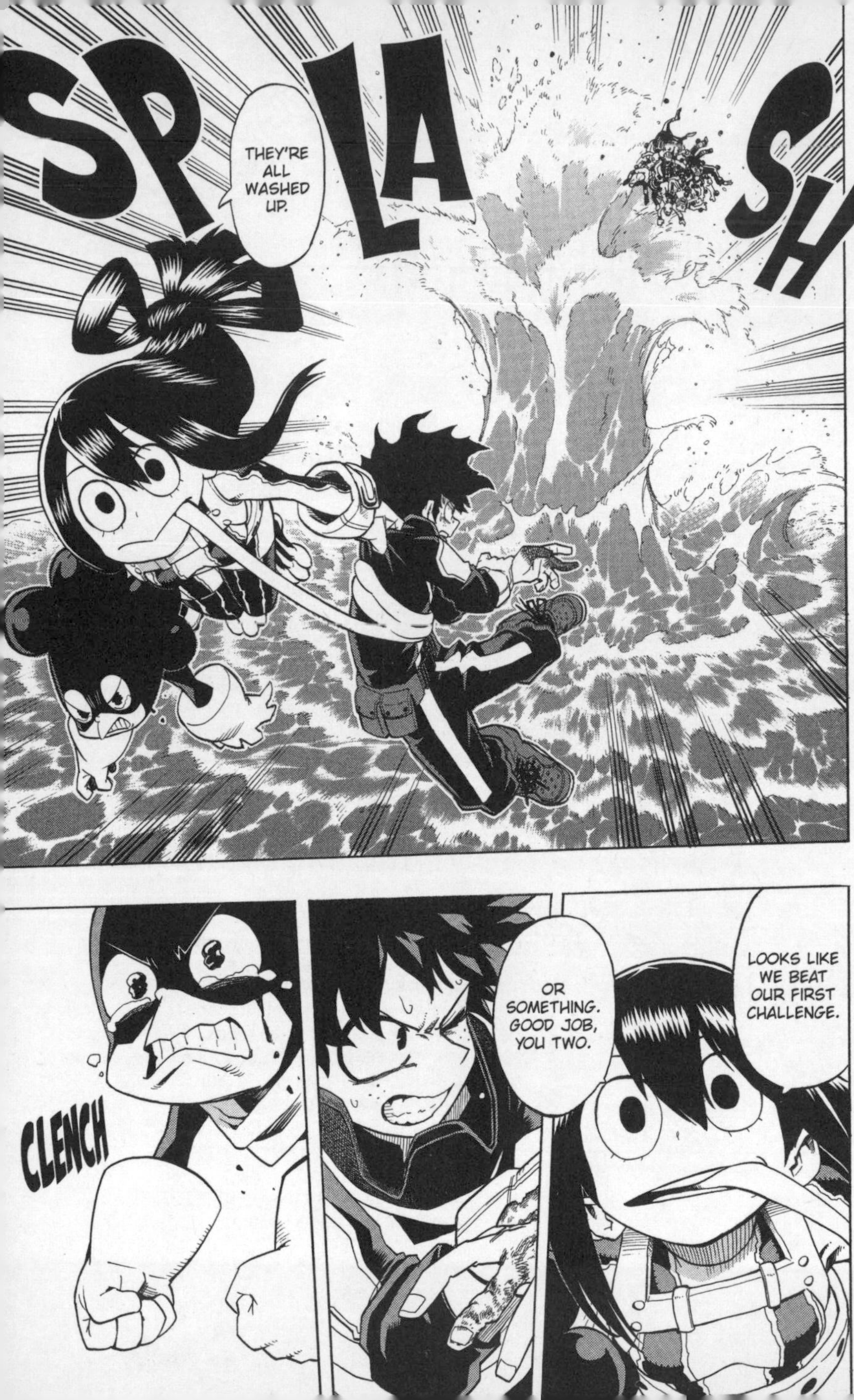
SPLASH
THEY'RE ALL WASHED UP.
LOOKS LIKE WE BEAT OUR FIRST CHALLENGE.
OR SOMETHING. GOOD JOB, YOU TWO.
CLENCH

LOOKING FASHIONABLE

Birthday: 10/8
Height: 108 cm
Favorite Thing: Women

BEHIND THE SCENES
This guy's design was decided early in the planning stage. I'm a perv myself, so he's always fun to draw, but I realize that some out there aren't big fans of pervs, so it's hard to find just the right balance.

THE SUPPLEMENT
I've gotten a lot of letters asking something along the lines of, "How the heck did this guy pass the entrance exam?" so I thought I'd address that here. As Izuku said, his Quirk's actually quite strong. The goal in the entrance exam was to incapacitate the faux villain robots, so Mineta stuck his balls to the ground and walls, essentially setting traps that would render the robots immobile. He also plugged their cannons with the balls. Both of these strategies earned him points. Facing an opponent head on and chucking them is hardly a winning strategy, though, given how easy it is to read, and that's a point that pains Mineta.

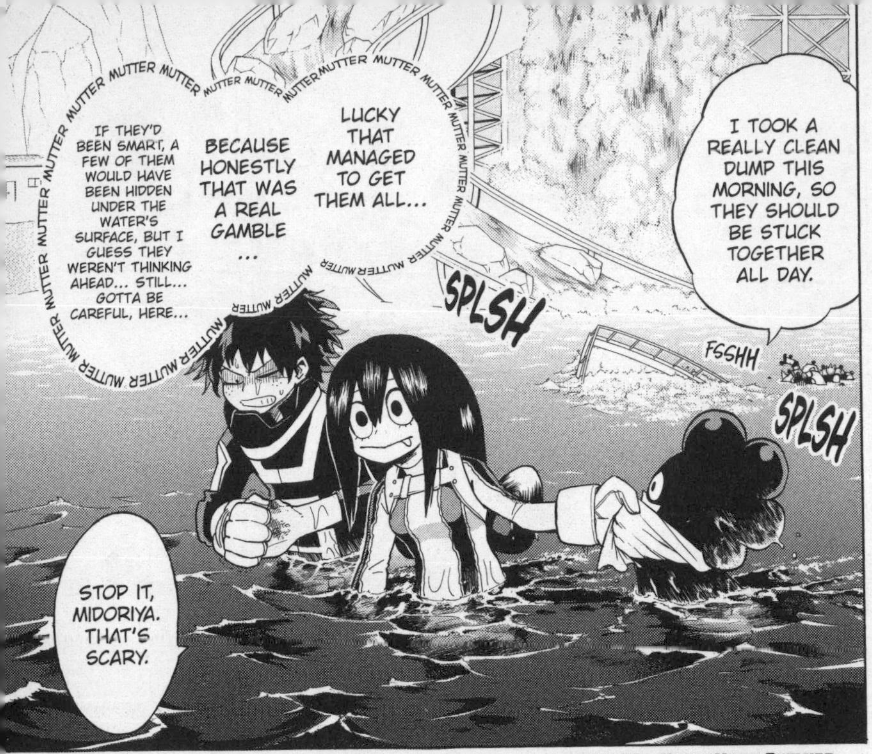
I TOOK A REALLY CLEAN DUMP THIS MORNING, SO THEY SHOULD BE STUCK TOGETHER ALL DAY.
SPLSH
FSSHH
SPLSH
MUTTER MUTTER MUTTER MUTTER MUTTER MUTTER
LUCKY THAT MANAGED TO GET THEM ALL...
BECAUSE HONESTLY THAT WAS A REAL GAMBLE ...
IF THEY'D BEEN SMART, A FEW OF THEM WOULD HAVE BEEN HIDDEN UNDER THE WATER'S SURFACE, BUT I GUESS THEY WEREN'T THINKING AHEAD... STILL... GOTTA BE CAREFUL, HERE...
STOP IT, MIDORIYA. THAT'S SCARY.

No.16 - Know Your Enemies

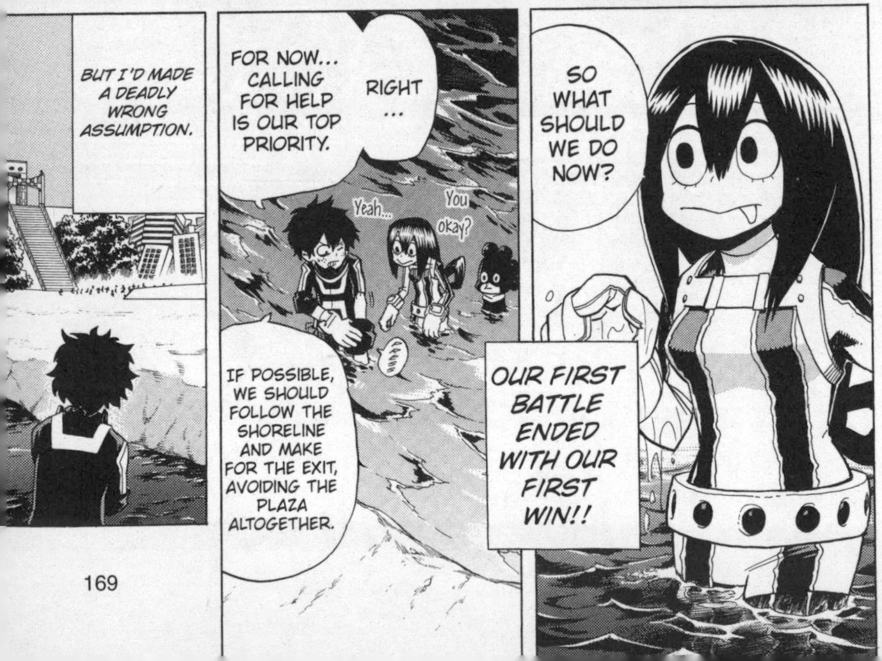
SO WHAT SHOULD WE DO NOW?
OUR FIRST BATTLE ENDED WITH OUR FIRST WIN!!
RIGHT ...
FOR NOW... CALLING FOR HELP IS OUR TOP PRIORITY.
You okay?
Yeah...
IF POSSIBLE, WE SHOULD FOLLOW THE SHORELINE AND MAKE FOR THE EXIT, AVOIDING THE PLAZA ALTOGETHER.
BUT I'D MADE A DEADLY WRONG ASSUMPTION.

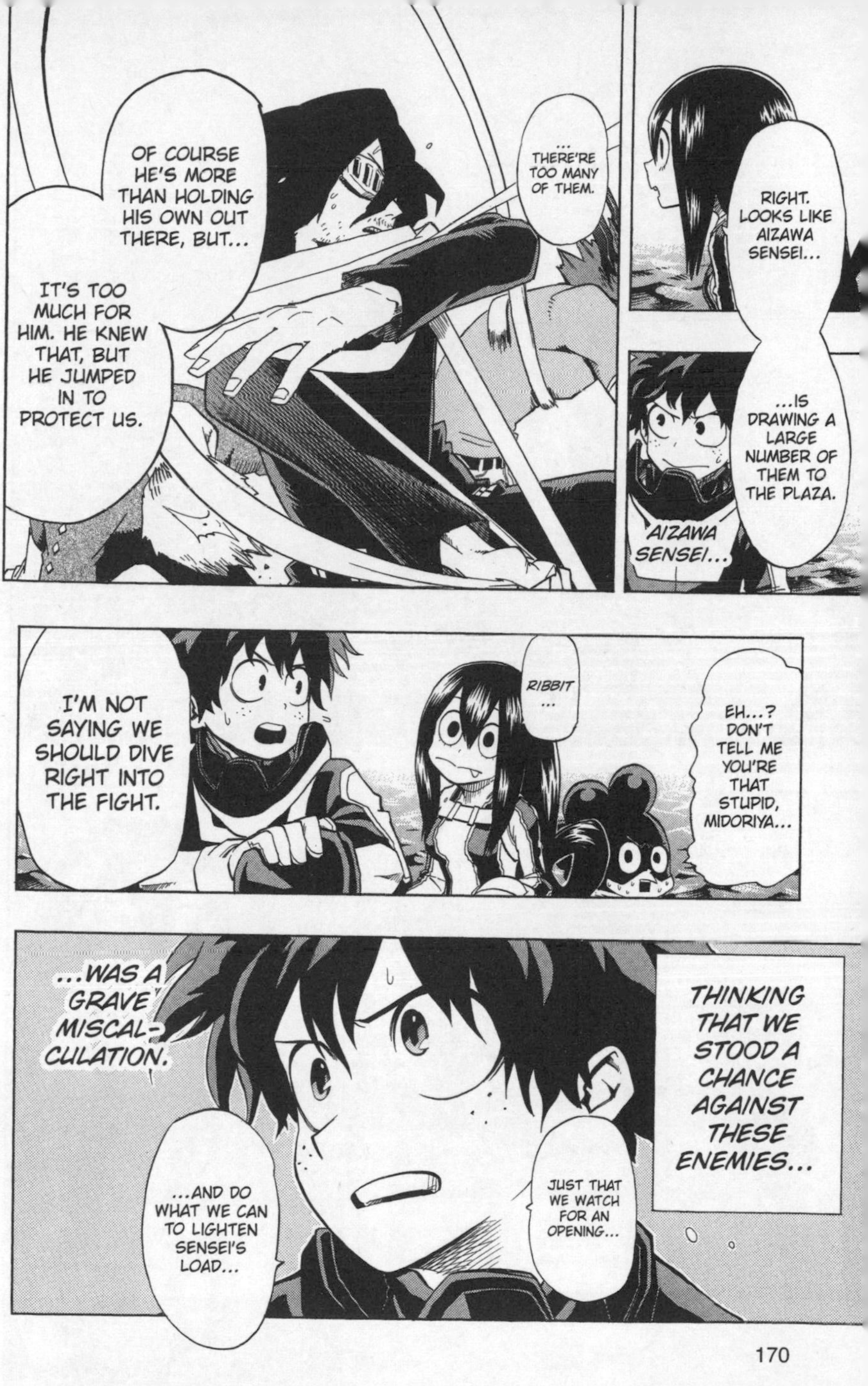
RIGHT. LOOKS LIKE AIZAWA SENSEI...
...IS DRAWING A LARGE NUMBER OF THEM TO THE PLAZA.
AIZAWA SENSEI...
...THERE'RE TOO MANY OF THEM.
OF COURSE HE'S MORE THAN HOLDING HIS OWN OUT THERE, BUT...
IT'S TOO MUCH FOR HIM. HE KNEW THAT, BUT HE JUMPED IN TO PROTECT US.
EH...? DON'T TELL ME YOU'RE THAT STUPID, MIDORIYA...
RIBBIT...
I'M NOT SAYING WE SHOULD DIVE RIGHT INTO THE FIGHT.
THINKING THAT WE STOOD A CHANCE AGAINST THESE ENEMIES...
JUST THAT WE WATCH FOR AN OPENING...
...WAS A GRAVE MISCALCULATION.
...AND DO WHAT WE CAN TO LIGHTEN SENSEI'S LOAD...

No.16 - Know Your Enemies

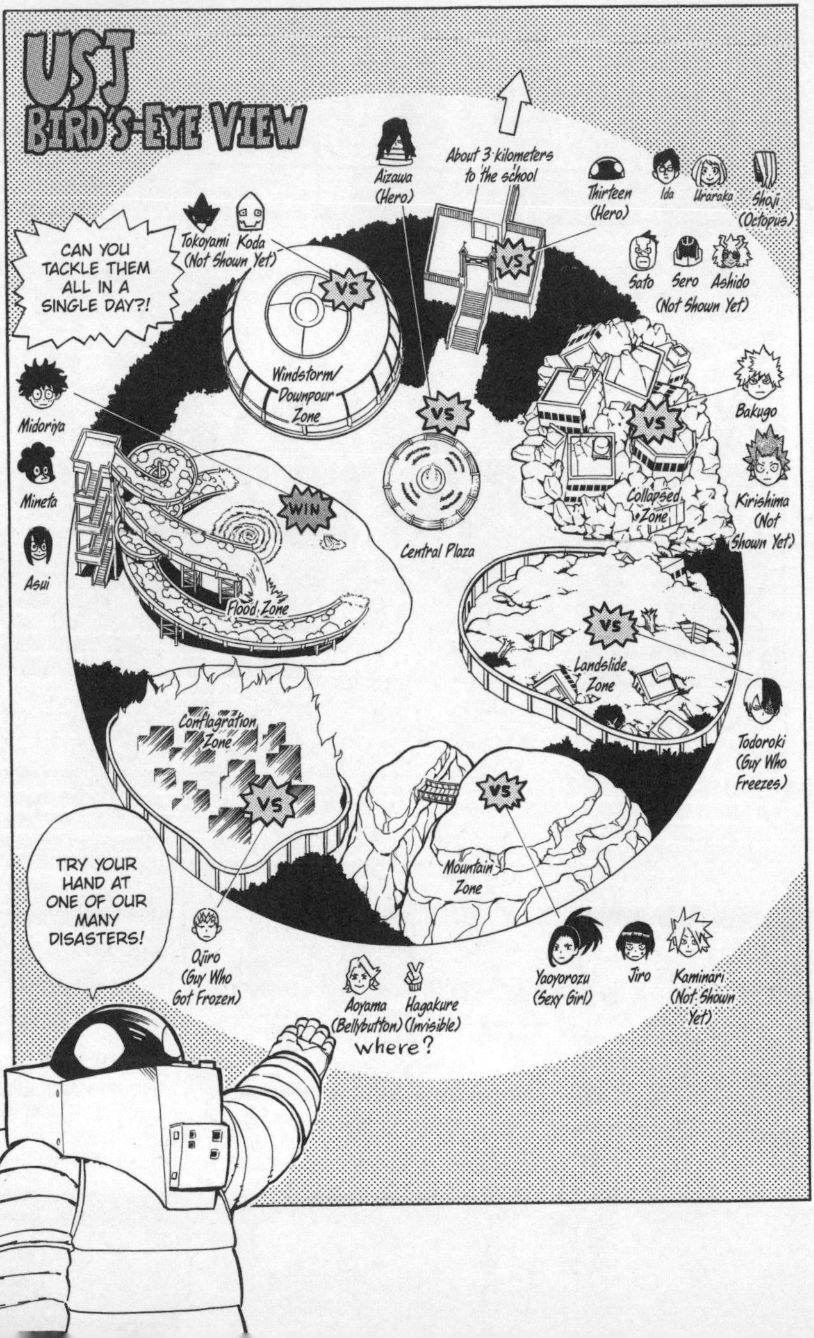

USJ
Bird's-Eye View
About 3 kilometers to the school
Aizawa (Hero)
Thirteen (Hero)
Ida
Uraraka
Shoji (Octopus)
Sato
Sero
Ashido
(Not Shown Yet)
Tokoyami
Koda
(Not Shown Yet)
CAN YOU TACKLE THEM ALL IN A SINGLE DAY?!
VS
Windstorm/ Downpour Zone
Midoriya
Mineta
Asui
WIN
Flood Zone
Central Plaza
Bakugo
Kirishima (Not Shown Yet)
Collapsed Zone
Landslide Zone
Todoroki (Guy Who Freezes)
Conflagration Zone
Mountain Zone
TRY YOUR HAND AT ONE OF OUR MANY DISASTERS!
Ojiro (Guy Who Got Frozen)
Aoyama (Bellybutton)
Hagakure (Invisible)
where?
Yaoyorozu (Sexy Girl)
Jiro
Kaminari (Not Shown Yet)

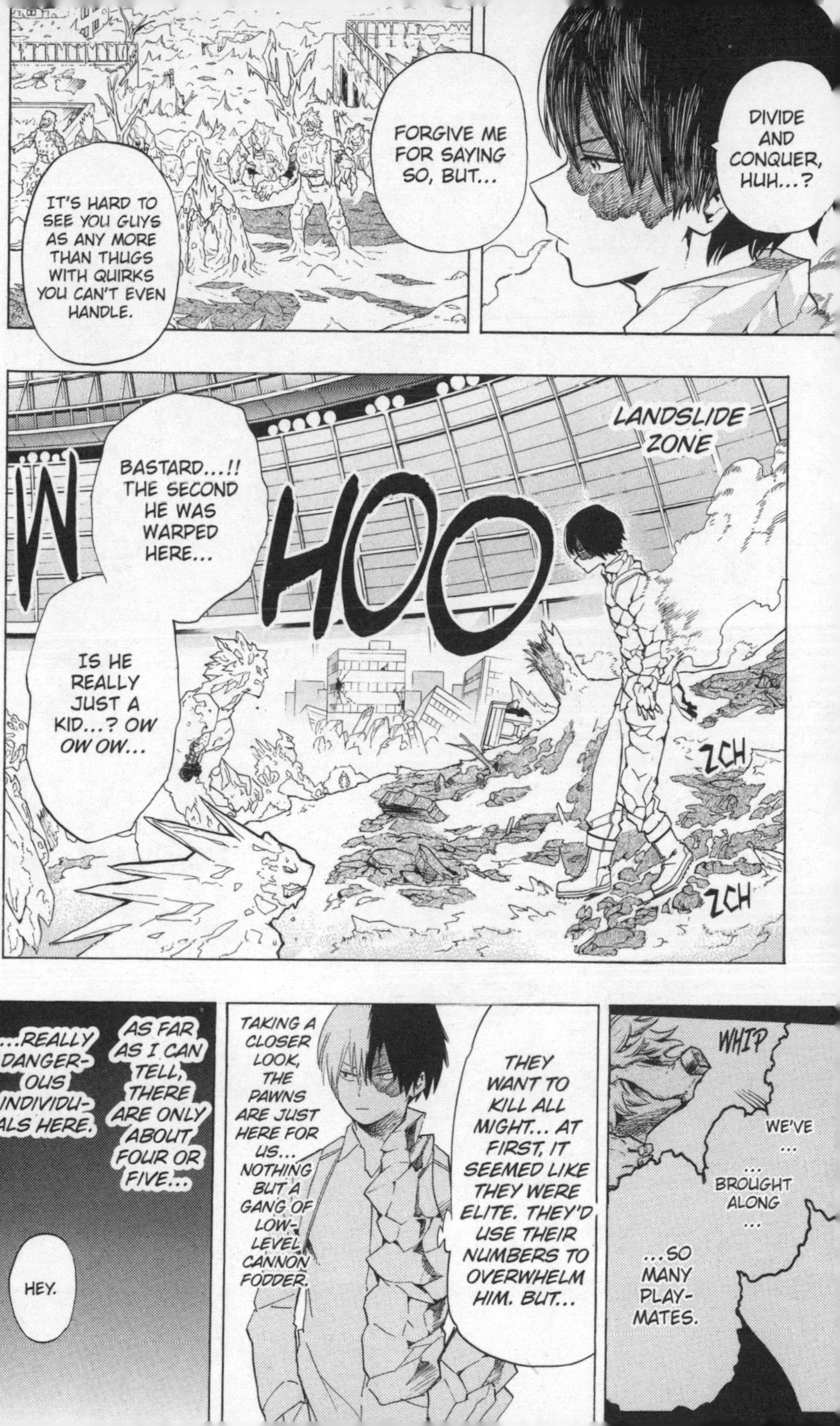
DIVIDE AND CONQUER, HUH...?
FORGIVE ME FOR SAYING SO, BUT...
IT'S HARD TO SEE YOU GUYS AS ANY MORE THAN THUGS WITH QUIRKS YOU CAN'T EVEN HANDLE.
LANDSLIDE ZONE
WHOO
BASTARD...!! THE SECOND HE WAS WARPED HERE...
IS HE REALLY JUST A KID...? OW OW OW...
ZCH
ZCH
WHIP
WE'VE...
...BROUGHT ALONG...
...SO MANY PLAY-MATES.
THEY WANT TO KILL ALL MIGHT... AT FIRST, IT SEEMED LIKE THEY WERE ELITE. THEY'D USE THEIR NUMBERS TO OVERWHELM HIM. BUT...
TAKING A CLOSER LOOK, THE PAWNS ARE JUST HERE FOR US... NOTHING BUT A GANG OF LOW-LEVEL CANNON FODDER.
AS FAR AS I CAN TELL, THERE ARE ONLY ABOUT FOUR OR FIVE...
...REALLY DANGER-OUS INDIVIDU-ALS HERE.
HEY.

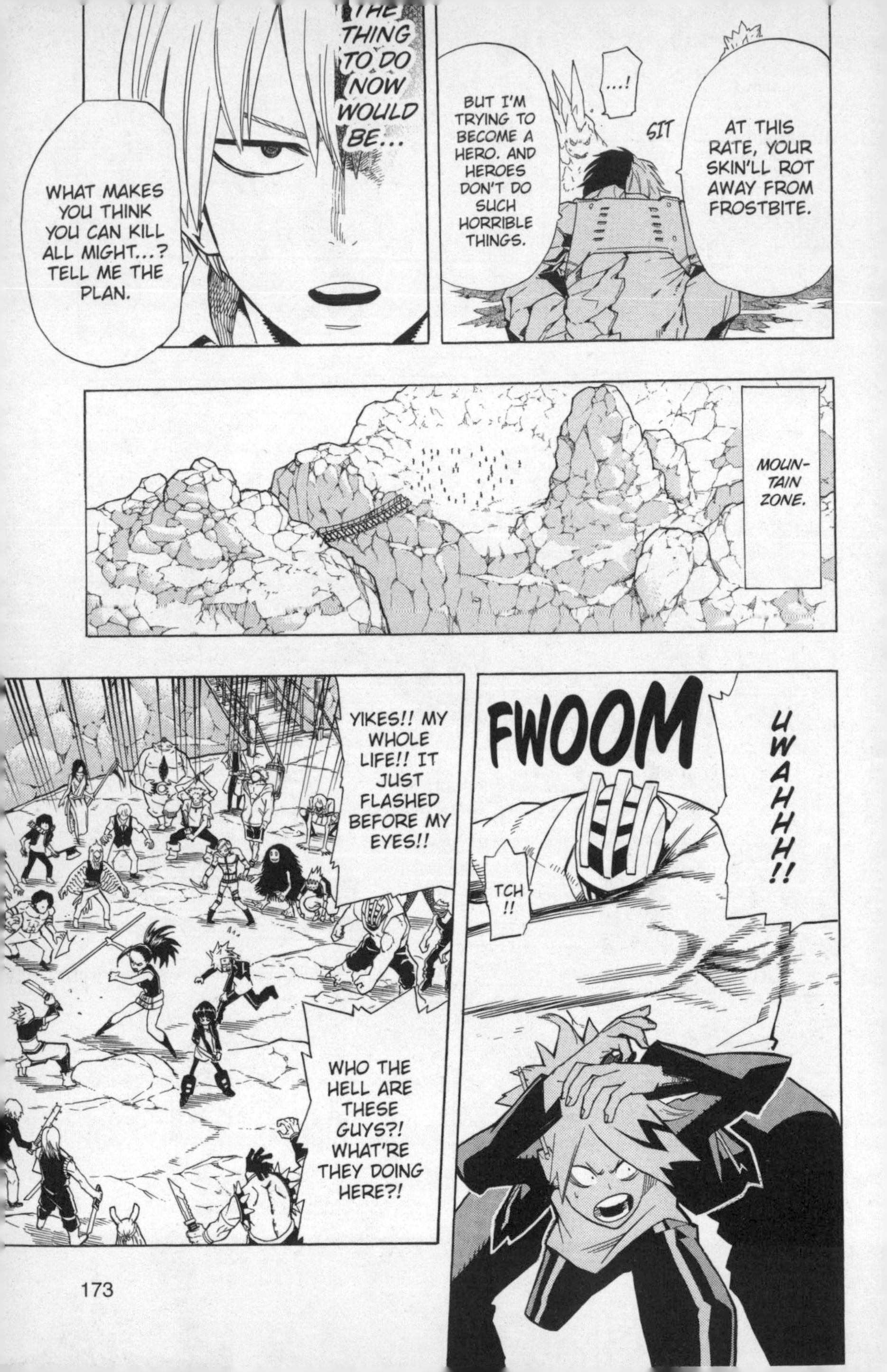
AT THIS RATE, YOUR SKIN'LL ROT AWAY FROM FROSTBITE.
SIT
...!
BUT I'M TRYING TO BECOME A HERO. AND HEROES DON'T DO SUCH HORRIBLE THINGS.
THE THING TO DO NOW WOULD BE...
WHAT MAKES YOU THINK YOU CAN KILL ALL MIGHT...? TELL ME THE PLAN.
MOUN-TAIN ZONE.
FWOOM
UWAHHH!!
TCH!!
YIKES!! MY WHOLE LIFE!! IT JUST FLASHED BEFORE MY EYES!!
WHO THE HELL ARE THESE GUYS?! WHAT'RE THEY DOING HERE?!

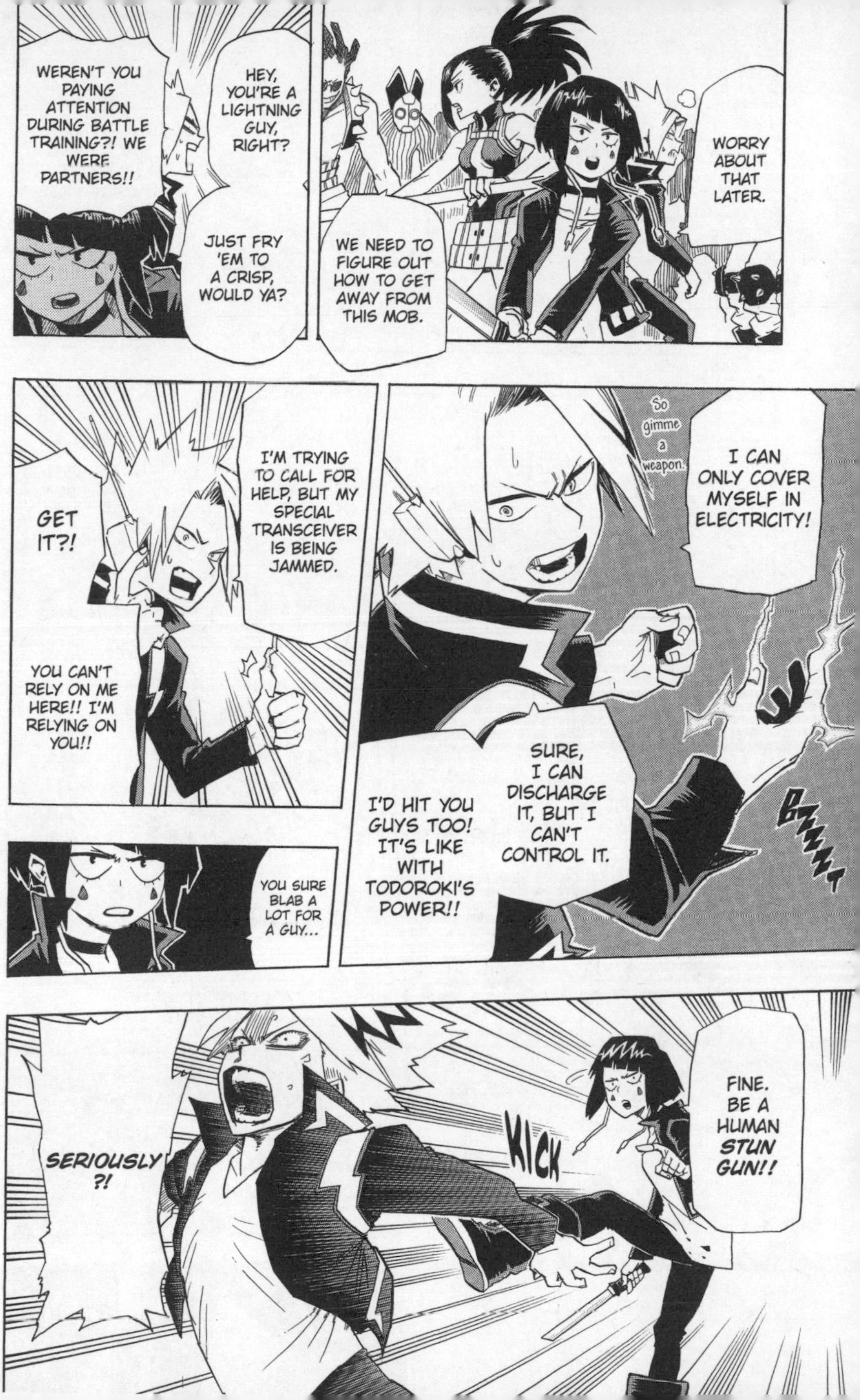
WORRY ABOUT THAT LATER.
WE NEED TO FIGURE OUT HOW TO GET AWAY FROM THIS MOB.
HEY, YOU'RE A LIGHTNING GUY, RIGHT?
JUST FRY 'EM TO A CRISP, WOULD YA?
WEREN'T YOU PAYING ATTENTION DURING BATTLE TRAINING?! WE WERE PARTNERS!!
I CAN ONLY COVER MYSELF IN ELECTRICITY!
So gimme a weapon.
SURE, I CAN DISCHARGE IT, BUT I CAN'T CONTROL IT.
I'D HIT YOU GUYS TOO! IT'S LIKE WITH TODOROKI'S POWER!!
BZZZZT
I'M TRYING TO CALL FOR HELP, BUT MY SPECIAL TRANSCEIVER IS BEING JAMMED.
GET IT?!
YOU CAN'T RELY ON ME HERE!! I'M RELYING ON YOU!!
YOU SURE BLAB A LOT FOR A GUY...
FINE. BE A HUMAN STUN GUN!!
KICK
SERIOUSLY ?!

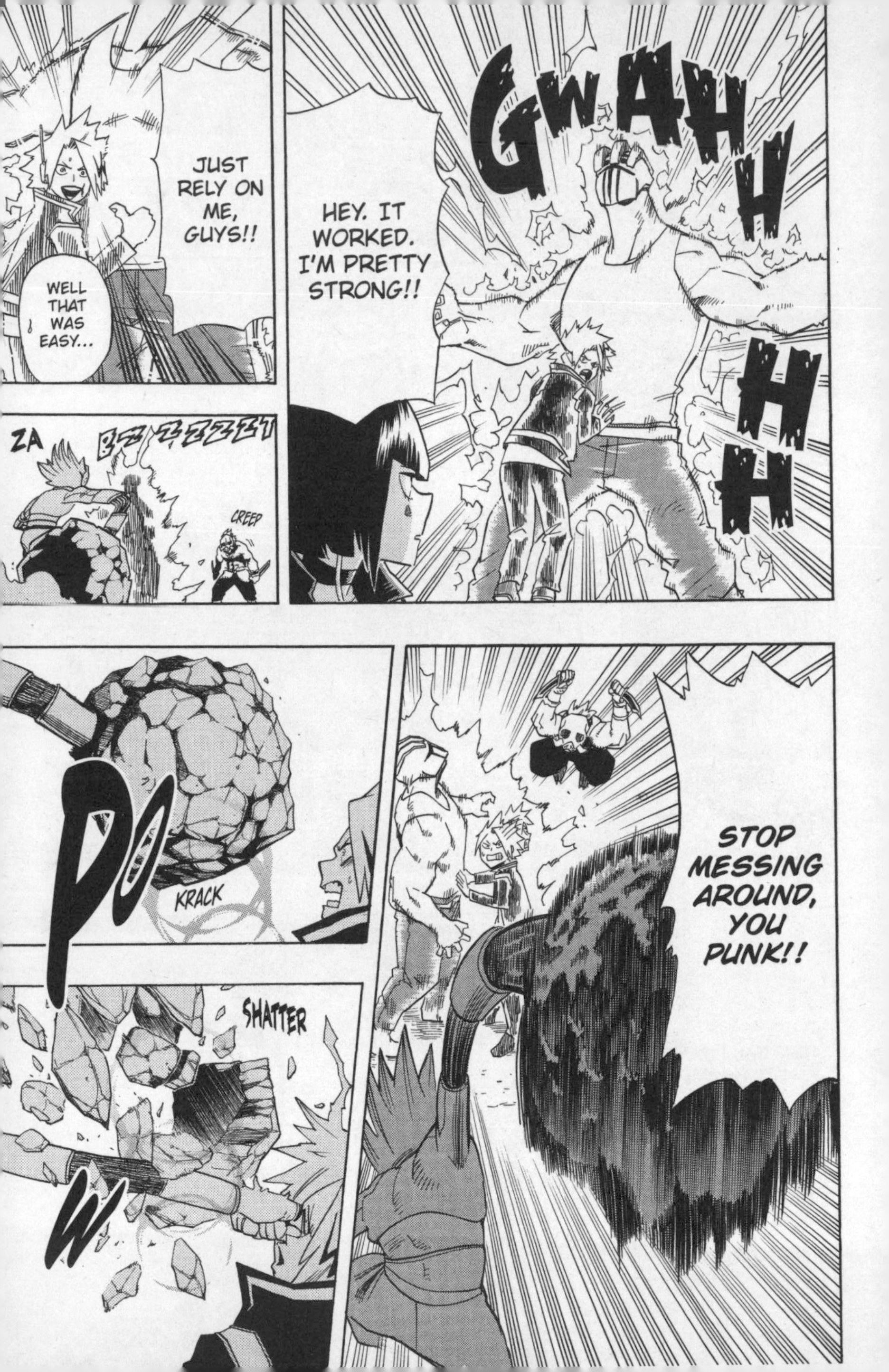
GWAHHHH
HEY. IT WORKED. I'M PRETTY STRONG!!
JUST RELY ON ME, GUYS!!
WELL THAT WAS EASY...
ZA
CREEP
STOP MESSING AROUND, YOU PUNK!!
PO
KRACK
SHATTER
W

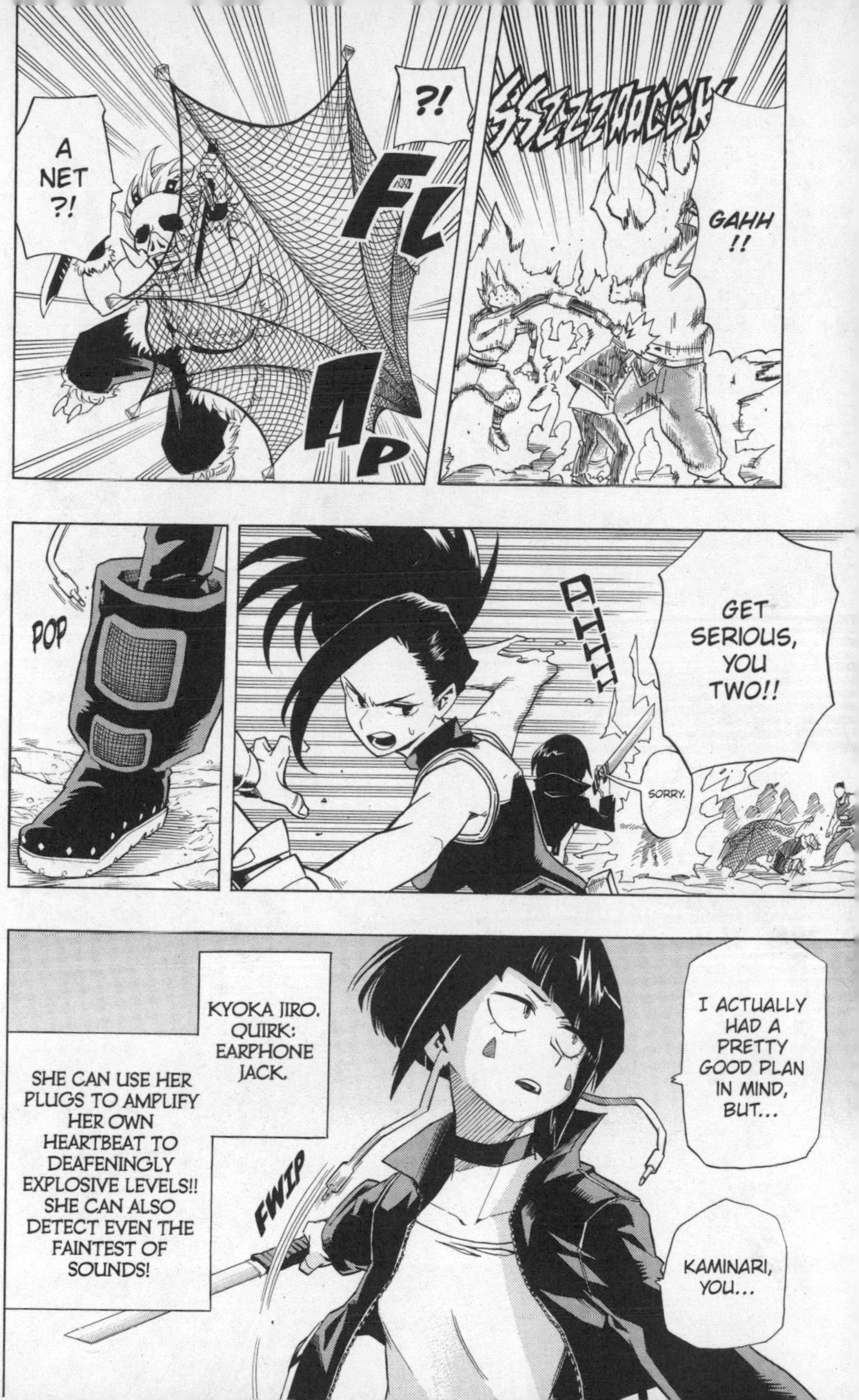
SSZZZWOCCK
GAHH!!
?!
FLAP
A NET?!
GET SERIOUS, YOU TWO!!
AHHH
SORRY.
POP
I ACTUALLY HAD A PRETTY GOOD PLAN IN MIND, BUT...
KYOKA JIRO. QUIRK: EARPHONE JACK.
SHE CAN USE HER PLUGS TO AMPLIFY HER OWN HEARTBEAT TO DEAFENINGLY EXPLOSIVE LEVELS!! SHE CAN ALSO DETECT EVEN THE FAINTEST OF SOUNDS!
KAMINARI, YOU...
FWIP

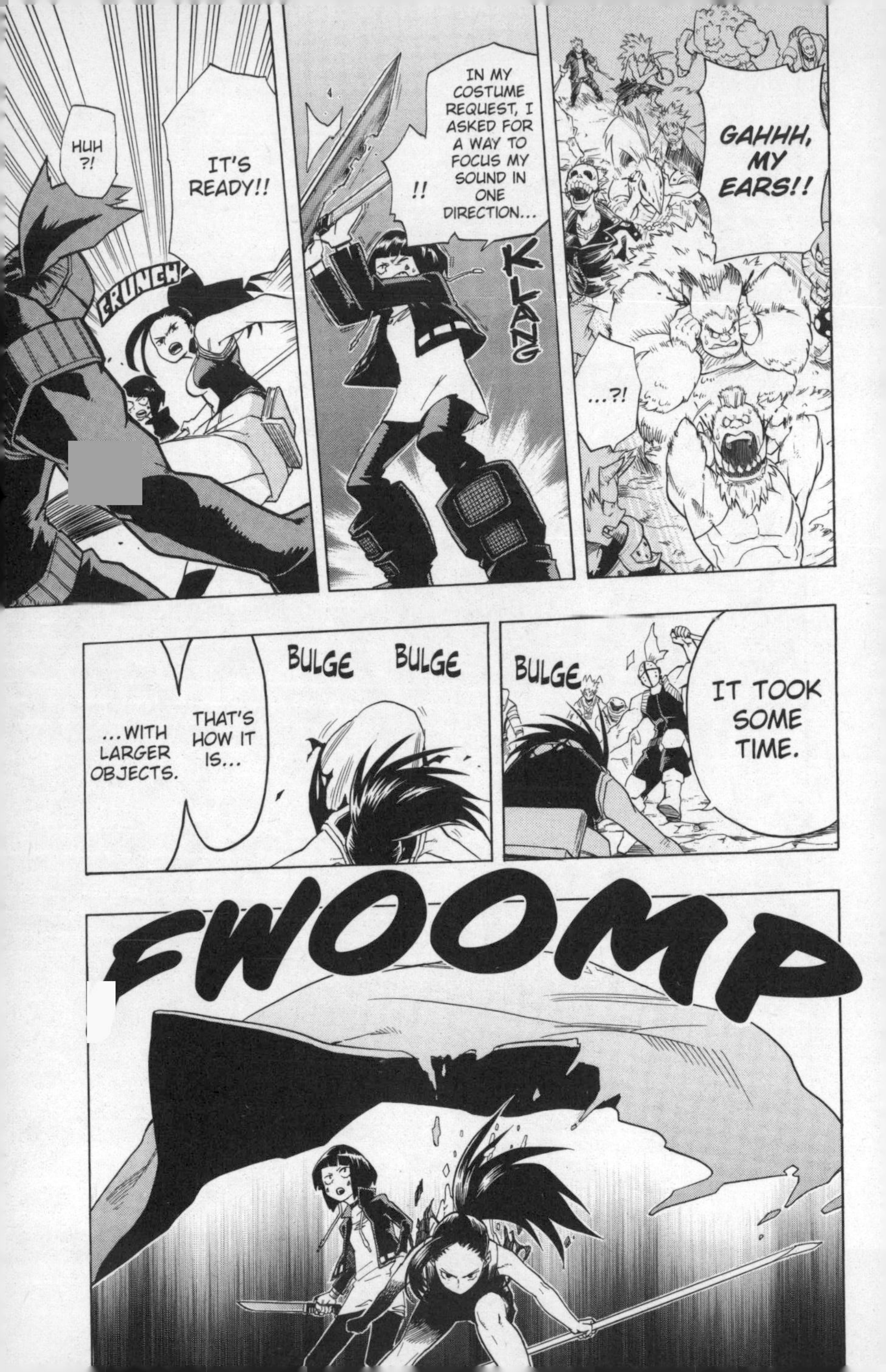
GAHHH, MY EARS!!
...?!
IN MY COSTUME REQUEST, I ASKED FOR A WAY TO FOCUS MY SOUND IN ONE DIRECTION...
!!
KLANG
IT'S READY!!
HUH ?!
CRUNCH
IT TOOK SOME TIME.
BULGE
BULGE
BULGE
THAT'S HOW IT IS...
...WITH LARGER OBJECTS.
FWOOMP

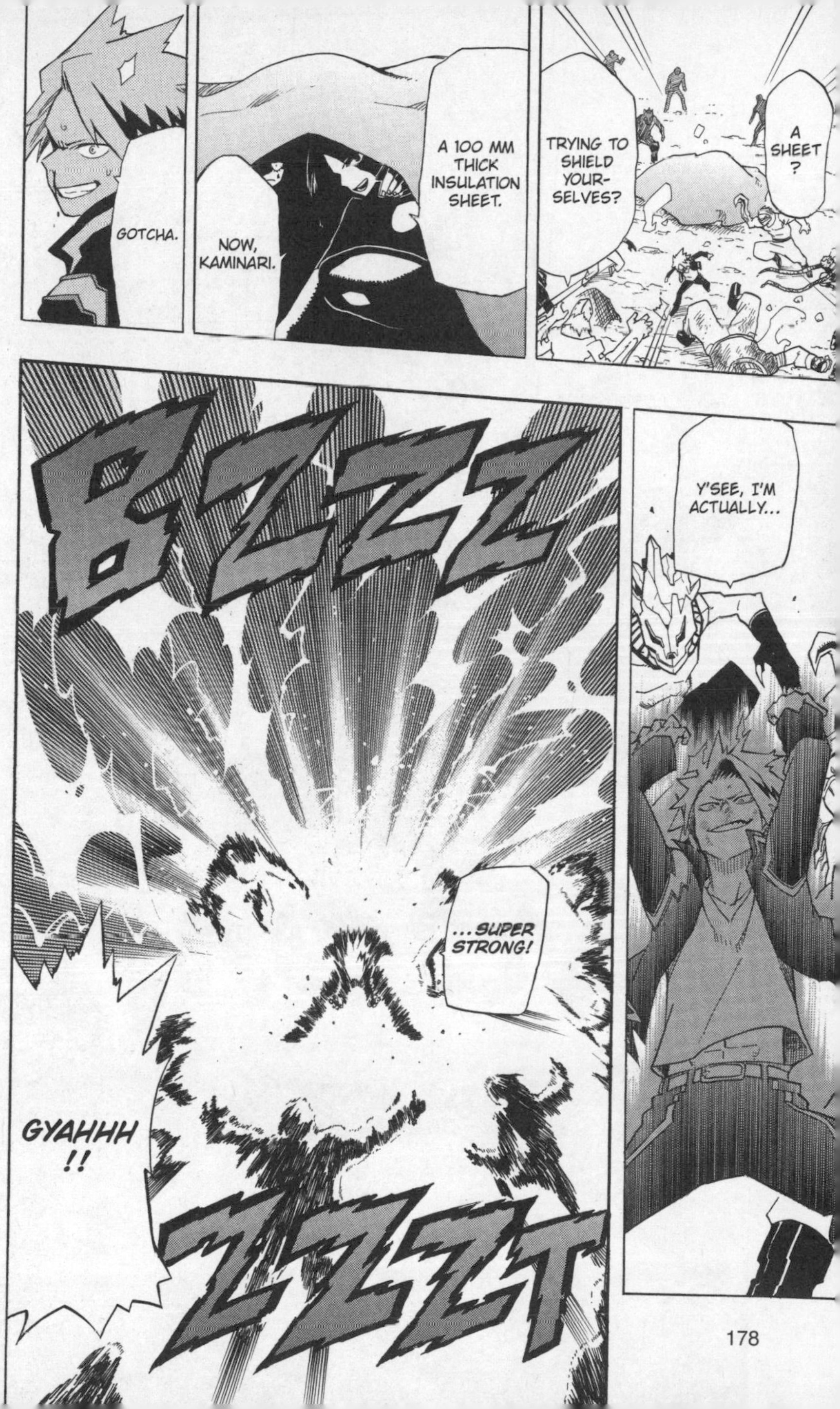
A SHEET?
TRYING TO SHIELD YOURSELVES?
A 100 MM THICK INSULATION SHEET.
NOW, KAMINARI.
GOTCHA.
Y'SEE, I'M ACTUALLY...
BZZZ
...SUPER STRONG!
GYAHHH!!
ZZZZT

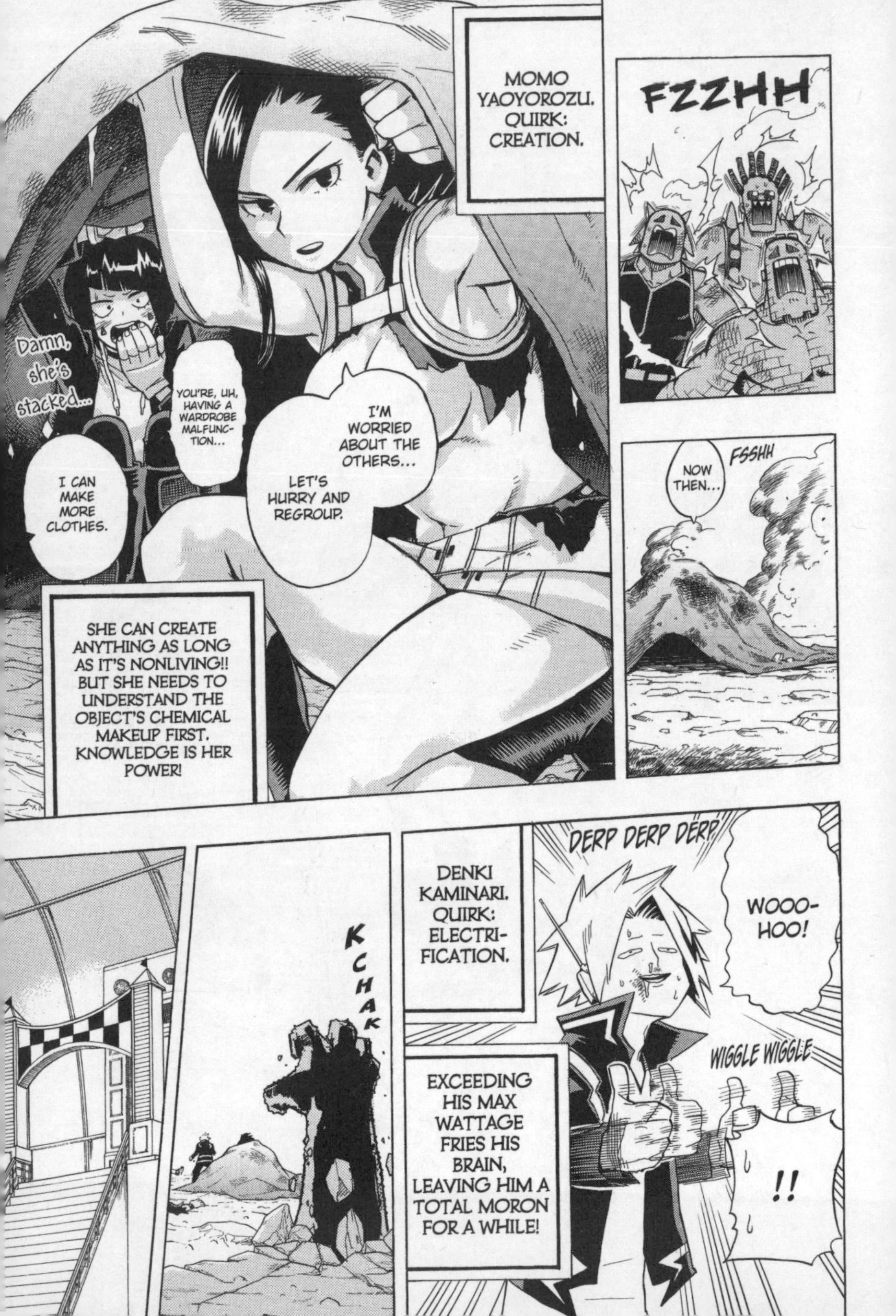
FZZHH
FSSHH
NOW THEN...
MOMO YAOYOROZU. QUIRK: CREATION.
I'M WORRIED ABOUT THE OTHERS...
LET'S HURRY AND REGROUP.
YOU'RE, UH, HAVING A WARDROBE MALFUNCTION...
Damn, she's stacked...
I CAN MAKE MORE CLOTHES.
SHE CAN CREATE ANYTHING AS LONG AS IT'S NONLIVING!! BUT SHE NEEDS TO UNDERSTAND THE OBJECT'S CHEMICAL MAKEUP FIRST. KNOWLEDGE IS HER POWER!
DERP DERP DERP
WOOO-HOO!
DENKI KAMINARI. QUIRK: ELECTRIFICATION.
WIGGLE WIGGLE
!!
EXCEEDING HIS MAX WATTAGE FRIES HIS BRAIN, LEAVING HIM A TOTAL MORON FOR A WHILE!
KCHAK

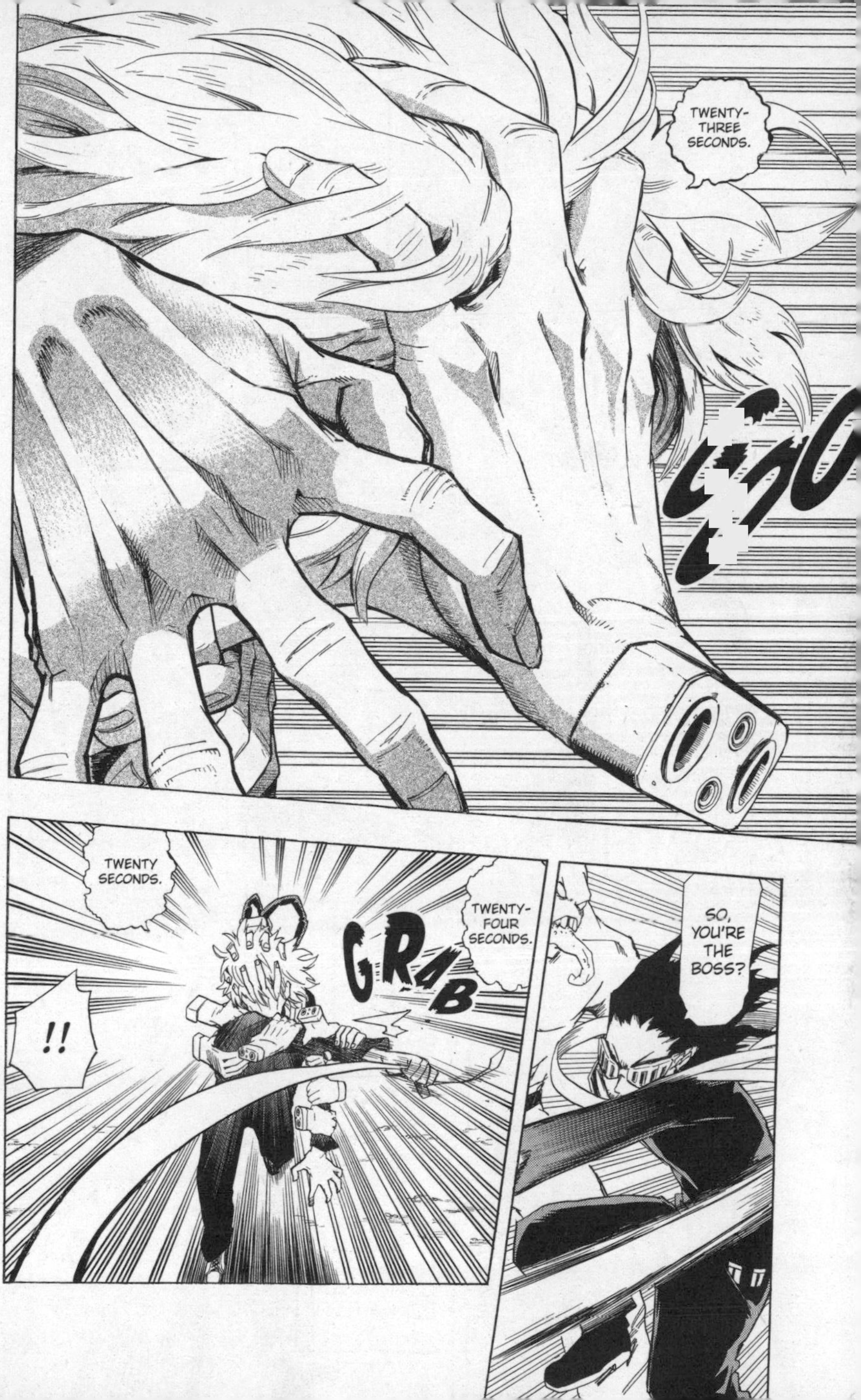
TWENTY-THREE SECONDS.
SO, YOU'RE THE BOSS?
TWENTY-FOUR SECONDS.
GRAB
TWENTY SECONDS.
!!

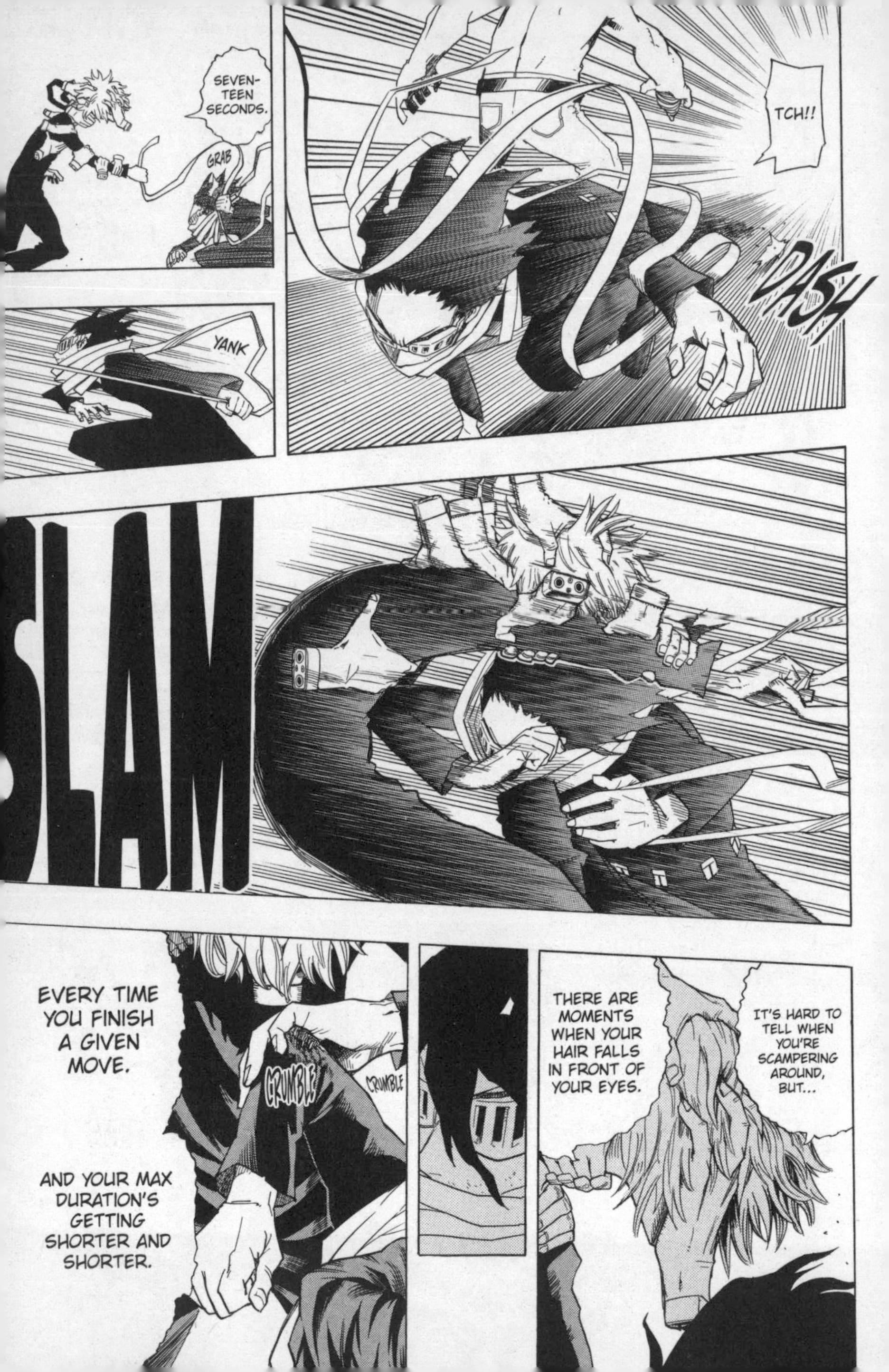
TCH!!
DASH
SEVEN-TEEN SECONDS.
GRAB
YANK
SLAM
IT'S HARD TO TELL WHEN YOU'RE SCAMPERING AROUND, BUT...
THERE ARE MOMENTS WHEN YOUR HAIR FALLS IN FRONT OF YOUR EYES.
CRUMBLE
CRUMBLE
EVERY TIME YOU FINISH A GIVEN MOVE.
AND YOUR MAX DURATION'S GETTING SHORTER AND SHORTER.

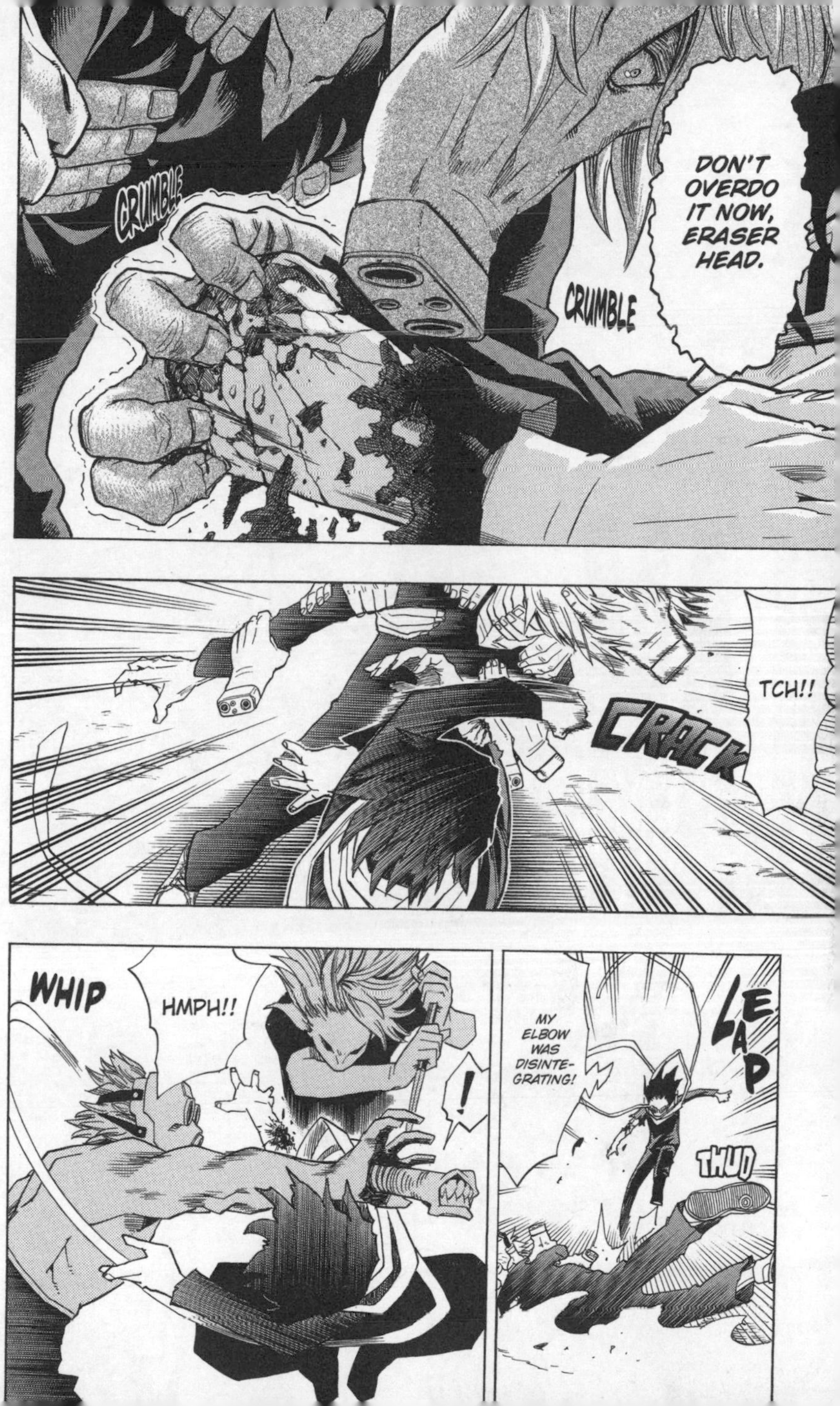
DON'T OVERDO IT NOW, ERASER HEAD.
CRUMBLE
CRUMBLE
TCH!!
CRACK
LEAP
MY ELBOW WAS DISINTE-GRATING!
THUD
HMPH!!
WHIP
!

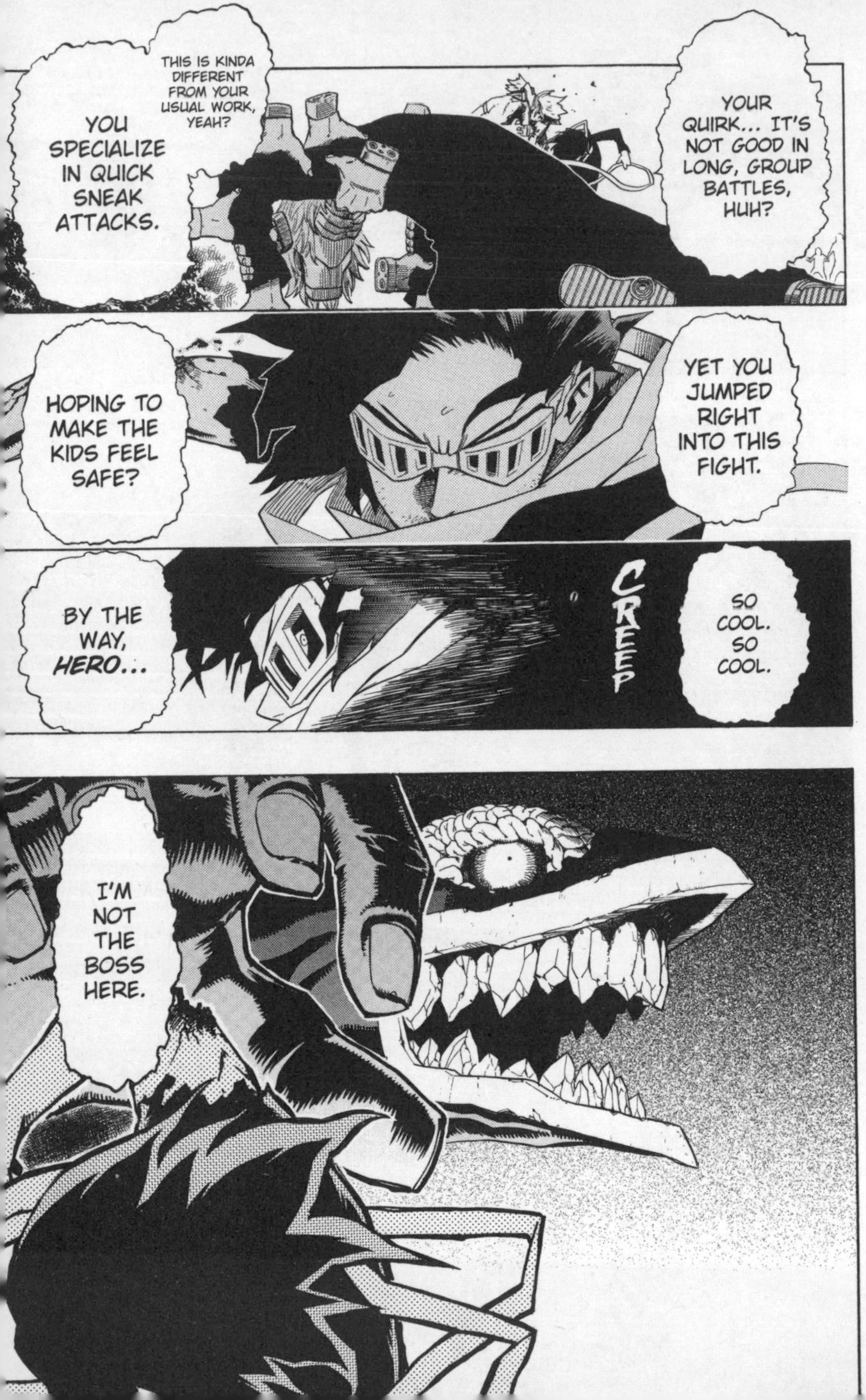
YOUR QUIRK... IT'S NOT GOOD IN LONG, GROUP BATTLES, HUH?
THIS IS KINDA DIFFERENT FROM YOUR USUAL WORK, YEAH?
YOU SPECIALIZE IN QUICK SNEAK ATTACKS.
YET YOU JUMPED RIGHT INTO THIS FIGHT.
HOPING TO MAKE THE KIDS FEEL SAFE?
SO COOL. SO COOL.
CREEP
BY THE WAY, *HERO*...
I'M NOT THE BOSS HERE.

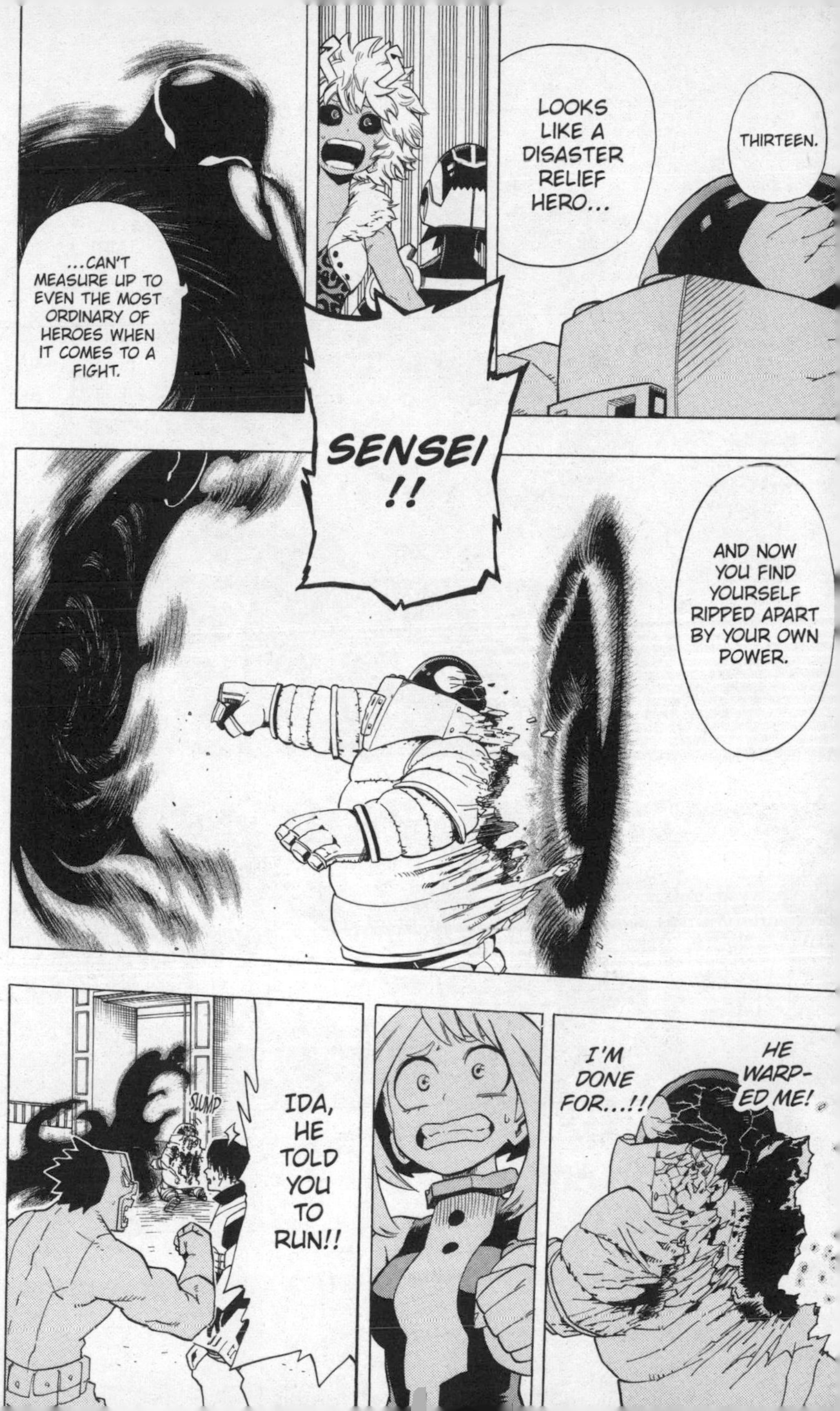
THIRTEEN.
LOOKS LIKE A DISASTER RELIEF HERO...
...CAN'T MEASURE UP TO EVEN THE MOST ORDINARY OF HEROES WHEN IT COMES TO A FIGHT.
SENSEI!!
AND NOW YOU FIND YOURSELF RIPPED APART BY YOUR OWN POWER.
HE WARPED ME!
I'M DONE FOR...!!
IDA, HE TOLD YOU TO RUN!!
SLUMP

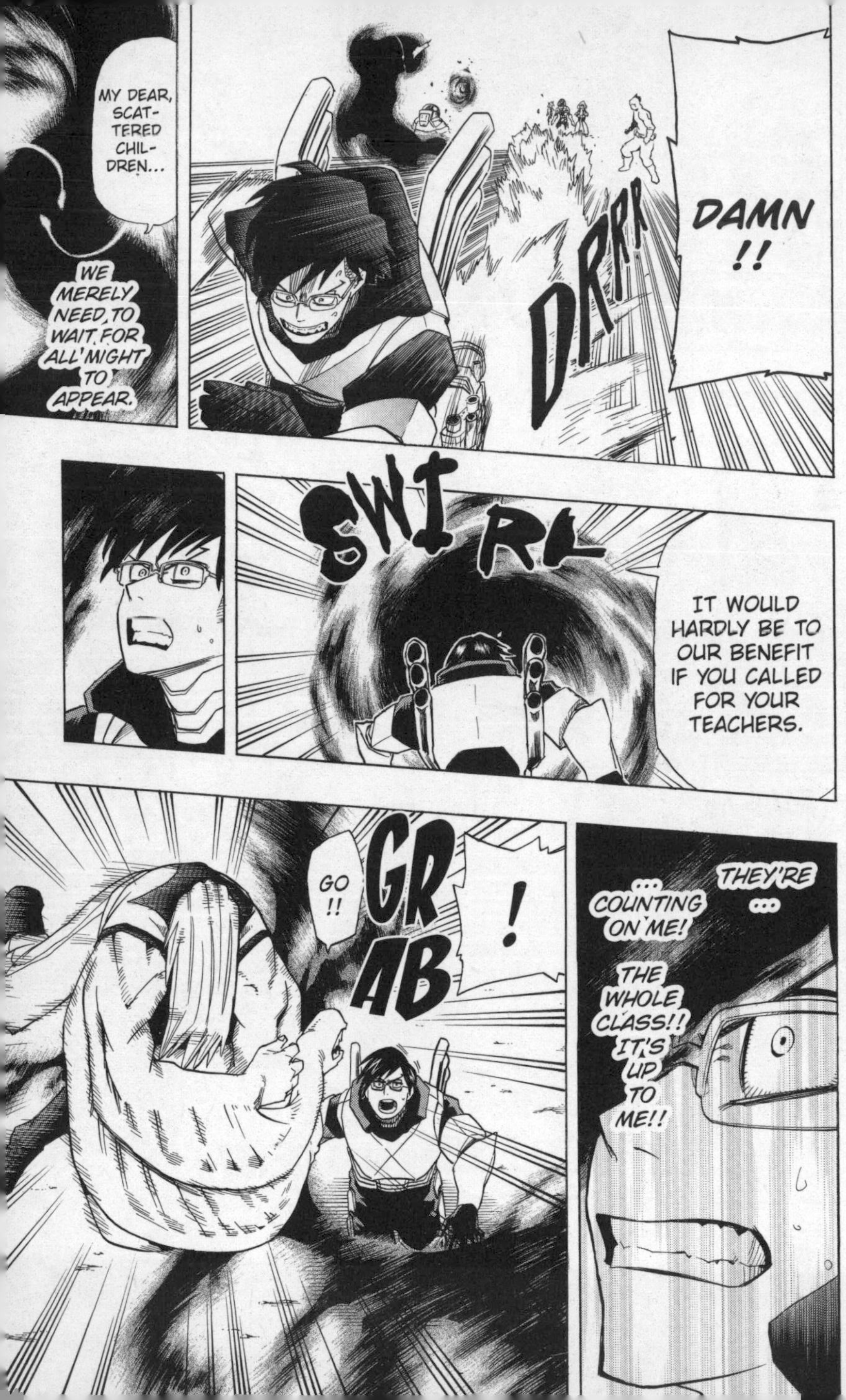

DAMN !!
DRRR
MY DEAR, SCATTERED CHILDREN...
WE MERELY NEED TO WAIT FOR ALL MIGHT TO APPEAR.
SWIRL
IT WOULD HARDLY BE TO OUR BENEFIT IF YOU CALLED FOR YOUR TEACHERS.
THEY'RE ...
... COUNTING ON ME!
THE WHOLE CLASS!!
IT'S UP TO ME!!
!
GRAB
GO !!

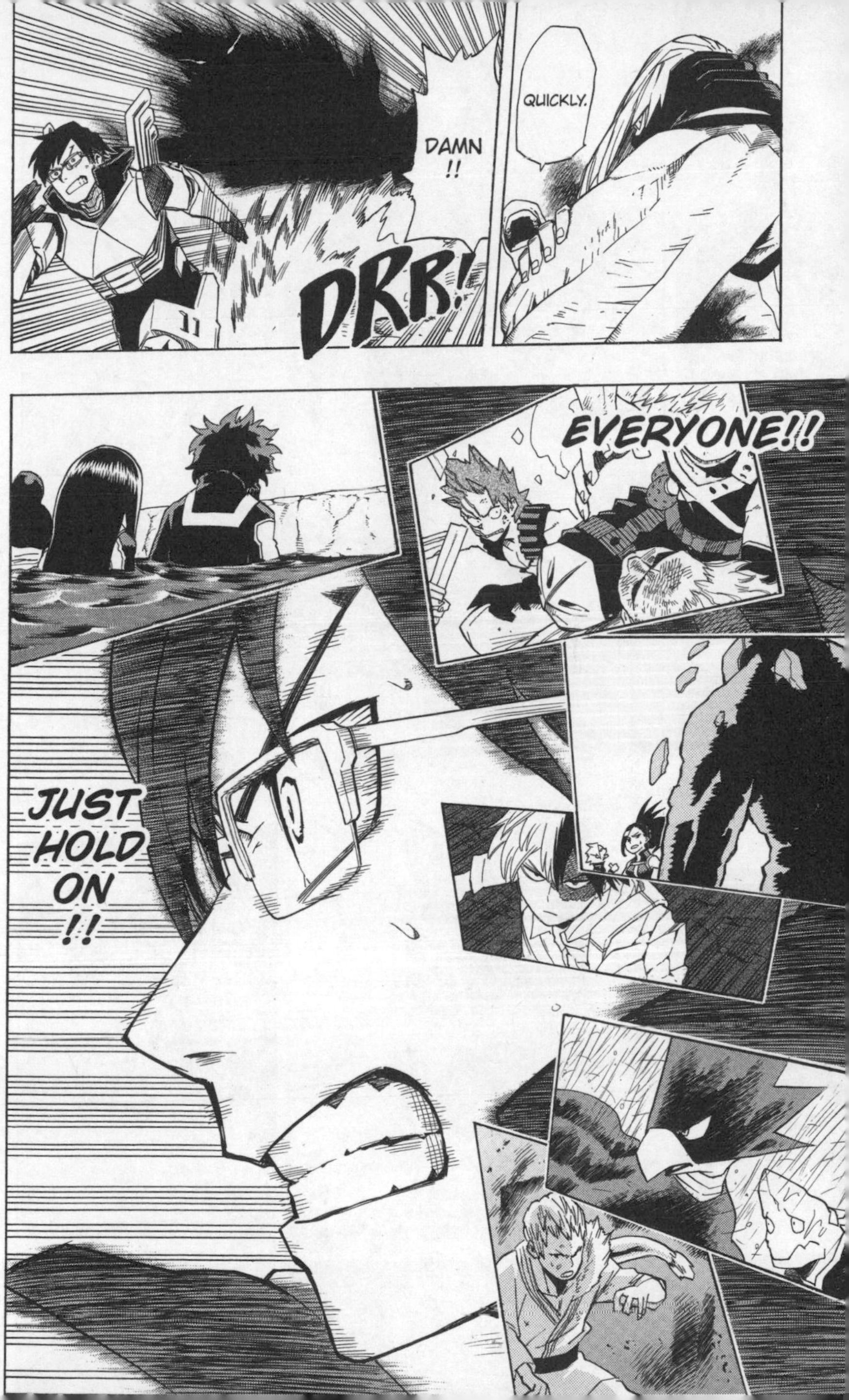
QUICKLY.
DAMN !!
DRR!
EVERYONE!!
JUST HOLD ON !!

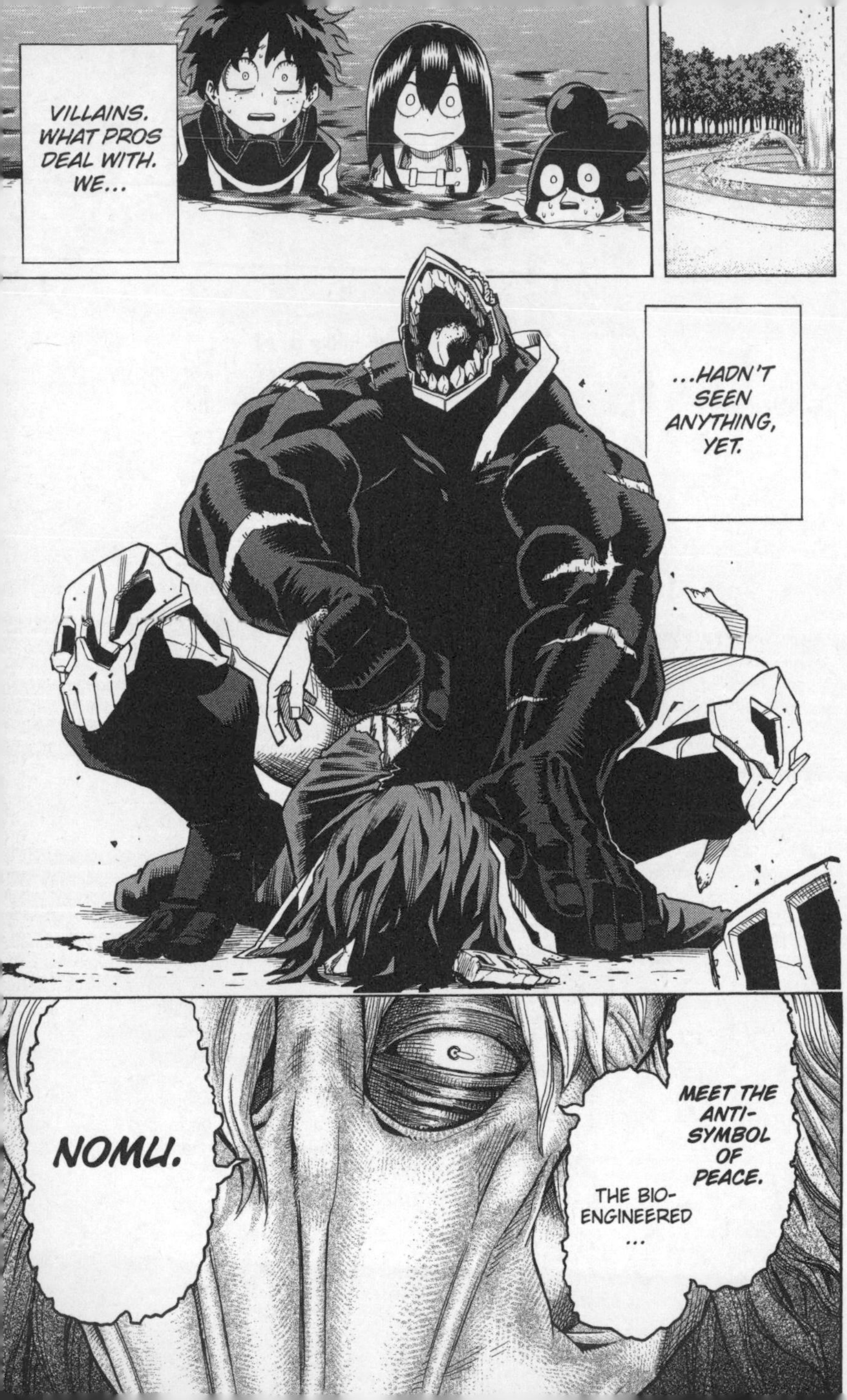
VILLAINS. WHAT PROS DEAL WITH. WE...
...HADN'T SEEN ANYTHING, YET.
MEET THE ANTI-SYMBOL OF PEACE.
THE BIO-ENGINEERED ...
NOMU.

MOMO YAOYOROZU (15)

RELATIVELY CASUAL

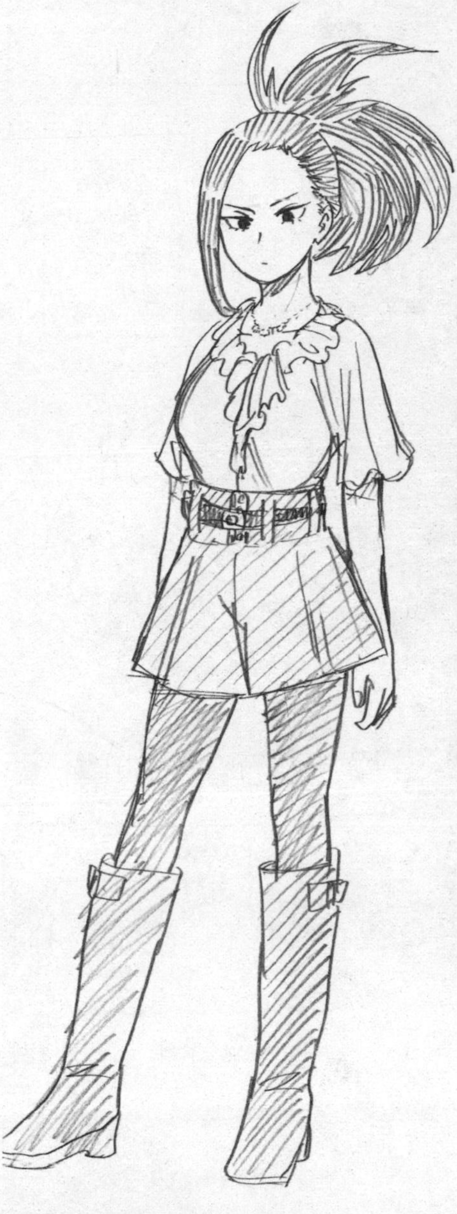

Birthday: 9/23
Height: 173 cm
Favorite Thing: Reading (especially illustrated encyclopedias)

BEHIND THE SCENES

First, I have to apologize for something. When the chapter with the explanation of her ability was first published in *Jump*, I wrote that she couldn't produce "organic matter." It should have been "living things." I thought I could fix it in the editing stage, but the error wound up getting printed. If she couldn't produce organic matter, then the insulator sheet and clothing would be impossible. Anyhow, getting the explanation of a superpower wrong in a manga about superpowers is unforgivable. I can't apologize enough. If she knows the chemical makeup, she can produce any nonliving thing.

BEHIND THE SCENES

Just like with Ida, I originally thought to give her Quirk to a pro hero, but I made the change when I realized that such an almighty ability would be much more interesting in the hands of someone less experienced.

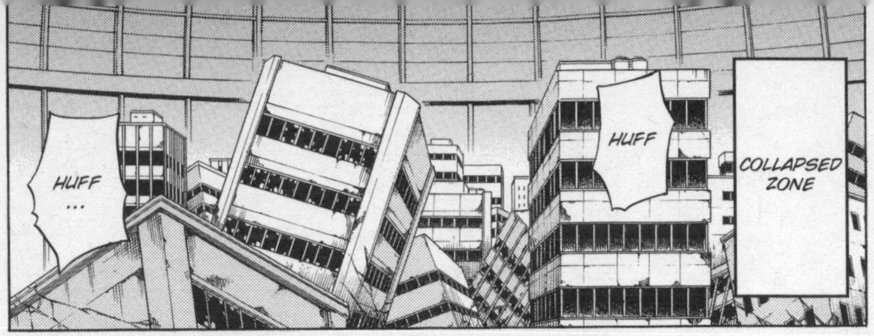
COLLAPSED ZONE
HUFF
HUFF ...

No.17 - Game Over

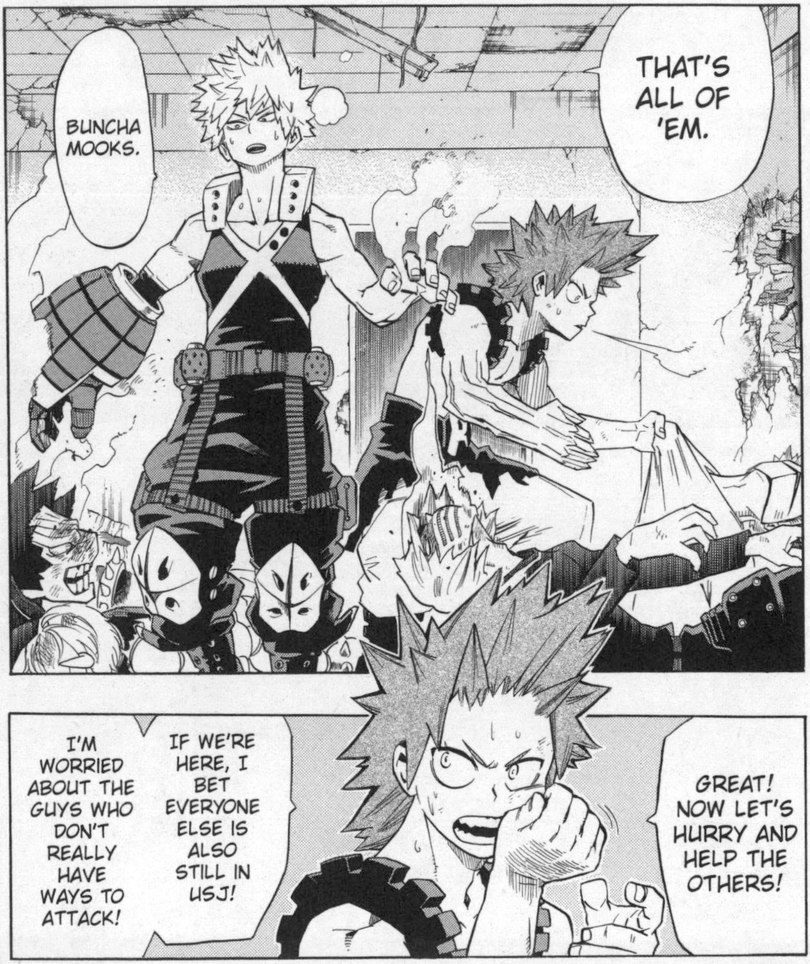
THAT'S ALL OF 'EM.
BUNCHA MOOKS.
GREAT! NOW LET'S HURRY AND HELP THE OTHERS!
IF WE'RE HERE, I BET EVERYONE ELSE IS ALSO STILL IN USJ!
I'M WORRIED ABOUT THE GUYS WHO DON'T REALLY HAVE WAYS TO ATTACK!

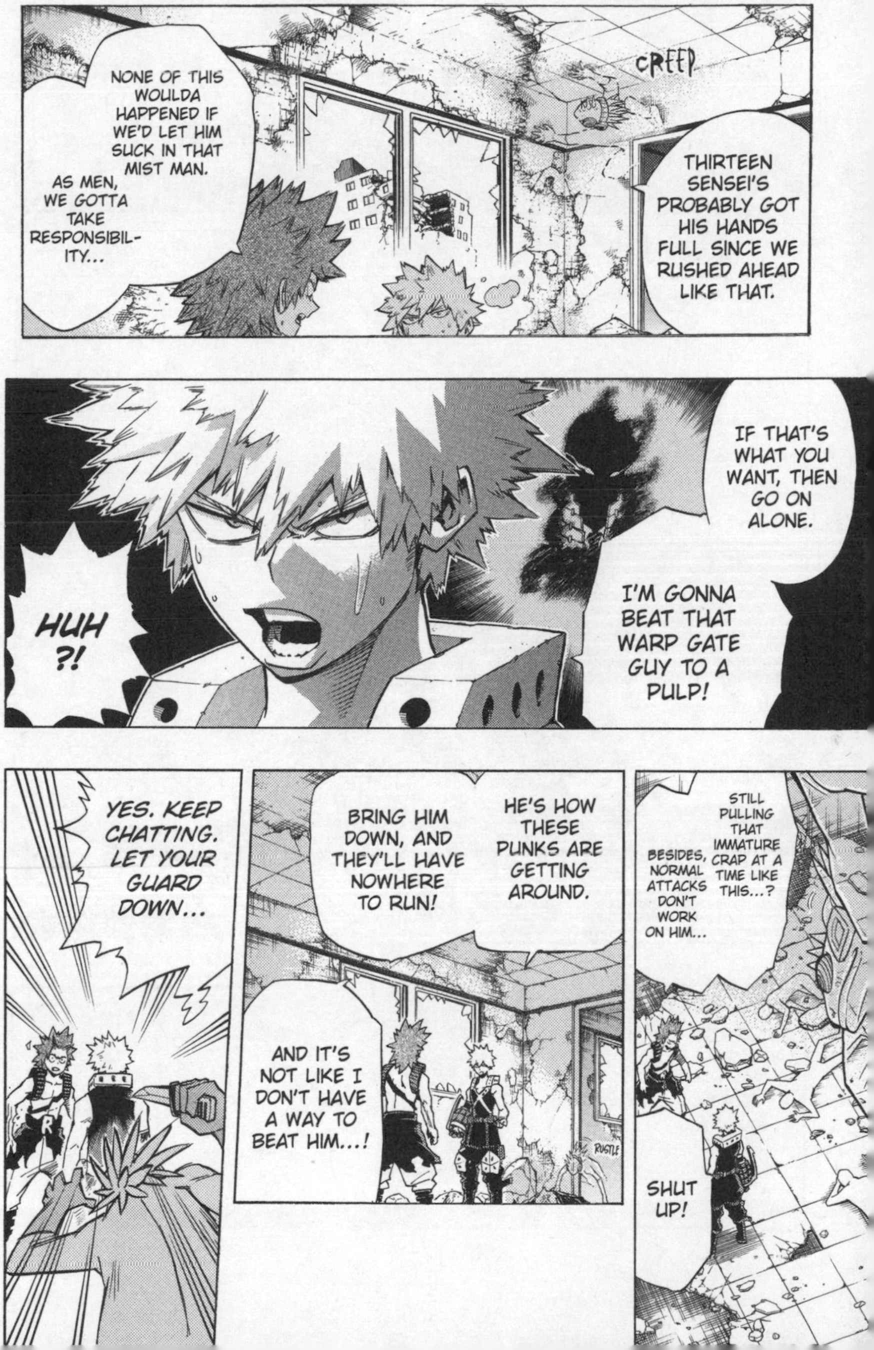
CREEP
THIRTEEN SENSEI'S PROBABLY GOT HIS HANDS FULL SINCE WE RUSHED AHEAD LIKE THAT.
NONE OF THIS WOULDA HAPPENED IF WE'D LET HIM SUCK IN THAT MIST MAN.
AS MEN, WE GOTTA TAKE RESPONSIBIL-ITY...
IF THAT'S WHAT YOU WANT, THEN GO ON ALONE.
I'M GONNA BEAT THAT WARP GATE GUY TO A PULP!
HUH?!
STILL PULLING THAT IMMATURE CRAP AT A TIME LIKE THIS...?
BESIDES, NORMAL ATTACKS DON'T WORK ON HIM...
SHUT UP!
HE'S HOW THESE PUNKS ARE GETTING AROUND.
BRING HIM DOWN, AND THEY'LL HAVE NOWHERE TO RUN!
RUSTLE
AND IT'S NOT LIKE I DON'T HAVE A WAY TO BEAT HIM...!
YES. KEEP CHATTING. LET YOUR GUARD DOWN...

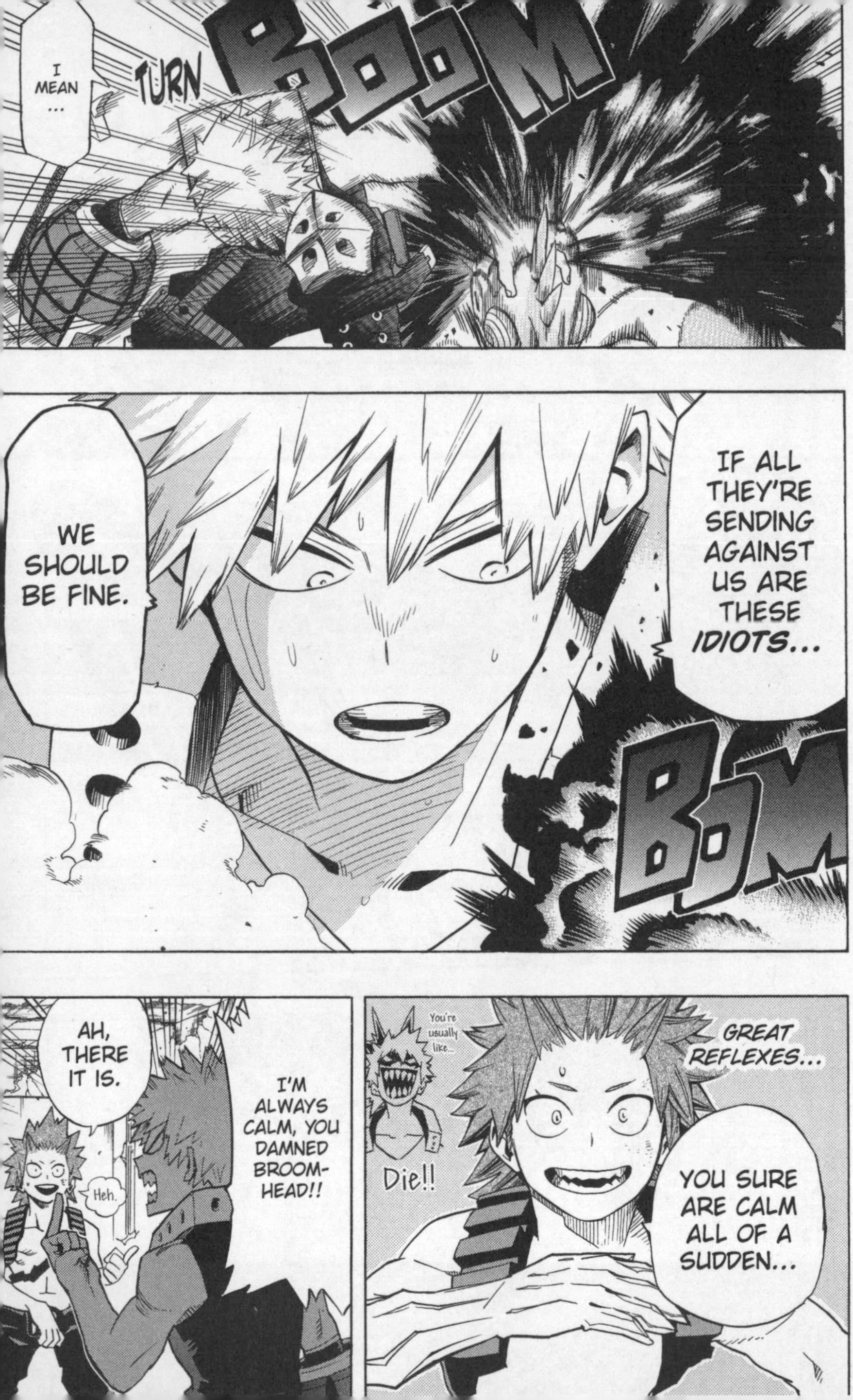

BOOOM
TURN
I MEAN ...
IF ALL THEY'RE SENDING AGAINST US ARE THESE *IDIOTS...*
BOOM
WE SHOULD BE FINE.
GREAT REFLEXES...
You're usually like...
YOU SURE ARE CALM ALL OF A SUDDEN...
Die!!
I'M ALWAYS CALM, YOU DAMNED BROOM-HEAD!!
AH, THERE IT IS.
Heh.

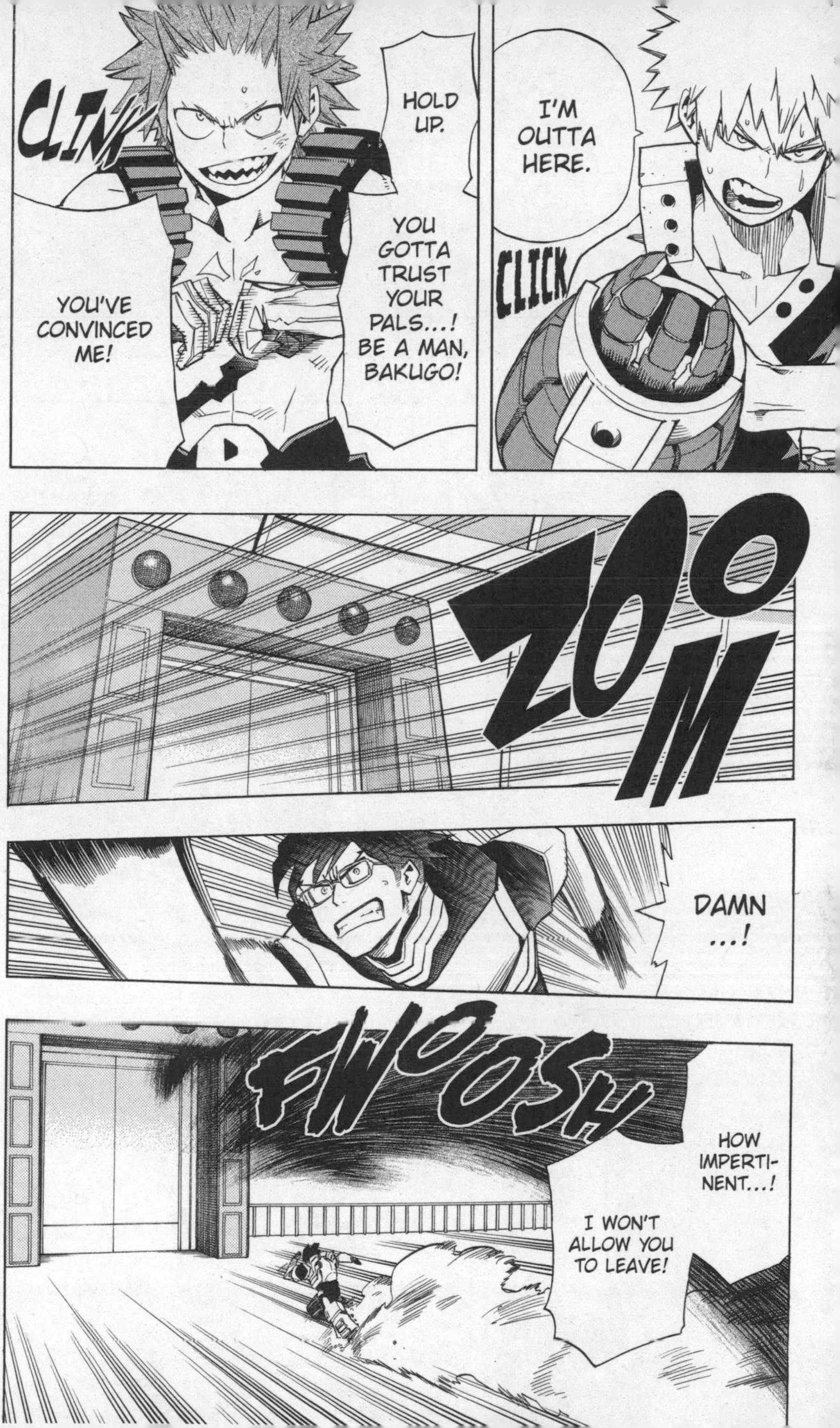
I'M OUTTA HERE.
CLICK
HOLD UP.
CLINK
YOU GOTTA TRUST YOUR PALS...! BE A MAN, BAKUGO!
YOU'VE CONVINCED ME!
ZOOOM
DAMN ...!
FWOOOSH
HOW IMPERTI- NENT...!
I WON'T ALLOW YOU TO LEAVE!

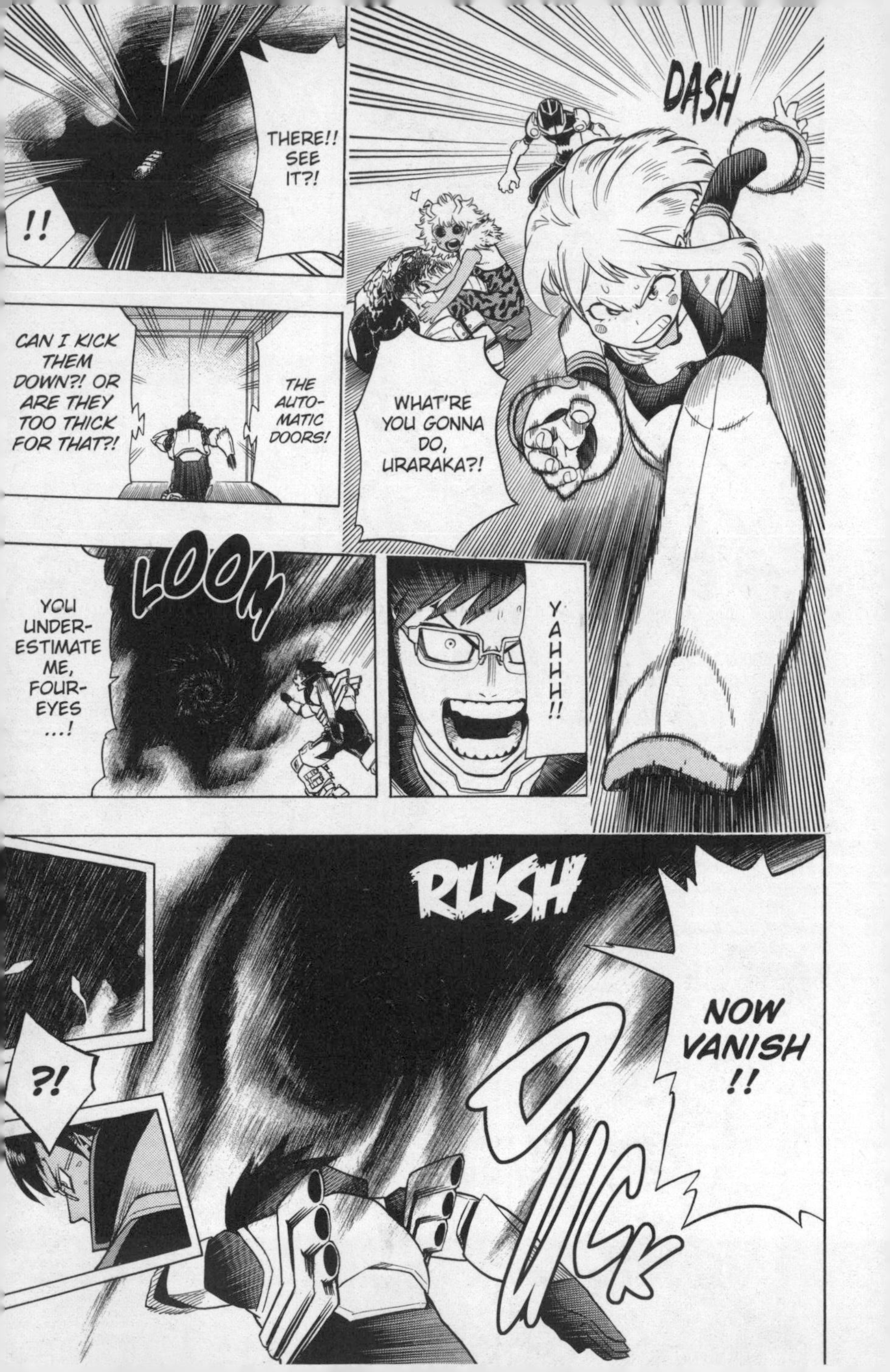
DASH
WHAT'RE YOU GONNA DO, URARAKA?!
THERE!! SEE IT?!
!!
THE AUTO-MATIC DOORS!
CAN I KICK THEM DOWN?! OR ARE THEY TOO THICK FOR THAT?!
YAHHHH!!
LOOM
YOU UNDER-ESTIMATE ME, FOUR-EYES ...!
RUSH
NOW VANISH !!
?!

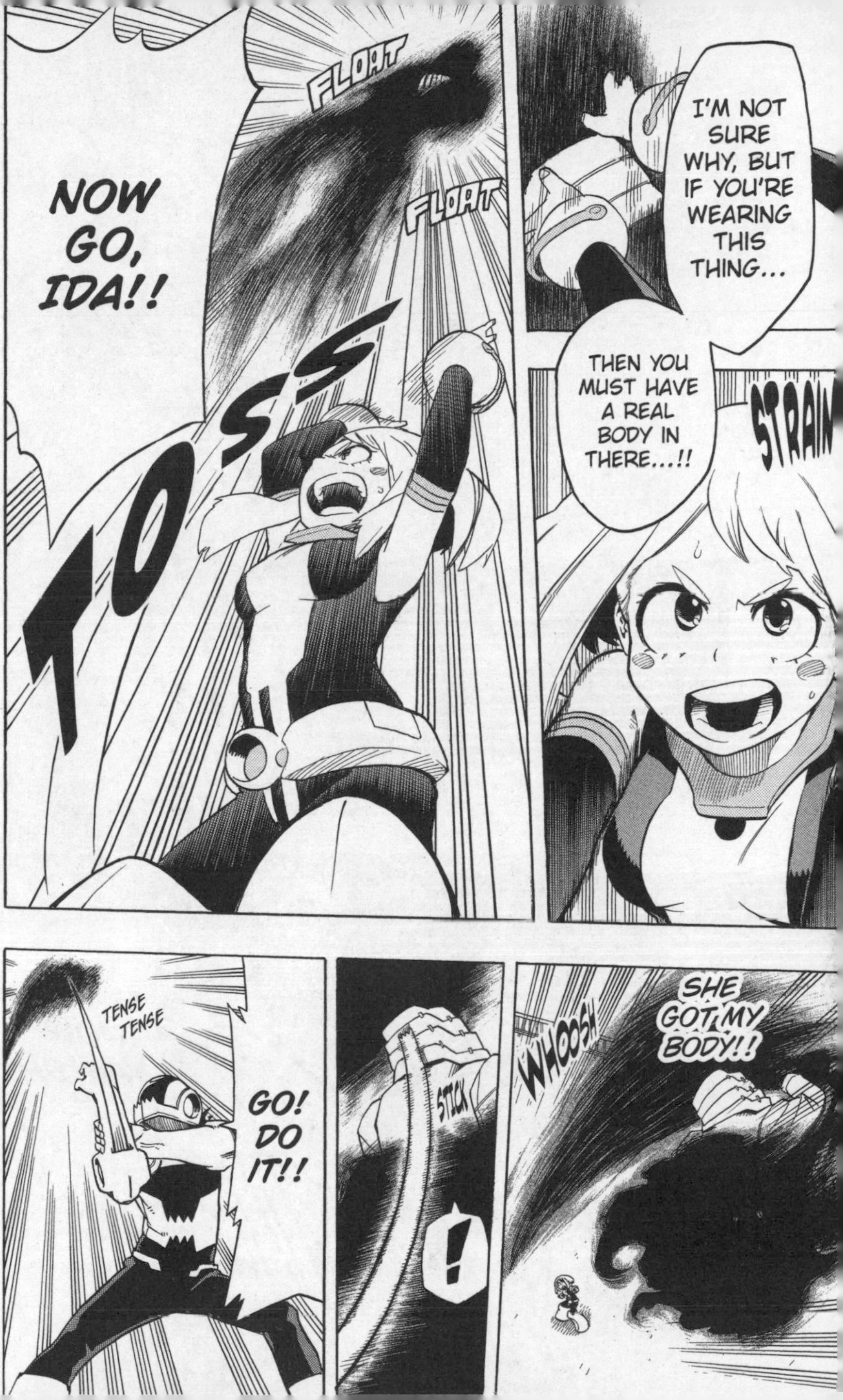
I'M NOT SURE WHY, BUT IF YOU'RE WEARING THIS THING...
THEN YOU MUST HAVE A REAL BODY IN THERE...!!
STRAIN
FLOAT
FLOAT
NOW GO, IDA!!
TOSS
SHE GOT MY BODY!!
WHOOSH
STICK
!
TENSE TENSE
GO! DO IT!!

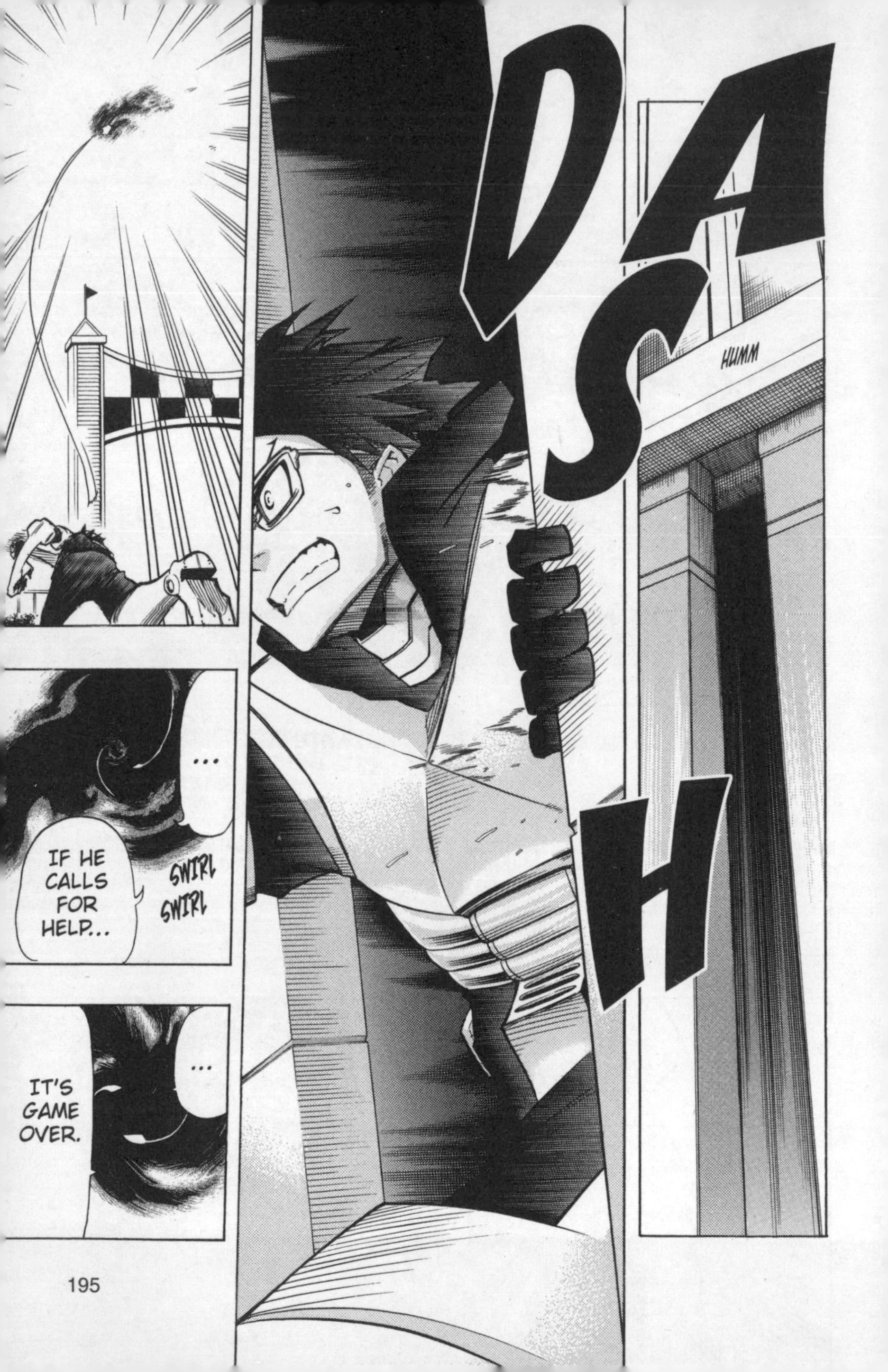
HUMM
DASH
...
IF HE CALLS FOR HELP...
SWIRL SWIRL
...
IT'S GAME OVER.

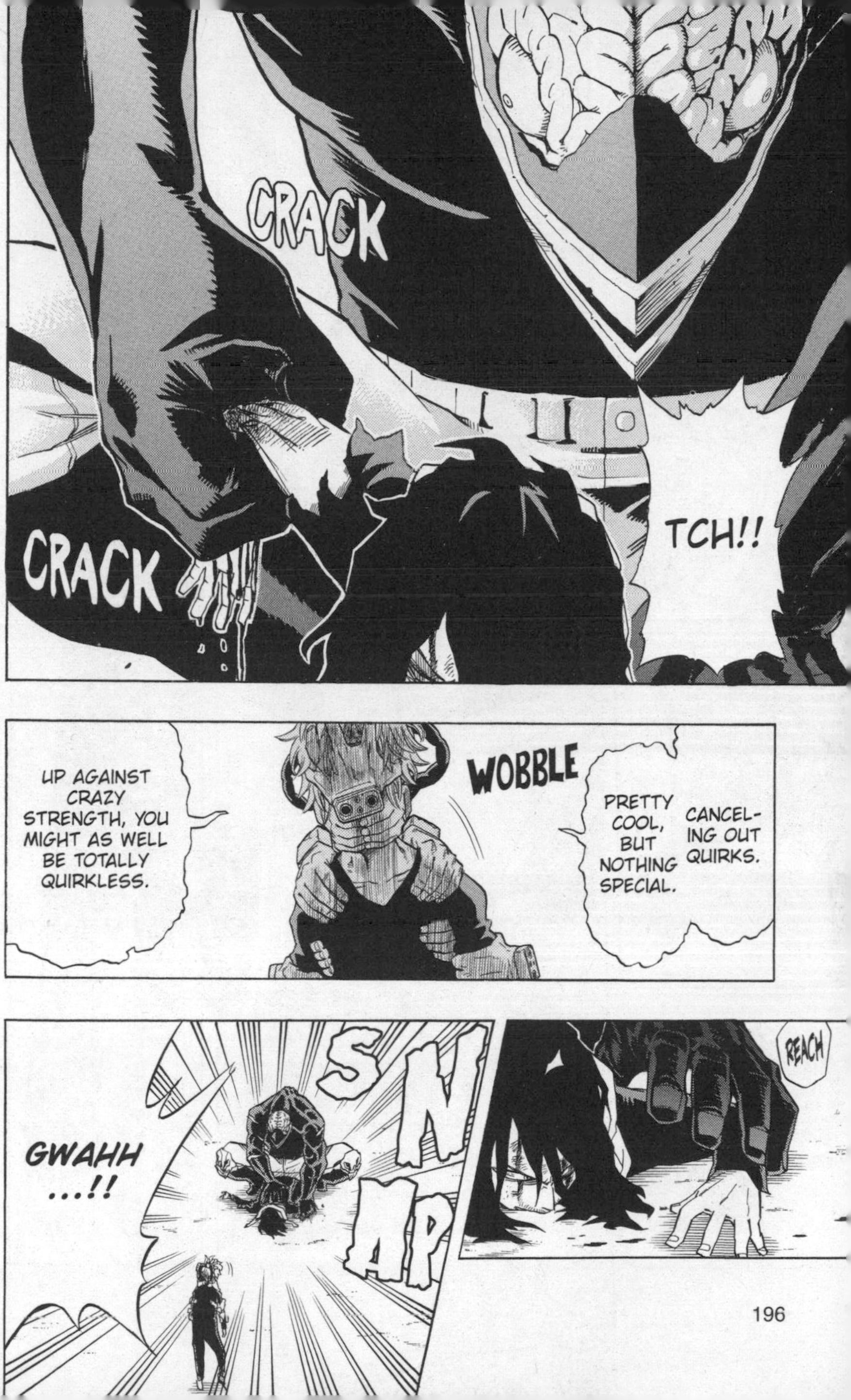
CRACK
TCH!!
CRACK
CANCELING OUT QUIRKS.
PRETTY COOL, BUT NOTHING SPECIAL.
WOBBLE
UP AGAINST CRAZY STRENGTH, YOU MIGHT AS WELL BE TOTALLY QUIRKLESS.
REACH
SNAP
GWAHH ...!!

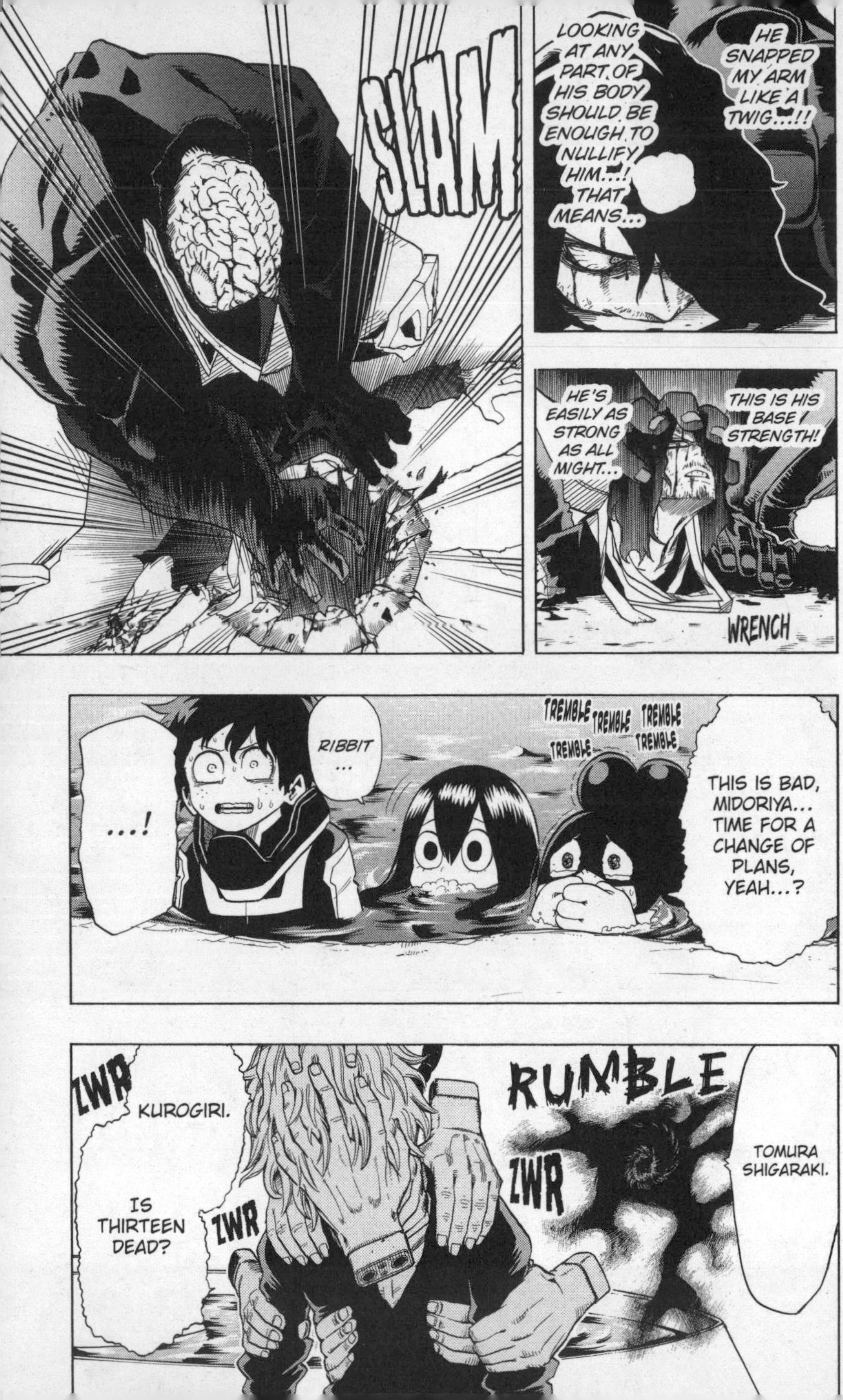
HE SNAPPED MY ARM LIKE A TWIG...!!
LOOKING AT ANY PART OF HIS BODY SHOULD BE ENOUGH TO NULLIFY HIM...! THAT MEANS...
THIS IS HIS BASE STRENGTH!
HE'S EASILY AS STRONG AS ALL MIGHT...
WRENCH
SLAM
TREMBLE TREMBLE TREMBLE TREMBLE TREMBLE
THIS IS BAD, MIDORIYA... TIME FOR A CHANGE OF PLANS, YEAH...?
RIBBIT ...
...!
TOMURA SHIGARAKI.
RUMBLE
ZWR
ZWR
KUROGIRI.
IS THIRTEEN DEAD?
ZWR

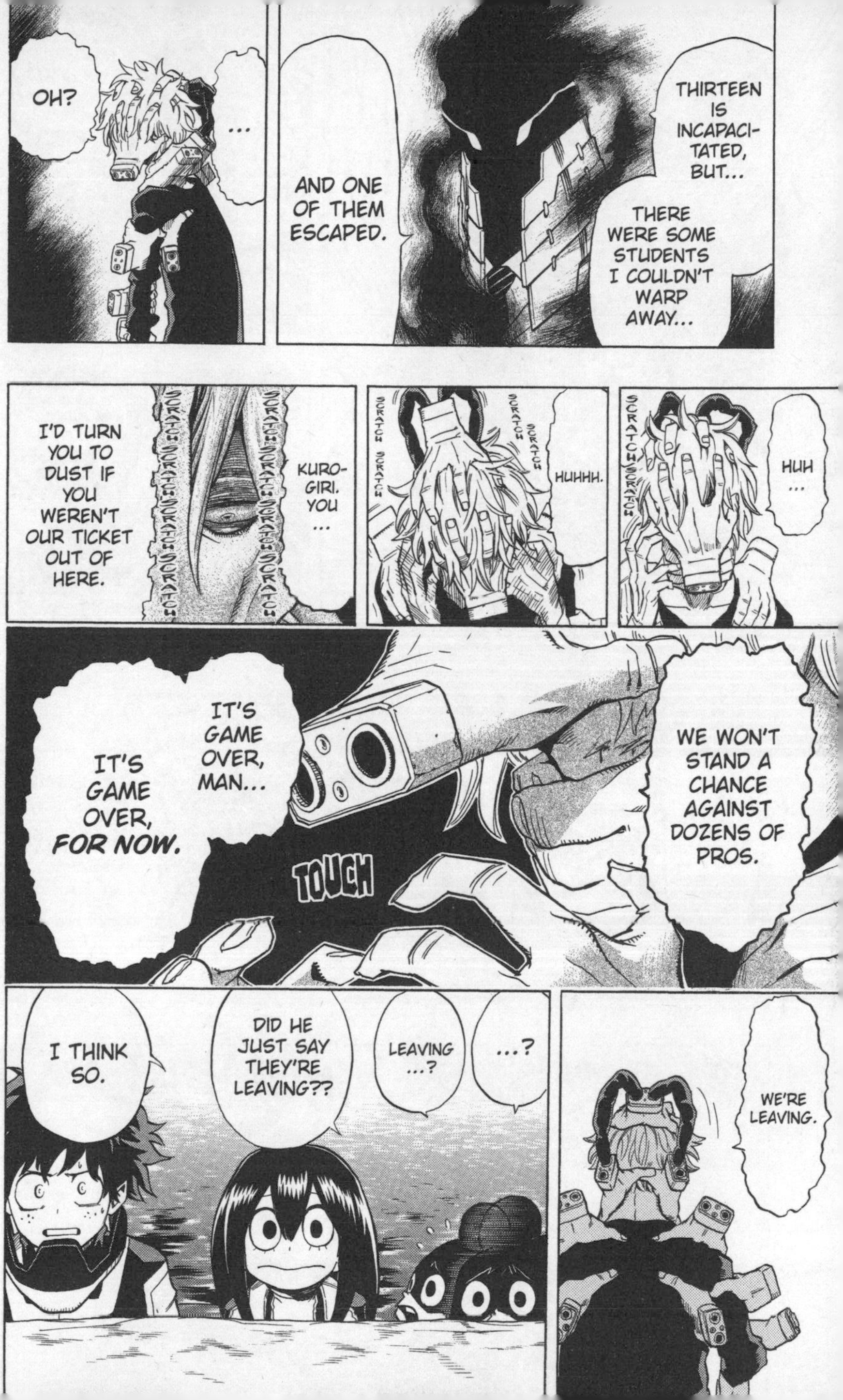
THIRTEEN IS INCAPACITATED, BUT...
THERE WERE SOME STUDENTS I COULDN'T WARP AWAY...
AND ONE OF THEM ESCAPED.
OH?
...
SCRATCH SCRATCH
HUH ...
SCRATCH SCRATCH
SCRATCH SCRATCH
HUHHH.
SCRATCH SCRATCH SCRATCH SCRATCH
KURO-GIRI. YOU ...
SCRATCH SCRATCH SCRATCH SCRATCH
I'D TURN YOU TO DUST IF YOU WEREN'T OUR TICKET OUT OF HERE.
WE WON'T STAND A CHANCE AGAINST DOZENS OF PROS.
TOUCH
IT'S GAME OVER, MAN...
IT'S GAME OVER, *FOR NOW.*
WE'RE LEAVING.
...?
LEAVING ...?
DID HE JUST SAY THEY'RE LEAVING??
I THINK SO.

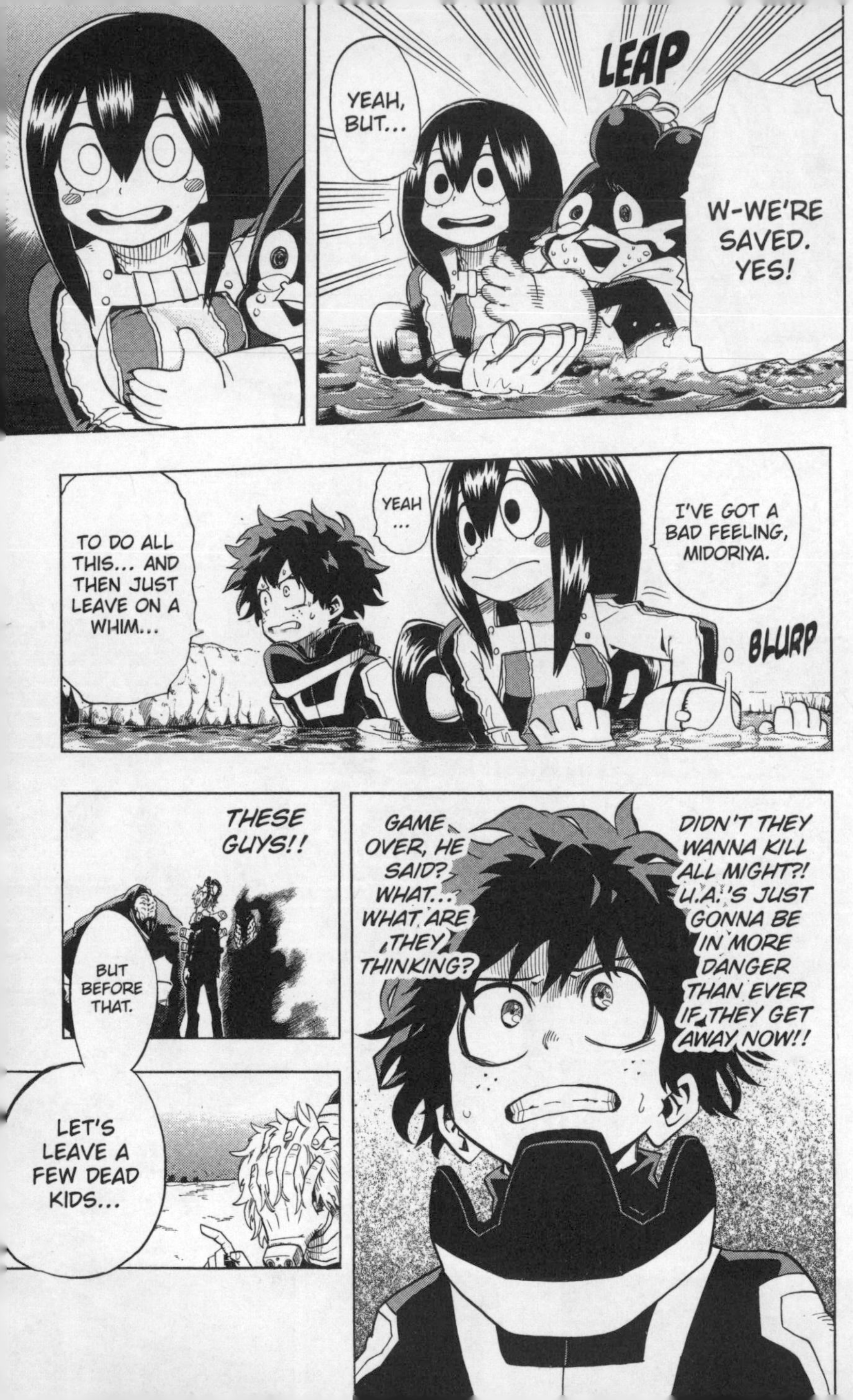
LEAP
W-WE'RE SAVED. YES!
YEAH, BUT...
I'VE GOT A BAD FEELING, MIDORIYA.
BLURP
YEAH ...
TO DO ALL THIS... AND THEN JUST LEAVE ON A WHIM...
DIDN'T THEY WANNA KILL ALL MIGHT?! U.A.'S JUST GONNA BE IN MORE DANGER THAN EVER IF THEY GET AWAY NOW!!
GAME OVER, HE SAID? WHAT... WHAT ARE THEY THINKING?
THESE GUYS!!
BUT BEFORE THAT.
LET'S LEAVE A FEW DEAD KIDS...

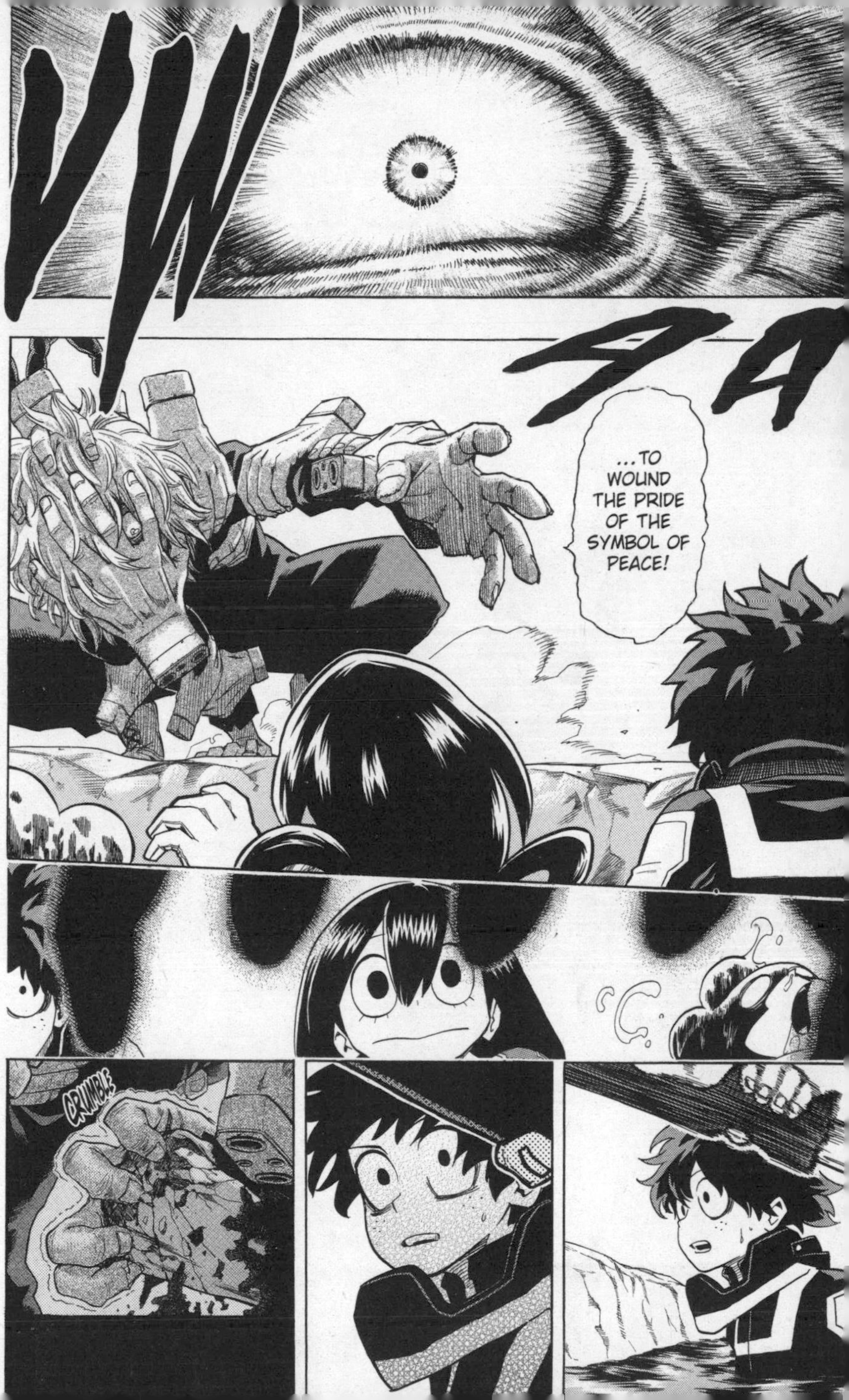
VWAA
...TO WOUND THE PRIDE OF THE SYMBOL OF PEACE!
CRUMBLE

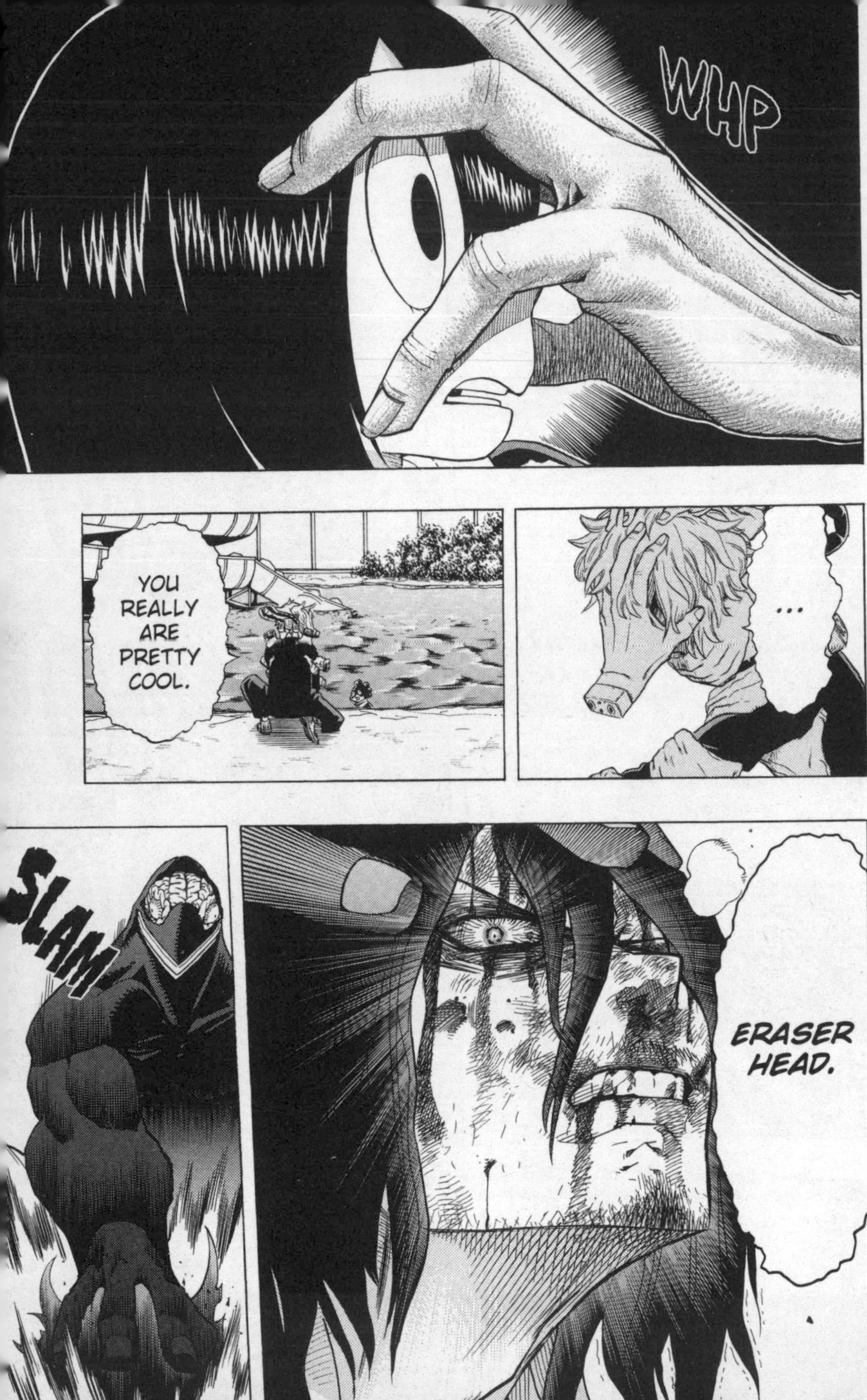
WHP
...
YOU REALLY ARE PRETTY COOL.
ERASER HEAD.
SLAM

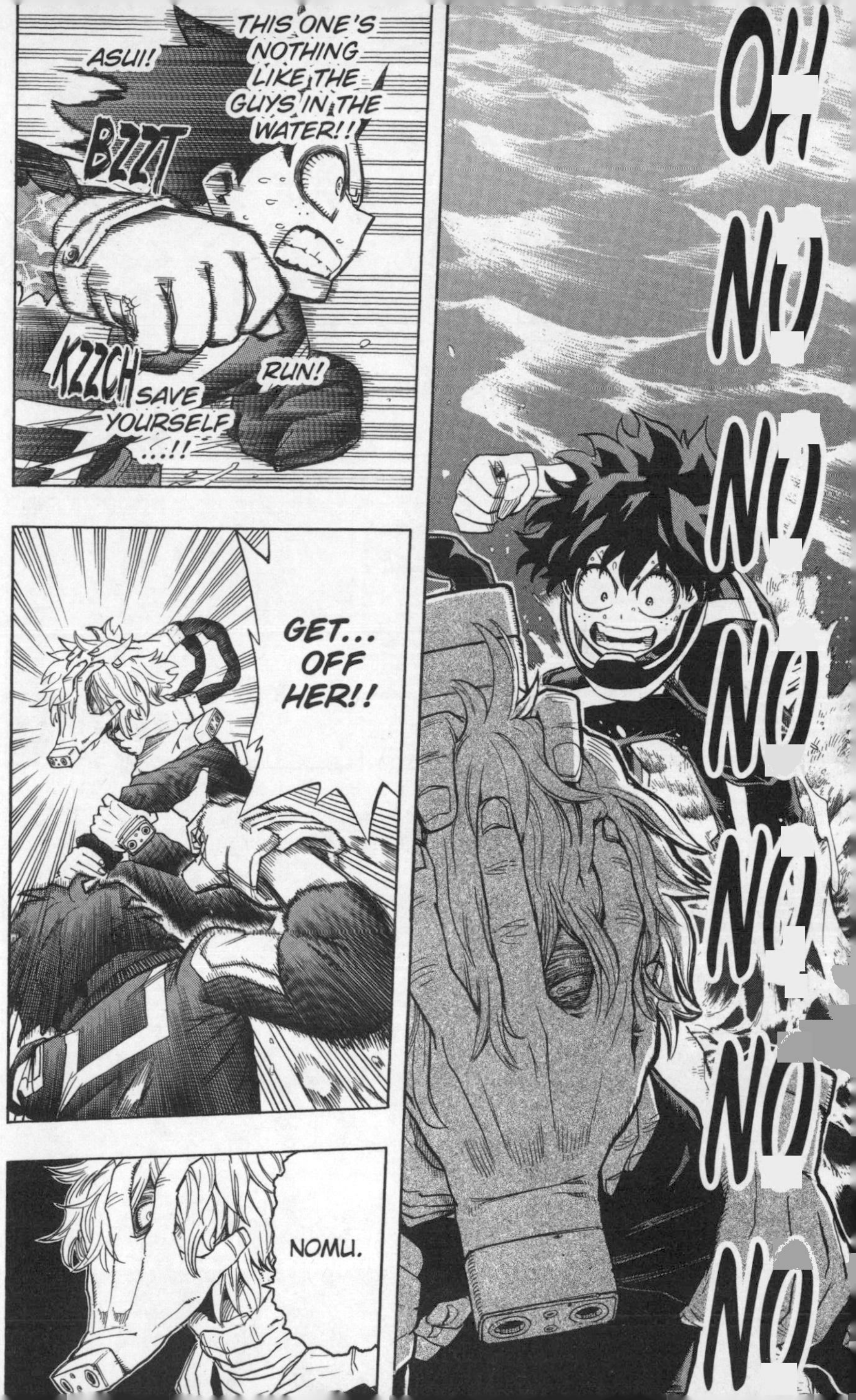
OH NO NO NO NO NO NO NO
THIS ONE'S NOTHING LIKE THE GUYS IN THE WATER!!
ASUI!
BZZT
RUN!
KZZCH
SAVE YOURSELF...!!
GET... OFF HER!!
NOMU.

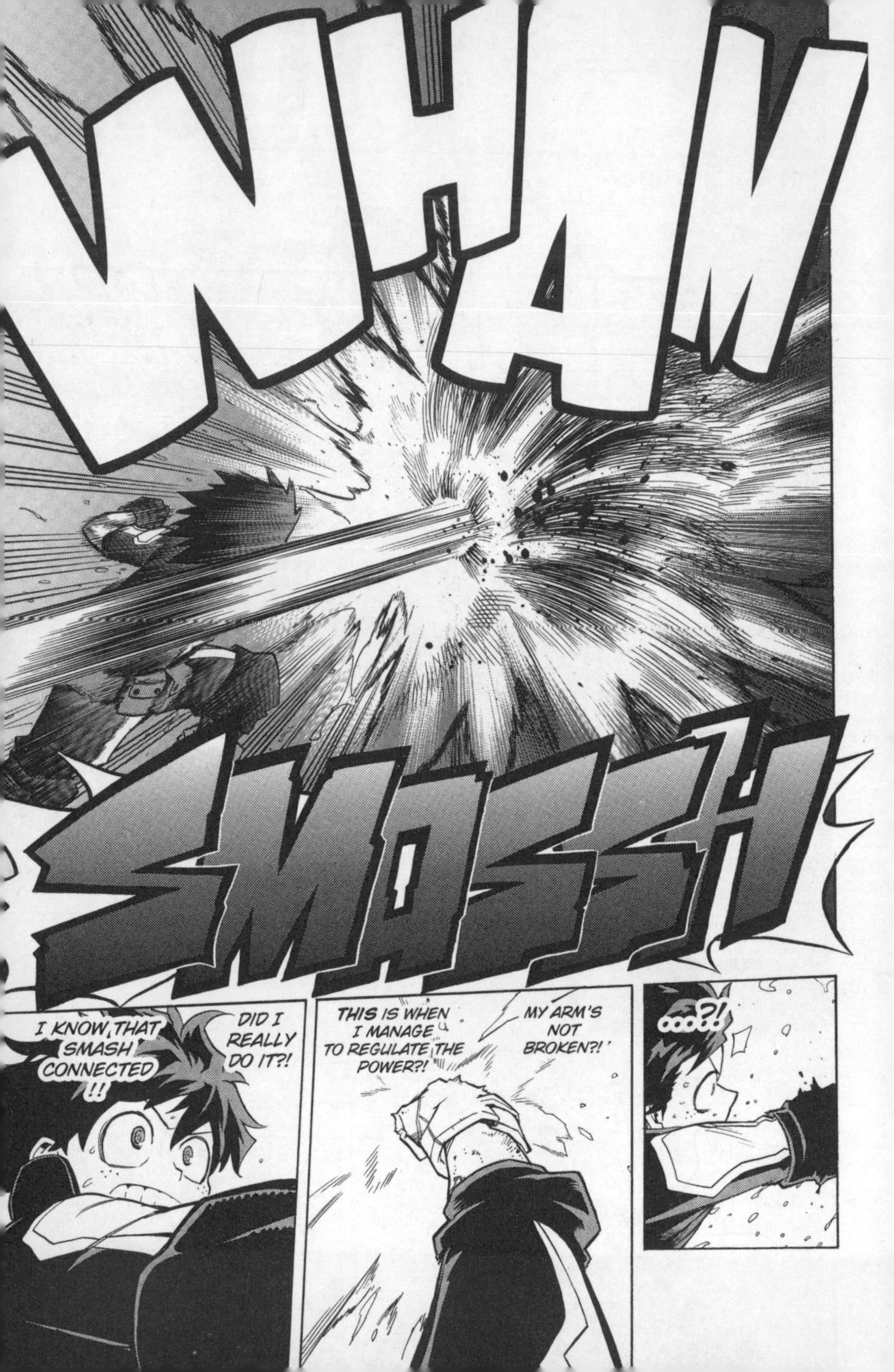
WHAM
SMASH
...?!
MY ARM'S NOT BROKEN?!
THIS IS WHEN I MANAGE TO REGULATE THE POWER?!
DID I REALLY DO IT?!
I KNOW THAT SMASH CONNECTED!!

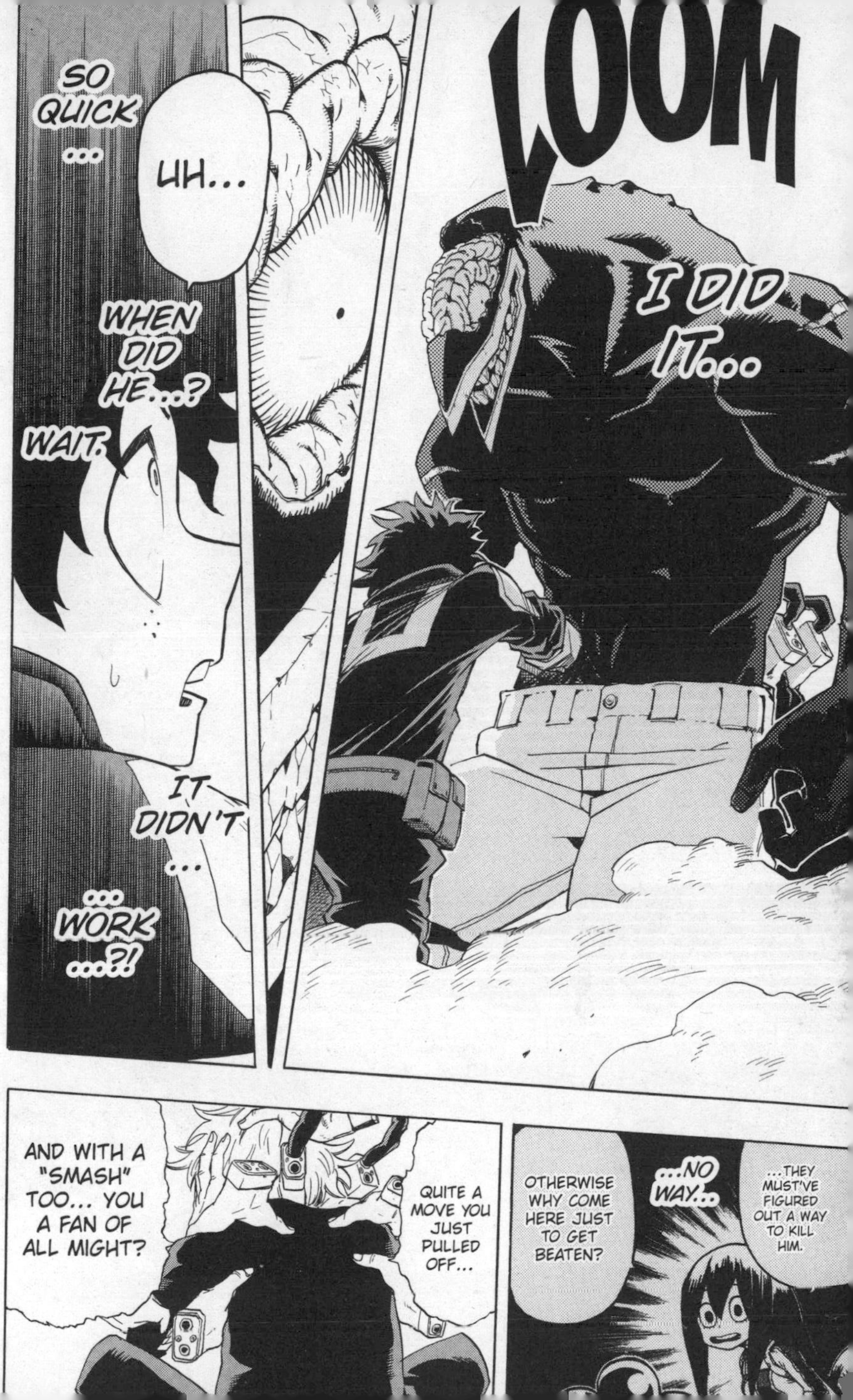
LOOM
I DID IT...
UH...
SO QUICK...
WHEN DID HE...?
WAIT.
IT DIDN'T...
...WORK...?!
...THEY MUST'VE FIGURED OUT A WAY TO KILL HIM.
...NO WAY...
OTHERWISE WHY COME HERE JUST TO GET BEATEN?
QUITE A MOVE YOU JUST PULLED OFF...
AND WITH A "SMASH" TOO... YOU A FAN OF ALL MIGHT?

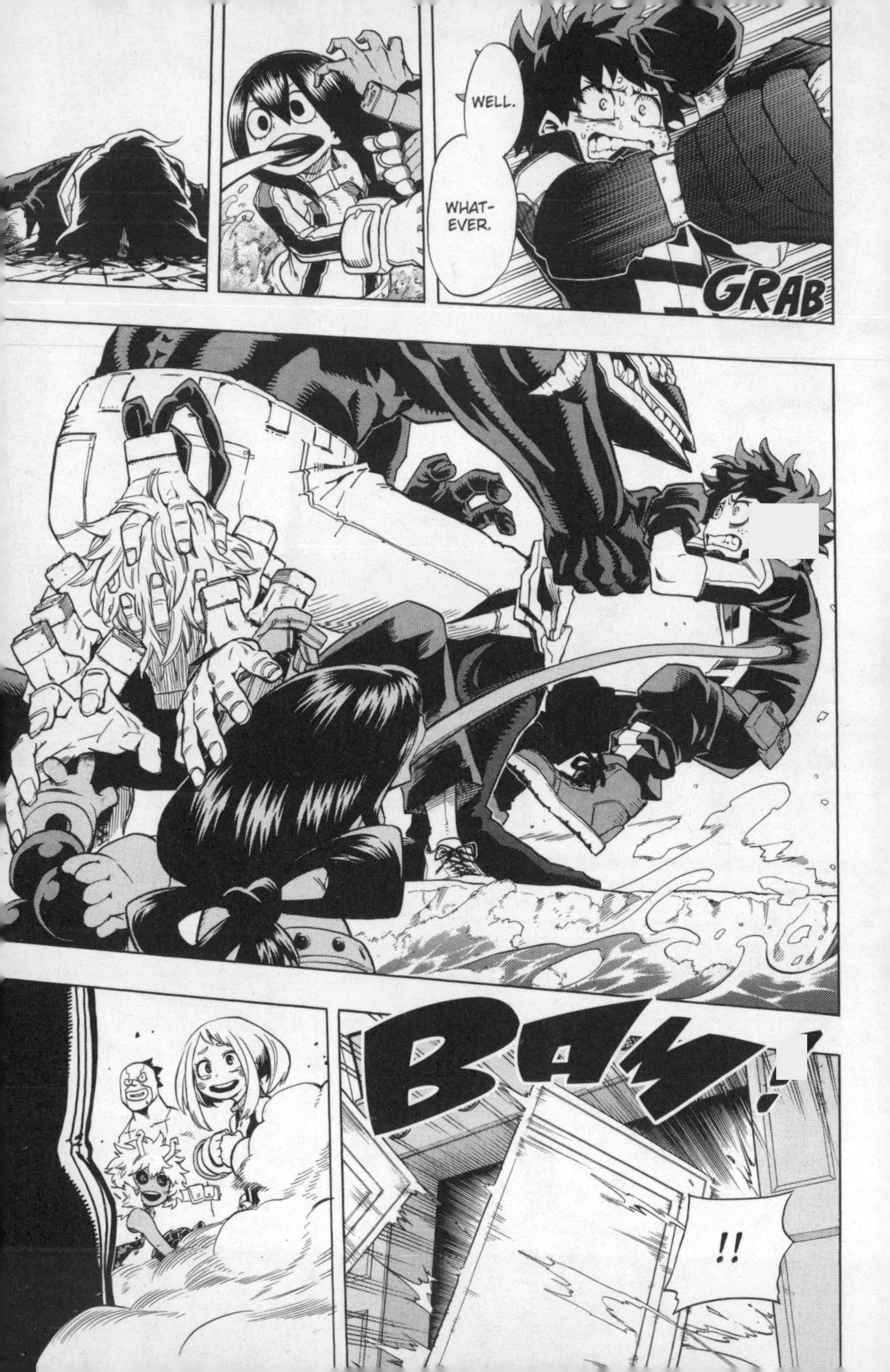
WELL.
WHAT-EVER.
GRAB
BAM!
!!

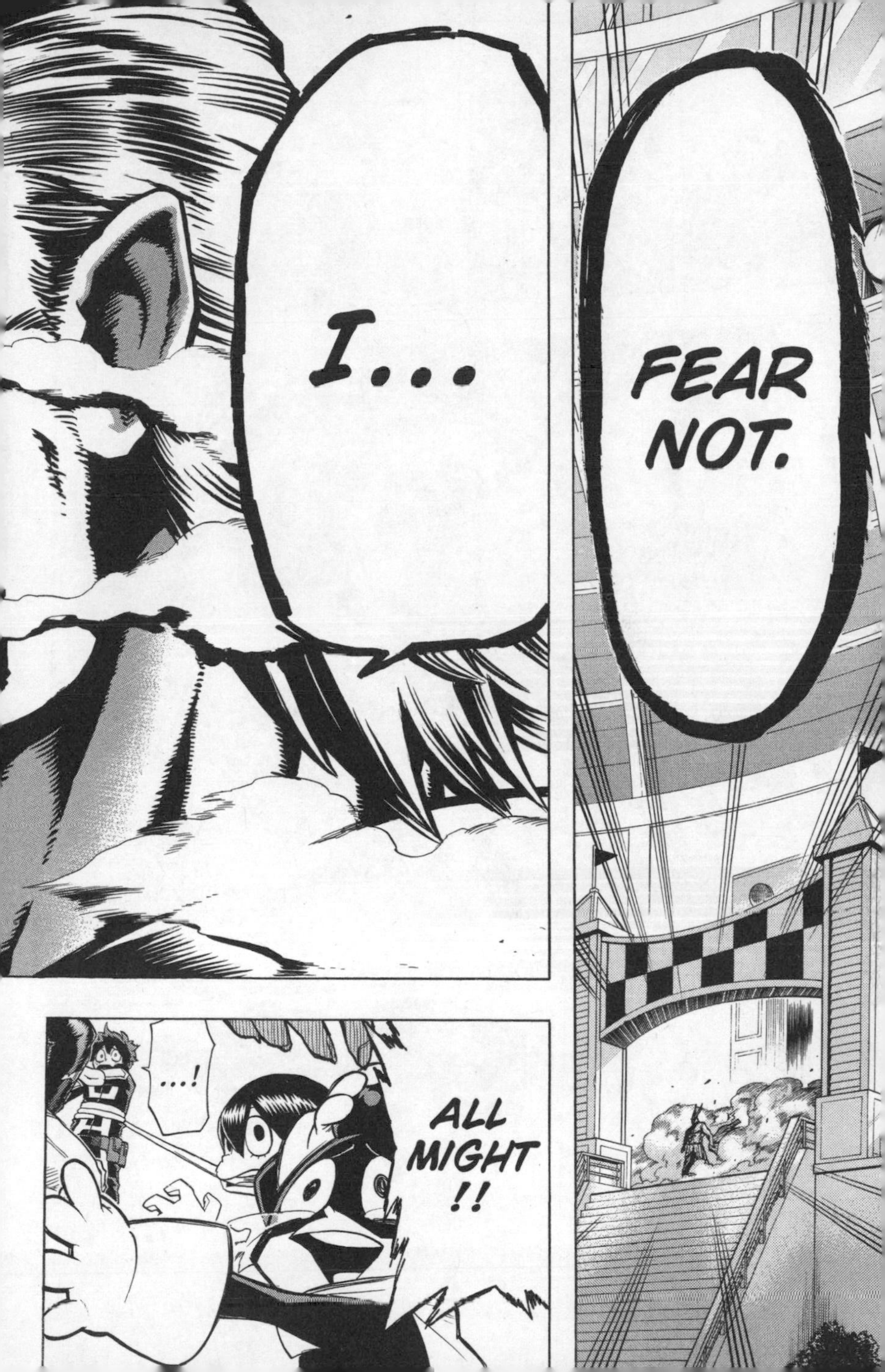

FEAR NOT.
I...
ALL MIGHT !!
...!

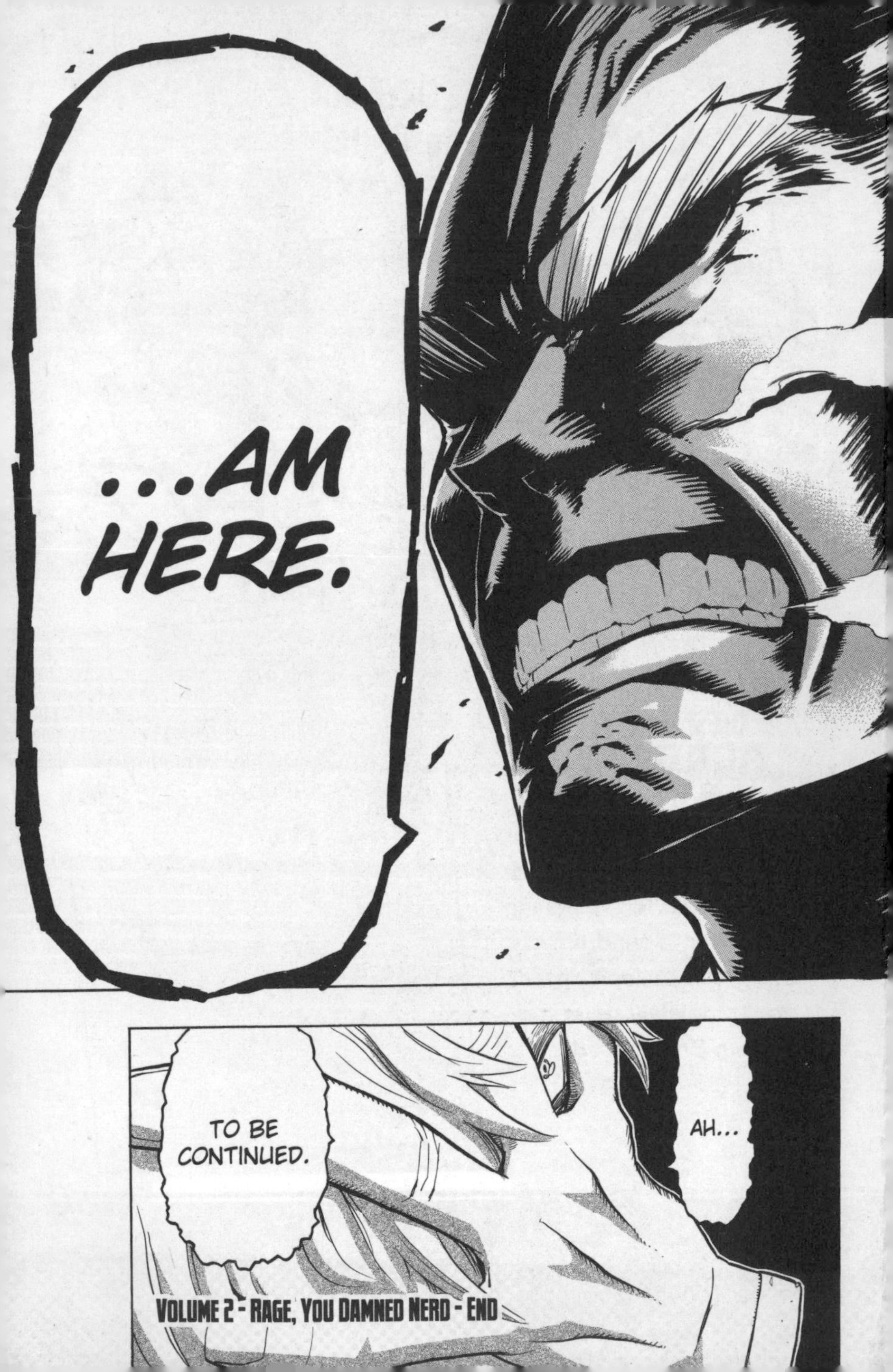
...AM HERE.
AH...
TO BE CONTINUED.
VOLUME 2 - RAGE, YOU DAMNED NERD - END

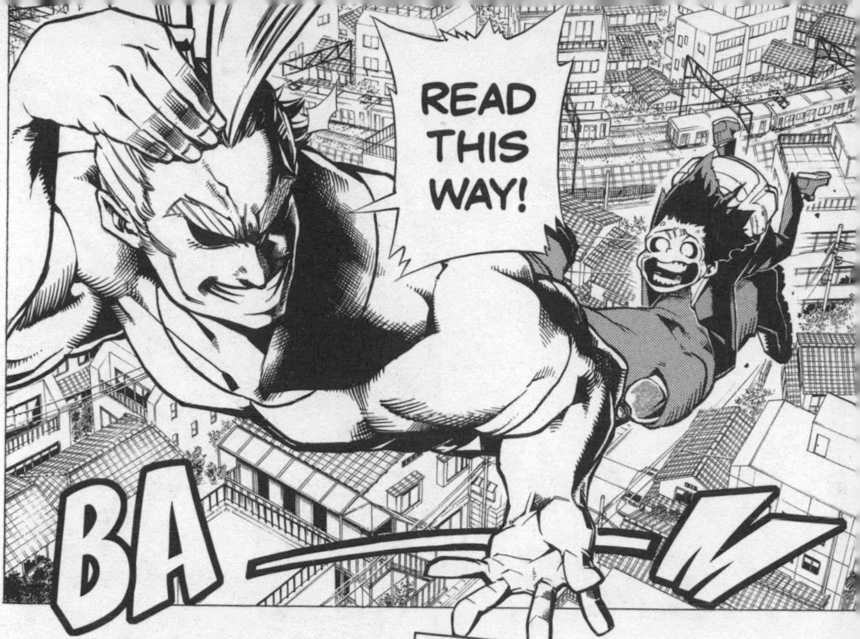
READ THIS WAY!
BA-M

MY HERO ACADEMIA

reads from right to left, starting in the upper-right corner. Japanese is read from right to left, meaning that action, sound effects and word-balloon order are completely reversed from English order.

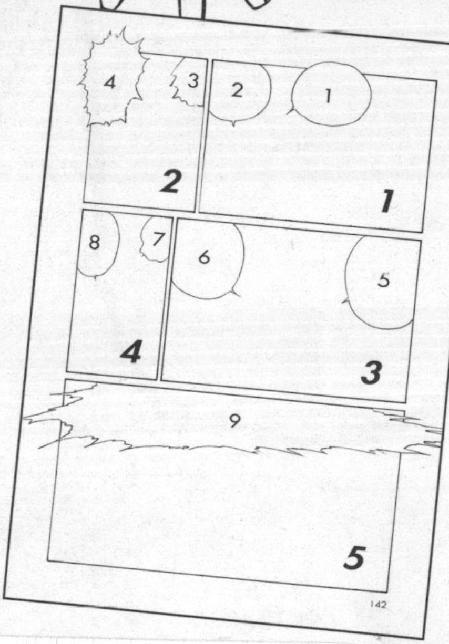
1
2
3
4
5
6
7
8
9
1
2
3
4
5
142